DELIVERING LONDON'S OLYMPIC DREAM

A LONG LIFE IN SPORT

CRAIG REEDIE

FONTHILL

To all those who love to play sport, to those who make sport a major feature of their lives by giving of their time and energy to organise sport for others, and to those special few who are fortunate to be invited to protect sport by promoting the values and success of the Olympic movement.

Fonthill Media Language Policy

Fonthill Media publishes in the international English language market. One language edition is published worldwide. As there are minor differences in spelling and presentation, especially with regard to American English and British English, a policy is necessary to define which form of English to use. The Fonthill Policy is to use the form of English native to the author. Sir Craig Reedie was born and educated in Scotland; therefore, British English has been adopted in this publication.

Fonthill Media Limited
Fonthill Media LLC
www.fonthill.media
books@fonthill.media

First published in the United Kingdom and the United States of America 2022

British Library Cataloguing in Publication Data:
A catalogue record for this book is available from the British Library

Copyright © Craig Reedie 2022

ISBN 978-1-78155-883-6

Typeset in 10.5pt on13pt Sabon
Printed and bound in England

Foreword

Shortly after the closing ceremony of the London Olympic and Paralympic Games, I met Craig Reedie for a family-sized whisky—an essential ingredient for the decompression phase we had all entered. As we greeted each other, I instinctively called him 'Governor'. It is an epithet that stuck.

For many years and well before the London Games, Craig had become the senior partner in the hierarchy of UK sport. I for one was immensely grateful that on so many occasions, private and public, I had been the recipient of Craig's shrewd observations and wise counsel, and he has at all times been a friend.

My respect for what he has achieved in globalising and gaining Olympic status for his beloved sport of badminton, for the status of British sport in general, for the Olympic movement, and for the well-being of the athletes is unbounded.

His legacy will flower with time as his achievements become better appreciated, the most significant of which was to pave the way for our successful bid for the London Olympic Games of 2012. But more than that, during the entire process from that unforgettable day in 2005 in Singapore, when we snuck across the line and won the right to host the Games, to London's closing ceremony, he was a constant source of wisdom and advice throughout the extraordinarily complex business of delivering the Games.

I was also particularly grateful that, as president of WADA, Craig stood resolutely behind the stance adopted by the then IAAF, now World Athletics, in the defence of sporting ethics during the stressful and seemingly interminable crisis of the Russian doping scandal.

I am delighted that he has now told the story of his long life in sport. It is a story that needs to be told. For those plying their trade in the world of sports administration and aspiring to pen their own memoir, it will be a vital 'how to'. It is a chronicle that makes a seminal contribution to the distinguished history of British sport.

Seb Coe

Preface

I am delighted that Craig Reedie has decided to write an account of his long life in sport and his outstanding commitment to British and international sport.

It is important to remember that, during his tenure as president of the British Olympic Association, the performance of our athletes at the Olympic Games went from modest to outstanding.

I have fond memories of working with Craig on our challenging journey to win London the right to host the 2012 Olympic Games. Without his experience and wisdom, our bid would never have succeeded and without his subsequent guidance and expertise, those wonderful Games would not have been as memorable as they were.

We all owe him an enormous debt of gratitude.

Tony Blair

Acknowledgements

An attempt to write a memoir with a memory not as abundant as once it was, is a challenge. To have any kind of success depends on access to younger people or those with access to the required information. I have been hugely helped by both.

I owe a debt of gratitude to many. From Badminton Scotland to its long-serving player, former doubles partner and enthusiast Mac Henderson, and to Judy Budge and Leon Douglas, the author of its excellent centenary history.

From the British Olympic Association, I am indebted to Simon Clegg, David Luckes, and Mark England, and from the International Badminton Federation, now the Badminton World Federation, to Torsten Berg, Stuart Borrie, and its conscientious archivist Pierre Sibert.

I am also grateful to the following: Brian Agerbak from the European Badminton Union, the Secretariat in Rome of the European Olympic Committees, Philippe Gueisbuhler of the General Association of Sports Federations, Gunilla Lindberg from the Association of National Olympic Committees, Pamela Vipond and Makara Fitzgerald from the International Olympic Committee, Chris Harvey from UK Sport, Sir Keith Mills, Jackie Brock-Doyle, Debbie Jevans and Alison Nimmo from LOCOG, Olivier Niggli and Maggie Durand from WADA, and, at home, to Brian Cairns, my IT man.

In particular, I owe a huge debt to my wife and lifelong companion, Rosemary, whose scrapbooks from 1992 provided a constant and fascinating collection of articles from media sources and correspondence. Her diligence allowed me to recall vital details about my time at the BOA,

Britain's Olympic bids, the challenges and successes of London 2012, and the less happy times when I struggled with the outrage of the Russian doping saga.

Finally, my thanks to my old friend, Olympic enthusiast and inspiring historian, Stewart Binns, for all his encouragement and wisdom.

CONTENTS

1

In Braveheart's Shadow

The first time I ever hit a shuttlecock was in Logie Parish Church Hall, Causewayhead, in the autumn of 1951. Originally a small village, Causewayhead was rapidly becoming a suburb to the north of Stirling, the historic Scottish city famous for the towering presence of its legendary castle. It is said that 'Stirling, like a huge brooch, clasps Highlands and Lowlands together' and, 'he who holds Stirling, holds Scotland'.

I was born in the city ten years earlier and then lived comfortably in the family home at 35 Easter Cornton Road in Causewayhead. It was a four-room, newish bungalow my parents could not afford to buy for £350 when they moved from Glasgow in 1937. As was typical of most families at that time, we lived in only three of the rooms, keeping one as a parlour for important guests, who rarely, if ever, came. The area has been built up over the years, but when I was a wee lad, we were surrounded by green fields, with Stùc a' Chroin mountain looming in the distance.

Neither of my parents came from a moneyed background. My father was a surveyor by training but had moved to join the valuation department of the Inland Revenue and my mother was a housewife. One salary was insufficient to fund such a large purchase, so the house was rented and not bought until 1965, when its price had escalated to £3,500, a small fortune at the time.

My original primary school was at the High School of Stirling, housed in an ancient building below Stirling Castle in which Mary Queen of Scots, aged just nine months, was crowned in 1542. As I walked to school every day, I looked up to the Wallace Monument, the towering edifice to commemorate Scotland's great hero, Sir William Wallace, whose mighty two-handed broadsword is on display within the monument. Hardly surprisingly, I have been a proud Scot ever since.

Even in those days, schools could run out of room. My primary department was closed, and all the young children were farmed out to neighbouring schools. My luck was that I was sent to Causewayhead primary school under the supervision of Headmaster Robert Johnston. We moved into a building that had four classrooms for eight classes, so my last two years of primary school were taught in the same room. Robert Johnston was the man who organised my first badminton moment. Quite apart from badminton and in addition to normal schoolwork, he taught two senior classes in woodwork, metalwork, and—believe it or not— dancing, the Scottish country version. His wife even taught us how to use the telephone, which was quite a novel device at the time.

They were really formative years with tangible benefits from increased personal attention at school and through falling under the influence of a committed and enthusiastic teacher. Family life was greatly enhanced by the purchase of our first car—another technological wonder that few people possessed at the time. Regular Sunday trips up to Glasgow to visit my grandmother in Govan followed. Although the roads were nothing like as busy as they are now, there were no motorways then, and the route was complicated. Not only that, my father drove very slowly.

Govan was that other Scotland. My home in Stirling, which is often called the 'Gateway to the Highlands', was peaceful, ancient Scotland. The Highlands began just to our north. Govan was on the Clyde, Glasgow's dingy waterfront. It was urban, industrial, and poor. The docks and the shipyards supplied work, although that, sadly, would soon change, but not much by way of wages. In those post-war days, there was still rationing, and the residue of the war was plain to see. My grandmother still had an Anderson shelter at the back of her house. The economic recovery had not reached the area and the welfare state had yet to be launched. My Sunday trips to the west gave me a very early insight into the stark contrasts in Scottish life.

I never knew my grandfather, who had died in 1935. He was a ship caulker at Stephens of Linthouse (one of the major Clyde shipyards), a trade union representative, and very much a child of urban Scotland. As a caulker, he would spend his days with a large caulking hammer, a flat chisel, and yards of hemp to make a ship's hull watertight. It must have been hard labour and tediously repetitive. On his retirement, he was presented with a silver tray; family rumour suggested that this was in recognition of being one of the few men never to have stolen any of the union's money.

Family holidays took us to St Andrews, where the stunning West Sands, which were to become famous around the world as the setting for the opening scene of the 1981 film *Chariots of Fire,* were of much greater interest for me at the time than the magical golf course that the Sands bordered. Nevertheless, the seeds of my interest in golf were sown by my father's decision to take me to Dunblane Golf Club for the first time. Looking back, those years were among the happiest of my young life.

When it was time to go to secondary school, I went back to the senior part of the High School of Stirling. The standard curriculum in Scottish schools at that time included English, maths, history, geography, Latin, and French, with additional classes in art, music, and physical education. The object of the whole exercise was to obtain suitably high standards in the 'Higher' examinations, which would lead to university. Six happy years passed very quickly. I have fond memories of an excellent history teacher, the likeable Miss Jessie Thomson, the less likeable but very able maths teacher Miss Hamilton, and the highly regarded Latin enthusiast Mr Murray, who doubled as a rugby coach on Wednesday afternoons and Saturday mornings.

Sport for boys was rugby, cricket, and the occasional athletics event. I made the 1st XV for rugby as a wing forward and was much derided for being very quick at moving away from the ball. Our fixtures were against a range of different schools from Buckhaven High School in industrial Fife, where the goalposts were designed for both football and rugby, to the Queen Victoria School in Dunblane, a school for the sons of military servicemen, where everything was first class and the opposing team was as hard as nails. Somewhere between those two extremes was the annual away match against Alloa Academy. It had a pitch that appeared to be used for rugby on a Saturday and for grazing cattle on the other six days of the week. The playing surface could only be described as unusual for its unique method of fertilisation.

A great thrill was the annual visit to the schoolboys' enclosure at Murrayfield in Edinburgh. It was always packed, but four rows of seats around the whole pitch were reserved for schools for Scotland's home international rugby matches. They were wonderful occasions, involving rail travel to Edinburgh, by steam locomotive of course, a packed lunch, and a seat to watch international sport for the first time. The crowds were huge. On one occasion, the total attendance was 104,000, much to the embarrassment of the overwhelmed police of Edinburgh.

I have a clear memory of a celebrated try by Scotland's winger and captain Arthur Smith during a famous victory over Wales. Smith was a remarkable man. A farmer's son from Galloway, as well as captaining his country thirty-three times, he was an excellent footballer and long-jumper, and got a PhD in maths from Cambridge. Sadly, he died of cancer aged just forty-two.

As an enticing alternative to more physics and chemistry, I was the official scorer of the cricket team and a 100 yards hurdler for the school's athletics team. In my last year, I was asked to anchor the school 4 × 100 yards relay team at the Stirlingshire school championships. Three excellent sprinters gave me a comfortable lead for the last leg, but my vision of glory was ruined when passed by the 'Balfron Bullet', a youngster called Mike Hildrey who was to become one of the leading sprinters in Britain.

The school had only one football match. It was against St Modan's Academy in Stirling, which did not play rugby. The match was played at Stirling Albion's ground. Our opposition included a fiery little red-haired individual. He was such a good player that we could not get near enough to kick him. St Modan's won easily, but I can always think back proudly in having once played against the great Billy Bremner, who was to have a stellar career as captain of Scotland and the famous Leeds United team of the 1960s and 1970s.

Throughout those relaxed six years at school, I continued my badminton education by playing in the Stirling and district leagues, then as a member of the Saint Columba's church team. Saint Columba's was a classic one-court club that played on a Wednesday evening in the church hall. Matches were also played in the local drill hall, which had the luxury of three courts, allowing three different matches to be played at the same time. All matches were played as mixed doubles and were keenly contested. It was a different experience but added greatly to the skills necessary to play the sport well.

The last year at school was dominated by thoughts of progress to university. Applications were submitted to St Andrews, Scotland's oldest, where students are granted low-cost golf, and to Glasgow, Scotland's largest. There was a nervous two-week wait for replies. To their great misfortune, St Andrews declined the opportunity to benefit from my intellectual prowess, so Glasgow it was. On 5 October 1959, I set off with my dapper university blazer and brand-new leather briefcase to start what was to become another six years of utter joy.

The University of Glasgow, founded in 1451, is the second oldest university in Scotland. It has a distinguished list of graduates, including three former prime ministers and seven Nobel laureates. Among its most famous graduates are Adam Smith, the famous philosopher and economist, and James Wilson, who emigrated to the United States of America in 1766 and went on to sign the Declaration of Independence and helped write the United States Constitution.

I had no particular preference for the course I should take, but my father suggested an initial degree in arts followed by a degree in law. Without giving it much thought, I decided to accept his advice and I was lucky to come under the care of Professor Esmond Wright in his modern history class. He was an expert in American history and probably the best lecturer at the university at that time. University life suddenly became interesting. Wright was to become a Conservative member of parliament for the Glasgow Pollock constituency for three years before returning to academic life as director of the Institute of US Studies and professor of American history at the University of London. I was fortunate to be a student when he was at his academic best.

For my first year, I decided to stay at home and travel to Glasgow each day by train. It turned out to be a less than ideal option as the west of Scotland rail service was seriously affected by periods of very thick fog and proved to be unreliable. Many morning lectures were missed while sitting in a stationary train outside Buchanan Street railway station. The frustrating experience led me to realise that living closer to the university was maybe a good idea.

So, in October 1960, I moved into one room at 1253 Argyle Street, a large sandstone typical Glasgow terraced row. It was owned by Mrs McCulloch, who was to be my landlady for the next seven years. Her charges were more than reasonable at £3 per week, including lunch, and £3 10 shillings if I stayed all weekend. I found out that Frank Kennedy, the university badminton team captain, was looking for digs and he joined me in our new home. Mrs McCulloch was a widow who had lived a difficult life. She had a daughter who visited infrequently and who was described to us as an 'elocution teacher', which was a bit of a surprise as she had the broadest Glasgow accent I had ever heard. Perhaps she specialised in Glaswegian, what the locals call the 'Glasgow patter'.

Sadly, we knew that our landlady's eldest and favourite son had died early in life and that alcohol had played some part. We had our own rule that if we were to be out late at night and anywhere near a beer, we would go home after Mrs McCulloch had gone to bed. She also believed that no man should go to work without a good breakfast, so bacon and eggs were served every morning, including those weekend mornings when we might have been rather late getting into our beds. I had a front room overlooking the busy Argyle Street, where I learned to tell the time by the number of

Glasgow's famous yellow and green trams that passed below my window. Glasgow Corporation Tramways, one of the largest urban tramways in Europe, with over 1,000 trams and 100 miles of rails, went out of service in September 1962. I missed their distinctive bells—their trundling, clattering, and banging—and had to resort to a modest investment in an alarm clock.

There was an interesting social history aside concerning the closure of the tramway. At that time, the trams were a rare example of gender equality in the workplace. During the First World War, the corporation had allowed women to become tram drivers. After the war, in what was an unusual decision, women were allowed to keep their jobs. This continued until the system closed. Afterwards, women took a backward step. In the absence of power-steering, women were not allowed to be bus drivers because, it was said, they did not have the strength to control the steering wheel.

Without the tedious journey back and forth from Stirling to Glasgow, university life became much easier when I could walk to classes or to the sports club. At that time, University of Glasgow was expanding its halls of residence but still had a large core of students from the city and the west of Scotland. Social life revolved around the university union with its restaurants, coffee rooms, bridge rooms, and library. It held dances and debates, and it had a very popular beer bar.

Dance nights featured the conversion of one library room into a smooching den with little or no light known as 'The Squeezy' for those lucky enough to have a girlfriend. The beer bar was the centre of intellectual argument on profound themes like football and popular music and served a special pint of draft cider for the very reasonable price of one shilling. The football debates, often very heated, revolved around the merits of the 'Old Firm', Rangers and Celtic. In music, the Beatles and the Rolling Stones had not yet surfaced, so the big hits were mainly from America by stars like Roy Orbison, Patsy Cline, and Chubby Checker and his new craze, 'the Twist'.

It was easy to make new friends, and a helping of haggis at lunchtime, the cheapest and most filling dish on the restaurant menu, kept you going for the remainder of the day, while its price helped to fund the rest of your social activity. Our lives revolved around the university and its activities, all without a television set in sight.

I completed my arts degree in 1962 and moved to the faculty of law. I found myself in distinguished company. My fellow students included John Smith, Donald Dewar, and Menzies Campbell. Smith was to become the leader of the Labour Party and almost certainly prime minister if he had not tragically died at just fifty-five, Dewar became the first minister of the new Scottish parliament, and Campbell went on to be a member of the 1980 British Olympic Team and leader of the Liberal Democratic Party.

Those talented students all made their mark in the tradition of political debating, which was a feature of life at University of Glasgow. There were six political clubs, and at each debate, one formed the government, while another formed the opposition. The president of the University Union acted as the speaker. Debates were held on a Friday in the first two university terms. During the evening session, the government had to produce a stunt as part of a mock version of *Question Time*. On one famous occasion, the government of the day managed to persuade a donkey up the stairs of the Union to the second-floor debating chamber. The donkey proceeded to foul the carpet underneath the speaker's mace. Quick as a flash, one of the opposition speakers leapt to his feet and made the proposal: 'Mr Speaker. There is a motion before the house.'

My university life was bound to include the sport of badminton. On arrival in 1959, one of my first tasks was to find the university badminton hall. To my surprise and disappointment, it was a one-court hall in a small building behind the botany department. On the opening day of the badminton year, I turned up eager to take part and managed to complete only two games in a period of three and a half hours. Fortunately, the second game involved the then captain of the university badminton team and future housemate, Frank Kennedy. As I was lucky enough to have the better partner, I managed to beat him and clearly made an impression. This resulted in an invitation to attend team practice the following week and my university badminton career was underway.

In the 1959–1960 season, the university team, playing men's doubles, competed in the fifth division of the west of Scotland leagues. We then proceeded to move in successive years to the fourth, third, second, and finally the first division, then managed to stay there. Looking back, we had as much fun as any group of young students could have had. They were some of my happiest days in sport. That small group, all of whom were involved in long degree courses, became the best of friends and we share those happy memories to this day.

In 1961, University of Glasgow sport dragged itself into the twentieth century by opening the Stevenson Building, known as the 'Stevie'. It contained a 25-m swimming pool, squash courts, a gymnasium, and a main hall with three badminton courts. In addition, students were able to enjoy warm and clean showers after training or competition. The facilities were so attractive that we decided to host our own University of Glasgow open doubles tournament, which ran very successfully for a number of years.

There were domestic matches against other Scottish universities, but international matches were restricted to two events against Irish universities as each sport at Glasgow was granted a tour grant every second year. In 1962, we set off to play matches in Ireland against University College Dublin and Queen's University Belfast. In those days, travel to Ireland was in very small cabins at the back of the Burns and Laird overnight ferry service from the Broomielaw pier in central Glasgow to Belfast. Each cabin consisted of four small bunks with a night light and no other facilities. The light above my bunk was not working, so, in possession of a fine university education, I worked out that the obvious solution was to replace the dud bulb by 'borrowing' a good one from the cabin next door.

As I did so, the cabin door flew open and in poured four members of the Queen's University women's hockey team, who, complete with 'jolly' hockey sticks, a mountain of kit and piles of luggage, were returning from their Scottish tour. Later, in an attempt to recover from the embarrassment of being caught in the act, I tried to make friends with the girls upstairs on deck. I was particularly impressed by an attractive brunette who seemed very friendly. On arrival the following morning in Belfast, we hired a car and set off for Dublin for the match against UCD. On returning to Belfast, my new friend turned up to watch our match against her university.

Having found out that her name was Rosemary Biggart, whose father was a big cheese in medicine in Northern Ireland, I invited her to the after-match dinner on the advice of Queen's Belfast player, David McCullough. David told me she was a medical student and added a few interesting details based on his admiration for her. So, I took the plunge and phoned her; slightly to my surprise, she turned up in a new red dress, over which I promptly managed to pour a drink. A splendid evening ensued, and I borrowed £2 from Frank Kennedy to take her to lunch the following day. We are still together fifty-eight years later.

The competitive system in badminton in Scotland was based on a series of open tournaments around the country almost every weekend. Most were well organised, and all were highly competitive, with entries up to and including the Scottish international team. My standards improved. I was a reasonable singles player but was much stronger as a doubles player. Playing some of the best players in the world, I entered two of the major tournaments in England, the Northern Championships at Birkenhead, and the London Championships at Crystal Palace. At home, a win in the Glasgow Open with Scottish international, Mac Henderson, proved to be a good example of the theory that success in doubles is down to the intelligent choice of one's partner.

During those years, I became involved with two men who became my mentors in both sport and in life, David Bloomer and John McCarry. Bloomer was a friend of my parents and a past president of the Scottish Badminton Union and the International Badminton Federation. McCarry was introduced to me by Bloomer as a 'slow speaking inhabitant of Dennistoun' (an inner-city area in the east of Glasgow). McCarry was also a former international and president of the SBU.

Although very different characters, they were close friends and had made a major contribution to the sport in Scotland. McCarry in particular was blessed with an unusual turn of phrase. A fellow international badminton player, Murdo McLean, had disappeared. When Bloomer asked McCarry if he had seen Murdo recently, he said: 'Well David it is a very sad story. Unfortunately, his father died and left him £87,000. He was so overcome by grief that he had to go on a world cruise.'

While still at university, and still a playing enthusiast, I was given an unusual opportunity to watch world-class badminton. In 1949, Scotland had been asked by the International Badminton Federation to stage a match between Malaya and the United States of America. It was the semi-final of the first ever Thomas Cup competition. The two Scottish officials invited to organise the event were Messrs Bloomer and McCarry. They chose to use the 3,000-seat arena in the Kelvin Hall in Glasgow. Bloomer commented:

> With the confidence of ignorance the inexperienced impresarios had undertaken to sell 6,000 tickets for a match in an unknown sport between foreign teams to an uncaring public in a soccer besotted city.

The event was sold out. The match featured one of the few occasions when the Malayan legend, the 'Great Wong', Wong Peng Soon, met the equally formidable David Freeman of the United States. The quality of play stunned and then enthralled the crowd in what was probably the best badminton match in the history of the sport. Freeman beat Wong, but the Malaya team won the tie and won the inaugural Thomas Cup by beating Denmark in the final.

It was clear that there was a future for this type of international competition in Scotland and the event led to the creation of the World

Invitation Tournament. This was first played in 1951 and on seventeen subsequent occasions and featured many of the top players in the world. It was the badminton event which started the practice of international players travelling on a worldwide basis. The Kelvin Hall organisers met the travelling expenses of the players, particularly those from Asia. To defray some of the cost of travel the organisers then 'sold' the players to a tournament in Denmark, an exhibition match in Ireland and eventually to the All-England Championships in London. Although there was no prize money, an invitation to Kelvin Hall became much valued by many of the great players: Finn Kobbero and Erland Kops of Denmark, Rudy Hartono of Indonesia, Noriko Takagi and Hiroe Yuki of Japan, and the Choong brothers from Malaya.

My first active involvement in Kelvin Hall was as a volunteer linesman sitting on a small stool in a draught, which, given Glasgow's climate, often felt like a howling gale. More importantly, the current of air did little for the accuracy of the players' long shots to the baseline. Eventually, I graduated to be an umpire. In those days, the microphone was handheld and possessed a small switch to the 'on' position, making it a source of nervous fumbling in the hand of a novice. The tournament referee was John McCarry, who offered some of his normal precise advice: 'If you follow Donald Ross into the umpire's chair you will find that the microphone will smell strongly of drink.'

The Kelvin Hall tournament was to make most of the money the Scottish Badminton Union received and made a huge contribution to the promotion of the sport for many years. It became clear to me that the sport had become an integral part of my young life. I managed to graduate from university and undertook an apprenticeship with Glasgow solicitors, Tindal Oatts & Rodger, and then moved to become the young assistant in the office of financial advisers, DL Bloomer and Partners. By then, it was clear that, despite every effort, I was unlikely to become a world-beating player. Dreams of badminton stardom began to fade, and the sad reality dawned that working for a living was likely to be my best option in life.

2

The Young Administrator

In 1965, while settling into my law apprenticeship with Tindal Oatts & Rodger, the temptation to become involved in the administration of badminton in Scotland became more than a little attractive. Both Messrs Bloomer and McCarry were encouraging. In retrospect, the offer of an annual honorarium of £200 became almost irresistible when added to my salary of £350. It was a financial arrangement that probably represented the biggest percentage increase in my income in my whole career.

I took over the position of secretary and treasurer of the Scottish Badminton Union from John McCarry, who himself had agreed to serve the union on one final occasion after the retirement of its longstanding secretary and treasurer, Mr W. F. G. Normand. Fitz Normand had been the senior partner in a firm of chartered accountants in Edinburgh and fitted his badminton involvement into time at his three distinguished golf clubs: Bruntsfield, Gullane, and Muirfield. He was a delightful man. However, I suspect that, in practice, since 1946, the sport had been run by his secretary in his Edinburgh office.

The move of badminton's administrative centre from Queen Street, Edinburgh, to my digs at 1253 Argyle Street, Glasgow, was easily achieved. In those less automated days, the principal duty of the office was to send out the annual subscription notice to each of the affiliated badminton clubs in Scotland. This was never the most exciting part of sports administration, and it became clear that these duties should be moved to an organisation that would be more efficient. A small office was taken in the Scottish Council of Physical Recreation building in Royal Crescent in Glasgow. An enthusiastic badminton player called Liz McFarlane became the only employee of the Scottish Badminton Union and undertook the main administrative work. The room in the office was shared with the Scottish Sub-Aqua Association. Liz, being a young mother, had to bring her baby daughter with her to the office, where, on occasions, the little one provided a unique atmosphere.

Having a proper office allowed me freedom for another change in my life: Rosemary and I decided to get married. She had been working as a resident doctor in Glasgow Royal Infirmary and we purchased our first home in Herries Road for £3,500, and then painted it from top to bottom. The wedding ceremony was arranged for Belfast on 9 September 1967 with a reception in the Culloden Hotel. The name was unfortunate as Culloden was the scene of the legendary military defeat of Bonnie Prince Charlie's Scots by the English in 1746, but the hotel was splendid.

Visiting guests from Scotland enjoyed a memorable four-ball at County Down Golf Club on the 8th, the day Rosemary passed her driving test. The happy couple and their families and guests enjoyed a special day, although weddings in Ireland did not then finish with a party and dance. To deliver an alternative, David McCullough, an old Irish badminton friend, hosted most of the younger Scots at his house in the evening. One of them, who should remain nameless, was seen to emerge from a steamed up mini car, where he had been with one of the bridesmaids, asking, 'Does anyone know her name?'

Without the need to attend the evening event, Rosemary and I flew to London to spend two nights in the very up-market Carlton Tower Hotel in Sloane Street, London, then the showpiece of the Hotel Corporation of America, before heading for our honeymoon in Austria. For both of us, the hotel room was the first we had stayed in that had the luxury of a television set in the room. At that time, there were only three channels—BBC 1, BBC 2, and ITV.

BBC 2 was building an audience in the London area only for its 'midnight movie' programme. So, as my new bride prepared herself for her wedding night, I asked her, 'Would you like to watch the Midnight Movie?' To which, in what I assumed was in the same tongue-in-cheek vein, she replied, 'Yes!' The set took some time to warm up and the sound could be heard before the pictures, as the commentator said, 'And here is Nicklaus on the fourteenth green'. It was the World Series of Golf from Akron, Ohio. I was tempted but decided that duty called and that it was wise to turn the television off.

Back in Scotland with a proper office, I identified that the advantage of working through the documentation for each of the 600 clubs in Scotland would give me a clear picture of the current strength and weaknesses of the sport. In those days, almost all clubs played in one-court halls, many attached to churches, as evidenced by strong local church leagues all around the country.

However, a major change in the provision of indoor sports facilities was underway. Cities were beginning to construct multi-purpose sport complexes. There was a new sports centre in Glasgow with eight badminton courts, a cafe, and warm and pleasant showers. The challenge to the sport was to understand how individual players would react to the opportunity to book their own courts at their own time and, perhaps, to abandon their previous club loyalties. To assist in understanding the implications of this change, we put together a group of current and recent top players, my first ever Athletes' Commission. As you would imagine, the feedback was very full and frequently variable in quality, but when you gather a portfolio of ideas, some of them can be really outstanding.

It became clear that we had to change the attitude towards the union of all its previous players by offering an attractive series of potential benefits as well as improving the status of top-class and international competition for both senior and junior players. The old funding system that had operated for years and compelled each club to pay a subscription to the union was likely to be unsuccessful in the new era. To replace funding from one system to another involved a host of different models, including discounts on equipment, booking fees, and other items of interest. In reality, most of these ideas were overtaken by the introduction of direct funding by national and local government and over the years this has become the base funding model for most amateur sports. The Scottish Sports Council was not established until 1972, so we were on our own and did not have access to the kind of advice now freely available.

We also understood that a successful sport in a small country like Scotland would require a strong grassroots element and that we should pay attention to encouraging as many young people as possible. We decided that the best way to do this would be to set up some form of activity for badminton in schools. Before we took the delights of badminton to them, perhaps naively, we decided to introduce a new competition rather than seek some form of organised structure for schools. In that enthusiastic spirit, we decided to hold the first ever Scottish schools badminton championship in the new Bellahouston Centre in Glasgow.

To say that we were overwhelmed is only part of the story. We received entries for each of the three different age groups we planned and from many more schools than we could have hoped for in our wildest dreams. Literally hundreds of young schoolchildren appeared clutching a range of badminton rackets from ultra-modern to distinctly antique. Our plans, which allowed each match to be played over three games, would have meant using the sports centre for at least a week instead of the two days we had anticipated. In practice, each match was reduced from three games of fifteen points to one game of eleven points. The sports centre staff thought we were crazy as the exhausted organisers departed. However, the weekend led to the formation of the Scottish Schools Badminton Union, which was to become a successful organisation. It not only delivered joy to generations of young people, but also produced a stream of young talent for the sport.

Our international matches were limited to matches in the Thomas and Uber Cup competitions, the worldwide men's and ladies' team championships. There were also annual matches against England or Ireland. The home matches tended to be played in the Cornmarket in Edinburgh and almost always on the Thursday of the week of the Scottish Open Championships. That meant that the visiting players could stay on and play in the Scottish event, the third oldest championships in world badminton.

The Cornmarket was not an ideal venue as it provided exactly what its name implied: a corn market with a stone floor, a glass roof, and an array of wooden stands for the corn traders. It did hold six courts and offered the very welcome asset of a good pub right next door. The pub was a boon, but the venue was not ideal for spectators beyond the usual badminton enthusiast. To change our strategy, we approached Charles Munro, who was one of the two sport producers at BBC Scotland.

Charlie became a close friend and understood that badminton was a relatively inexpensive and attractive television event featuring Scottish and some major international players. We began to look for possible new venues that would allow us to develop our modest international match portfolio. Over the years, matches travelled to the City Hall in Perth, the new Bells Sports Centre in that city and to the village of Brae in Shetland, 110 miles from the Scottish mainland.

This last and distant match was a first-round match in the Ladies' Competition for the Uber Cup between Scotland and Norway. The intrigue in the venue was the historical fact that Shetland had been ruled by Norway and only became Scottish in the fifteenth century. Shetland was benefitting from the boom in North Sea oil but had a very tense relationship with the Scottish administration in Edinburgh. Much to the irritation of Edinburgh, the Shetlanders were experts in extracting money from oil companies for social improvements or events.

Shetland was also the home of the new Sullom Voe oil terminal, a multimillion-pound project bringing both men and money to the island. The local organisers were very successful in selling tickets for an all-female sporting occasion to the lonely male labourers building the oil terminal. The Norwegian players were not the greatest exponents of the game but scored highly in their on-court appearance and demeanour, so they were well supported by the ticket holders and the locals. Both teams, and most of the crowd, came to the after-match party when the Scottish victory was tolerated rather than celebrated with a selection of less than congratulatory political speeches. It was a very bizarre experience in one's own country to be described as a group of 'Sooth Moothers', a less than friendly yet widely used Shetlandic term to describe anyone from the mainland. By coincidence, the final of that Uber Cup competition was held in the Badminton Hall in Auckland, New Zealand—a venue that would play another part in Scottish badminton history.

As with many of the good experiences in life, I found that one of the best aspects of this new world of administration was the opportunity to meet, learn from, and enjoy the many different characters and personalities that crossed my path. Moving on from a playing career made it possible to invite friends from the badminton court to help in plans for a better court experience.

Good Scottish players like Ian Hume, Bob Fowlis, and, in particular, Mac Henderson were valuable sounding boards. Our best player in that era, and arguably the best of all time, was Robert McCoig. Originally from the badminton hotbed of Greenock, he took a sojourn in London working with Burroughs machines. Robert was the top singles player in Britain. He had travelled the world representing the sport and his country in tournaments, impressing everyone with his play and his personality. He was able to make many balanced suggestions for improvement in our work and to do so from the basis of personal experience at the top of the sport. He would have made an excellent member of an 'athletes' commission' had the concept been invented at that time. One possible flaw in his character was a tendency to suffer from the customary Scottish trait of being careful with money. On his first ever visit to Sweden for a Thomas Cup match, Robert was horrified at the price of a pot of tea in the hotel and decided that in order that his expenses would stretch a little further, he would dry his used tea bags on the radiator in his room.

Even more wisdom was provided by John Best, who was a former winner of the all-England mixed doubles title and a regular member of the English international team. John had studied at Cambridge University in the era when, benefitting from a group of excellent players from Malaya, Cambridge could probably have played the rest of Europe and won. Almost certainly arranged by David Bloomer, John had taken up a professional appointment with a Scottish whisky company and played regularly in Scottish tournaments and in the Glasgow leagues.

He was the most delightful of companions. As a convinced bachelor, he was easy to entertain, and we enjoyed his sense of humour. After some years in his original flat in Marywood Square, he moved to a much better apartment in Pollokshields and called us to say that we were invited to his new home where he thought he had everything in place. I asked, 'Television?' He said, 'Yes,' and I said, 'Colour?' He said, 'Brown, I think.' However, his observations on Scottish badminton were a more than reasonable reward for buying him dinner. His reflections on people he met could be incisive and, on many occasions, remarkably accurate. His description of David Bloomer as 'A man who, despite every effort of that luminous intelligence, still allowed his heart to rule his head' stays with me to this day.

Unexpectedly, 1965 was to bring about one of the major changes in the history of Scottish badminton. The sport had been included for the first time in a multisport event: the Commonwealth Games to be held in Kingston, Jamaica, in 1966. Edinburgh wanted to submit an application to host the next celebration four years later. In those days, the host city, or its Commonwealth Games Association, had the option to submit in its application the programme of sports to be included. That was a crucial feature of a number of meetings in 1965 as well as the selection process of the athletes to represent Scotland in Kingston.

The first draft selection for Kingston included three badminton players, Robert McCoig, Mac Henderson, and Muriel Ferguson. After all the first selections from all the sports were noted, there were, from memory, eleven available additional places. My case for a fourth badminton player, a woman, was strong, as she could then play singles, doubles, and mixed doubles, giving three more medal chances. The logic of this was accepted and Cathie Dunglison was selected, creating, in particular, a strong mixed doubles pairing with Mac Henderson. Having made my mark, I was then expected to be completely silent on any choices for the other sports. In reality, the badminton selection worked and brought home a mixed doubles bronze medal, on this occasion won by the McCoig and Ferguson pairing.

The next meeting to nominate the sports for 1970 was a much more troubled occasion. One of the popular sports which bid for inclusion in the programme was rowing. Its problem however was the proposed venue.

Rowing could not be accommodated in Edinburgh, so the alternative was to hold the sport at Loch Lomond, provided the wind blew from the right direction. As you might expect, the other sports representatives were less than enthusiastic about this proposal and the risks of holding the rowing competition on wide open water and with variable wind conditions counted strongly against it.

It seemed to me rather obvious that badminton would fit very well in Edinburgh. It could be played in the newly planned Meadowbank Sports Centre. This new development would contain at least three main halls, one of which would have movable seating and could become a stadium holding around 2,300 people. This would allow badminton a practice hall and an excellent arena for the Commonwealth Games.

After initial success in Kingston, badminton found itself as a prime Commonwealth Games sport with a venue at the very heart of the Edinburgh Games planning. At the Commonwealth Games General Assembly in Kingston in 1966, Edinburgh defeated Christchurch by eighteen votes to eleven to win the right to host the 1970 Games.

To complete this exciting change in the future of the sport, it seemed appropriate to be in Edinburgh to wish the team good luck before they headed for the airport for their flight to Kingston. As I waved goodbye to the bus, the rain came on and I got very wet on my way to a meeting with the city architect in Edinburgh, Alex Steele. We were to discuss the lighting plot options for the new Meadowbank Sports Centre, but only after he had borrowed some of my Benson and Hedges cigarettes.

Meadowbank was to revolutionise sport in Scotland. As the complex built for the Games, it provided a complete set of options for indoor sport, plus an athletics stadium with a central pitch for football or rugby and a velodrome, open to the fresh air, which turned out to be occasionally difficult in the wrong weather.

For badminton, the flexibility provided by the three indoor halls gave us a whole range of options, from simple individual court bookings to the use of one or more halls for different sizes of tournament competition. The main hall could be set up as an arena with ample seating for major events. This might attract a varied number of spectators at different times over a few days with an emphasis for finals, frequently on a Saturday evening. Modern changing rooms, showers, medical facilities, and a full-service cafeteria moved us into the new century. The centre of badminton in Scotland moved back to Edinburgh and would be our regular venue for many years.

As a new Commonwealth Games sport, we found ourselves subject to a new set of regulations. For years, we had developed our own processes, governance and systems for tournament play dedicated to our sport. We now had to fit the organisation of the sport into the wide-ranging Commonwealth wrapper, which placed on us a whole range of responsibilities we had never had to deal with before. Much of this work was allocated to two of our Edinburgh-based senior officials, Jake Simpson and David Laidlaw, who manfully attended the never-ending meetings of the local Scottish Commonwealth Games Association. As Games' time approached in 1970, we pulled together the team who would organise the actual playing of badminton. This then released Jake and David to undertake the onerous task of attending an almost infinite list of parties hosted by each of the attending countries—forty-two in total—during the period of the Games. By the end of the Games, they looked like they had run a marathon a day for ten days.

As we gathered in Meadowbank, we first discussed how we would be able to fill the time given to us. We were used to holding tournaments in the Cornmarket on six courts over Friday evening and all-day Saturday. We now had three courts and six days to complete the event. Our first practical problem emerged when a gentleman appeared with a filing cabinet. We had never used a filing cabinet at a badminton tournament before but one of our number came up with the inspired idea that we should place it in the storage cupboard behind the organising committee table.

We then asked Ian Hume, a member of the Scottish badminton team who worked for Haig Whisky, if we could use his connection to establish a small 'committee bar', which seemed an ideal use for the filing cabinet. Our approach provided an occasional wee 'comfort' for the badminton organising committee, and we soon found we had a number of guests who declined their comfortable seats in the VIP section, preferring to frequent the delights of the badminton storage cupboard. A regular visitor was the 2nd Earl Beatty, who suddenly seemed quite keen to improve his knowledge of badminton by regularly adopting the famous Haig slogan, 'Don't be vague, ask for Haig'.

Our next problem was the appearance of an unknown Edinburgh official who asked us where 'Stand AD' was. We suggested to him that it might be in one of the other halls as presumably all the seats in the badminton hall had been sold to spectators. He explained that Stand AD was the area for the players, and we had to admit that no plan had been made for this eventuality. To resolve the issue, we suggested that somebody should find the closest school to Meadowbank and seek a supply of school chairs. To his credit, the official did just that and Stand AD was created, although over the next six days, very few players actually used it.

On the very first morning of competition, we were all sitting ready for play. At the end of the first match, when Robert McCoig had kept his opponent on court long enough to entertain the duke of Edinburgh, our first royal visitor, we were faced with our first result. The official referee accepted the umpire's score sheet, passing it to a recorder on his left, who in turn passed it to a second recorder on his left, and finally to a volunteer who took it away. Ten minutes later, the volunteer returned with about 100 copies. Unsure about what to do with the pile, we asked the volunteer to return to the copy office and dispose of at least ninety-nine of them.

Overall, the Games were a great success, with Scotland finishing fourth in the medals table behind Australia, England, and Canada. Famous athletes like Kip Keino, Ron Clarke, David Hemery, Lynn Davies, Raelene Boyle, Mary Peters, Michael Wenden, and David Wilkie all took part. Badminton too played its part, with a strong English team and a men's doubles gold for Ng Boon Bee and Punch Gunalan of Malaysia.

Each of the badminton sessions was well supported, and finals night was packed. Jamie Paulson of Canada won a surprise gold medal in the men's singles, and we successfully navigated our first medal presentation ceremony. Protocol and ceremonial were the responsibility of an army detachment taking instructions from the Commonwealth Games Federation. Its secretary general, Sandy Duncan, the old British Olympic Association Secretary, decided to change the medal presenters for the final event, the mixed doubles. He replaced our own Jake Simpson with our now regular friend and filing cabinet stalwart, the Earl Beatty. I fought the decision as hard as I could as few had worked harder for the event than Jake Simpson, but I lost. Jake was broken-hearted. After the hall emptied, we all repaired to a flat in Edinburgh with the remains of the contents of the filing cabinet.

Our reflections on the Games clearly indicated that as a reasonably efficient national governing body, we had little or no contact with the organising committee but plenty with the local Commonwealth Games Association, the interest of which was the success of the local team. We were experienced at organising major events, from the annual Scottish Open Championships to the World Invitation Tournament, but the now accepted close relationships between organising committees and the international federations had yet to emerge. However, the Games must have shown a small organising profit as, some months later, each Scottish National Federation of the nine sports in the Games programme received a cheque for £100. Badminton has been a core sport in the Commonwealth Games ever since.

3

Progress To Our Own Home

Following the excitement of 1970, badminton continued to boom. All the normal activities had to be continued, but with ever more pressure on the volunteers to deliver an increased workload, it became clear that it was necessary to move to a more professional style of management. It was natural that increased activity would require a major increase in communications. There was also a clear demand for the creation of some form of magazine that would allow the SBU to spread the word on badminton around the country.

To achieve this, as well as meeting the growing demands in organising the sport, more people needed to be involved and the organisation improved. A new secretary and treasurer, Stewart Coghill, was appointed and the offices moved to Frederick Street in Edinburgh to shared space in the building owned by the Scottish Sports Council.

The move to a more professional system involved the search for a full-time administrator, a decision which was to revolutionise the whole organisation. When the position was advertised, we received a glowing recommendation from Altham Turner, the director of the Scottish Sports Council training centre at Inverclyde in Largs. His secretary of some years was a young woman called Judy Budge from the Highlands of Scotland. Altham made constant efforts to ensure that her name would be included in the shortlist. This list resolved itself to three women, and after the necessary interviews and processes, Judy was appointed. She took up her position in mid-1973. Judy brought professional and interpersonal skills to the job, which allowed the sport to deliver the type of organisation it wanted.

In addition to the normal administrative duties involving subscriptions, keeping records, and attending meetings, Judy was able to achieve regular press coverage from the Scottish newspapers. One further and important administrative duty was to improve the organisation of tournaments run by the SBU. This led to a successful application to organise the 1973 European Junior Championships.

The long-awaited and much anticipated badminton magazine— *Badminton Scotland*—first appeared in 1974. Sandy Sutherland, a former Scottish track and field athlete, was the first editor but most of the organisation printing and distribution was handled by the SBU.

We must have been doing something right in our move toward professional administration as I received an invitation from the Badminton Union of Ireland to speak at a conference they were organising in Galway on the same subject: professional administration. The conference was organised by Frank Peard, who had been one of the leading Irish players in the mid-1950s. He had formed an excellent doubles partnership with Jim Fitzgibbon which led them to a ranking at the top of world badminton.

In his professional life, Frank became one of the four executive directors of the Guinness company. We met in Dublin on the way to the conference in Galway. At that time, he was in charge of production at the St James Gate Brewery, where the famous black stout was brewed. In a reflective moment, he confided in me that at that time he was, 'With the possible exception of the Pope, the most important man in Ireland.'

The conference turned out to be well attended and I assumed that the enthusiasm to develop badminton that existed in Scotland was as strong in Ireland. The impact of a conference speech on a topic like professional administration can run the risk of being a little less than exciting. To try to make the subject only marginally more interesting, I shared with my audience the detail of our experience in Scotland, when we appointed Judy Budge, one of three women candidates.

One was middle-aged and intended to return to England at an early stage, which rather reduced her attraction to the interviewing panel. The second was a very attractive young lady wearing a mini skirt who was the secretary to a medical professor at the University of Dundee. The problem the panel had with her was perhaps the naïve, and these days the politically incorrect, assumption that she would find a boyfriend and a future that might reduce the length of her stay in the job. The winner, Judy Budge, as I explained, was already bringing her many skills to the new appointment.

At the end of the presentation, Frank asked the audience if there were any questions. Immediately, a hand was raised at the back of the room from a man who I later found out was called Pádraig McNally. His question was clearly relevant to everything I had said when he asked, 'I don't suppose you could give me the phone number of the good looking one?' Sport in Ireland has always been full of fun.

The impact of the appointment of Judy Budge became apparent when we had to employ two additional part time assistants. One of the long-held aspirations in the SBU was the wish to establish a proper coaching organisation. There was the inevitable debate on whether such a new organisation should concentrate on coaching coaches or coaching players. In practice, the only practical way forward was to try to incorporate an element of both philosophies.

The driving force behind the initial coaching effort was Mac Henderson, ably assisted by three other good former players: Douglas Henry, Ian Hume, and Ian Young. In their own time, they headed south to the well-established coaching system in England and sat their initial coaching certificate examination. On their return, their aim was to provide a supply of coaches in each of the original groups affiliated to the SBU. It also became clear that there was a need to provide detailed coaching services for our top junior players. In 1976, the appointment was made of Roger Mills, a well-known English international player, to a part-time position with the junior players at the National Training Centre at Inverclyde.

Yet again, as activity increased, we changed the structure of the organisation by splitting the roles of secretary and treasurer. Neil Cameron took on the role of secretary and Stewart Coghill stayed on as treasurer. Hugely encouraging results were obtained on court with a bronze medal in the mixed doubles at the first world championships in Malmö in 1977 and a medal at the European Junior Championships in Malta. I became president of the SBU in 1977 and worked with Neil Cameron in presenting a new strategic plan that set a clear direction for future progress. The plan was based on the following:

1. Efforts to improve facilities for the playing of the game and specially to provide specialist halls.
2. Improving communication and engagement with clubs and members in order to overcome apathy.
3. Improving the image and profile of the sport.
4. Improving the standard of play.

The first of these was a challenge that took over my life for at least six months.

There had been a rumour that the first occasion at which the idea of building its own hall had appeared in the minutes of the SBU was around 1934. Despite repeated searches, no evidence of this plan had emerged. In 1964, the dynamic pair of Bloomer and McCarry had established a plan to purchase the ground in Pollokshields in Glasgow, which had been occupied by the local tennis club. The purchase price was £2,000, and the challenge was to raise another £50,000 for the building costs over the next two years. David Bloomer undertook most of the efforts to raise the additional funds required and to do so from his contacts and business friends.

In spite of considerable efforts, the challenge was greater than we had expected and the ground was eventually sold at a modest profit. It was a disappointing outcome, as the position of the ground in a pleasant residential area not far from the city centre, would have been ideal. The long-standing proposal remained unfulfilled.

In 1974, by virtue of my position on the International Badminton Federation, I was lucky enough to attend the final matches in the Uber Cup competition in Auckland, New Zealand. The competition was held in the Auckland Badminton Hall, a construction based on corrugated iron but well-preserved, well-maintained, and well-used.

New Zealand is a country with a distinguished sporting tradition, an ability to organise events, and a propensity to produce champions in a number of different sports. The population of Scotland was only marginally greater than that of New Zealand, and it occurred to me that if New Zealand could build a perfectly suitable badminton hall, then Scotland should be able to do so as well. As is often the case, coming up with the idea was far easier than executing the delivery.

Glasgow had once been the second city of the British Empire, with a population of just under 2 million. The city was based on heavy industry, much of which produced the materials for a world-leading shipbuilding industry. By the mid-seventies, much of the shipbuilding infrastructure was either empty or in poor condition. However, it seemed it might be possible to find a substantial building with, above all, enough height and sufficient space for six badminton courts. This number was an aspiration as the tradition of tournament play in Scotland involved a minimum of six courts in the Cornmarket in Edinburgh.

It took much research to unearth suitable buildings and to find one that would meet the basic specification. Eventually, I was directed to look at an unused paint works in Bogmoor Place in Govan, an area where some of the major shipyards had been built. A brief examination of the dimensions of the building indicated that it was high enough for badminton, big enough for six courts, and with other parts of the building that could be used for our other requirements. I found out exactly where Bogmoor Place was and set out to go and see it.

In a phrase to be used many years later, my initial reaction was that a lot of imagination was needed to envisage how this was going to work. The first surprise was that the potential hall was upstairs on the second floor. There were three industrial units on the ground floor and a two-storey extension at each end. After the initial sense of disappointment, I realised that at least the main hall was high enough and big enough. Closer instant examination revealed a large mezzanine platform, the whole length of the hall, constructed of concrete on a large steel framework. This would have to be removed, and it looked very permanent. The two buildings at the end were a mix of unused rooms at one end, and, at the other, with a connecting door at first floor level to the hall, a suite of offices with a small carpark. There was much to be thought through.

A personal friend and architect, Scott Calder, agreed to have a look at the building and its prospects. He was encouraging in that the two end buildings could be used for the ancillary requirements of a sports hall, or as offices with unspecified future use. Most important was his view that the large mezzanine level could be removed. We decided to ask him to draw up the necessary plans. We were directed to a demolition company to remove the mezzanine level and to work out what the market value might be for the industrial units on the ground floor.

Finance was the next challenge. We were recommended to a firm of quantity surveyors and over several weeks we finalised a set of plans. Demolition costs and all other items produced an estimated final cost of around £54,000. At the time, I was aware of the funding rules of the Scottish Sports Council and the reality that if they did not make use of their total government grant for the financial year, they would lose the funds. This somewhat draconian policy resulted in an enthusiasm for acceptable projects towards the end of the financial year. We fitted the bill beautifully—a progressive sport trying to better itself and in so doing providing new facilities in an inner-city area. Glasgow City Council was also helpful and the combined grant offers allowed us to proceed.

The demolition was undertaken and completed. The concrete floor then needed rather more attention to recover from the demolition. Dropping large lumps of concrete on it was not floor-friendly. We blacked out the roof windows and painted the walls the ideal dark green background. The separate building at the north side of the project became changing rooms, showers, toilets, and a small but adequate cafeteria.

We even managed to convert a small room up an internal staircase into an office for the hall, which eventually became a small shop selling badminton equipment. We purchased six portable mat courts and designed a simple lighting plot at the side of each court right over and beside the net. Even for tired eyes like mine, the shuttlecock stood out spectacularly well. Slightly to my surprise, the SBU decided to clean up the offices at the south end of the building and moved their staff to the new premises.

Looking back, the whole building effort was completed pretty much on time, until work was needed for the provision of the main public services of power and water. That was when we ground to a halt. Despite any number of calls to a variety of officials in these public services, I was getting nowhere. A knowledgeable and sympathetic badminton friend came up with the solution. 'You must have some badminton players who work in either of the two utilities,' he said. I did, and the problems were solved.

In retrospect, it was inevitable that the final costs would rise, but the successful negotiation of grants of £67,000 made the project costs of £74,000 viable. In my innocence, I had forgotten the financial instincts of the rates department of Glasgow City Council. When its first attempt at placing a rateable value on the hall produced an initial rates bill of £12,000 *per annum*, I could only assume that the department's officers did not know that the City Council had given us a grant of £5,000. In simple terms, the project was in liquidation before it opened. Fortunately, a full and frank meeting with members of the rates department made them see sense. Perhaps they realised that if I handed them the keys to the building, they would have no idea how to run a badminton hall. Our new and long-awaited hall opened in 1980 and, after a lick of paint, our new offices, also opened for business.

The project was very time-consuming and not as fully designed and costed as it should have been. There was inadequate heating, especially through a Glasgow winter, which made playing conditions marginally less than ideal, but the cost of full central heating for a hall of that size would have made the initial construction cost beyond our means. However, being able to play in our own premises from 9 a.m. to 10.30 p.m. without any other sport intruding on us was a real luxury.

I moved on to other sporting duties and the hall, now known as the Cockburn Centre, fell into the caring hands of the Glasgow Group of the SBU and in particular to its Chairman Tom Pettigrew. He virtually took the building into his family as one of their property investments and personally managed any repairs. The initial legal holding was by a twenty-five-year lease, but Tom raised the necessary funds to purchase the building for the SBU. Over the years, proper heating was installed, a new floor built, and finally a new roof erected. The hall has been the centre of badminton for the last forty years and an asset beyond price. The building is now named the 'Sir Craig Reedie Badminton Centre'. It was a kind gesture as, gratefully, for the time being, it is not the 'Sir Craig Reedie Memorial Badminton Centre'.

4

The IBF

The International Badminton Federation had been founded in 1934 with the membership of nine nations. These included the four home nations, as well as Ireland, Denmark, Canada, France, the Netherlands, and New Zealand. The list was not unusual as the organisation of international sporting bodies and the development of their sports were principally European efforts and, in particular, based on foundations from English national federations.

David Bloomer was president of the IBF from 1965 to 1969 and, as the new young secretary of the Scottish Badminton Union, took me to my first meeting in 1968. At that time, the IBF held only one meeting, an annual general meeting, and, the following day, a meeting of a newly elected council. These meetings were always held in London and the reward for election to the council was to be entertained at the All-England Club at Wimbledon by Rene Gathier of RSL (Reinforced Shuttlecocks Ltd) and Bow Brand Gut, businesses much involved in racket sports.

By then, membership had grown to fifty countries. The secretary was Herbert Scheele, the secretary of the Badminton Association of England. There was only one official language, English. No travel or other expenses were paid, and it became common that member countries would invite a friend or contact from England to represent them at the annual meeting in London. Probably due to his arrangement of the first Thomas Cup semi-final in 1949 in Glasgow featuring a team from the United States, David Boomer himself had represented the United States.

This may have provided his explanation of why he was elected president when he said that it was because he was one of the few candidates who spoke English, but it was not. It was his talents as a leader, not his linguistic skills, that got him elected. It was at that particular visit to London that I first met Stellan Mohlin from Sweden, with whom I become closely involved for many years. At the annual meeting in London in 1970, I was proposed and elected to the council by June Wheating, the delegate from South Africa.

In those more innocent times, it would be fair to say that the main items of discussion involved the laws of the game. As the nominated delegates of many distant countries came almost exclusively from England, a number of the debates involved arguments between different schools of thought within the game in England, as opposed to opinion from the rest of the world. The most acute at that time was a regular argument over the 'wood shot rule'. It was a fault under the laws of the game if the shuttlecock was struck with the wooden frame of the racket rather than the strings.

In those days, all rackets were made of wood. The general opinion from Asia was that the wood shot rule should be changed, and this case was argued constantly by K. B. Oon, a Malaysian living in London. He was well known in badminton circles as his three sons all played to a high level while at an English University. K. B. even once tried to convince me of his case by inviting me for a drink in the London Hilton along with his wife. To my surprise, Mrs Oon left the discussion every fifteen minutes and retired to powder her nose. Eventually, her husband felt compelled to explain this behaviour by telling me the hotel played her favourite music in the ladies' room every fifteen minutes.

The demand for change became ever stronger when technology started to be applied to badminton rackets. The Carlton company produced a revolutionary racket with the frame made of steel and covered in red plastic. This development started the trend towards using more modern materials in racket manufacture, a trend that has developed constantly and improved the enjoyment of the sport for literally millions of people. Stronger and lighter rackets have been of huge benefit, particularly to women players. To no one's surprise, the wood shot rule disappeared.

I also have happy memories of a prolonged debate over the serving regulations. Two of the more pedantic English delegates held a detailed discussion on whether a change to the laws should use the words 'each foot', or the words, 'both feet'. As the ultimate arbiter in any such debate hinged on the translatability of any new rule, this particular question was raised. I happened to be sitting beside Ole Mertz, the Danish delegate, who was a teacher of English in Copenhagen. I asked him if there would be a translation problem into Danish and he replied, 'Not really, as we have one word for foot and another word for feet in our language too.'

Of much more relevance was the news that along with the sport of water skiing, badminton had been declared a demonstration sport at the Munich Olympic Games in 1972. For your information, demonstration sports were officially introduced in the 1912 Summer Games when Sweden decided to include glima, traditional Icelandic wrestling, in its Olympic programme. Most organising committees then decided to include at least one demonstration sport at each edition of the Games. They were usually popular sport in the host country, like baseball at the 1984 Los Angeles Games and Taekwondo at the 1988 Seoul Games. Some demonstration sports eventually gained enough popularity to become an official sport in a subsequent edition of the Games. Traditionally, the medals awarded for the demonstration events followed the same design as the Olympic medals, but of a smaller size. They were never included in the medal count.

Demonstration sports were suspended after the 1992 Summer Games as the Olympic programme grew much larger. It is unlikely that they will be reintroduced as a requirement for future games. However, the Beijing organisers received permission from the IOC to run a wushu (Chinese martial arts) competition parallel to the 2008 Beijing Games.

The IBF had applied for programme status at the International Olympic Committee Session in Luxemburg in 1971. It had been rejected on the grounds that the games were becoming too unwieldy and that their size should be diminished—sounds all too familiar. The application was deferred until the next meeting in February 1972, to be held in Sapporo, Japan.

Efforts by the German Badminton Association and the IBF president, triple Thomas Cup winner, Indonesian Ferry Sonneville, were successful and badminton became a demonstration sport in Munich later that year. Arrangements were in the hands of the German Badminton Association. Twenty-five players from eleven countries were invited to take part in a one-day tournament. The players involved many of the world's best, including Rudy Hartono, Christian and Ady Chandra from Indonesia, Svend Pri and Ulla Strand from Denmark, Noriko Nakayama and Hiroe Yuki from Japan, Sture Jonsson from Sweden, and Derek Talbot and Gillian Gilks from England. Four events were planned, but without women's doubles, and a very suitable hall for badminton was prepared.

The council decided to hold its meeting in Munich at the time of the demonstration event and we all set off to a modest hotel in Gmünd, on the

Tegernsee, about 30 miles from Munich. I was now moving in circles with which I had no familiarity. After our first day of meetings, I found myself involved in a brand-new experience, a visit to a casino.

The party consisted of Sushil Ruia from India, very rich; Ferry Sonneville, reasonably rich; Stellan Mohlin from Sweden, quite rich; and me, definitely not rich. You had to present your passport to purchase any chips and I managed to drop my passport so that my very modest chips purchase would not be noted by any of my colleagues. I then had to learn the rules of roulette. After a couple of lucky bets on red and then black, it became clear that success depended on an intelligent selection of numbers. That was easy, as I used number nine, Rosemary's birthday, and twenty-four, our wedding anniversary.

Spectacular success followed with a win totalling $35. That paid my bed and breakfast bill for the three days, a drink with friends, and—by Reedie standards—a very expensive bottle of perfume on the way home. Despite the generous surprise, Rosemary destroyed my new gambling theory by reminding me that nine was our wedding anniversary and twenty-four her birthday. The moral is, whatever system you develop, just believe in it totally.

The venue for the demonstration event was a well-organised badminton hall. However, at the last minute, just before we had left for Germany, we discovered a basic flaw in the arrangements. A call had come to me from Germany to ask if I could bring with me a sufficient supply of shuttlecocks. No one at airports or customs had seemed to be remotely concerned that I was struggling along with a box containing sixteen dozen, which I hoped were the correct speed.

The hall was well filled with spectators on 4 September—the auspicious day of the tournament—and the standard of play was high and impressive. I have no particular recollection of seeing many members of the International Olympic Committee in the stands, but I do clearly remember a short visit by Avery Brundage, president of the IOC with IBF President Ferry Sonneville. It seems clear in retrospect that we should have made more effort with IOC members, but even that may not have been sufficient to gain us permanent acceptance onto the Olympic programme.

The players were all living in the Olympic Village but were entertained to a post-match reception before being taken back to the village by a special bus clearly marked with the Olympic rings. As we approached the village, the security at the entrance simply raised the red and white barrier and we drove straight through. Just a few hours later, the attacks on the Israeli athletes started, and the world of sport changed forever.

The IBF officials had returned to their hotel in Gmünd, and when we rose the following morning, we found the hotel full of athletes and coaches from different sports in the German team who had all moved out of the village. We followed the course of the attack, the moving of the hostages, and the final disaster at Fürstenfeldbruk military airport with an increasing sense of dread. Before returning the following day, we followed the ceremony at the stadium, when it was declared that the Games would continue. This was a controversial decision as the IOC had never faced a similar situation. I was in favour of continuation, but the memories of that terrible event remained with the IOC and were subsequently officially recognised at a special ceremony in the Olympic Village in Rio de Janeiro in 2016.

Our journey through Munich International Airport was not a happy experience as all security was now in the hands of the army and could only be described as very thorough. One very large soldier gave me a body search, and after reaching one spot, I thought to myself, 'should I ask if he wants me to cough?' Silence was golden.

At the IOC Session during the Games, the IBF application to be included in the next summer Games in Montreal in 1976 was, once again, deferred. Looking back at the whole exercise, it is easy to claim that the IBF missed a chance to have their sport taken into the Olympic programme. Yet the reality was that after the nightmare of Munich, the last thing the IOC was concerned with was an extension to their Games programme. However, it can never remove the sad feeling I have that my first Olympic day was 5 September in Munich.

Although Munich was a disappointment for badminton, the sport's inclusion in the Olympic programme had not seemed to be a major political priority for the IBF Council.

However, badminton was involved in the political situation in South Africa. The IOC had banned South Africa since 1964, but players from that country had competed for many years in major badminton events. In a sense, this was a political situation that the IBF managed with some success. There had been only one formal proposal to expel the South African Badminton Association, which had not been successful.

To my surprise, I was invited to visit our friends in South Africa, who explained in detail that membership of an international sports federation like the IBF was very important to them. This was despite the fact that there were huge difficulties for any South African player actually taking to the badminton court in major events.

My trip to South Africa started in Johannesburg, where I found the game organised and played almost entirely by the white community. Their facilities were excellent and well-used. I moved on to Durban where the Indian community organised and played the sport. Once again, I found the facilities to be excellent and local competition to be well-organised and popular. The next stop was to fly down to Cape Town where badminton was in the hands of the Cape Coloured community. I attended an evening match in their splendid hall when the best cape-coloured girl beat the second-best white girl and both teams and all the officials then went to a party.

The local organiser was a lawyer called Huxley Joshua and he spent many hours explaining the practical legal issues he had living in Cape Town, very few of which affected his badminton. The overall political system of the country was the long-term problem. The fee to be paid for what were a delightful few days with badminton friends was to end the visit by attending meetings with South African sports officials in Pretoria. Most were from the white community, and all were anxious to renew international competition for their athletes rather than token membership of the relevant international federations. As is often the case, the athletes were the losers. It was also very clear that badminton was not a sport played in the black communities. Although the IBF did not become involved in the very public protests against apartheid, the lack of membership from Africa was a clear weakness for the IBF, which took many years to resolve. All this was a useful learning process.

However, a serious political situation was about to raise its head within international badminton in a way that challenged the whole future of the IBF. The basis of the situation was what many people saw as the legitimate aspirations of the Badminton Association of China, but in reality, it was the whole sporting structure of the People's Republic of China. China had begun to emerge into the world sporting community at the Asian Games of 1974 and began to argue for its place in the world of international sport. It was clear that China possessed many of the best badminton players in the world, a number going to China from Indonesia in the early 1960s after the political disturbances in Indonesia.

With such playing strength, it became important that China was represented in the various international sports federations. In badminton terms, and in fact in many other sports, the problem was that the existing member of the IBF was the then Taiwan Badminton Association, the representative of the communist mainland's bitter rival, nationalist Taiwan. Mainland China argued in political terms that Taiwan was part of China, occupying its rightful place on the IBF, their case strengthened by Taiwan calling itself the 'Republic of China'.

The argument was made at a number of IBF annual general meetings by an unusual advocate, a former Wimbledon junior tennis finalist who lived in Iran and who had been involved in the 1974 Asian Games (of whom more later). Taiwan was represented on the IBF by two senior officials, individuals who were much liked, even though their country produced no great players from a very enthusiastic badminton populace. The IBF began to face a situation where the China dilemma became the only real issue at successive AGMs and threatened the whole existence of the organisation. Different skills and actions would be required.

5

War and Peace

China—the People's Republic of China—has become one of the leading countries in the world in hosting major sports events, from regional to national to international and to the Olympic Games. It now seems strange to record that around forty-five years ago, China was just emerging into the sporting world and demanding the status to which it believed it was entitled. By doing so, it caused distinct problems for sport's international federations and for sport at the highest level.

The Republic of China (ROC) National Olympic Committee had been recognised by the IOC and took part in the Olympic Games of 1932. However, that was before war with Japan and the vicious civil war that followed. Prolonged war and political upheaval in China meant that when Mao Tse Tung's communists were victorious and the People's Republic was declared in 1949, the original ROC was to be limited to the island of Taiwan, to where Chiang Kai Shek's nationalists had escaped. In effect, this meant that the world had two 'Chinas'—the mainland communist People's Republic and Taiwan's pro-Western nationalists. It was a dilemma for the world and for sport.

The People's Republic immediately demanded what it saw as its rightful place in the sporting world. In 1954, the IOC recognised the National Olympic Committee (NOC) of the People's Republic. It was invited to the 1956 Melbourne Games but did not attend and subsequently withdrew from the Olympic movement.

In the early 1970s, its priorities clearly changed. In 1979, the IOC again recognised the People's Republic's NOC, which agreed that Taiwan could also compete in Olympic Games, but on condition that it did so as

Chinese Taipei, with an appropriate name, flag, and anthem. Following an executive board meeting in Nagoya, the IOC accepted that under the 'Nagoya Resolution'. However, Chinese Taipei did not attend the Montreal (1976) or Moscow (1980) Olympic Games.

Badminton was one of the most popular sports in China and so the IBF became deeply embroiled in the political history of both 'Chinas' and their international ambitions. At the Asian Games held in Tehran in 1974, the Asian Badminton Confederation (an international organisation and part of the IBF) decided to expel the Taiwan Badminton Association and to admit the Badminton Association of the People's Republic. It was a rule of the IBF that any continental body could enjoy IBF membership if all their members were also members of the IBF. Clearly, the new arrangements within the Asian Badminton Confederation did not meet IBF rules.

To deal with this, the IBF called an extraordinary meeting in London on 30 June 1975 to amend its rules to allow for the change introduced by the Asian Badminton Confederation but with the proviso that any such membership was subject to the approval of the IBF Council. Any new member of the ABC would be denied access to the Thomas Cup, Uber Cup, and world championships. At the extraordinary general meeting, the council proposal was substantially watered down by an amendment from Pakistan.

At the full annual general meeting the following day, under the new rules, Pakistan proposed that the People's Republic should be admitted to membership of the IBF by a simple majority. Sweden also proposed that Taiwan should resign, somewhat to the embarrassment of Stellan Mohlin from Sweden, who was a senior vice president of the IBF. The Asian view was argued and presented by Richard Avory, a former Wimbledon junior tennis finalist who was resident in Tehran and who had been a supporter of Chinese status at the 1974 Asian Games. Richard was to become something of a fixture at IBF events on this subject before he was forced to leave Iran when the Shah was removed from office in that country.

In a significant later change of direction, Richard joined IMG, the Mark McCormick organisation, in Hong Kong and was to become instrumental in assisting the development of sport and other events in China. The proposal from Sweden was carried by a majority but did not reach the required two-thirds majority and was lost. The proposal in favour of the People's Republic was ruled out of order.

As you might imagine, the Asian members were not best pleased. With their long-term friends from Taiwan in the room, the general view of many was that the whole process was unfair and that 'politics should not interfere with sport'. Attitudes might well have been hardened by the unsuccessful nomination of Teh Gin Sooi from Malaysia to replace Herbert Scheele, the long serving secretary of the IBF. The president, Stuart Wyatt from England, was pleased to see that a decision to award the hosting of the first world championships to Sweden was passed and he spoke warmly about the chances of Olympic programme inclusion. Asian feelings were greatly enhanced by a final decision to award the 1976 AGM to Bangkok, with Hong Kong as the alternate.

The decision to hold an annual general meeting in Thailand meant that the IBF would travel outside London for that purpose for the very first time. The 1976 AGM was held in the Erawan Hotel in Bangkok on 2 June. As the chairman of the finance committee, I was delighted to see a more normal item being approved in that the unit value of the subscription to the IBF would be changed from £10 to 80 Swiss francs. The change of currency and the change in amount were both pleasing as we moved to a currency with fewer political overtones.

Of course, the principal item on the agenda was the proposal to expel the Badminton Association of Taiwan. This was carried by forty-five votes to thirty-five but once again did not achieve the necessary two-thirds majority. The meeting then turned to the application for membership of the People's Republic Badminton Association. What might be described as the Asian case was made on this occasion, and very eloquently, by George Candappa, a barrister from Sri Lanka. He was relatively small in stature but had a very round head and face with the most pleasant of golden suntans. This, added to his smiling delivery, meant that he well-deserved his new name: 'Sunshine'.

All the known arguments were used but George insisted on the reality that Taiwan, although wishing to be known as Republic of China, did not represent mainland China. The People's Republic claimed that their application made in 1974 was 'still effective'. Stuart Wyatt, whose company acted as factors to the Mountbatten Estates in Hampshire, allowed a prolonged period for the debate and announced that he would give his ruling after lunch. To the surprise of some delegates, he ruled that to resolve the problem, both badminton associations would re-apply and that a future full meeting of the IBF would decide. This decision was greeted with some reserve on both sides, which probably meant that it was correct.

By virtue of holding the meeting in Asia, there were lots of nominations of Asian personalities for election to the council, and again that Teh Gin Sooi should become secretary. Herbert Scheele, almost certainly unhappy with recent AGM proceedings, wanted to retire and the council preferred Herman Valken of the Netherlands, the current treasurer, to take on a combined honorary role of both secretary and treasurer. Another election was pending.

The main election was to appoint Stellan Mohlin of Sweden as president—unopposed, I am happy to record. Stellan had been a top player in his own country and a former president of the European Badminton Union. He had been active in the push for Olympic status and his enthusiasm was a major factor in the award of the world championships to Malmö in 1977. He had also been a client of D. L. Bloomer and Partners, my own firm, which had at one time held a whisky broking licence. This was not part of my portfolio, but we had become golfing mates on his visits to Scotland. His command of the English language was impressive as he used to send messages to tell me that he 'would bring me a bottle of my water', to which I would reply, 'Thanks but I prefer a single malt.'

When election time came, Herman Valken defeated Teh Gn Sooi and no Asian candidate for the council was elected. A new generation of Europeans, Commonwealth officials, and, unusually for a new member country, Oleg Markov from Russia were all successful. It seemed to me that during a pleasant post-meeting drink with 'Sunshine', I should explain to him that for many years, no one had appeared in London until the morning of the meeting, but that in Bangkok, many delegates had been in the hotel for several days before the meeting and had every opportunity to fully discuss all the options in advance. Sunshine listened with interest and then said, 'Really?!'

The results from the Bangkok AGM deferred the hot issue of China for a year and almost certainly allowed the first official world championships to proceed in Malmö in 1977. Asian opinions were divided as there had been rumour of an Asian championship in 1976 at the same time as the famous all-England championships, which would have been an aggressive clash of dates. However, despite confident statements to the contrary, the troubled division in the sport did nothing to promote Olympic inclusion.

Everybody appeared to understand that the date Stuart Wyatt's famous ruling would be tested would be 6 May in Malmö at the AGM held in conjunction with the first world championships. The atmosphere was tense as it became known that the Taiwan Badminton Association had appointed London solicitors who intended to raise an action in the High Court to the effect that the ruling was illegal. There was a certain irony in the appointment of a firm run by Stanley Jones, the brother of Arthur Jones, recently elected to the IBF Council. Despite this threat, the meeting proceeded with the necessary approval of the previous year's Bangkok minutes, which led to consideration of the effect of the ruling. The Taiwan Association had not made the requested application for membership, and this allowed the Chairman to declare that Taiwan was no longer a member of the IBF. Legal consequences were sure to follow.

The Championships themselves were a huge success: well-organised and with a full and international entry. Finals' day was a triumph for Denmark, which won both singles titles and the mixed doubles. Flemming Delfs and Lene Koppen were the singles stars, with Lene also part of the successful mixed doubles pairing. Indonesia provided both pairs in the men's doubles final and Japan won the ladies' doubles. There was no connecting bridge between Malmö in Sweden and Copenhagen in Denmark in those days, so the successful Danish contingent had to take over one of the regular ferries for their homeward party. Ole Mertz, their senior badminton official did not like parties, so he waited for the next ferry.

The threatened court case was called in the High Court in London on 5 July 1977, before Mr Justice Goff. I had hoped that the court might not accept jurisdiction to hear such a politically based case, but the IBF was still resident in the UK and jurisdiction was accepted. The IBF was represented by Miss Hilary Heilbron, the daughter of Dame Rose Heilbron, a very famous barrister and judge in England. In a case lasting all day, Hilary made very good arguments and maintained a strong defence in what increasingly appeared to be a difficult situation.

The judgement was a clear defeat for the IBF with their actions against the Taiwan Association declared illegal. Taiwan's membership was reinstated, and injunctions were granted against Stellan Mohlin, Herman Valken, and Stuart Wyatt to prohibit them from taking any actions that could give effect to the expulsion of Taiwan. Costs were awarded to Taiwan.

This judgement inspired an almost instant extraordinary meeting of the council, except for those named in the judgement, in the Normandy Hotel at Glasgow Airport. It may not have been the best hotel in the world, but it had the huge advantage of not being subject to the jurisdiction of the High Court in England. The small council was clear that further legal and regulatory process would have to follow. This had to be yet another extraordinary general meeting in London on 29 September to formally close the saga.

The council had re-instated Taiwan and now made a formal proposal that Taiwan be expelled, but did so with a clear statement that, despite the motion being in the name of the council, it did not have the council's support. On this occasion, Richard Avory represented the Asian Badminton Confederation and spoke at length against the council and its processes. He claimed that the meeting might be illegal, and that the council did not have the necessary powers. Significantly, he threatened that the reinstatement of Taiwan would have the effect of establishing a rival world federation. After long and acrimonious debate, the motion was lost by thirty-six votes to nineteen—a result that reflected the public instruction to the Asian Badminton Association members to not cast their votes.

To illustrate the degree of dissent and confusion, the meeting decided to accept the eligibility rules of the International Olympic Committee for players at almost the same time as the Asian delegates, and some others, held their own meeting to discuss the establishment of a new world badminton federation.

The Asian Badminton Confederation then went to work. A series of a preliminary meetings were held, and the new World Badminton Federation came into being at an official meeting in Hong Kong on 28 February 1978. The attendance and membership list were interesting. It contained, of course, mainland China, Thailand (which was particularly sympathetic), Hong Kong, Singapore, Malaysia, North Korea, South Korea, Pakistan, and five African countries. The meeting coincided with a 'World Badminton Invitation Championships', sponsored by Hong Kong. Of interest was the fact that Malaysia and South Korea did not take part in the tournament. The president of the new body was Air Marshal Dawee Chulaspaya of Thailand, and the secretary was Tim Fok from Hong Kong, who in later years was to become a member of the IOC.

The first world championships of the new WBF were held in Bangkok and Chinese players were almost universally successful. It became clear that China had a playing standard superior to all other countries. It also seemed apparent that much of the funding for WBF came from China. However, it was very significant throughout the early years that the major Asian badminton countries—Indonesia, Japan, Malaysia, and India—took no part in WBF events.

The IBF side of the sport continued its own programme and successful Uber Cup Finals were held in New Zealand in 1978, when Japan beat Indonesia five–two, and Thomas Cup Finals in Indonesia in 1979, when the home team beat Denmark nine–nil. The star players from China could only watch from a distance. The WBF organised a small number of events and found that the entry was not geographically representative and that China totally dominated every competition.

Stellan Mohlin, as president of the IBF, made constant efforts to maintain a connection with badminton officials in Asia. In parallel with the 1979 Thomas Cup Finals, a friendly meeting was arranged between badminton officials of both sides. This was held in Bandung, a provincial city in Indonesia, very much at the request of and organised by the Indonesian Badminton Association. The attendance list showed that officials from Asian countries on both sides of the argument were joined by IBF officials and two men who were to play a part in the future discussions. For the WBF was Henry Fok from Hong Kong (Tim Fok's father), who was an important businessman with close ties to Chinese authorities in Beijing. For the IBF was Suharso Suhandinata of the Indonesian Badminton Association, who had wide experience and knowledge of Asian opinion across many different matters.

Henry Fok had significant sporting experience with FIFA, football's governing body, and helped and advised the Chinese delegates throughout what became a unification process. The Bandung meeting came up with the proposal that a joint study group be established, and this was eventually agreed by both organisations. Along with Fok and Suhandinata, I joined the group and watched with interest as progress was slowly made.

As you might expect in any negotiation with a political element, it became clear that agreement would involve some acceptance of both positions but also that the important issue in Asia of 'loss of face' should be understood wherever possible. Debates were to continue about whether a completely new body was to be formed; how its membership would be established; voting rights; and the size of its committee structure. Both sides were aware of the Nagoya resolution in the Olympic world, where it was agreed that the National Olympic Committees of both the mainland and Taiwan could both enjoy Olympic membership with Taiwan adopting the name Chinese Taipei and with agreed flag and anthem.

Taiwan had also lost a court case in Switzerland against the IOC. With this background, it became possible to resolve a number of the main issues, but progress seemed to be slower than hoped. At one meeting of the study group in Hong Kong, Zhu Tse, president of the Chinese Badminton Association, seemed unsure about how he should proceed and was carefully protected in his remarks by Henry Fok. Their Chinese interpreter was a lady called Lu Shengrong and I was not always convinced that her interpretation was actually what was said but may have been what she thought her president might have wanted to hear. I managed to speak to her privately, not an easy thing to do, but with enough time to ask the question. 'What actually do you want?'

Rather carefully, she replied, 'Could we have one vice president and two members of the council?' From that moment, we were in business. Shengrong was to have a long and distinguished badminton history.

It took another study group meeting, in Copenhagen, to finalise the agreements and some correspondence with the Chinese Badminton president before both organisations agreed that WBF would unify with IBF subject to the following four principles:

1. The modified voting structures would provide for one member one vote on membership matters and proportional voting on all other badminton matters.

2. The South African Badminton Union would continue its policy of not taking part in the Thomas Cup, Uber Cup or world championship competitions.

3. The Taiwan Badminton Association would change its name to Chinese Taipei Badminton Association along similar lines to the IOC position.

4. The number of positions on Council would be extended to provide an additional vice presidency and two additional Council members.

Both organisations held their respective general meetings and approved the principles. The badminton world came together in Tokyo on 26 May 1981 in a ceremony of unification. The extended and united body held its first annual general meeting two days later.

When the practical interests of the Chinese badminton authorities became clear and were limited to mainly structural governance changes, my earlier blunt question to Lu Shengrong was reciprocated: 'What did I want?'

My reply was succinct and easy for China to accept: 'I want your players to enter and play in the following list of major badminton events.' The list included the top competitions of the IBF and the major national tournaments in the big badminton countries. China met its side of the bargain, and the sport was ready to boom. I wrote the deed of unification in Copenhagen, in the back garden of Denmark's Poul Erik Neilsen, three times winner of the doubles at the all-England and my successor as president of the IBF. It was after a splendid lunch, washed down with several gins and tonic, making easier the composition of a legal document full of long legal words like 'heretofore' and 'thereanent'. The final document read rather well. In an elegant gesture, Taiwan met the IBF's legal costs.

After seven years of discord, all the world's best players could play in the same events and standards were bound to rise. The split in the badminton world did nothing to help Olympic inclusion, but the opportunities presented by a unified sport were significant. Badminton had learned a rather painful lesson. In much of the world, it was impossible to separate sport and politics, especially geopolitics affecting large nations. For example, at the first WBF world championships in Bangkok, China's leader, Deng Xiaoping, flew down from Beijing to present the trophies.

It was also clear that, after the work of IOC president, Lord Killanin, and the diplomatic skills of his successor, Juan Antonio Samaranch, over the Taiwan issue, that the IOC was becoming a yet more powerful authority in sport.

Closer to home, in 1976, despite being free to play in the Danish, Swiss, and French championships, the British government did not grant visas to players from Taiwan who had entered the All-England Championships on a timely basis, leading them to have to withdraw. Badminton was in a new world.

6

The New Leader

After the excitement of the unification ceremony, I became the twelfth president of the IBF exactly twenty days after my fortieth birthday. I had inherited the chairmanship of the council from Stellan Mohlin in 1980, so I had a clear idea of my priorities for the sport, although in those days, there was no need for a prospectus or a strategic presentation of intended achievement. The IBF had a tradition of their presidents having short terms in office, with two years being the usual duration. Stellan had been a member of the council and a vice president for many years but had, by 1980, completed four years as president. It was seen as an elegant move to promote his likely successor to the position of chairman of the council for one year while allowing Stellan to complete the unification of the sport in his last year.

As chairman of the council, I knew what was required was an improvement in our administration. We had operated for at least two years out of the fourth bedroom of the house in Cheltenham in England owned by Ronnie Rowan, who was our only salaried administrator. Ronnie was a good player and both knowledgeable and enthusiastic as a badminton official, but she was seriously overworked. We had to move quickly into the twentieth century and employed Wendy Bennet as her assistant and opened a formal office in Cheltenham, which was to become our home for many years.

It was also a real pleasure to welcome one of the new council members. It was Tom Bacher of Denmark, with whom I had worked when we were members of the European Badminton Union (EBU) executive committee. I first met Tom in 1970 at the dinner at the end of the All-England

Championships when, unseeded, he and his partner Poul Peterson reached the men's doubles final. I had been sitting beside Ole Mertz, the senior Danish official, and asked him if the two young Danes had a chance. With his normal cynicism, he replied, 'You should see our fifth ranked couple.' The young Danes won fifteen–eleven and fifteen–nil. I was lucky enough to be at the Danish celebration table at the dinner and a close friendship was born. I had helped Tom with a partner for a visit to the Scottish Open Championships a few years later when Punch Gunalan of Malaysia became available and together they added to their list of badminton titles. Tom, a world class player in his own right, grew into one of the best sports officials I ever met.

He maintained a skilful balance between the interests of players and the commercial realities and organisational responsibilities of elected international representatives. Like many Danes, he possessed a good sense of humour and a splendid playfulness, which made him excellent company and a good friend. His distinguished playing career with Denmark gave him status within the IBF, which became a real asset in both debate and decision-making. He enjoyed the Danish habit of a morning or late evening beer and added a love of good red wine and small cigars to his personal preferences. We were to share many experiences together, not least a commitment to the charitable sponsorship of young orphaned girls in Indonesia.

In some ways, it was pleasing, after years of politics, that an IBF annual general meeting discussed the laws of the game. We were concerned at the potential development of what was known as the reverse spin serve. Conventional thinking indicated that the shuttlecock should only ever be struck on the base. We knew that experiments had taken place to develop a serving action that involved striking the shuttlecock on the feathers, thereby creating reverse spin on the shuttle, which made it almost impossible for the receiver to play a legal stroke. The suggested rule change was not accepted, and the problem remained.

At the All-England Championships in 1982, the Malaysian Sidek brothers and the Chinese ladies' doubles pair of Lin Ying and Wu Dixi had clearly developed the reverse spin serve to an unplayable level. If a player won the toss and chose to serve, the game was over. Both pairs won their doubles' finals easily. It became vital that the law had to be changed. I had always believed that instant legislation was bad legislation, but the requirement that the shuttle would always be hit on the base was being proved to be a serious omission in the laws of the game. Change to the serving laws had become a priority. The laws were changed, but probably one year too late.

The debate on Olympic inclusion as the best route for the sport had been challenged in a rather unusual way. Over the previous two or three years, an alternative route had been presented by a number of the better players who wished to see the future development of the sport based on tournaments offering cash prize money. Regulations had been put in place to allow for cash payments in an event where prizes were below 1,000 Swiss francs. Developments in events above that limit were considered under the heading of 'Open Badminton'. One tournament had been organised in London sponsored by an insurance company with a prize fund of a very substantial £20,000.

It was clear that a decision on the overall direction of the sport was needed. To make sure that the opinions of the players were considered, Tom Bacher and I met with leading players at the National Badminton Centre in Copenhagen. We soon understood that the opinions expressed by the players came from envy of the apparent success of the major tennis players and golfers, who, in truth, were independent contractors. Freedom of action like this was very attractive to the best European players. Control by the national federations in Europe was limited to the main IBF events, world championships, and team competitions, when players represented their countries.

In Asia, all the top players were contracted to their national badminton federations, which provided all travel expenses and a whole range of coaching, medical, and other performance services. Players were constant members of the national team. Direct payment of prize money to players was not permitted. Any decision to agree a preferred route for the sport had to have universal effect. A practical solution was found to legislate that all prize money would be paid to the national federation of the winning players and the federation would distribute this under its own national regulations. This would allow the IBF to have regulations acceptable to the IOC, but also allowed it to develop the range of commercial opportunities becoming available to the sport.

An early example of these commercial opportunities had been presented to me at a meeting with two representatives from IMG, the Mark McCormack organisation, then the largest and best known of the sports marketing agencies. One of them was Barbara Wanke, who was to make her name in the tennis world. They explained the benefits of becoming an IMG client, all very impressive and how important we would become in the world of sport. I happily agreed to consider their promised written report.

This arrived a few weeks later, along with a draft contract which gave only examples of the 'Promised Land' and explained why a modest fee of only 20 per cent of any revenue generated would apply to much of our activity. This clearly needed mature thought. While I was thinking, and not for too long a period, a letter was received from Ian Todd, the senior official in IMG London. It was addressed to me as 'Chairman, International Badmington [*sic.*] Federation'. The letter expressed some irritation at the length of time I was taking to 'think' and rather obliquely suggested that failure to respond to their original efforts might have legal consequences.

A reply was required, and I wrote politely to thank Mr Todd but to make the point that while I had only qualified in Scots Law, and was not familiar with English Law, it did occur to me that the fact he could not properly spell the name of the federation he purported to advise rather reduced his chances of obtaining satisfactory legal opinion. A few days later, I took a call from Alistair Mackay Forbes of IMG who said, 'I have just picked up the smallest and funniest file we have in our office. Can we please come and see you and start again?'

This contact and subsequent meeting led to a long-term arrangement with IMG and a personal friendship with Alistair that lasts to this day. The IMG office in Hong Kong became fully involved in badminton as we developed our commercial interests with a united sport and a huge Chinese market. Ian Todd became a good friend and our old adversary Richard Avory, who was based in Hong Kong, made a real contribution to badminton's business efforts.

Only two months after unification, the IBF took part in the first World Games with a top group from China among a high-quality list of players. The World Games was the inspiration of the General Association of Sports Federations (GAISF). This was the worldwide body, members of which were all international sports federations, from the major Olympic sports to the much more modest, but ambitious all the same.

Established in 1982, the World Games was an attempt to create an alternative and smaller multi-sport event than the Olympic Games for both summer and winter sports. The clear promise made to prospective member federations was the opportunity to present their sport in an arena that, if successful, could lead to inclusion in the full Olympic programme. Stellan Mohlin had become a member of the executive committee of the World Games and was very enthusiastic. He clearly believed this was an interesting new route to the Olympic Games.

The organisation of the first World Games was entrusted to Santa Clara in California, with badminton to be held in the Civic Auditorium in neighbouring San Jose. They were both areas that would, in years to come, develop into Silicon Valley. As our first thoughts were to run a tournament with decent prize money, the IBF passed its own organisation to the Open Badminton Committee. I travelled to Los Angeles to make provisional arrangements. It was clear at this early meeting that the organisers were enthusiastic but overconfident about what they believed they could achieve.

The hall in San Jose was adequate for the sport but there seemed to be little attempt to market the event and spectator attendance in any numbers was unlikely. Despite that early impression, the IBF was able to arrange invitations to many of the top players in the world. The numbers included entries from China only two months after unification, which added very considerable interest in the tournament. The Chinese entries included Zhang Ailing, who would, almost immediately, prove to be the best ladies' singles player in the world. Indonesia agreed to send its top singles and doubles players, as did Denmark and England.

The tournament then planned on allowing further entries that would be dealt with in a qualifying event. Regrettably, the arrangements for qualifying could not be delivered as the hall was not ready for play and practise until the date of the event itself. Nevertheless, after more than a few organisational challenges, excellent badminton was played, and the considerable interest in having top Chinese players was vindicated when they won four of the five events.

Despite all the good intentions of the first attempt, the concept of the World Games struggled to make an impact. There were few spectators and only minimal media coverage. There was a lack of experienced organisers, which resulted in rather poor delivery of the hoped-for services. The event ran at a substantial financial loss, which was eventually covered by Patrick Nally of West Nally and Co., the marketing agent of GAISF. West Nally was to meet similar financial obligations for the next two World Games, and the concept took some years to fully match its founders' intention. The badminton world reflected on its experience and, as will become clear, decided not to take part in future World Games, but to approach the IOC in a different way.

This different way was to prove more difficult than expected. Stellan Mohlin and I attended the 1981 IOC session and Olympic congress at Baden-Baden in Germany. Neither of us had attended an IOC meeting before, and in all honesty, we made more than a few mistakes. We were allocated hotel accommodation in a small hotel on the outskirts of Baden-Baden, which was some distance from the central meeting venue.

We spent at least two days trying to reach the IOC sports director, former Hungarian footballer Árpád Csanádi, in the mistaken belief that he would be the logical and most effective route to bring about the move of badminton onto the Olympic programme. Our attempts to interest members of the IOC made us realise that badminton was clearly not at the top of their priorities at this particular meeting.

We were not accredited for the full session meetings and missed the most interesting moments involving the contributions from the new athletes' committee. After two or three unproductive days, we left and I came back to London to attend a badminton tournament in the Albert Hall. On the following day, I read in the British media that the IOC had decided to include the sports of tennis and table tennis in the 1988 Games in Seoul. My embarrassment was complete. This saga left a deep impression on me. It was clear that holding and promoting a good idea, supported by all sides in our sport, was one thing, but actually delivering the required result was quite another.

For almost ten years, without having any day-to-day responsibility for bringing it about, I had been aware of attempts to persuade the IOC of the benefits to its Games' programme by including badminton. In retrospect, our efforts, although well-intended, had been rather naive and ineffective. We had been unlucky in Munich in 1972 as our demonstration sport status was completely overshadowed by the horrors of the terrorist attack on the Israeli athletes. However, on my first attempt in a fully responsible position, I had overseen a complete failure. My lack of knowledge of the inner workings of Olympic sport had been a major factor and this gap in knowledge had to be faced.

I made a call for help to Tommy Keller, the president of FISA, the International Rowing Federation, and the long-standing president of GAISF. I asked him that if I came to Zurich, would he meet with me and offer advice? We met in a Japanese restaurant near Zurich Airport and over a prolonged dinner, I got him to take me through the labyrinthine world of international sport, the place of the Olympic movement within it, and the role of the many international sports federations. Those five hours proved to be the most beneficial I had ever experienced. I had a much better idea of what was necessary.

7

The Thomas Cup and
a Step Towards Olympia

The premier event in badminton is the Thomas Cup. Otherwise known as the World Men's Team Championship, it was first played in the 1948–49 season for the trophy presented by Sir George Thomas, the founding president of the IBF. The first semi-final was played in Glasgow in 1949 with the subsequent final in Preston, England, a few weeks later.

The first winner of the trophy was Malaya, which had beaten a strong team from the United States in the Glasgow semi-final and Denmark in the final. The trophy was taken to Kuala Lumpur and effectively stayed in Asia for most of its subsequent life. The Thomas Cup was dominated by Malaya, later Malaysia, and thereafter by Indonesia, where badminton is the national sport.

The early competitions were established with a series of matches between national teams in different continents with the winner going through to contest the 'challenge round' against the holders—a system clearly based on the Davis Cup in tennis. Perhaps due to the dominance of Indonesia, the rules were changed so that a winner of the trophy could not defend it twice in succession in its own country.

For the final stages of the cup in 1981–82, the event was awarded to the Badminton Association of England, which was delighted to welcome back the world's biggest badminton team competition. The final stages were spread over four different venues in England. The final was played in London's famous Albert Hall, where the teams were presented to her majesty the queen and his royal highness the duke of Edinburgh.

There was much excitement among badminton supporters in England and indeed throughout the world at the prospect of Indonesia defending the Thomas Cup against, for the first time, a team from China. Regrettably, there arose a difficult problem with the Indonesian team before the competition started. At the All-England Championships in March 1982, one of the Indonesian selected players, Hastomo Arbi, had tested positive for a prohibited substance. In the context of the current sporting environment, it seems bizarre that the IBF had no doping regulations in 1982 and rather assumed that any breach would be dealt with by the player's own national federation. It was clear that a decision had to be taken before the start of the sport's leading event.

I called a meeting of the Indonesian team management before the first match of the final series. The team's manager was an old friend and a former president of the IBF, Ferry Sonneville. Ferry had a distinguished record in the Thomas Cup when playing for his country in several previous competitions. The drug issue was a problem and it had to be addressed.

While trying to agree with Ferry and his management colleagues, I knew the situation had a personal dimension for Ferry and his team. Some years before, his son and first child had died of an overdose of drugs in his own country. I greatly respected the way in which the Indonesians accepted the decision that their player would have to be withdrawn from the event with the inevitable media consequences back home. Despite my many years' experience to come in the anti-doping world, I find this episode unsettling to this day.

As holders, Indonesia was seeded to the semi-final stage. Its challengers were Denmark, Japan, England, Malaysia, and the People's Republic of China. I set off in my car to the Huddersfield Sports Centre to watch the first match between Denmark and Japan, comforted by the presence of a case of the Famous Grouse whisky, a gift from Matthew Gloag and Sons, the sponsors of Scottish badminton.

The gift allowed me to 'entertain' the court and equipment management team as they travelled all around England to the final in London. Denmark won the opening match by five–four in a very close encounter and qualified to meet China in the semi-final. We then moved south to the Gloucester Leisure Centre, where England were to play Malaysia. Another close and excellent match ensued with England coming through five–four and qualifying to meet Indonesia in their semi-final.

Under this original format, each match took two days; this allowed sufficient time to discuss, finalise, and oversee the sponsorship and marketing exposure associated with the whole event. For the first time in badminton, certainly in Europe, the matches were sponsored by companies from Indonesia and the final in the Albert Hall was televised by

Indonesian television. The combined sponsorship and television rights fees from TVRI (Television of the Republic of Indonesia, the country's public broadcaster) made the whole event possible.

With the organisers, I then travelled back up to Preston for the first of the semi-finals on 14 and 15 May, when China appeared for the first time and made short work of beating Denmark eight–one. Two days later, we were in Birmingham at the Ashton Sports Centre, when Indonesia played for the first time and recorded a similar result, beating England eight–one.

So to London. As you might imagine, the list of arrangements to present top-class badminton in the Albert Hall with royalty in attendance was long and complicated. Fortunately, there was just enough Famous Grouse to encourage the badminton technical team to keep going, and all the necessary security arrangements were completed in time. Play started at 6.30 p.m. on Thursday 20 May, and Indonesia won three of the first day's four matches, no doubt to the delight of a major television audience watching in the middle of the night in that huge country.

On Friday 21 May, play was timed to start at 6 p.m. The extra time was needed to allow for two presentations to be made. The first was done by my ten-year-old daughter, Catriona, who presented a bouquet of flowers to the guest of honour. Resplendent in her new Harrods dress and very expensive Mayfair hair-styling salon, Catriona did this with charm. The second presentation allowed the players of both competing nations to shake hands with her majesty the queen and his royal highness the duke of Edinburgh. Her majesty later told me it was the first occasion she had left her normal seat in the royal box and walked on the floor of the Albert Hall.

In discussions during the evening with our royal visitors, we were delighted to discover that there was a badminton court in Buckingham Palace, and I arranged that a donation of some top-class shuttlecocks was subsequently made. In what was an epic final, the Chinese team made a spectacular recovery from the deficit from the first night and won their first ever Thomas Cup, five–four. The famous trophy was presented to Wang Wenjao, the Chinese team manager, and the unification of our sport was complete.

During the evening, and at his request, I was able to present Han Jian, the top Chinese singles player, to Mrs Betty Uber who had donated the Uber Cup for international competition for women's teams. Han Jian spoke little English, and Betty Uber spoke no Mandarin. Despite that, in common with many meetings between eminent sportsmen and women, there was nevertheless a rather special moment of complete mutual interest.

During the queen's visit, who graced a special evening, no one in badminton, nor any spectator, would have known that HMS *Ardent* had been sunk that day during an incident in the Falklands War in the South Atlantic. I have never had a suitable opportunity to ask if the queen had been informed of the incident. At the time, she had a son, Prince Andrew, who was flying Royal Navy helicopters during the conflict. Her presence at a badminton event during those most difficult of times is to her great credit. It was typical of her that she would fulfil a diary commitment that must have been made many months before.

After two exciting and fulfilling weeks, during which badminton made considerable strides, I jumped back into the car and drove home from London to Glasgow. With me was Ian Palmer, our council member from New Zealand and a future president of the IBF, who had travelled over to watch the Thomas Cup finals. He was good company on the long drive as we reminisced about the matches we had watched.

We reached home late in the afternoon, when the washing machine was filled. On the following day, I was to leave him with Rosemary as I left for Rome and the IOC session. I had a real feeling of excitement after the international success we had just enjoyed and rather assumed that a further approach to the IOC could bring about results that had been sadly lacking in Baden-Baden the year before. This naïve assumption was to become another disappointment.

The 1982 IOC session was a smaller affair than in 1981 as there was no IOC congress at the same time and venue. Access to the official hotel was possible but access to the session room was not. People like me, and there were a few, were limited to coffee and lunch breaks as the main opportunities to approach and to speak to members.

On the first day, I arrived from my small local hotel in time for the first coffee break and began my sales pitch for badminton's inclusion on the Olympic programme. The advice from Tommy Keller on the identity of members who might be more interested or even more amenable proved to be more than a little relevant. However, I did not have photographic records of all the members and had to develop a style of introduction that was as much for my benefit as I hoped it would be for theirs.

It also became clear that most opportunities for meeting and discussion were very short. Coffee breaks were brief, and lunch breaks almost always removed the members to a room in the hotel to which I was denied access. From memory, I managed to speak to no more than three members at the first coffee break, all without making any real impression. In particular, I tried to find specific members who had some knowledge of the popularity of badminton in their countries, and this further delayed the efforts to make any meaningful impression.

The first lunch break was even less successful than morning and afternoon coffee and left me with the unfortunate experience of speaking to members who were not interested in badminton, certainly not involving any change to the Olympic programme. This taught me a lesson that I tried to remember when I later became an IOC member. It is a very dispiriting experience for enthusiastic sports people who have passionate convictions to ignore or dismiss them. As a complete novice at this new game and with only very limited connections I had a lonely dinner after my first ever day in Rome.

Day two was not much better, but I did manage to meet Dadang Suprayogi, the IOC member in Indonesia, who seemed an obvious potential ally. He told me he was an enthusiastic supporter but had no real advice about how I could achieve the inclusion of badminton through the IOC processes. A similar reaction was received from Tan Sri Hamzah from Malaysia, but at least I had made contact with two members from badminton countries.

Some other members were polite but not interested and it began to dawn on me that the current tactic of individual discussion was unlikely to be effective. However, the experience was useful as it introduced me to some of the realities of dealing with the IOC. Throughout those two days, all members seemed to be aware of the importance of the new IOC president, Juan Antonio Samaranch of Spain. It appeared that he had much power in any discussions or proposal on issues much wider than a particular sport and its ambitions to be on the programme. I decided that it might be worth trying to arrange a meeting with the president.

I found that his personal assistant was called Alain Coupat and I sought him out. He was personable and friendly. I asked about the possibility of meeting, and he said, 'Of course. How about tomorrow at 6 p.m.?' The date was made and dinner on the second night tasted much better.

I had never met Samaranch, but I was an avid follower of Olympic news. I had listened to President Avery Brundage during his address to the special ceremony in Munich after the terrorist attack and had followed the presidency of his successor, Lord Killanin, throughout the 1970s. I had read the almost constant reports in the British media about financial problems in Montreal for the 1976 Games and the major issue the IOC had with the boycott of the African nations over sporting links with South Africa. I had also followed the build-up to the 1980 Moscow Games and the major boycott instigated by US President Jimmy Carter over the Soviet invasion of Afghanistan. It soon dawned on me that running world sport involved a lot more than checking on the height of a badminton venue.

I was aware that Samaranch had been the Spanish Ambassador to the Soviet Union but had little knowledge of his sporting history, other than his appointment to the presidency of the IOC. I was soon to find out that not only was he incredibly knowledgeable about sport, he was also a consummate diplomat, highly proficient in the dark arts of international affairs.

However, having arranged a meeting with the president, my plans for day three had to be changed. This involved changing hotels and flights back from Rome to Glasgow. Rather than continuing as a lobby rat, I decided to become a tourist. The day was hugely enjoyable. I walked all around the Eternal City as a young impressionable visitor; St Peters, the Vatican City, the Trevi Fountain, the Colosseum, and all the other delights made for a memorable experience.

At 6 p.m., I presented myself at the president's office in the official hotel, and to my surprise, our meeting lasted for forty-five minutes. Samaranch began the meeting with the encouraging words, 'I know your sport.' We discussed at length the process of unification of the badminton world using the Chinese/Taipei formula with which he was very familiar. He asked several questions on the presentation of the sport before we got on to more international and political matters.

I explained in detail that badminton is a simple sport with the no need for expensive technical facilities; it is played by both men and women in equal measure and is fully international and compliant with the membership rules of an international federation, as required by the rules of the IOC. I made the point that any city wishing to host an Olympic Games would certainly have any number of indoor halls in which badminton could be played; the only issue was spectator capacity.

This point led on to a discussion of the geographical popularity of the sport and the clear evidence that this lay in Asia. It was easy to point out that much playing strength was situated in Indonesia, Malaysia, Thailand, and Singapore, in addition to further north in Asia with the game centred on Japan, Korea, Hong Kong, and recently China. I made the point that a sport popular in southern Asia would be of real interest to the IOC as its current reach and influence was not great in those countries. The point was not lost on the president. It was clear that the meeting was making progress.

He left his desk and from a table behind produced a small gift. He then said, 'When are your next world championships?' I told him that they had been allocated to Denmark in May 1983. 'I will come,' he said. I responded by asking, 'Do you have your diary?' That was produced immediately, and the dates were inserted. The happy accident of having chosen a European venue for 1983 became clear when we then discussed his future travel commitments around that time. Fortunately, Copenhagen is relatively close to Lausanne. To my surprise, Samaranch then gave me a direct telephone number and a direct fax number to his office in Lausanne for all future communications.

At that time, I was unaware of the tensions between the relatively new IOC president and the long-serving director general and former Olympic swimmer Monique Berlioux. I also knew from occasional communications with her that Madame Berlioux, who used to be called 'The Iron Lady' by insiders, was not interested in the sport of badminton nor its Olympic aspirations. Fortunately for badminton, Samaranch was far too astute even for the formidable French woman and she was replaced by the suave and very clever Swiss lawyer, François Carrard, a few years later.

Looking back, the decision to seek a meeting with the new president of the IOC was a game-changer. Quite apart from his personal reactions, it was clear that, for him, sport had a higher priority than I had expected. Having taken tennis and table tennis into the programme the previous year, it was clear he was more than happy to expand it. The meeting and his subsequent visit to a World Badminton Championships helped to allay my fears that taking a third racket sport into the programme might have been a step too far for him.

Having made an impression, and my experience from direct lobbying in Rome, it was important that the IBF organised a campaign to inform IOC members about the progress of the sport. This was put in hand. Any opportunity to meet with and inform the top echelons of the IOC should be taken and some of this became possible through attendance at other sporting events or organisations.

The success of those four days in Rome has always been a happy memory and is, perhaps, the reason why Rome is one of my all-time favourite cities. After many visits over many years, I still wonder how Rome manages to bring joy out of its endemic chaos. You can park your car anywhere you like as long as you leave just enough room to allow anything else to pass. In our over-regulated world, it is a freedom to be cherished.

8

New Friends and New Money

To my pleasant surprise, there was no need to remind the IOC of the agreed dates for the visit of President Samaranch to the World Badminton Championships in Denmark in May 1983. We were delighted to receive confirmation of his arrival on the Friday of the finals' weekend. The event was held in the Idrettens Hus of the Danish Sports Confederation in Brondby, just outside Copenhagen.

It was a well-known badminton centre with a main hall large enough to contain the necessary five courts for the early rounds and a centre court for the finals with 3,500 spectators. I had known the centre for a number of years as the host of different badminton meetings, not least the meeting with the top players to discuss 'Open Badminton' when an overnight stay was required. The modern Danish architecture had designed small rooms with metal bars on the doors giving the distinct feeling of staying the night in prison.

As a venue for major sport events, the centre contained practice courts, accommodation, training facilities, medical facilities, and the administration offices for the combined Danish National Olympic Committee and Danish Sports Confederation—an unusual sporting marriage in those days.

Danish sport was delighted to have the president of the IOC at its headquarters. The local organising committee under the leadership of Frede Kruse-Chritiansen, president of the Danish Badminton Association, had selected the Admiral Hotel in the city centre as the base for the IBF council and any guests. The Admiral was a converted eighteenth-century shipping warehouse on the harbour in Copenhagen. It featured the style of the best of modern Danish designers and their tendency to use minimal bedroom furniture beneath the old oak beams, which were a feature of the individual rooms.

Perhaps it was an error of omission, but I had not checked up on the suite for our important Olympic guest. As I showed him to his room, I was a little surprised to find that it contained a round bed and few other facilities. I wished him a pleasant 'good night' and returned to my own room, when the telephone rang. It was Samaranch. 'How do you get an outside line?' he asked. This seemed an unusual request but became clearer at the end of his visit.

On the following day, we took him to Brondby Hall and explained the organisation of the world championships via a conducted tour of the facilities. In those days, there was huge interest in people recording sports events or family experiences on small video recorders. The Danish organising committee had placed a fixed video camera, just a standard video recorder, behind each of the five courts. At the end of each match, the tape was taken by a volunteer to the pressroom, identified, and placed in a timed storage system. This allowed the attending journalists to remove and watch the tape from any match while enjoying the comfort and facilities of the pressroom, which just so happened was sponsored by the Carlsberg brewery.

Along with Tom Bacher, I had been watching a singles match involving Liem Swie King of Indonesia. When we explained the system to Samaranch, he immediately understood that the system was an important innovation and particularly attractive. When he asked if he could have a tape of the match we had we had been watching, Tom Bacher asked, 'Would you prefer a tape in the NTSC (American) format or the PAL (European) format?' This knowledge of the different television formats from around the world clearly left a very favourable impression on a president who understood the media world exceptionally well and who, over his future career, became very aware of a need to have and to maintain good relationships with the international media.

One unexpected benefit of living in the Admiral Hotel was the quality of the splendid buffet arrangements available to its guests. This allowed Samaranch to eat only the relatively small amounts of food, which he preferred. Despite this, he still attended the special dinner arranged by the IBF at the famous Langelinie Pavillonen, a fine restaurant close to Copenhagen's famous *Little Mermaid* statue. Being a Catalan with a taste for the *avant-garde* and design, Samaranch may well have been impressed by the chosen venue.

Still there as a wedding venue, it is a fine example of Danish modernism. The Danes are very fond of modern design and are particularly keen on contemporary light fittings. Apparently, the Pavillonen has a specially commissioned gem—the world-famous Poul Henningsen 'Artichoke Pendant', which, hardly surprisingly, looks just like an artichoke hanging from the ceiling. I cannot remember if artichoke was on the menu, but the owners were clearly missing a trick if it was not. An excellent evening was enjoyed by all, even though the timing probably kept the IOC president from his circular bed a little longer than he would have preferred.

As a highlight of the final day, the Danish Badminton Association had invited the Danish queen, Margarethe II, to attend, along with many other Danish dignitaries. Every one of the 3,500 spectator seats was filled. As is often the case in indoor halls that have multi-purpose uses, there is a special entrance for vehicles.

The royal car arrived exactly on time and was met by Frede, president of Danish badminton, and me. Queen Margarethe had chosen to wear a large hat and as we waited behind the curtain, which blocked final entry to the hall, the inevitable strong wind tried to remove her headwear. By this time, Frede had disappeared, presumably to give a sign to the assembled crowd that her majesty had arrived. At that point, the queen said to me, 'Why can't we go in?' to which I was forced to reply, 'I'm so sorry your Majesty, but I don't know the answer to that question.' To save any further embarrassment, Frede made a rapid recovery, the curtain opened, and the crowd was able to welcome their queen.

After the formalities, we all settled down to watch the five finals. To open conversation with the queen, I asked her, 'Do you know much about badminton?' I received the immortal reply, 'No. Except that we're rather good at it.'

The queen had to wait some time for confirmation. In the women's singles, Li Lingwei beat her Chinese teammate, Han Aiping. Lingwei was by then the best singles player in the world, only narrowly better than Aiping; she was to go on to become a leading figure in badminton, Chinese sport, and eventually the IOC. The result between the two best players in the world was not unexpected.

In the following men's final, Liem Swie King of Indonesia, who had beaten Han Jian of China in the semi-final, played the young Icuk Sugiarto, also of Indonesia, who had beaten the Danish favourite Morten Frost in the quarter final and then Prakash Padukone of India in the semi-final, to make it an all-Indonesian contest. In common with many others, I thought this might have been a disappointing final, but everyone was to be proved wrong. In one of the genuinely great matches, the young Icuk beat his senior teammate 15/8, 2/15, 17/16 in a classic that engrossed the Danish full house. After one very long and outstanding rally, Samaranch turned to me and said, 'We must have this sport!'

Clearly enjoying himself, he asked many questions about the strength of the sport in both Asia and Europe. He asked about the training and the apparent efficiency of the umpires and linesman around the court. The service rules, especially the rule to strike the shuttle below the waist, encouraged a long discussion and a clear understanding from the newly interested observer about the complexities of this rule and the difficulties in being a service judge.

Samaranch was impressed by the atmosphere in the hall created by a full house of spectators and the preference within badminton to have a smaller stadium full of spectators rather than a larger stadium half empty. He liked the confirmation that television coverage was delivered by DR (Danmarks Radio), the national TV station, and by a crew that clearly knew all about the sport.

After watching the top world pair from China, Lin Ying and Wu Dixi, winning the ladies' doubles, we all went upstairs to the lounge, where I was asked to present to him the Danish players in the tournament. He forgave me when, towards the end of a line of players, all of whom I knew by name, we came across a young woman I had never seen before, and she immediately became 'Another very good player!'

The queen's royal conviction on Danish standards was well proven when two Danes—Steen Fladberg and Jesper Helledie—won the men's doubles title against Martin Dew and Mike Tredgett of England. The crowd loved it. The extraordinary speed at which top-class doubles is played was on display again when Thomas Khilstrom of Sweden and his English partner Nora Perry won the mixed doubles. The Danish crowd went home thrilled by the mix of great play and national success they had enjoyed.

Samaranch left after the finals directly to the airport but not before we enjoyed a few reminiscences of a very successful weekend. From that visit, and well before any formal decision by the IOC on our programme ambitions, the president always seemed to make a special effort at many a future IOC or international federation meeting to go out of his way to shake hands, say hello, and speak briefly about badminton.

I interpreted these gestures to indicate his continued approval of our discussions in Copenhagen. Some weeks after the world championships, when signing off on expenses, I began to understand the reason behind the telephone request for 'an outside line'. His telephone bill turned out to be more than his room charge in the Admiral Hotel. On reflection, I realised that, even in May 1983, in reaction to the boycott in Moscow in 1980, the president of the IOC was very occupied in trying to prevent a boycott of the 1984 Games in Los Angeles. It was yet another small insight into the complexities of the Olympic world.

The introduction of individual world championships, all three events having been successful, encouraged a review of our longstanding major events, the Thomas Cup for men and Uber Cup for women, both of which were team sports. The distribution of matches was based on geographical rules and each individual match was played over two days. Tradition and history were all very well, but as international sport was developing very rapidly and changes in content and presentation becoming more accepted, it was time for a close examination of potential options.

There was also a clear disparity in popularity of the Thomas Cup over the Uber Cup, this despite the inclusion in world badminton of the Chinese female stars and the rapidly developing team in Korea. The 1982 Thomas Cup competition had twenty-six countries, while the Uber Cup competition in 1981 had only thirteen. It was clear that more entries from more affiliated member countries would be a good thing, but the two-day format of nine individual matches was not ideal. Also, the entry and travel costs were significant.

In a truly international competitive sport, but with relatively few sub-committees in its administrative structure, our practice of putting together a small but expert working group had been developed and accepted. The working group charged with what was a major change was entirely European—an unusual situation for a sport dominated by Asian countries. However, having gone through a painful unification process and then skilfully brought players and nations together, this reflected the lack of nationalistic or political issues in badminton, much to the benefit of the sport in those days.

Entirely coincidentally, it allowed the small working group to meet very informally in Tom Bacher's garden in Greve, a suburb of Copenhagen. A combination of constant coffee, sunshine, Carlsberg with the open sandwiches at lunch, a good red wine with the evening barbecue, and total relaxation throughout produced the kind of revision of regulations that is rarely achieved. Tom and Poul-Erik Nielsen from Denmark, Arthur Jones from England, Roger Johannson from Sweden, and myself become a close and effective group.

We changed the rules so that both Thomas and Uber Cup competitions would be played at the same time, in both the qualifying and final events.

Ties would be reduced from nine matches to five and would be played in one session and on one day. Each tie would have three singles matches and two doubles matches, which would reduce the minimum number of players in any team. Matches would be organised in groups using a pool system. Qualifying venues would be selected on a more practical basis and would not necessarily be continentally based. It was our firm belief that the finals events of both competitions would become a very attractive proposition to our member nations.

For the first of the new format competitions in 1984, thirty-four countries entered the Thomas Cup and twenty-three the Uber Cup. Qualifying events were to be hosted in New Delhi, Hong Kong, Toronto, and Ostend, bringing international badminton to new cities as venues. Strong Asian countries would exercise their right to qualify in different qualifying venues. The finals would be allocated to Malaysia and Kuala Lumpur after a break of fourteen years.

What looked like a really good development became an ever more exciting one. For almost all previous competitions, the finances of the qualifying or final ties were entrusted to the host badminton association. The working group had also planned for a more responsible financial situation for the IBF, which, if properly structured, would ease the burden on the host of the finals. I had developed some experience of the sporting sponsorship jungle through my annual attendance at the GAISF conference in Monte Carlo, when every novel sponsorship system and financial arrangement was a subject of discussion.

We were aware that in those more relaxed days, tobacco companies were big sponsors of international sport and that in Asia, and in particular China, the market was enormous. I had been approached by representatives from British American Tobacco and we were discussing the possibility of a sponsorship figure in the range of $150,000. With immaculate timing, I took a call from the Hong Kong officer of our new friends at IMG, asking if I had made any progress, then strongly suggesting that I should do nothing more until I heard from them in a few days.

Indeed, it was only a few days before they came back with the proposal that Philip Morris International was prepared to sponsor the finals using its Marlboro brand. The fee offered was $1 million. I called my contact in British American and made a fulsome apology, then went home, dropped to one knee, and thanked whoever had been watching over me for the previous few weeks.

A sponsorship deal with a company of that reputation and an amount well beyond any expectations would make the new Thomas and Uber

Cup competitions an opportunity for the sport that was unique. It was a dream come true: we could finance every part of the events; we could meet travel and accommodation costs for the finals; we could pay prize money; we could properly present the sport and with good court officials; and, above all, we could agree a favourable deal with our final host country.

This would allow us to reduce any hosting fee, control the advertising, and allow the host country to keep ticket sales, thus creating an excellent opportunity for the host country to benefit from the event in its own city. The opportunities were huge and every one of them would benefit the Uber Cup like nothing else. IMG was also happy; its commission was 15 per cent.

In addition to this mouth-watering prospect, the united IBF had decided to run a new grand prix event. Eight major tournaments, all over the world in singles only, were linked together as a means of promoting greater commercial interest and increased prize money for players. I had encouraged the Chinese badminton president, Zhu Ze, to include as many of these tournaments as possible in his annual programme. At a meeting in the Asian Games in Delhi in 1982, he had committed to the 1983 All England Championships and the world championships in the same year but the more exposure we could organise with our new Chinese member would be beneficial.

As it turned out, the timing of the 1983 council meeting could not have been better. We had accepted an invitation from the China Badminton Association to convene in Beijing in November that year. To our complete surprise, we received an invitation from the government of China to expand on our arranged visits to the Summer Palace, the Forbidden City, and the Great Wall, to include dinner with Li Mengwau, the Chinese sports minister. On 12 November, we were all received in Great Hall of the People by Wan Li, the vice premier of the State Council, the fourth highest-ranked Chinese official.

It was my first experience of a formal meeting with an important Chinese official with the formal seating arrangements: the horseshoe with the two senior attendees in the middle, and only those two as speakers. Wan Li offered a warm welcome and expressed his pleasure in being able to welcome people from sport, as opposed to those involved in the many intense domestic and international political issues, which were his normal daily diet. I managed to respond offering some sympathy for his position and responsibilities but assuring him that sports people also dealt with difficult and challenging problems, like the speed of the shuttlecock. He smiled graciously. This was a unique experience for a young IF president from a small town in Scotland.

The grand prix finals, sponsored by the Pro-Kennex Company, were allocated to Indonesia, to be held in its famous Senayan Stadium in Jakarta in mid-December 1983. Having qualified five of its top players, including all three of their great ladies' singles players, the prospect of top Chinese players returning to Indonesia was eagerly anticipated. However, Chinese memories of major political disturbances in Indonesia in the early 1960s, which caused an exodus of many ethnic Chinese people, including many who were top badminton players, made the prospect of a Grand Prix final in Indonesia more than a little problematical.

It would have been very damaging to the Grand Prix concept if the Chinese players withdrew. To avoid disappointment, I offered to travel to Jakarta for the finals and to undertake a responsible watching brief to ensure a peaceful tournament. In the end, all twelve men and eight women who had qualified appeared at the start of play.

The Senayan Stadium had a reputation as the most famous of badminton stadiums. It was an old building but attracted huge crowds when Indonesian players were on court. The lack of air conditioning, huge local enthusiasm, and the smell of the pungent aroma of clove and kretic (tobacco cigarettes) provided an atmosphere like no other.

The visiting players were all seated on the floor of the arena beside one of the two courts, and at the end of play on the first night, a sizeable number of local spectators gathered simply to watch the Chinese players as they gathered their rackets and bags before they left the hall. The players and their management found this disconcerting and I arranged that for the rest of the tournament a small detachment of the local riot squad was in position to ensure this situation did not happen again.

The four nights of play produced scintillating badminton and the reaction of the knowledgeable local crowd produced a welcome to the Chinese players which completely offset their opening night experiences. Li Lingwei, Han Aiping, and Zhang Ailing dominated the ladies' event. Luan Jin won the men's singles, beating Denmark's Morten Frost in the final, a result much influenced by Frost's incredible semi-final win over Malaysia's Misbun Sidek over three long games at 17/16 in the third game. Trying to fulfil my watching brief, I went to congratulate Morten on his huge effort, and he confided in me that, 'This place is not good for pale Danes.' The Pro Kennex Grand Prix had come of age.

On the following day, the Chinese party were to leave Jakarta airport on the morning Cathay Pacific flight to Singapore and on to Hong Kong, where they were to night-stop before returning to Beijing. There was a crowd of several thousand to see them off and passing through that tearful crowd was a very moving experience. Shou Fenshu, the Chinese ladies' coach, came up to me to say, 'Mr. Craig. Thank you for arranging this tournament here and for coming specially to look over us'. I told him that it was a real success to have the Chinese party and players there, but it was only a badminton tournament. 'No,' he said. 'What you don't know is that I see my family here for the first time in twenty-three years.' I can think of few better reasons for international sport than that.

9

IBF Changes and Other Tasks

The year 1984 was a significant year for the IBF and for the sport. The year was filled with the new structure for the Thomas and Uber Cups and their preliminary rounds. With Marlboro involved in its first finals under its sponsorship contract, our office in Cheltenham was in almost daily touch with the Malaysian Badminton Association, which was hosting the finals in their famous Stadium Negara in Kuala Lumpur. We may have underestimated the requirements of a major international company as a new sponsor, but the combined efforts put in place a framework for a major upscaling of a badminton event. However, we had a pleasant diversion.

1984 was the fiftieth anniversary of the International Badminton Federation. This was the reason behind the surprise suggestion that I should enjoy a third year of my presidency, as it was thought better to have an English speaker for that occasion. It was also decided to hold a short but very special tournament around the time of the All-England Championships but limited to previous players of distinction. To our surprise and delight, many famous players took the trouble to come to the Wimbledon Squash and Badminton Club, where many must have played in previous years, to renew friendships and enjoy the game they loved.

The Devlin sisters, Sue and Judy, were joined by many of their contemporaries with a substantial contingent from Denmark. Eddie Choong played, but more slowly than before, and Eva Twedberg and Etsuko Takenaka showed that they had lost none of their skills. I managed to pull rank and enter, playing with the winner of many major doubles titles, Poul Erik Nielsen, who was to be my successor as president of the

IBF. Unfortunately, we made an early exit by losing to a senior Danish couple featuring Jorn Skaarup.

As you might expect, the tournament ran into trouble with time, as the competitive instincts of the players had not diminished in any way. We had to reduce the individual games and matches to a shorter score, so that everybody would have time to recover and change for the fiftieth anniversary dinner to be held in the Park Lane Hotel in central London. We were joined by many of the current top players for a unique occasion. The dress code was formal, and I decided to wear my kilt.

The group of Chinese players was led by Li Lingwei China's top singles player, dressed in a grey trouser suit. As she looked across the room at the 'formal' dress of the host of the evening, I could almost hear her thinking, 'Why am I wearing the trousers and this man is wearing a skirt?' We have laughed together about that meeting over many subsequent years as she became a close and valued friend.

David Bloomer, the senior past president present, spoke in his normal amusing and relevant manner and Erland Kops, in his excellent English, spoke similarly on behalf of the players. Players from many countries mixed and chatted happily throughout the evening and left me with the strong conviction that the sport was in good spirits.

This feeling became even stronger as we gathered in the Federal Hotel in Kuala Lumpur for the first combined Thomas and Uber Cup competitions under the new format. Special editions of magazines and newspapers were produced as the enthusiastic Malaysian fans bought tickets in unprecedented numbers. The change in format to have eight teams in each competition with four matches on each night provided a feast of badminton for the many thousands of knowledgeable spectators. The Uber Cup was dominated by China, beating England five–nil in the final, with South Korea winning over Denmark by the same score in the third-place match.

In the Thomas Cup, Malaysia failed to qualify from its group, but this did nothing to reduce interest in the final stages. Indonesia won back the famous trophy by three–two in the final against China, reversing the result from London two years before. England won a very close third place match by the same score against South Korea. Packed crowds watched the final stages and there was blanket television coverage. There was little doubt in anyone's mind that the changes to the format had been a great success and sponsors, television, hosts, and the IBF could bask in everyone's reflected glory.

The 1984 annual general meeting was my last AGM in the chair of the IBF. The meeting dealt responsibly with the normal issues on finance, membership, and the laws of the game, but I was allowed a few moments at the end to offer my own thoughts. In my closing remarks, I said:

In 1981 I had three general ambitions:

a. To have all the world playing together after the disappointing period from 1977 to 1981 and, with very limited exceptions, I am delighted that this has been achieved.

b. To try to make badminton larger, richer, and more powerful. Our membership is on the increase. We have worked hard to absorb the commercial interests coming into our sport and this has resulted in much more international play on a truly world scale than ever before. And the impact of both in publicity terms makes us more powerful.

c. The third was to progress our Olympic inclusion. Despite the present troubles in the Olympic Movement, I am convinced that badminton will come to no harm by continuing its application. 1992 is a long way off and we live in a changing world.

International sport serves humanity, and, as one of the larger members of the international sport community, we also have that duty. In my view, we do it well and one of the prime reasons is that the IBF allows no gap to develop between those who administer the game and those who play. As long as you remember that your only duty as administrators is to make the game better for all those who play. Then, even more than now, the IBF will be admired by the international sporting community, and you will better serve humanity.

The minutes of that meeting also included a short piece of information from me to the members. It confirmed that the IOC programme commission intended to balance the sports in the Olympic programme at its meeting in November 1984 and that the results would be presented to the 1985 session of the IOC in East Berlin—most definitely a work in progress.

For quite long periods in the previous fourteen years, I had been serving on two other international sports organisations. The first of those was the European Badminton Union (EBU). Founded in Frankfurt in 1967 from the enthusiasm of the then German Badminton Association, it became the continental body for Europe. Stellan Mohlin had been its second and long-serving president from 1969 to 1977 and there was close integration with the progress of the IBF and a sharing of officials. I first appeared as a delegate representing Scotland in 1970 and chaired the umpiring sub-committee for three years from 1974. Everybody must start somewhere.

The EBU concentrated entirely on the organisation of the playing programme and for many years was happily free from politics. European championships started in Bochum in West Germany in 1968, with a spectacularly successful edition in Dublin in 1976, organised by Frank Peard, internationalist, and Guinness executive director, to be followed by the Helvetia Cup for smaller countries. Junior championships started in 1969 in the Netherlands, and Scotland hosted the second junior event in Edinburgh in 1973.

A Europe Cup for club competition was also started with its first finals in Bochum, but by 2007, this had extended as far as the Club Primorye in Vladivostok. This club had been developed by a few enthusiasts, perhaps from the naval base, an amazing nine time zones away from Moscow. It has also hosted the Russian Open Championship. A further healthy development was the creation of a development committee to help spread the game, mainly to eastern and southern Europe.

For many years, the driving forces behind the EBU both came from Holland: Herman Valken, the treasurer of the IBF, and Emile ter Metz, a talented and enthusiastic parent of a gifted daughter from Haarlem, who was also the organiser of the Flower Tournament in Dijnwuik. This event had a happy policy of offering visiting international players private hospitality in the homes of local people. Unfortunately, the men's singles one year was won by Elo Hansen of Denmark, and the elderly couple with whom he had been placed were so proud that their guest had won the event, they left the hall, rushed home, and prepared a special dinner for him. Unaware of their kindness, Elo celebrated at length and only staggered home at five o'clock in the morning. Private hospitality was less popular thereafter.

As the EBU grew and developed its own programmes, there was a clear feeling that too much discussion of IBF issues was unwelcome, and Poul Erik Nielsen and I resigned our EBU vice president positions to concentrate on IBF duties. Around that time, politics did emerge in the EBU with the usual Russian proposals that its language should become an official language of the organisation and that national flags and anthems should be involved in presentation ceremonies. Badminton had been wise to avoid such requirements for many previous years. Further strain was caused by turmoil in the Balkans and membership issues involving Yugoslavia. The EBU was later to develop into a very well-organised, professionally run, and effective continental body.

The second of these organisations was GAISF. Founded in 1967 as the General Assembly of International Sports Federations, it became the General Association of IFs in 1978. Formed to be a relatively small grouping of international sports federations, it organised an annual assembly for discussion of matters of mutual interest and effectively became a system of transfer of knowledge between IFs. Badminton's IBF joined in 1978 and found an ever-growing organisation with members sharing common interests which included all the sports on the Olympic programme and many others who harboured that ambition.

Originally based in Lausanne, the organisation opened a small administrative office in Monaco, one of the first sports organisations to do so. It was encouraged by Prince Rainier, who saw attracting sports organisations as part of the long-term development of his principality. Monaco became a very popular venue for the annual general assembly, which attracted almost all the most important office bearers of the IFs and increasingly their sponsors, advisers, and supporters.

In 1978, the GAISF president was Tommy Keller from FISA (the International Rowing Federation). A polished, multi-lingual Swiss, he appeared to be allowed much free time from the family business to develop his sport and to encourage the complicated and expensive business of building rowing courses. He also had time to oversee GAISF, a position from which he often tried to curtail the growing power of the IOC, when Samaranch became its new president. It was a political battle that Keller would eventually lose. His secretary general was Charles Palmer from the UK, who was also secretary general of the IJF, the International Judo Federation, as well as a leading official in several British sports organisations.

I was asked to serve on a small sub-committee to review the English version of the GAISF statutes, with one sensitive problem to face. The IJF had lost confidence in its secretary general and no longer wished him to hold the same position with GAISF. There was always great interest in who might stand for or be elected to international positions. There was also a feeling that some elegant way should be found to deal with an official who had served the organisation in a leading position. The solution finally agreed was to recognise that a new secretary general would have to be elected but that a new position of vice president would be created, clearly to allow Palmer to move, probably sideways, but still retaining a significant position.

There was much informal debate among members and interested parties with a view to accept the changes in the statutes, but no comment came from Palmer about his intentions. In reality, he took much time to decide that he would not stand for the new vice president position, and at the very last minute, a nomination appeared for Un Yong Kim from South Korea, president of the World Taekwondo Federation, who had been a major influence in the successful Seoul bid for the 1988 Olympic Games. Kim was to become president of GAISF in 1986 but significantly a member of the IOC, chairman of its radio and television commission, and a vice president who developed a very close relationship with Samaranch. He was a candidate for the presidency of the IOC in 2001.

At the same time, GAISF was presented with comprehensive structural change. In part to thwart Keller's aim for independence, the IOC had established: the Association of Summer Olympic Federations (ASOIF), a grouping exclusively for sports on the summer programme; the Association of International Olympic Winter Sports Federations (AIOWF), a similar organisation for sports on the winter programme; and the Association of IOC Recognised International Sports Federations (ARISF), a group of sports recognised by the IOC but not in either programme.

The effect of the above was to concentrate discussion on Olympic matters to those specific groups, as opposed to the full GAISF membership in an open session. Sceptics argued, not without justification, that the moves were designed to restrict the growing influence of GAISF and some personality issues between Keller and Samaranch. The IOC countered with its own view that the development of international federation (IF) involvement in the Olympic Games would be an ongoing process best discussed with only those sports with specific interests and on the programme. In truth, the answer was somewhere between those two views. The commercial development of sport was of growing interest to IFs and also to the IOC. At that time, there was no worldwide sponsorship programme and the commercial rights in the Olympic Games were developed mainly by the host city organising committees.

For its annual general assembly in the sun of Monaco, GAISF would allocate a different theme for each year. I also became involved in preparations for those assemblies, and in 1984, the theme selected was 'the Commercialisation of Sport', designed to provide interesting content for all participants. We put together an impressive group of speakers with different skills and different business models.

My own contribution was to ask Ian Todd of IMG to speak. We had become friends after our shaky start, and he represented the then leading agency in world sport. To give an alternative view, I invited David Hill, who was the director of the Open Golf Championship for the Royal and Ancient Golf Club in St Andrews. David made a clear case that an IF should embrace all its commercial interests itself and deliver them in-house, rather than outsourcing to an agency, a more than interesting alternative. To speak on behalf of the world of television, where rights fees seemed to be expanding exponentially, we were delighted to welcome Neal Pilson, head of TV for CBS in the United States, the US rights holder for recent Olympic Winter Games. He caught the instant attention of his audience by his opening remarks:

> My name is Neal Pilson, head of TV for CBS. There are many changes in our business at the moment and my assistant is sitting upstairs in the balcony and will give me a sign if I am no longer head of TV for CBS by the end of this presentation.

At the end of an excellent and relevant day, the IFs had been presented with much food for thought.

Perhaps due to the success of that assembly, I became more involved with efforts to provide services to GAISF members and with its finances. There was a small study group to look at styles for television contracts, which resulted in an initial TV manual. There was also a need for improvement in membership fees and financial controls and I was asked to help the secretary general, Luc Niggli, and the treasurer. There is an abundant history of Scots being placed in positions of financial responsibility, due perhaps to our national characteristic of possessing short arms and deep pockets. I eventually inherited the treasurer's role. The importance of an interesting theme at the annual assembly was central to the success of GAISF. Assemblies in Colorado Springs, Lausanne, and Budapest, where the theme was 'Sport and Media', maintained interest and the 1990 assembly in Monaco was given the theme of 'Women in Sport'.

That was probably one of the first major sport conferences recognising the issue of gender equality, although the conference might have been remembered more for proving that sport showed a distinct lack of it. Anita de Frantz from Los Angeles and the IOC made the opening keynote speech as chair of the IOC Women in sport commission and was supported by several other female representatives of different women's groups. Their enthusiasm and requests for greater involvement and exposure were clear. Regrettably, the topic did not seem to excite the audience in the same way as did sponsorship and TV rights. Specifically, the habit of Primo Nebiolo, president of the International Athletics Federation, spending all day during various presentations in close and constant discussion with one of his entourage, seriously upset some of the presenters.

During the coffee breaks and the post-assembly drinks, I was subject to several complaints about the apparent lack of enthusiasm among the audience. One enraged woman went as far as saying that men showed an inability to consider inequality probably because they could not even sew a button on. I pointed out to her that being married to a busy doctor meant that I had mastered the art of button sewing many years ago, but that if the case for gender equality in sport was to be based on intellectual assertions like that, there would be little chance of any sympathy. She apologised and calmed down; we then became campaigners together in the UK to develop women's sport. It was a conference theme that may have been before its time, but I was subsequently presented with a financial report that indicated that the 1990 assembly had shown a loss of over $40,000 due to high travel and accommodation costs of the number of speakers invited. This caused a hole in the annual accounts.

For 1991, it was clear that we needed a conference theme that would engage all the participants. I had been speaking to John Coates, the president of the Australian Olympic Committee, about the possibility of Sydney hosting an assembly. As we considered what, at first, seemed a rather remote location, it became clear that many IFs saw a Sydney venue as an opportunity to meet with their national federations in that part of the world. Sydney was also toying with the idea of a future bid for the Olympic Games and a GAISF assembly could fit well with its aspirations.

We decided that if suitable arrangements could be made, we would use the theme of 'International Federations in the Olympic Movement'. Research quickly indicated that Qantas, Australia's national airline, was flying with many empty seats down to Sydney. The Intercontinental Hotel in Sydney could hardly believe its luck when asked to quote for suitable accommodation for such large numbers. Our friends in the Australian Olympic Committee were hugely helpful in the more detailed arrangements for the actual assembly and its preparation.

So, Sydney it was. Attendance was high. Qantas met the travel costs of the GAISF council, and the Intercontinental Hotel proved to be a friendly and cost-effective home. The Sydney Convention Centre hosted an excellent assembly, and the theme involved every attendee in some way or another. Sydney is one of the great cities and the hospitality was splendid. By pure chance, the organisers managed to get 'Round the World' racing yachts into the famous harbour and Jacques Rogge, a future president of the IOC and an Olympic sailor, had the thrill of captaining one. Sydney seemed happy to enjoy the presence of another seventeen IOC members.

When we added up the final costs, we found to our delight that the 1991 assembly produced a surplus just higher than the $40,000 loss on the 1990 event. At the following year's annual general meeting, I retired as treasurer of GAISF to take on the chairmanship of the British Olympic Association, but my newfound reputation as a financial genius was rewarded with the presentation of a large silver salver.

It was a fascinating period in the development of major sport. There were many new events, new personalities, and major commercial interest. Samaranch, the enthusiastic and talented new IOC president, was on a mission to develop the IOC across all its interests, especially its finances. International federations were equally intent on enhancing their own commercial interests, launching or expanding their world championships, and growing their sports. The overall mood was one of real progress and I confess that I enjoyed being part of it, despite my absolute priority of achieving Olympic programme status for badminton. Similarly, the leading personalities became figures of interest to the media whose own agendas coincided with the sporting boom.

Samaranch was seen as the ringmaster, and his many moves to develop the Olympic movement were followed and analysed closely. Un Yong Kim was a 'coming man' with close links to Samaranch and the IOC through the organisation of the 1988 Olympic Games in Seoul, and no one seemed concerned that, when he had become president of the Korean Taekwondo Federation, he had ceased any contact with the International Taekwondo Federation, the North Korean-supported organisation, thereby maintaining a split in the sport which lasted for many years. Kim was later to receive a formal warning from the IOC over the Salt Lake bidding scandal which was to cost him much loss of status.

Primo Nebiolo was another dominant figure in the sporting world. A long jumper in his athletic career and a successful businessman, he became president of the Italian Athletics Federation in 1961. He joined the IAAF Council in 1972 and became its president in 1981, an election delayed for over a year due to the US-led boycott of the Moscow Olympic Games in 1980. The election campaign involved a concerted effort to defeat the long-standing President Adriaan Paulen of the Netherlands.

Nebiolo, a controversial character, made many changes to the IAAF, introducing world championships and payments to athletes but was accused of involvement in the rigging of the long jump event at the 1987 world championships to ensure a bronze medal for Italy's Giovanni Evangelisti. He became president of ASOIF in 1983 and was seen to be in frequent opposition to Samaranch until he became an IOC member in 1992.

One name behind the development of international federation influence and success was Horst Dassler. Before becoming chairman of Adidas, his father's German sports goods manufacturer, he had established the first sports marketing business with Patrick Nally. Together they developed a successful relationship with Joao Havelange, the new president of FIFA, and brought several major companies to be worldwide sponsors of football. In 1982, minus Nally, Dassler established ISL Marketing to continue the original sponsorship arrangements but added television rights to make the revenues even greater.

In May 1985, ISL was appointed as the marketing agency of the IOC, a contract and decision that was not put out to tender. Dassler also acted for the IAAF and was believed to have close relationships with Nebiolo, developed during his long running election campaign in 1981. In all these corporate contracts with leading sports organisers, there was the clear possibility of conflicts of interest, but the new riches greatly outweighed any 'questionable' complications in their delivery.

Over the years, there has been much journalistic scrutiny of the influence that Horst Dassler had over the key figures in the higher echelons of world sport, particularly his role in the ascendancy of Havelange, Nebiolo, and Samaranch. British journalism in particular was critical of the influence of a German marketer over three 'Latin' individuals who had replaced the previous leaders of sport who probably were above any form of wrongdoing but also had lacked an ambitious vision for their sport and had failed to grasp the potential of commercial opportunities. It is a complex issue.

On the negative side, there is little doubt that Dassler's influence, particularly in the Third World, was a major factor in advancing the careers of the 'big three' in world sport and in the commercialisation culture in sport in those years. On the other hand, the sports marketing revolution was an important and timely transformation. Before it, most sport was in need of development, growth, and needed money. The sport we enjoy today—its scale, its presentation, both in venues and in the media; its grassroots base and its many social and health benefits, physical and mental—is directly a result of the changes that took place in the 1980s.

To be blunt about it, while Dassler and others were wheeling and dealing, my priorities were to maximise prize money in badminton, get it onto the Olympic programme, and grow the game around the world.

10

Olympics at Last and New Business

It was very unusual for the IBF to offer a position to a retiring president, but in my case, they did. At the 1984 annual general meeting, they established the 'business committee' with me as chairman and made Tom Bacher from Denmark and Titus Kurniadi from Indonesia members. Tom and I had known each other for several years and worked closely together. Titus was one of the newer members of the Indonesian Badminton Association but a man with much experience of business in Asia.

The composition of the new committee clearly indicated the areas of the world in which it would be most involved and recognised the importance of the major sponsorship possibilities in that part of the world. I had a second but equally important role in promoting the IBF's Olympic ambitions, particularly programme inclusion and any resulting developments. To balance both activities was to create diary and travel challenges but also opened up a whole new world in international sport.

The first of these challenges was to influence in some way the November meeting of the IOC programme commission when badminton's future was on the agenda. Contact had been established with Walther Troeger, the IOC sports director, who had been consistently helpful in understanding our aspirations. The programme commission meeting must have been successful, as we were informed that the inclusion of badminton would be on the agenda of the 1985 session of the IOC to be held in East Berlin in June. I was just a little irritated at the relatively slow progress in the Olympic world in matters that I considered to be of great importance but in later years learned to understand the system. The formal invitation to attend the session was gratefully received and accepted.

Travel to East Berlin involved arrival in West Berlin and special documentation giving access to the session via the famous Checkpoint Charlie, the most public entry to East Germany at that time. For anyone who has walked through the infamous crossing between the West and the Eastern Bloc, it is quite an experience. Images of exchanges of espionage agents in spy novels and films, and the affluence of West Berlin compared to the run-down drabness of East Berlin, come flooding into one's imagination while walking past heavily armed guards and looking up at dilapidated buildings still bearing the scars of the Second World War.

Despite some initial concerns, the actual process was slow but safe and I found myself happily installed in the Palasthotel as a guest at the ninetieth session of the IOC. Although better designed than most East German buildings, the Palast was an enormous concrete and glass block of over 1,000 beds. As well appointed as anything could be in the Eastern Bloc, its food was a little less elaborate than the cosmopolitan offerings on the other side of the Berlin Wall. Nevertheless, it was comfortable enough.

What I did not know at the time was the hotel's nickname, the 'Stasi-nest'—an important part of the Stasi-surveillance of all foreigners who entered East Germany. At all times, there were four Stasi officers employed to monitor the hotel. With Stasi recording suites on the fifth floor and using cameras and microphones throughout the building, the spooks kept the reception hall, lifts, corridors, and several rooms under strict surveillance. Twenty-five to thirty rooms in the hotel were technically equipped for the 'necessary monitoring' of especially 'interesting' guests. However, I am fairly certain I was not one of them. On the other hand, I am equally certain that President Samaranch, a former Spanish ambassador to Moscow, was one of the 'interesting' guests, as must have been some of the assortment of sheikhs, princes, princesses, generals, and prominent businessmen among the IOC membership.

It was my first ever visit behind the Iron Curtain and it was interesting to see that the hotel was happy to receive US dollars, British pounds, Swiss francs, and most other convertible currencies but had a reluctance to accept Ostmarks (the East German currency). This was of course to ensure that the state maximised its revenue in valuable foreign currency. Needless to say, ordinary East Germans were not allowed to stay at the hotel. Credit cards were fine but mine was in my own name and not in the name of the IBF, so, as a Scot, I was somewhat 'conservative' in its use.

Agendas for IOC sessions are inevitably long as the meeting is the annual opportunity for discussion and debate on the broad range of Olympic and sporting issues. However, in those days, meetings had to be prepared and conducted without the benefits of the instantaneous methods of communication we have today.

As always, an agenda is only a list of subjects, not a chronological list of when they will be discussed, so I found myself outside the session room for several days waiting for the programme decision. Waiting was tolerable in the company of British journalists or other interested parties, and I listened with interest to their analysis of the rumours filtering from the Session room or from their own contacts. Discussions with experts like John Rodda of *The Guardian*, Ian Mcleod of *The Telegraph*, and David Miller of *The Times* were always stimulating. They were very well informed on all matters Olympic, and their reports were read widely by an interested audience in Britain.

One major topic was the strong rumour that Samaranch was considering a change of executive director at the IOC, and much debate ensued on the level of compensation to be paid to the formidable Monique Berlioux, the 'Iron Lady' of the IOC, who had held the post since 1971 and had much influence in the Olympic movement. I did not know Madame Berlioux well but knew that she had not been interested in any expansion of the Olympic programme.

The advice from Samaranch, given to me in Copenhagen in 1983, that contact with him should be through his own private telephone or fax lines, rather reinforced the point that Berlioux was a significant obstacle on badminton's path to Olympic inclusion.

A second subject of session gossip was the possible IOC decision on the host city for the 1992 Olympic Games. The intrigue centred on the contest between Barcelona and Paris, with the potentially fascinating duel between the powerful French influence within the IOC and a new Catalan president from Barcelona. The outcome was of interest to me as I was beginning to believe that badminton would appear for the first time in one of those cities.

The badminton agenda item on the Olympic programme eventually came up for discussion late on the afternoon of 5 June. I was asked to wait outside the session room, presumably until the report from the programme commission had been dealt with. Then came the long-awaited decision that badminton would be included in the programme of the Olympic Games to be held in 1992. I was asked to enter the session to receive the excellent news from the president and to make the following short remarks:

Mr. President, Ladies and Gentlemen of the International Olympic Committee. On behalf of literally millions of badminton players all round the world, can I thank you for the decision you have taken this afternoon to admit their sport to the programme of the Olympic Games in 1992. I would like to reassure you, just as these players have been telling me, that we will be a good Olympic sport. Badminton fits in almost precisely with your definition of what an Olympic sport should be and we are now ready to accept all our obligations and to become a credit to the Olympic Movement. Like you, the International Badminton Federation puts its athletes first. We have made strenuous efforts to ensure that there is no gap between those who administer the sport and those who play, and for that reason we are one of the happiest families in the international sports community. I leave this week for Calgary, for the Olympic Saddledome, in which we play our World Championships. After your decision today we look forward to welcoming your representative to what will be one of the happiest events in the history of our sport. Mr President, we wish you every success in your efforts to promote the Olympic ideals and we are delighted to be part of your family.

After receiving congratulations from my new media friends, I made arrangements to meet with Walther Troeger to thank him for his help and to have him join me in a small celebratory drink. We settled down in the bar with two large whiskies at a price of £7 each—no small sum in 1985. Such a momentous decision deserved a second round, and we were joined by Sir Lance Cross, IOC member in New Zealand. Lance always liked to be associated with success, especially when he was able to celebrate with large whiskies at £7 a time.

During the conversation, Walther, a proud German, who was a teenager during the war, asked Lance if he had ever been to Berlin before. Lance swallowed another gulp of Scotland's finest and then confessed, somewhat sheepishly, that he had travelled to Berlin twice a week for eighteen months during the 1940s. In fact, Sir Lancelot Cecil Stewart Cross had been a bomb-aimer in Lancaster bombers during the war and may just have been personally responsible for the vast area of devastation that could be seen outside the grounds of the Palasthotel.

Perhaps as a result of the blows to my credit card, I slept blissfully well and on the following day headed for Calgary and our world championships. *En route*, I stayed for one night at home and was able to write formally to the IOC, acknowledging their decision, to which Samaranch replied in a short formal letter, which contained his own handwritten note below his signature which read. 'I know that Olympic badminton owes you very, very, much. JAS'. It is a letter I cherish to this day.

The IBF office, now relocated to Calgary, received and passed on to me a whole range of letters and telegrams of congratulation. For me, the telegram from Stellan Mohlin was special but just as pleasing was a handwritten letter from Noriko Nakayama in Japan. Under her maiden name, Noriko Takagi, she was one of the first of the great Japanese female players. She had played and won all-England championship titles and played at the World Invitation Tournament in Glasgow's Kelvin Hall. She also won the singles event in the Demonstration Tournament organised by the IBF at the Munich Olympic Games. We remain friends to this day.

Another late arrival in Calgary was James Worrall, the senior IOC member in Canada, who made the journey from the IOC session in East Berlin to formally present the Olympic flag to Poul-Erik Neilsen, the president of the IBF. We managed to arrange that this was done during a short break in play in the Saddledome to a warm reception from all the many spectators.

Jim had been supportive of the sport as it worked its way through the IOC processes, and we were delighted to welcome him. However, he presented a very particular problem. Jim, a former Olympic hurdler, was a giant of a man—at least 6.5 feet tall—and we had to arrange an especially large bed for him in the hotel, a task that challenged the hotel staff almost to their limits. Stellan Mohlin, who had worked so hard on our inclusion, and I had our own special moment holding the Olympic flag, but it was an equally special moment to be able to share the flag and the excitement with Betty Scheele, whose late husband Herbert had been secretary of the IBF for many years and one of the initial campaigners for Olympic status.

Perhaps as a reality check during the Olympic celebrations, the commercial arrangements for the Calgary world championships had presented more than a few challenges. We had decided that taking the world championships out of Asia and Europe to a new continent would be a wise decision in terms of the development of the sport. Advice from Canada was that badminton was played enthusiastically in Calgary due at least in part to the presence of former international players from Thailand as coaches at that city's famous Glencoe Club.

Cities in Canada had developed big indoor clubs as a means of providing sport, entertainment, and social facilities throughout what can be their long and demanding winters. The Glencoe Club was a good example and was run very professionally by a badminton enthusiast called Jim Powell. As a matter of policy, we had decided that the commercial arrangements in Calgary would be different from the scale of commercial arrangements to which we were becoming accustomed in Asia. We made formal approaches to the Canadian Badminton Association, which was supportive but happy to leave all the practical arrangements to Jim Powell at the Glencoe Club. It was the Glencoe Club that agreed to meet a relatively modest facility fee to the IBF of around 50,000 Canadian dollars.

The venue chosen was the Saddledome, which was to be the centre of the 1988 Olympic Winter Games. This huge indoor stadium could accommodate 18,000 spectators—a capacity necessary to cater for the huge enthusiasm in Canada for ice hockey. There was no difficulty in fitting in the required number of badminton courts, and for the final day, we managed to sell almost all the seats in the two main sections of the stadium. It was only a modest problem that the floor-mounted television cameras showing action close to the net also showed large banks of empty seats at either end of the stadium.

The championships were a success, with China winning both singles titles and the first world medals for Park Joo-bong of Korea, who was to become one of the great doubles players of all time. The Glencoe Club was a generous host to the extent that I reduced the facility fee by around 20 per cent when it became clear that no financial assistance would be available from the National Badminton association, despite previous promises.

An early challenge to the business committee was to agree a structure and sponsorship guidance for the main events we would be promoting in Asia. Our three-year contract with Philp Morris and Marlboro brought financial stability but also the need to ensure that the presentation of the events and advertising in the stadium were under control and made to look attractive. The principal method of delivering the marketing return to sponsors was to place well-designed advertising boards around each court in the initial stages and specifically on the final day. Marlboro was quite happy that one board would be allowed for a selected equipment supplier and, for the three Thomas/Uber Cup events in Asia, a soft drink sponsor.

For many years, equipment for badminton included rackets and shuttlecocks. In later years, these requirements were extended to specially made moveable courts and to nets and posts, but a supply of high-quality shuttlecocks was essential. Traditionally, the best shuttlecocks had been provided by an English company, RSL Ltd—Reinforced Shuttlecocks Ltd. Shuttles were made from sixteen white goose feathers inserted into a small piece of Portuguese cork, covered with a small piece of goat kid leather. RSL moved its production from Kent in the UK to China, where its manufacturing equipment had to be modernised.

The development of the sport brought new producers into the potentially large and expanding market. The essential ingredient was goose feathers. Traditionally supplied from Eastern Europe, it became clear that a business supplying white goose feathers might not be the most attractive of enterprises and new sources of feathers would be essential.

As RSL production declined and the company eventually went out of business, the best shuttles were manufactured in China by the Yonex Company, a Japanese sports goods business concentrating on badminton, tennis, and golf. We were well aware of the quality products it made, especially excellent rackets, but a reliable supply of their top range shuttles was required. It also became clear that Yonex understood the potential advantage of the sport's Olympic inclusion and was interested, even in those early days, in becoming a supplier of the necessary sports equipment to the 1992 Olympic Games.

During a planned visit to Japan, I had made arrangements to meet with the senior management of the Yonex Company. In a friendly *quid pro quo* arrangement, so that we could learn from one another, I was invited to play golf with the founder of Yonex, Minoru Yoneyama, at Narashino Golf Club, the home course of Jumbo Ozaki, the most famous golfer in Japan.

We left the Keio Plaza hotel at 7.30 a.m. and worked our way through the Tokyo traffic to the course. Minoru was waiting with several assistants and a new set of Yonex golf clubs, which he claimed were 'guaranteed to make ball go 12.5 per cent further'. Luckily, my first drive ended somewhere near the middle of the fairway, but as we walked down the course, there was a small but noticeable earthquake. I was a little disconcerted as the ground beneath my feet moved, but my host, living in a country that has approximately 2,000 earthquakes a year, did not bat an eyelid. As golf is challenging enough when the playing surface remains still, this did not augur well for the rest of the round.

After nine holes, we paused for lunch, then played the back nine, which was followed by an exhaustive traditional Japanese bath and shower. I returned to the hotel at 8.05 p.m. in the evening. Twelve hours thirty-five minutes is still my longest ever round of golf.

However, the long haul proved to be important. Yonex shuttles were used exclusively at top badminton events. One Yonex board was strategically placed around each court at the big events. Yonex developed its own portable badminton courts, which were to provide an almost standard playing surface at major events all over the world. The courts even allowed for the inevitable problem of sweat from players falling on the playing surface at the events in the tropical climates of Southeast Asia.

Many top players, or their badminton associations, became contracted to Yonex for rackets or clothing and its badminton business boomed. For the first renewal of the IBF/Yonex contract, we invited Kei Yanagi, Yonex's European managing director, and his assistant to the Old Course Hotel at St Andrews. I managed to arrange a deal on a suite overlooking the Old Course, with lunch in the Royal and Ancient Golf Clubhouse, all of which resulted in a draft contract with revenues well above those we thought we could achieve.

Our celebrations on a deal well done were soon to be disappointed when Yanagi-san informed us that when Mr Yoneyama saw the draft contract, he refused to sign it as it was too generous to the IBF. The relationship with Yonex was too important to allow an argument over money to cause problems and it was fairly easy to agree a figure that allowed both sides to claim that they had snatched victory from the jaws of defeat. In 1992, the Barcelona organising committee selected Yonex as its badminton equipment supplier.

Soft drinks are an essential element of sport in the heat of Asia, and badminton and its big events were to become a very attractive marketing opportunity. Perhaps naively, we assumed that the local Coca Cola agents would be the obvious route to follow, but in Kuala Lumpur, we were approached by the company that made and distributed Milo.

This was a rather thick, sweet, chocolate drink that, to European tastes, could not be described as the ideal tropical thirst-quencher. However, its marketing director, Dino Rizal, had different views. Visits to his office in Kuala Lumpur were easy as the IBF frequently held council meetings in Singapore, and a twenty-minute flight in the morning allowed for a full day of marketing visits with Malaysian companies.

Dino was the most enthusiastic salesman I ever met and, almost by full force of personality, convinced the business committee that the future of badminton for events held in Malaysia rested entirely on the opportunity to put a Milo board in a good position around each court with some additional banner advertising in the stadium. He backed up his arguments with serious money, and we agreed to a contract that did not include any obligation on any player to carry a can of Milo or even drink one. This was good business.

The main event in 1986 was the Thomas and Uber Cup finals in Jakarta, the second event in the Marlboro sponsorship contract. Once again, the advantages of the new system, which involved many more competing nations in the finals, proved to be a success. Television was in the hands of TVRI, the Indonesian state television company, which presented our first problem in dealing with television rights fees. The director of TVRI seemed to indicate that a small commission for himself would ease negotiations. The solution to the problem was to remove the IBF from the detailed discussions, which were handled very capably by Titus Kurniadi, our local member.

It also became clear to us that television would play an ever more important role as the viewing figures in China were huge. Our relationship with IMG proved to be beneficial in the supply of coverage to which we were contracted. Perhaps in recognition of our efforts, I was invited to play for IMG in the Pro-Am golf competition at the Island Club in Singapore for the Dunhill Cup, a tournament that finished each year on the Old Course at St Andrews. I enjoyed two days away from my busy life in Jakarta, but the IMG team failed to qualify.

One of the unusual challenges in promoting major sporting events in Indonesia was the habit of different companies trying to use a presence at the event in their marketing efforts without the courtesy of paying for the opportunity to do so. It is called 'ambush marketing' in the competitive world of sports marketing. It got to the stage that before play started each evening, I would go to the Senayan Stadium in Jakarta and count the number of advertising banners so that I could spot the two or three new ones that had almost miraculously appeared overnight and had to be removed from the walls of the stadium. After excellent preliminary rounds, China retained both Thomas and Uber Cups, proving beyond doubt that they had become the top nation in world badminton.

However, Olympic matters were never far from our thoughts. In November 1984, the IOC programme commission had noted the request from Korea that badminton might be an exhibition sport during the 1988 Seoul Olympic Games. This was slightly confusing as IOC rules made provision for 'demonstration sports'. In his letter to me in June 1985, confirming our status for the 1992 Games, Samaranch had mentioned the possibility of demonstration status for badminton, so attendance at the Asian Games in Seoul in September 1986 was important.

I had travelled to Seoul in early 1985 in the pursuit of programme status and in the hope of persuading Korea that badminton would be a good fit for the 1988 Games. Our Korean Badminton Association had arranged a meeting with Roh Tae Woo, the president of the Seoul Olympic organising committee, and I was able to present to him a gift of a bottle of Special Glenfiddich Malt Scotch Whisky with a label that stated that it had been specially bottled for him. Like any good diplomat in his position, he smiled appreciatively.

However, new sports were not high on his order of priorities. In moments of realism, I was aware that the building of a 52,000-seat baseball arena in the Seoul Olympic Park and the demands of Taekwondo, their national sport, made badminton third favourite. My guess is that the request for a badminton exhibition was a political arrangement that the IOC would quietly live with. On that trip, I had also attended the Japan Open Championships in Tokyo and had met with Yoshio Sakarauchi, the foreign minister of Japan, seeking the support of his government for badminton's inclusion.

The 1986 Asian Games were, in fact, a test gathering for the 1988 Olympic Games and would use the same facilities and sporting infrastructure. Some 296 events for twenty-five sports were planned with twenty-seven countries taking part in the biggest test event in history. Korea finished second in the medal table to China. In the Seoul National University Gymnasium, Poul-Erik Neilsen and I watched Korea win the badminton team event and two individual gold medals, both featuring Joo Bong Park in both men's and mixed doubles. Zhao Jianhua of China won the men's singles, and the women's final continued the long running rivalry between Han Aiping, the winner, and Li Lingwei, the two best players in the world. The standard of play was at the highest level and proved that Korea had become a major force in the game.

Poul-Erik looked after all the purely badminton matters, and I tried to make use of the time available to have discussions on topics that were my detailed responsibility. It came as no surprise that a 1988 Exhibition was of no interest to organisers, who were flat out with a huge test event. They were also hosting a series of IOC meetings that demanded their full attention. Negotiations on what looked like a modest Olympic project would have to wait.

My increasing knowledge of Asian names and systems was put to the test in trying to fix an appointment with Jim Bukata, one of the top IMG television executives, with whom I had built a good relationship. I knew he was staying in the Shilla Hotel, but they appeared to have no record of him. After several failures to trace him, I asked the hotel to try again and waited with some irritation at the desk. In a flash of inspiration, I suggested they try 'Mr Jim' and instantly their computer produced his name, room number, and the annoying information that he had checked out that morning.

I did, however, manage to speak to Mary Glen Haig, a British official from the sport of fencing, who had become an IOC member in 1982, one of the first female members to be elected. She was familiar with the badminton campaign and explained to me the opportunity which would occur for the sport to become a full member of the British Olympic Association, of which she was a director. To my complete surprise, she suggested that I might consider a future with the BOA, presumably with the impression that, having been an IF president, I would have lots of free time.

In October, Veronica 'Ronnie' Rowan, the IBF's first professional secretary general, and I attended the IOC session in Lausanne when the host city for the 1992 Olympic Games would be decided. The IBF, as a recognised international federation, was invited to these occasions, and to my great surprise, I found out that Birmingham was one of the bidding cities. I had not been aware of the candidature as all my attention had been focused on sports programme issues, but it rather reflected the lack of promotion within Britain of the Birmingham campaign.

The bid was led by Denis Howell, the former Labour minister of sport, whose party was then in opposition to the Conservative government. In Lausanne, the Birmingham team seemed to be mainly local officials, although Sebastian Coe was a member of the presentation team. At the start of the Birmingham presentation, Denis Howell opened with the formal words, 'Mr President, distinguished members of the International Olympic Committee, good morning.' Then, suddenly, the lights went out—unfortunate in the extreme. Their competition was strong, with bids from Barcelona, Paris, Brisbane, Belgrade, and Amsterdam.

The intensity of the campaigning in Lausanne was markedly different from the efforts in Britain. Barcelona and Paris were favourites and the order of presentation rather benefitted Paris as the timing allowed Jacques Chirac, mayor of Paris, to make a powerful speech with some dramatic promises. A guarantee was given to close the Paris streets. At sessions in those days, the actual vote was taken on the day following the presentations, which may well have diminished the impact of the Chirac *tour de force*.

The results showed early exits for Amsterdam, Birmingham, and then Belgrade, Brisbane, and Paris, as Barcelona won with forty-seven votes in the third round of voting. I am sure Birmingham was disappointed but one of the positives was the construction in the city of the National Indoor Arena, which has been a real benefit to sport and to Birmingham for many years.

So, Barcelona it was—a decision that began many years of work to deliver our Olympic debut.

11

Progress on Both Fronts

Over the previous years, we had certainly made our mark on the promotion of the sport, and we had finally won over the IOC and joined the programme of the Olympic Games. It was slightly disappointing that badminton's acceptance was for only four events: singles and doubles for both men and women, but omitted mixed doubles—a discipline of equal importance to us.

The IOC's justification was that it meant that badminton had the same number of events and athletes as the four events already accepted for the other racket sports: tennis and table tennis. However, neither of our sporting cousins hold mixed doubles in the same esteem as we do in badminton. Nevertheless, having our sport in the Games was important and we resolved to make further efforts to bring mixed doubles to its rightful place.

On assuming the presidency of the IOC, and conscious of its close relationships with the city of Lausanne, Samaranch spoke to many of the Olympic international federations and suggested that they might consider bringing one of their top events to the expanding sports facilities in Lausanne. The *Capitale Olympique* was happy to contribute.

I knew that a similar request would be made to the IBF, but our major efforts and contracts were all concentrated on Asian venues, and it would be some time before such an event would return to Europe. However, there was a sixteen-court private badminton centre in Lausanne. Developed by the Duboux family, the Mally Centre was a new option in Lausanne. When taken to see it, I was impressed by its size and popularity and it gave us an opportunity too good to miss, so we organised an exhibition match.

I had been aware that the sport was played in Lausanne by some IOC staff as I had been able to provide some rackets to people like Marta Salsas, one of President Samaranch's private secretaries who was later to marry Michael Payne, the IOC marketing director. Good relations with the IOC seemed to be a wise move. One small effort in that direction was, before our exhibition match, to hold a short cocktail party in the foyer of the IOC's headquarters on the outskirts of Lausanne at Vidy, on the shore of Lake Leman. It is a wonderful location with views across the lake to the French Haute-Savoie.

We took over one of the four halls in Mally and set up an arena for around 1,500 people. As always, our national badminton associations helped by sending some of their top players; Morten Frost from Denmark as well as Liem Swie King and Icuk Sugiarto from Indonesia joined Li Lingwei from China in an exhibition evening that delighted a packed crowd and the watching President Samaranch.

In truth, the hall was just a little too low for world class players, but they all joined me in a pre-match discussion and understood the need to make the exhibition as dramatic as they could. Without doubt, the closing men's doubles match between Li Yongbo and Tian Bingyi of China and Joo Bong Park and Moon Soo Kim of Korea, the best two pairs in the world, demonstrated the amazing speed and reactions of the top players. Everyone went home happy, including the guest of honour who was asked for his autograph by a charming Li Lingwei. All in all, it was a very worthwhile initiative.

Over the years following unification, the China Badminton Association had fulfilled all its obligations in sending its top players to compete in IBF events and had enjoyed great success in both team and individual competitions. It was almost inevitable that China would wish to host and organise a major event, and its first choice was the 1987 world championships, to be held in Beijing. Since that date, greatly to the benefit of world sport and not least to badminton, China, has become a regular host of major sporting events on an Olympic and worldwide basis. However, it was an interesting challenge to be an early promoter in May 1987.

To our surprise, we were approached by British Airways with a sponsorship offer which, as the fee was acceptable and they seemed to understand the system we had developed to provide a good commercial return, we were happy to accept.

BA's sponsorship department for the Championships was led by a young English woman who rejoiced in the name of Penrose Courtney-Wildman, who understood the basic agreement but seemed unsure about how it could be applied to the benefit of both parties. For example, she suggested that BA would announce its sponsorship at a press conference in Hong Kong. However, at that time, there was only one return flight per day from Hong Kong to Beijing. Not only that, the handover of Hong Kong from Britain to China was imminent. I insisted that she change the venue of the media conference to Beijing, and we arranged that some top Chinese players would attend.

It also became clear that BA had no great demands for hospitality for guests or clients and did not need any special allocation of tickets at different times during the week of the championships. It was easy to build BA identification on accreditations, tickets, and in the event programme, but there seemed little effort being made to advertise the event and thereby increase visibility of the sponsorship. Eventually, I had to ask, 'What exactly do you want to achieve from your sponsorship?' After a short lull in proceedings, the answer came back: 'Maximum television exposure.'

Our host broadcaster, for the first time, was CCTV, the huge state television operation in China, and with a particular focus on Asia, we started to ensure as much coverage of the championships as possible. We also decided that we would make a special one-hour highlights programme after the event, which we would distribute, free of charge if necessary, to any interested television company, as a means of promoting the sport, to say nothing of BA, our main sponsor. This meant arranging that we could have television quality tapes of the finals, which we would take back to Hong Kong for editing and the production of our own programme.

I had some experience of commentary work but needed professional assistance to deliver a quality programme and to provide English commentary during the finals. To meet these requirements, I arranged for Gerald Williams, one of the leading BBC commentators for the Wimbledon Championships, to fly out to Beijing with me and provide the professionalism we required. To my surprise, Gerry had never been to Hong Kong, or to China, during his tennis career and we held preliminary meetings in Hong Kong at the local office of IMG, which was heavily involved in the TV sales.

On our first evening in Hong Kong, I took Gerry down to the Captain's Bar in the Mandarin Hotel, a popular watering hole for expats. We had only just ordered our first drink when someone came over and said, 'Gerry. Is this really you?' An old friend from London had recognised him, but Gerry was so surprised and pleased that he said to me, 'Did you set this up?' His rather boyish enthusiasm was nice to see, but somewhat of a surprise as I had assumed he would be more worldly wise.

The championships were held in the old Capital Indoor Stadium in central Beijing, an arena with all the space we required and with seats for around 15,000 spectators. We had been allocated the Yanjing Hotel for the IBF party and officials. It was not the best hotel in Beijing, and it became a rather challenging experience to return after a long day at the stadium to find only very basic services of food and drink available.

The local bureaucracy in both the stadium and hotel became an irritating fact of life, based mainly on the language problem, which required almost constant translation to get anything done. I had invited Jim and Penny Powell, our organisers in Calgary in 1985, but could not find them for their first two days. Eventually, Jim appeared and told me that their complimentary tickets were so high up in the stadium that his nose bled, and he could only just see that the sport being played was badminton.

The IBF commentary position was at a table on the same floor level as the referee's table with only one microphone and one TV monitor set. I was not required for any of the first few days, so I had time to complete the modest improvements we needed. I did not really notice that Gerry seemed to have disappeared until contacted by Alistair McKay Forbes of IMG with the reason. One of the Chinese officials had complained that Gerry had been found in the foyer and coffee shop of one of the top Beijing hotels where he had gone for some European food. However, as a devout Christian, he had also taken the opportunity to distribute a selection of Christian religious texts—a move that was not well received by the Chinese authorities.

When I managed to find him, he understood the sensitivity of his actions and agreed to desist. That was a relief as I did not want to explain to the BBC why one of its leading tennis commentators was unfortunately unable to attend Wimbledon that year as he had been incarcerated in a Beijing dungeon. A less dramatic piece of information came from him when he told me that he would not be able to commentate live on the finals if any of the matches were covered live by BBC. As a result, he was demoted to being my adviser.

Perhaps predictably, Chinese players, playing at home, dominated the Championships. The women's singles was an all-China event with all four semi-finalists from the home country, with Han Aiping just beating Li Lingwei for gold. In men's singles, Morten Frost from Denmark fought his way through the draw to meet Yang Yang of China in the final. Morten had been the leading European player for several years and the only one who seemed able to withstand the strength and depth of the Asian players in almost every tournament. He was rightly top seed but only just lost an epic final fifteen–twelve in the third game, having recovered from eight–nil down.

The Sidek brothers from Malaysia won silver medals in men's doubles perhaps giving notice of good results to come. The remaining two doubles finals both went to China, resulting in the first ever clean sweep of titles to one country.

It took some time to collect the television viewing figures, but they were good enough to allow me to tell BA that we had delivered on its request for television exposure from the Beijing world championships on every television set east of the Middle East. I was told that the BA marketing director was delighted. Gerry Williams and I returned to Hong Kong and spent the best part of two days in an editing suite at local broadcaster, with TVB producing our first one-hour programme. We had been provided with copy tapes with international sound (action and crowd effects) but none of the English commentary I had laboured so hard to produce. It was a difficult enough task, not made any easier by some enthusiastic Chinese supporters squeezing into the space just in front of my table and managing to pull out the TV monitor cable with irritating regularity.

In those days, television tapes did not have inbuilt computer timing, so we had to watch every one of them manually to extract the periods of play containing the best action. We were then able to produce a one-hour highlights programme, with suitable breaks to allow for the insertion of any local advertising. Finally, we then had to put an English commentary on the final version, where Gerry's skills could be fully used. The final tape was sold or supplied to various television stations all around the world and was a good exercise in promoting the sport.

Having an international airline as a sponsor, and a happy one, brought about one unexpected advantage. All our routine travel in these days was in seats at the back of planes in what was known as 'monkey class'. Tom Bacher and I amused ourselves by holding a personal challenge to see which of us could arrange the best possible upgrade. As we normally travelled together, upgrades had been thin on the ground.

However, on 10 October 1987, I was to take a commanding lead in our challenge when a grateful BA upgraded me on to Concorde to go to New York on my way to a GAISF meeting in Colorado Springs. Upgrades to Concorde involved a seat in the very back row but the flight was only three hours and eighteen minutes from wheels up to wheels down in New York. There was just enough leg room, the food was good, but the wines were outstanding, especially the Meursault with the fish course.

All the other passengers had paid an extortionate price for their tickets, including the two elderly Americans I followed onto the plane. Concorde was a one class, first only, plane but it had a galley area after about eight rows of seats. As the American women walked through the galley area towards their seats, she turned to her husband and said to him 'George, are we travelling coach [American for economy]?' I thought he was going to kill her.

Anyone fortunate enough to travel on one of the most remarkable technological achievements of our time—an aeroplane rightly called one of the 'Seven Wonders of the Modern World'—will surely agree with me that flying Concorde is an awesome experience. As the speedometer in the cabin reached Mach 2 (twice the speed of sound), a glance out of the tiny passenger window revealed a sky that was closer to deep purple than sky blue—not surprising, given that the beautiful bird cruised at 56,000 feet. How sad it was when the tragic crash on take-off from Charles de Gaulle airport in July 2000 heralded the end of the wonderful machine. Perhaps my fortunate supersonic experience will be available in the future, but it certainly will not be in my lifetime.

The last event in the badminton year was the Grand Prix finals in a new venue: Hong Kong. It was pleasing that the climax of the season could be held in another major Asian city, but for the first time in Hong Kong. The results continued to show that after their complete success in the world championships in Beijing, players from China continued to dominate the sport.

The two decisions, taken in 1985 to admit badminton to the Olympic programme and in 1986 to award the hosting rights for the 1992 games to Barcelona, meant that the IBF had to contact the organisers in the Catalonian city. We were unsure of our detailed involvement and equally unsure whether our national association in Spain would be able to play a major part. Badminton was not a popular sport in Spain with only thirty clubs and less than 1,000 players, and we assumed, rightly as it turned out, that the Barcelona Olympic organising committee (COOB) would not be well briefed on the requirements for a new indoor sport on the Olympic programme.

Ian Palmer of New Zealand, our then president, and I made our first visit to Barcelona in February 1988. We received a warm welcome and were given what later transpired to be the standard tour for first time visitors to the Olympic city. We saw the construction and alterations to what was to become the main stadium and the large indoor hall beside it which would be the home for gymnastics. We were shown the site of the village, which was close to the beach. The village would become a feature of the extensive development of the whole beachside area, which, along with the building of the Olympic facilities, would be the outstanding lasting legacy of the Games.

When we got down to detailed discussion about the physical requirements for badminton, we realised that our hosts had only the most rudimentary knowledge of the sport. There were no existing badminton facilities in Spain which could serve as an example for them. We had to explain that we would require a floor area big enough to take three badminton courts. The requirement of a suitable height came as something of a surprise, along with our comment that it would be better if the background in the hall was a dark colour and without natural light.

The biggest surprise of all for them was when we told them that their assumed spectator attendance of 7,000 would be many more than we thought to be realistic for a tournament in Spain. We suggested that their plans might be based on spectator attendance of 4,000, a number we thought that we could fill at least for the days of the semi-finals and finals. It was clear at once that we had made an impression when they told us that we were the only international federation that had asked for a smaller number of spectators, and thus a smaller venue.

With no tradition of badminton in Spain and without any purpose-built venues that they could use, the challenge was to find an existing structure that could be converted to the size and height we required and in a suitable area of the city. Their first suggestion was to use the city's old fish market. However, the building would have presented a number of difficulties in the necessary conversion and was probably not in the ideal place in the city. In many ways, it was encouraging to see that when we made comments that outlined the difficulties, they abandoned the fish market site and suggested a building that housed all the vehicles that had been impounded by the Barcelona police.

It required considerable imagination to envisage sport being played in a huge, dusty, almost black building, which contained literally hundreds of old cars. While we gave the organisers full marks for effort, it was clear that neither of their first two suggestions would be suitable. Either venue might have been big enough, but the cost of conversion would have been very high or there was no detailed legacy use for such a badminton hall after the Games. We left Barcelona encouraged in many ways but realised that we had left COOB with a real dilemma in finding a suitable hall.

The major event for 1988 was the combined Thomas Cup and Uber Cup finals, which would return to Kuala Lumpur and would complete our three-year contract with Phillip Morris under the Marlboro brand. Clearly, the enthusiasm for badminton in Malaysia made the Stadium Negara a popular venue for major sporting events and for our combined championships. Thirty-two countries entered the Thomas Cup with thirty-three for the Uber Cup. There was a surprise result in the semi-final of the Thomas Cup when, to the delight of the large audience, Malaysia beat Indonesia by three–two to proceed to the final. At that stage, it lost to China by four–one—a result that gave the Thomas Cup to China for the third successive competition.

In the Uber Cup, there was a strong performance from South Korea, which reached the final for the first time but lost to the strong Chinese contingent. After an excellent event, the two major trophies in world badminton returned to Beijing and many thought that this might become their permanent home. Our host broadcaster was RTM (Radio Television Malaysia), which was happy to work in what appeared to be organised chaos. Nevertheless, excellent coverage was produced, which was the basis of our second IBF highlights programme.

Throughout the year, I was in regular contact with the Seoul Olympic Organising Committee over arrangements for our one-day exhibition in the Seoul National University Gymnasium during the 1988 Games. The event would be held on 19 September, two days after the opening ceremony. After our use of the gymnasium, the venue was to be re-configured to host the Olympic table tennis event four days later.

An initial letter from the organising committee suggested that the IBF should make a contribution to the costs of the exhibition, an amount they claimed should be $321,000. This caused not a little consternation in badminton circles, and I was instructed to negotiate as strongly as possible. Surprisingly, the negotiations were completed relatively quickly, as I was able to explain that the commitment of the IBF to send the world's best players to Seoul was a considerable contribution to the estimated costs. It was a huge relief when the Seoul organisers agreed that, having examined their original budget, the IBF should meet a payment of just $10,000. In any language, that could only be described as a result.

We invited eight of our national associations to send players to take part in this important Olympic exhibition. Players from China, Indonesia, England, Japan, Denmark, Sweden, and Canada joined the top South Korean players in an impressive international list. The IOC charter recognises demonstration sports but not exhibition events. This meant an element of confusion as national Olympic committees were not prepared to include in their official delegations to the Games the small number of invited badminton players, thus the players were not able to stay in the Olympic village.

So, with the assistance of the Korean Badminton Association, the IBF created its own little village in six apartments in the Olympic family town, an additional accommodation area for those attending the Games but without village access. The accommodation proved to be excellent and provided all the facilities of a good hotel, allowing us to create a small happy badminton 'home' for our players.

As the badminton players were not part of an official delegation, they could not march in the opening ceremony. Being aware of this restriction, I arranged tickets for all thirty players for the opening ceremony. With major help from China and Indonesia, I bought the tickets from NOCs in different parts of the world and arrived in Seoul with twenty-six of the necessary tickets in my briefcase. The last four tickets were purchased from the BOA, the NOC in Great Britain—an organisation I knew well and which I assumed would present no difficulties.

Despite regular efforts to make contact beforehand, I was told these tickets would be with me in Seoul. At least three days of reminders were sent, but it was not until around 11 p.m. on the night before the opening ceremony that the last four tickets were delivered from the office of the BOA, also situated in the Olympic family town. The feeling of relief was enhanced by the surprise to find that the envelope contained five tickets, one more than agreed or even paid for.

Now there was a problem. Tickets for an Olympic opening ceremony are always in high demand, and I now found myself in the very unusual position of having one spare ticket. We had been greatly helped by our Korean liaison person, a delightful young woman called Miss Chun, so I decided that it would be a nice gesture if the additional ticket was given to her. From that moment, I had a very happy young Korean on my hands, and over the next six or seven weeks, she rewarded me by writing kind and personal letters thanking me for all my kindness.

This caused a moment of tension on my return to Scotland when my wife said, 'Who the hell is Miss Chun?' The momentary discomfort was worth it as the badminton players were the only athletes at the Olympic Games who saw all of the Seoul opening ceremony from their own seats in the stadium.

Two days after the splendid opening ceremony with its vibrant colour, stunning illustrations of Korean culture, and the celebrated vision of a completely empty stadium with a solitary child dressed in white running across the stadium floor, our exhibition attracted a crowd of around 5,000 to watch some excellent badminton. The two courts were presented in exemplary style and a full team of volunteers, all immaculately dressed, presented the event with true Olympic panache.

Many guests appeared and all were delighted. The famous American tennis commentator Bud Collins spent the whole day watching badminton and was hugely impressed. NBC television covered the event and put together four separate slots that were shown on the network in the USA. This was an unexpected bonus, which we hoped would help create an upsurge of American interest.

Korean badminton had a great day, with Hye Young Hwang winning gold by beating China's Han Aiping in the women's singles. That was followed by a second Korean win in the women's doubles against the top Chinese pairing in an outstanding match. A third Korean gold came from Joo Bong Park and Myung Hee Chung in the mixed doubles. This was a sadly ironic result as, with no mixed doubles in our first full Olympic tournament in Barcelona in 1992, Myung Hee Chung would be unable to play in the event with her partner, the best mixed pairing in the world. Yang Yang in the men's singles and the doubles pair of Li Yongbo and Tian Bingyi won the other two gold medals for China.

The preparation for the exhibition was slightly troubled as the players could not be included in their own NOC teams, which left an impression that we would not be 'quite at the party'. On the other hand, the positive impact of our days in Seoul was the presentation by our Korean hosts that made badminton look like an Olympic sport. I was also left with the clear impression that an Olympic Games is truly 'the greatest show on earth'. Seoul had 160 out of a total of 167 NOCs taking part in twenty-three sports on the official programme.

It was clear that the coverage and publicity the sport would receive in Barcelona in 1992 would be greater than we could ever have expected. We had to be ready to take advantage of the priceless asset of Olympic inclusion to make sure badminton became even better known. Proof of that future exposure was immediately reinforced by the return journey from Seoul, which involved thirty-six hours in a hotel room at Narita Airport in Tokyo. Three different television stations were showing blanket coverage of the Games, albeit with Japanese commentary. We were on our way.

12

New Olympic Tasks

One major effect of becoming an Olympic sport is that it promotes that sport's national federation to membership of its national Olympic committee (NOC). In Great Britain, our NOC is the British Olympic Association, the membership of which contains all the national federations of sports on the Olympic programme for the Summer and Winter Games.

With a history dating back to 1865, the BOA was founded in 1905, a few years after the establishment of the IOC, and is one of only five NOCs that have taken part in every Olympic Games since 1896. The BOA competes as Great Britain (GBR) with athletes from England, Northern Ireland, Scotland, and Wales, plus three Crown Dependencies (Guernsey, Isle of Man, and Jersey) and a small number of British Overseas Territories. Within the IBF, full membership existed for England, Scotland, Wales, and Ireland (the whole island of Ireland).

Perhaps mildly regrettably, the first thing we had to do was to create a new committee—a British Badminton Association, only for Olympic representation, and the necessary steps were taken. The Irish situation had to be understood; it was recognised that athletes from Northern Ireland were entitled to represent GBR or, at their choice, the Republic of Ireland. Needless to say, during Northern Ireland's Troubles, this created a few political issues.

Perhaps as a result of my Olympic experience, I was asked if I would be prepared to represent the new British badminton organisation (the BBA) on the BOA from October 1988 for the apparently compelling reason that, 'You know most about this!' NOCs operate on a series of four yearly cycles, which terminate after the summer Olympic Games. So, badminton's entry to the BOA was only available at the start of the four-year cycle up to the Barcelona Games. From years of experience, I had managed to avoid the role of selector for any badminton team for which I played and made it clear to the BBA that this decision would continue. Therefore, somebody else would have to keep the peace within the four Home Nations as we prepared for Barcelona.

I was told that there were only three NOC meetings each year, and I worked out how I could get from Glasgow to No. 1 Wandsworth Plain in London—a series of four small Georgian houses with connecting doors and outdoor storage areas, which made up the BOA headquarters. I was intrigued to find that No. 5 Wandsworth Plain was owned by the Mick Jagger Organisation.

The BOA was led by three volunteer officers—Sir Arthur Gold from athletics, Eileen Gray from cycling, and Robert Watson from hockey—but organised and run by Dick Palmer as secretary general. Dick was a vastly experienced administrator who had been with the BOA since 1976 and had been through all the trauma of the proposed boycott of the Moscow Games, which, despite the unwelcome attempts by the government of the day, the BOA strenuously opposed.

This decision, and the declaration of its freedom and independence, was greatly to the credit of the organisation and has served it well over many years. Dick was a Welsh rugby fanatic but an Olympic expert and one of the wisest and nicest of men. He was backed up by George Nicholson, fundraiser; Caroline Searle, communications; and Kevin Hickey, coaching and performance. This tightly knit little group was able to accomplish the whole range of its responsibilities with only minimal financial resources.

Beginning to understand the structure and operation of this small but effective group was fascinating. I started to see the many intricacies I simply did not appreciate during my work to gain Olympic recognition for the IBF. I found it quite old-fashioned that the BOA did not have an executive committee, but a finance and general purposes committee, which ran the day-to-day operations of the body, all skilfully implemented by Dick Palmer and his staff. To my considerable surprise, I found that, except for Dick, I probably knew more about international sport than my other colleagues around the BOA table.

The funding for the BOA came from minimal amounts of sponsorship and a well-organised appeal conducted in the year before the Games; it was traditionally led by a senior figure in one of the major British banks. George Nicholson was in control of the appeal; any rights held by the BOA were in his very firm hands and, in practice, raised sufficient funds to allow the BOA to operate. Mind you, had there been the present auditing requirement to declare a 'going concern' basis, we might have had some problems in presenting the annual accounts. This was an interesting new world, and I was asked to serve on the finance and general purposes committee.

The chairman, Sir Arthur Gold, was a gentleman of standing in the world of athletics. Among other things, he was concerned at the increasing evidence that his sport was being damaged by athletes using performance-enhancing drugs. He realised that this development could affect all sport and made the sensible suggestion that the BOA might be prepared to enhance its selection criteria by adding a rule that any athlete convicted of a positive drug offence would no longer be eligible for selection for a British Olympic team.

Legal advice was taken to produce the correct wording, with the necessary conditions and exceptions, and the final draft was submitted to a full NOC meeting for approval. It was strongly supported by a newly formed athletes' commission, chaired by Martin Cross, a rowing gold medallist from the 1984 Los Angeles Olympic Games.

The efforts were widely praised and accepted, and considering future interests in my own sporting life, my belief that the BOA by-law should be supported until it is declared to be bad law was a sound position to support. In a lighter vein, the first ever BOA meeting to be held outside London was arranged for Manchester with a distinguished guest speaker—Lord Killanin, the former president of the IOC. He enjoyed a glass of good scotch, which extended the social hours after the formal meeting. The choice of Manchester was significant for reasons to follow.

Back in the day job for the IBF, the 1989 world championships returned to Indonesia and the Senayan Stadium in Jakarta. As always in that badminton hotbed, the championships were well-organised and very well-supported. Asian dominance continued, and on that occasion, China came close to winning all five titles; only the wonderful Korean mixed doubles pair of Park Joo-bong and Chung Myung-hee denied them a clean sweep when they beat the Chinese pair in the semi-final. In China, from April that year, a student protest movement picked up momentum until the Chinese authorities, concerned at the scale of the numbers and the situation, decided to use military force to end the protest.

In Jakarta, in the normal bubble of a major sport event, we were not aware of the troubles in Beijing. The championship finals were arranged for the evening of 4 June, and earlier that day, in the Borobudur Intercontinental Hotel, we were amazed to watch on television the disturbing pictures from Beijing of what became known as the Tiananmen Square Massacre. It is not known how many died, but it is estimated that it was several hundred with several thousand arrests.

It was only days later that I read in the media the story that a Chinese soldier had allowed his orders to be overruled by a printed 'permit' to one broadcaster who continued to cover the scene. I am not sure how much of the previous protest was known to the Chinese players in Jakarta, but Wang Wenjao, their national coach, came to me and said that his players were very upset at what they had seen from home, and they could not possibly play the finals.

While sympathetic to the situation, the IBF was committed to delivering the finals to the Indonesian spectators and to a whole list of television stations all over Asia. Having quietly discussed the problem with Wenjao, I asked him just how many people in China he thought might have seen the pictures. My guess was that it would have been very few if any at all. That being so, I suggested that the worst thing the Chinese players could do would be to withdraw from the finals, as all that would accomplish would be to draw attention to the protests in their own country. It was unlikely that many of the local spectators would have seen the television coverage as we were living in an international hotel, one of the few places with international TV access. Wenjao considered this, left to speak to his players, and came back about an hour later to say that he agreed and that play in the finals would proceed. I admired him greatly.

Of course, sport is no more than a wonderful distraction in life. It is good for our bodies and for our souls. However, at times like the tragedy of Tiananmen Square, we are reminded of what are the really important things in our lives. Sport is not one of those 'really important' things, but it is really important in helping us come to terms with the things that are.

I have always had a fondness for Indonesia and its people all caused by the wonderful badminton experiences and friendships. Some years before, Tom Bacher had persuaded me to sponsor a young Indonesian girl called Saripah through a US-based charity called Christian Children's Fund. I had taken my son Colin to Jakarta on this occasion for his twenty-first birthday, and we arranged with the local office of the charity that we would try to visit Saripah.

After a long drive from Jakarta and a good trek off the road, we made it to her village. She was six years old and the tenth child in the family of a father, who, we were told, was seventy-two years old. Above the door of the little wooden hut where she lived were two little stickers of Rudy Hartono and Liem Swie King, Indonesia's top badminton players. When

I explained that I knew them, the assembled family were very impressed. Saripah told me the village had a badminton court, so hand in hand, off we went to find a court underneath a tree. It was marked out on dried mud with lines made from rattan cane—no wonder the national sport was popular and produced so many good players who were national heroes.

We visited her school, which she attended for only one half-day per week, but she wanted to be a doctor when she grew up. I was asked if I would like to make the family a gift, and after some discussion, I agreed to purchase a goat. They asked for a girl goat as they already had a boy goat, which seemed to me to be sensible. The cost was 30,000 rupias—about $3—so it was easy to say yes. On our return to the hotel, Tom Bacher had lots of questions, including 'What was the cost of the goat?' When I confirmed the price of $3, he said, 'Wow. That's cheaper than a massage!' Some years later, Rosemary and I visited Saripah to monitor her progress and meet the new goat, but regrettably, the charity had stopped operating in Indonesia, and we lost contact completely.

On the day after the finals, Colin and I travelled up to Hong Kong for two or three days as he had never been to that fascinating city. On the evening of our return flight to London, we were delayed at Hong Kong airport for roughly six hours as the plane on which we were to travel had been sent on a diverted route to Beijing. It came back to Hong Kong with members of the staff of the British embassy and other British citizens living in Beijing at the time who had been recommended to leave because of the unrest. He used his new camera, his twenty-first birthday present, to record what was just a little bit of history.

During the second half of 1989, the interests of the IBF and BOA coincided in two distinct ways. The first was the second visit of the IBF to Barcelona to meet with Luis Millet who oversaw the venue planning for the 1992 Games. After consideration of the old fish market and the police car pound we had previously been directed to, we visited the city of Sabadell. It is a city of around 175,000 people situated 15 miles north of Barcelona and with, at that time, a mayor who was a member of the communist party. We understood the potential political justification for taking an Olympic sport to a major regional city, but we had always hoped to have a venue close to the middle of Barcelona.

Sabadell showed us the several good existing sports facilities, including a major sports hall, which they assumed would be suitable for badminton. While some of the dimensions were sufficient, the hall was well below the minimum height for international badminton, and we broke that news rather gently. Undeterred, the Sabadell officials almost immediately offered to lower the floor to produce the required height. We were sceptical and, discreetly, reminded Luis Millet and Manuel Fonseca, the sports director, of our wish to be in the middle of the Olympic action rather than in a peripheral venue. To our delight, we were subsequently informed that the cost of the major structural conversion involved the not small issue of who would pay for it, making the Sabadell suggestion impractical. Luis Millet and his team went back to work.

The BOA had selected the city of Manchester to be a candidate to host the 1996 Olympic Games, a decision that would be taken at the IOC session in Tokyo in 1990. I was a little surprised that another British bid would follow so soon after the Birmingham disappointment four years before but was invited to join the bid team as they realised that the successful badminton programme campaign made me one of the very few people who could claim any success in selling to the IOC. This was my first experience of the extensive, complex, political, and (on occasions) marvellous world of Olympic bidding.

The bid was led by Bob Scott, a director of Manchester theatres, with Rick Parry as bid director, a qualified chartered accountant and management consultant who was seconded to the bid. They proved to be a good team. Parry was serious and organised and was later to become a major official in the world of football. Scott was emotional, excitable, but knowledgeable about the theatre and communications world—in many ways, an ideal combination. I once asked him what he did for a living, and his reply was typical of the man. 'I am a theatrical impresario,' he said, 'In fact, I am the most famous theatrical impresario in the world, because I turned down *Jesus Christ Superstar* when Andrew Lloyd Webber was writing it.' I asked how he managed that:

> Well, we met when we were at Oxford and I was Secretary of the University Drama Society and one day this man with very staring eyes came to me and said, 'Bob, I am writing a musical based on the early books of the New Testament'. And I said to him, 'Piss off you silly little man!' True story.

The Manchester team understood that their only chance of success was to have a good plan with a strong legacy for the potential host city, but then be able to sell that vision to the very diverse and idiosyncratic eighty-five members of the IOC. They arranged to attend as many meetings as possible, where they could speak face-to-face with IOC members. There was a good delegation sent to attend the IOC session in September in San Juan, Puerto Rico, and I was invited to be a helper.

The sun shone brightly over the Caribe Hilton hotel as we met members and digested the IOC decisions taken. Juan Antonio Samaranch was re-elected as president, which was important to any bid, and I was more than a little intrigued by the decision to remove demonstration sports from future Olympic Games—Badminton had got in just in time.

It was a joy to meet and get to know one of the best-known Manchester supporters, Bobby Charlton, who gave freely of his time and effort whenever he could. We were also assisted by Britain's new IOC member, the princess royal. I had met Princess Anne, as she then was, but not formally as president of the BOA, and our paths became intertwined for many years.

To my delight, I was asked to meet with and talk to Peter Tallberg, IOC member in Finland, and this became a real treat as we met on the local golf course. I was pleasantly surprised that several members remembered my IBF efforts and were friendly. Our opposition were the cities of Atlanta, Athens, Toronto, Melbourne, and Belgrade, all of which had sales teams in San Juan. The hotel lobby was a busy place.

We were conscientious in our efforts and made use of every opportunity to speak to the IOC constituency. On the morning of our last day, a breakfast meeting was arranged for Bobby Charlton and me with Günter Heinze, IOC member in East Germany. Our research indicated that he liked football, so the presence of Bobby Charlton was ideal. He asked many questions and seemed genuinely interested, so the breakfast lasted a lot longer than planned. We then said our farewells and headed for the airport to catch an American Airlines flight to New York and then on to Manchester as part of our sponsorship arrangements with British Airways.

For the San Juan–New York leg, we were in seats 44A and 44B at the very back of the plane, and due to our rather late arrival at the airport, we were close to the back of the queue to board the aircraft. We were dressed immaculately in the Manchester team uniform with jacket, white shirt, and bid tie—all necessary for the breakfast meeting. The girl in front of us in the boarding queue was dressed in a bikini top, hot pants, and a sombrero, carrying a huge canvas backpack that probably contained her worldly possessions.

When we handed over our boarding cards, the American Airlines girl looked us up and down and said, 'Gentlemen. You look as if you should be in first class!' and changed us to seats 1E and 1F. As we moved forward to our new seats, we joined a small group of French delegates and one of them came over to Bobby and said, 'We have not met but I have always believed you were a great player.' I was able to say, 'Bobby, can I introduce

Jean Claude Killy?' Two of the great sportsmen of the age sat together for some time and chatted amiably—a surprising but really good moment.

The next long trip was back to Indonesia as the Olympic Council of Asia was holding a meeting on the island of Bali and several IOC members would be in attendance. The meeting was held in the Pertamina Cottages, a rest and recreation complex owned by Pertamina, the state oil and gas company. All the Olympic guests appeared at roughly the same time to find that their rooms were not ready as the previous oil meeting had overrun. There was a large crowd of unhappy and seemingly important people becoming irritated in the foyer of the hotel.

I offered to go up to the desk and speak to the local official in charge and found that he was a badminton fanatic. Five minutes later, after disclosing a bit of discreet information on two of the best Indonesian star players, the three Manchester rooms suddenly became available. Everybody has his part to play. Once again, we made friends and believed firmly that we were making progress. On that occasion, the Olympic Council of Asia was hearing presentations from both summer and winter Olympic bidding cities as the decision for the 1998 Winter Games would be taken in 1991, and the Japanese city of Nagano was bidding.

It seemed to me to be a bit incongruous to have winter sport presentations, all featuring snow and ice, on a tropical island with a humid temperature of around 30 degrees. The young Japanese presenter for Nagano, after a particularly articulate verbal presentation, could not get his video player to work and suffered several minutes of acute embarrassment. He recovered beautifully by eventually giving up on the technology, turning to his audience, bowing very low and saying: 'Ah, sometimes even Japanese video does not work.' I was to watch him get his real reward when Nagano won at the IOC session in Birmingham in 1991.

Out of purely personal interest, I managed to arrange a multi-sponsored visit to Auckland for the 1990 Commonwealth Games, but on this occasion with a contract as a commentator for the BBC for the Commonwealth badminton events. I was delighted to be working with and advised by Barry Davies, probably the best voice in the BBC sports department. The tournament was played in the Auckland Badminton Hall, which had been the model for the development in Glasgow twenty years earlier. The hall had benefited from an upgrade, presumably paid for by the Commonwealth Games organising committee. We managed to cover most of the matches of interest to the BBC, and after doing so one morning, Barry left the hall, presumably to fulfil another commitment.

Perhaps thirty minutes after he left, the telephone rang on the commentary table. The executive producer, Martin Hopkins, was on the line telling me that there was a violent thunderstorm that had stopped all the Commonwealth sport apart from badminton, an indoor sport, as the only live action taking place. He gave me short but clear instructions and I managed to describe a men's doubles match without too many mistakes. A rather wet Barry Davies reappeared halfway through the match, but skilfully avoided joining in the commentary as it would have been difficult to explain the sudden reappearance of his voice. Despite such modest problems, the Games were relaxed and enjoyable.

The nest stop on a long tour was Melbourne. I understood it was also bidding for the 1996 Olympic Games, but my visit had nothing to do with Manchester, only an opportunity to see what plans were in place for badminton. The visit was organised by the Australian Badminton president, Roy Ward, a member of the Victoria State Parliament, who had kept the badminton interests at the forefront of the Melbourne bidding committee. It was interesting to see the master plans for venues, the village, and—as a highlight—a visit to the MCG (the Melbourne Cricket Ground), one of the world's great stadiums with its 100,000-spectator capacity.

Roy also delivered on a long-standing promise to arrange a game of golf at Royal Melbourne, a world-leading course. After completing our round, the day got even better when one of the staff came into the locker room to find out if there was, 'a guy called Reedie here'. He told me that I had to change quickly as I was invited to make up a dinner party as the partner of Mary Glen Haig, the senior IOC member in Britain who was also in Melbourne. We were picked up from the hotel by our hosts, Peter and Joan Clemenger, and taken to their impressive mansion in Toorak, the best suburb of the city. Peter was in the advertising business and a member of the Melbourne Bid Committee. Mary was an obvious invitee.

Our fellow guests who were waiting for us were John and Lynn Landy. John Landy was the Australian athlete who was the second man to beat the four-minute mile barrier and who competed against Roger Bannister in the 1954 Vancouver Commonwealth Games in what was billed as 'The Miracle Mile', which Bannister won by 0.8 seconds, but both broke the four-minute barrier again. Landy was later to become the governor of Victoria. The other couple were Peter and Mary Thomson. Peter, a golfing legend, had won the Open Championship five times between 1954 and 1965, and three times in a row in 1954, 1955, and 1956. He was my first sporting hero; it was like having dinner with God and the Archangel Gabriel.

The evening was even more enjoyable, as we did not just talk about sport. Memory reminds me that the Thomsons were interested in the use and protection of the English language. After the meal, Mary Glen Haig was taken away to look at Landy's scrapbook and I was not quite sure whether I was to be involved as she was the guest with the IOC vote, but Thomson solved the problem for me by saying, 'Stay where you are, Craig, I know where Clemenger keeps his good red wine!'

Peter was a proud Australian who tried politics but without success, although his son, Andrew, was to become Australia's sports minister. Peter's record makes him one of the best of the best golfers in the history of the game. We became good friends, and Rosemary and I were to spend holiday time with the Thomsons in their summer home in Port Douglas during a future visit and had regular meetings with them when they made their annual visit to the Open Championships and the house they purchased in St Andrews. After a wonderful evening, it is only fair to record that the Melbourne plans for badminton were satisfactory.

The Tokyo Metropolitan Gymnasium was the venue for the 1990 Thomas and Uber Cup finals—a move from south-east Asian venues and something of an experiment. Total entries held up well with fifty-three teams in the Thomas Cup and forty-two in the Uber Cup. China retained both trophies, beating a newly invigorated Malaysia in the final, which had beaten its old rivals Indonesia in the semi-final. Korea reached the final of the Uber Cup which, was a disappointment to the local fans as they had hoped that Japan might have been higher than fourth place. The IBF had no regrets as Japan organised the event supremely well and we enjoyed the support and television coverage of NHK, the national broadcaster. NHK's producer was a pleasant woman whose ambition was to play golf at St. Andrews. At the close of the coverage, she presented me with a gift that was a welcome difference from the usual production company envelope containing an invoice.

A second visit to Tokyo followed as the Manchester Olympic bid made its final presentation to the IOC at its annual session in the Takanawa Prince Hotel. We set up a model of the master venue plans showing the development—and legacy—of facilities built around the Manchester ship canal in an area called Dumplington, which was quickly renamed to something more pleasing: Barton Cross.

As we entered the final hectic lobbying days, the general impression was that Athens had a strong claim to host what would be the Centenary Games, but there were doubts about the capacity of the Greek city to deliver such a large project. The city of Atlanta, the home of the Coca-

Cola Company, was strong and there was a similar opinion about Toronto, tempered a little by the very aggressive sales campaign led by its leader Paul Henderson, president of the International Sailing Federation. Toronto saw its chances greatly affected by a protest from a group from Toronto who managed to erect a tent in the foyer of the hotel. Manchester presented well with senior British government support from Chris Patten, secretary of state for the environment (sport was part of the environment ministry at the time) who Bob Scott kept introducing to IOC members as a 'future prime minister'.

There were five rounds of bidding, with Belgrade eliminated in the first round with just seven votes, Manchester in the second with five votes (having received twelve in the first round), Melbourne in the third with sixteen votes, Toronto in the fourth with twenty-two votes, and Atlanta beating Athens in the fifth round by fifty-one votes to thirty-five. As usual, the detailed voting was kept secret until the announcement ceremony held that evening. As we all sat nervously waiting for the announcement, David Dixon, the BOA legal adviser, asked the question, 'What do we do if he opens the envelope and says Manchester?' It was a slightly cynical remark but perhaps representative of the reality of how a British bid was regarded by the international community.

The disappointing result from Manchester, following the same result from Birmingham four years earlier, did not seem to dampen the BOA's enthusiasm to host the Games. A decision was taken that, in future, interested British cities would be invited to make an application to be selected as a bidding city by 31 January 1991, with their plans to be outlined by mid-April. The IOC would decide at its session in Monte Carlo in 1993. I was to serve on an evaluation commission with Bill Slater, Peter Coni, and the BOA officers. The diary was beginning to fill up.

13

Towards the End with the IBF

The BOA appeared to have been relatively uninvolved in the previous two Olympic bids from Great Britain, involving Birmingham in 1986 and Manchester in 1990. It is a little difficult to find details, but it appears that both bids were conceived and established by the respective cities, with the BOA providing the formal approval necessary for IOC purposes.

After the IOC decision in favour of Atlanta to host the Centennial Games in 1996, the BOA made a formal announcement that it would be much more involved in the process if another British city was to be allowed to bid for the Games in 2000. A small evaluation committee had been set up and a timescale made public for interested cities to present their case. The final decision would be made by the IOC at its session in Monte Carlo in 1993, extending the period of preparation given to the selected city from six years to seven.

Both London and Manchester registered an interest. The London plans appeared to consist of a mixture of differing opinions from various sports organisations with their own specific interests. Leadership seemed to be vested in the Central Council for Physical Recreation (CCPR) and its secretary, Peter Lawson, but clear tensions existed between the CCPR and the BOA over their different responsibilities. At that time, there was no Sports Council, but the government kept some form of informal monitoring as there was no formal local authority for London.

The Greater London Council (GLC) had been dissolved in 1986 and its powers passed to the London boroughs. It was clear that a whole range of different priorities existed in any London plans. Manchester, on the other hand, presented plans that had been created for its 1990 bid and which had been further developed and improved. The evaluation committee made no recommendation, but on this occasion, the full BOA met in the Charing Cross Hotel to listen to the presentations from both cities and to formally reach a decision.

The London case was presented by Sebastian Coe, one of Britain's sporting heroes and among the greatest middle-distance runners of all time. A double Olympic gold medallist, his career on the track had ended and he was beginning to enter the world of politics. The Manchester case was presented by Bob Scott who had accumulated much experience in the world of Olympic presentations. It would be fair to say that the case presented by Manchester was much more realistic and properly researched than the rather uncertain and uncoordinated picture painted by London.

BOA members were entitled to ask questions and when raised, created some problems in eliciting detailed answers from London. This should have come as no surprise, as BOA members were all delegated by their own sports and their questions reflected personal interests. Don Anthony, the chairman of the BOA Education Committee, took a wider view. He asked, 'Mr Coe, why do you think that London should organise the Olympic Games for a third time, as opposed to Manchester who would be organising them for the first time?'

To this, Seb Coe replied, 'That is a very good question, and to answer it I am going to call on Ron Eames.' Eames was the president of the British Canoe Federation and a member of the London bid team but had not been paying too much attention. He struggled to answer, leading me to conclude that Coe was destined to have a good career in politics. Manchester won the vote easily, and a pathway was set for the next two years.

Although it did not involve me in any additional efforts, I was surprised to discover that the ninety-seventh IOC session in 1991 was to be held in Birmingham. I have been unable to find any copy of a letter of application to the IOC from the BOA to host the session and can only surmise that the IOC decision must have been based on a relationship developed by Denis Howell with President Samaranch of the IOC during the 1986 Birmingham Olympic bid. The actual venue was the new and very impressive International Convention Centre in the middle of Birmingham with delegates staying in the adjacent Hyatt hotel, an imposing blue-glass giant which had an air bridge joining the two venues over Bridge Street.

Responsibility for the session brought several organisational challenges for the BOA, which were solved by Simon Clegg, our new, young assistant secretary. Bids had been accepted from Nagano (Japan), Salt Lake City (USA), Ostersund (Sweden), Jaca (Spain), and Aosta (Italy) for the 1998

Winter Games. The successful city would then have seven years to prepare—exactly like the Summer Games.

Space was allocated for each city in rooms in the hotel for exhibition and entertaining purposes, while the convenience of walking from the hotel to the Convention Centre was much praised, especially as Birmingham's rainy weather regularly soaked the several hundred bid supporters from their cities who delivered noisy approval of their bids in Centenary Square outside. Security was organised and politely enforced but then criticised when the security man on the air bridge refused access to the president of the IOC as he was not wearing his official accreditation. To his credit, Samaranch simply returned to his room to retrieve the required accreditation and carried on as if nothing had happened.

There were five rounds of bidding, with Nagano holding a narrow advantage throughout. In the first round there was an unexpected tie on fifteen votes between Salt Lake City and Aosta, with the American city surviving after a run-off. Salt Lake City then grew in strength until the fifth round when Nagano won by forty-six votes to forty-two. The large group of soaked Japanese supporters outside in the square were delighted.

There was much media comment about the alleged lavish hospitality provided in their entertaining rooms by some candidate cities, not least from the Salt Lake City delegation; the lessons learned from their 1991 bidding experience may not have been completely helpful. Indeed, its next Olympic bid was to create a major scandal and a crisis for the IOC. The Manchester bid committee watched all of this with interest and benefitted greatly from having an IOC session almost on its doorstep. The session was well-organised and was not unhelpful to the BOA's status with the IOC.

The IBF world championships for 1991 were awarded to Denmark rather than Hong Kong, which city had held successive Grand Prix finals. So, the badminton world returned to the Brondby Sports Centre, the scene of the very successful and significant championships in 1983. Almost as expected, Asian players dominated the championships, winning all five gold medal events. However, our Danish hosts provided excellent competition in winning silver medals in two of the three doubles events. The traditional victories in singles events were maintained in both men's singles and women's singles by the top Chinese players.

Slightly surprisingly, the silver medallists in the two singles events came from Indonesia, perhaps their performance indicating a strong challenge at the Olympic Games in 1992. In the doubles events, the outstanding Park Joo Bong from Korea won both men's doubles and mixed doubles. In both finals, the Korean pairings beat Thomas Lund and his partners from Denmark. In the men's doubles event, Lund and his partner Jon Holst-Christenses beat the famous Chinese pairing of Li Yongbo and Tain Bingyi in the semi-final and then lost in three games to Park and Kim of Korea.

Not much later in the day, Lund and his partner Pernille Dupont lost in another three-game final to Park and his partner Myung Hee Chung, the best pair in the world. Thomas Lund had developed into a world-class doubles player, and after his playing career was finished, he moved into the administration of badminton. He became a highly competent and successful chief executive (secretary general) of the IBF, which was to move its offices to Kuala Lumpur in Malaysia, where it would be right in the middle of its most important market.

Having looked back at their arrangements for the 1983 world championships, the Danish organisers decided to improve their arrangements for hospitality and added a large tent at the back of the competition hall, where visiting IBF officials and sponsors could mix and mingle. This was regarded as a major development in the arrangements for major events and was much enjoyed.

The world championships coincided with my fiftieth birthday—6 May 1991—and to celebrate, I arranged a small dinner with badminton friends in an Italian restaurant in a neighbouring town called Taastrup. The guests met for drinks in the hotel, but one absentee was my close friend, Tom Bacher. Tom lived in a neighbouring village called Greve Strand and had a close group of friends who celebrated each other's birthdays with some special stunt to mark the day. During the welcome drinks, the door suddenly burst open and in came the missing Bacher with two of his close friends, all three dressed as doctors and pushing a hospital trolley.

They declared that I was a patient in need of some medicine and produced a special bottle of medicine called Johnnie Walker Black Label. They instructed the other guests to leave because I was to be taken to hospital. Too much hilarity, I was left in the tender care of the new Danish medical team, who dressed me in white hospital clothing, insisted on more medicine, and wheeled me into a waiting ambulance.

With a police outrider, we headed for an unknown destination. They had blindfolded me, and the medicine was beginning to work. My guess was that I might be taken to the bar in the neighbouring Greve Badminton Club, but when the ambulance stopped and the stretcher began to move, I heard Bacher call out, 'Are the surgeons ready?' The blindfold was removed, and I found myself in the middle of the packed entertaining tent at the championships with all of the members of the IBF and many Danish friends.

As the evening unfolded, if that is the appropriate word, I discovered that the Danish Badminton Association had paid for the jazz band and that one of Tom's best friends had donated the barrels of beer. The event featured in the sports pages of the following day's *B.T.*, the major Danish tabloid newspaper, and a good time was had by all. However, a little worse for wear, when I eventually got to bed in the wee small hours of the following morning, it took me some time and no small difficulty to extract myself from my hospital attire.

Planning for future Olympic bids was all very well but finalising arrangements for the debut of a new Olympic sport was much more pressing. The Barcelona organising committee, having struggled to find a home for badminton in converted premises in the city or in a neighbouring town, eventually took the brave decision to build a brand-new multi-purpose sports centre just to the east of the Olympic Village. This was a good example of how hosting the Games could be a catalyst for the development of venues to the benefit of sport in a host city.

The resulting indoor arena, the Paveló de la Mer Bella, is used as a badminton school and hosts basketball, handball, indoor football, and other sports to this day. The overall detailed plans provided for three courts in a large main hall into which we would put seating for 4,000 spectators. It also had a practice hall, a gymnasium, and a whole host of other smaller rooms that would cater for our requirements during the Games and for multi-purpose use thereafter.

We were a bit naïve at the time and did not place any priority on extensive private offices for IBF officials during the Games, but we were happy that the necessary space would be available for players, courts, and organising officials. The design certainly allowed for enough height for top-class badminton, and there were plans for additional areas for relaxation outside the building that would be well-used during a sunny Spanish summer.

The overall situation, beside the Olympic Village, was potentially perfect, but only if we could arrange a gate in the security fence around the village to allow the players and team officials to make use of the internal transport system to travel the short distance to their field of play. This request presented some real problems, as any decision would involve not just the International Federation, but the organisation for NOCs, the village management team, the Barcelona organising committee, and the IOC. There was an obvious potential security issue which was a priority for everybody after the horrors of the 1972 Munich Games. It was one of the best moments in the years of preparations when we found out that our proposal for ease of transport for our athletes had been accepted. It was hard to imagine a better possible venue for any Olympic sport.

On one of the regular visits to Barcelona to check on the progress in construction of the Pavelo, we were delighted to find that the architects and builders were fully committed to the necessary height of the main hall. To our surprise, however, we found that as the Pavelo was built overlooking the sea, the architects believed that those sports using the building would prefer to have a clear view of the sea. The result was that two of the sides of the main hall were designed to hold large areas of glass. This did provide a clear view of the sea but would have made the playing of top-class badminton almost impossible if the sun shone.

There was consternation in the venue department but almost instant relaxation when we replied to their question, 'Do we have to rebuild the whole Pavelo?' by suggesting that a more cost-effective solution would be to hang dark curtains over the glass window areas, and that this would solve the problem. The moral of this situation was that sports should make every effort to work in a collaborative manner with a local organising committee.

Good playing conditions for indoor sports are crucial to their success, and several years of effort had gone into providing the environment we required, all to be delivered by a sympathetic organising committee. We then needed to make sure that the high quality of badminton at the Games would be seen by the maximum number of Olympic television viewers, especially in Asia. Television coverage would be provided by a separate wholly owned subsidiary company of the Barcelona organising committee under the direction of Manolo Romero, one of the top Spanish television officials with wide experience of the Olympic Games. It was his role to invite television production companies from different countries that had experience of televising particular sports in their own countries and with particular expertise.

We were delighted to be told that, for badminton, television production would be in the hands of Danmarks Radio (DR), with which we had worked on many occasions, and for two world championships. Olympic television coverage in Denmark was split equally between DR and TV2, the main commercial station, so we understood that the choice of a Danish company would not present any difficulties in an important European country. DR had already told us that its appointed producer would be Hans Groenfeldt, and we decided to invite him, at our expense, to come out to some of the major Asian events to familiarise himself with the players who were likely to be medallists in Barcelona.

I also made it my responsibility to contact all the major TV stations in our major Asian countries. For many of them, the presence of badminton on the Olympic programme was of real significance as they prepared their plans for their Barcelona coverage. Having an expert production crew was good news, but there was a question of how much badminton coverage would be made available. In 1992, the amount of coverage of each sport was a decision of the IOC and the local organisers. Thereafter, the amount of Olympic coverage to be shown in a nation was under the control of the executive producer for each country. The IOC and organising committees were many years away from the blanket coverage of all sport in the Games that modern technology now allows, to say nothing of the different platforms for that delivery.

Part of my discussions with our Asian TV friends was to ensure that they were familiar with the dates in the Olympic programme for the badminton competitions, and that there would be one main court for TV coverage. I also made it clear that the order of play for the badminton sessions would, as far as possible, be based on Asian players in the morning and European players in the evening, hopefully making badminton coverage a central feature of prime time in the respective continental areas. It was also crucial that Asian broadcasters made the necessary requests to the host broadcaster for the detailed dates and times when they would wish to have coverage of badminton to show in their countries. This sounded easy to do but proved to be rather difficult to organise, as our contacts in the major Asian badminton countries tended to be TV producers as opposed to TV planners. Even so, the efforts were to prove worthwhile.

The Barcelona organisers selected the Yonex Company from Japan to supply its top-quality shuttlecocks and its portable courts for the Games. The decisions were the responsibility of the organisers, but they were happy to have our approval. We planned a test event, but almost as soon as the curtains had been installed, I was able to take a small group of the very best players to the Pavelo to check out the playing conditions. Sitting at the back of the planned centre court, I had a feeling that not everything was in perfect order and decided to walk around the hall and to the top seats in each seating block.

At the top of the side block to the left of the courts, I found that the three courts had been put down without lining them up accurately, which might just have affected the quality of the television lighting that had just been installed. I was not the most popular man in Barcelona by insisting that the courts be re-laid, and the lights checked. This was done and the players gave the conditions their approval.

While this was being done, late on a Saturday afternoon, to my complete surprise, Samaranch appeared, very casually dressed, and asked me if there were any problems. He asked why I did not consult the coaches or team managers but seemed relaxed when I explained that for lighting purposes the views of the players were paramount. Team managers normally used lights only as an area for complaint. We chatted for a time, and I was very impressed that he would take this type of interest in the build-up to the Games.

The Barcelona Games were always going to be my swansong with the IBF as I had committed myself to take over the chairmanship of the BOA the following October. However, the IBF business committee had to supervise the 1992 Thomas and Uber Cup Finals, which we decided to allocate, once again, to Kuala Lumpur and Malaysia. The decision was a marginal one. Everyone remembered the successes of the same events staged in the Stadium Negara in 1984 and 1988 as important occasions in the three-event contract with Philip Morris and its Marlboro brand, which had revolutionised the IBF major team events.

Malaysia had been placed third in the 1986 contest, then runners-up to China, in 1988 and 1990. In the last two contests, the final score had been 4–1 to China. They were close results but still a gap in standard between the two countries.

Malaysian badminton had seen the rise of the Sidek brothers. The oldest, Misbun, was probably past his best but Razif and Jalani had been producing great doubles results and Rashid, the youngest of the brothers was showing great promise. The Malaysian Badminton Association had also employed Han Jian and Yang Yang as coaches—previous world class players from China. We decided that Malaysia had a team that might just be good enough to win the Thomas Cup at home, which would be a good result for the sport. The decision in favour of Kuala Lumpur presented us with a second benefit when Rothmans agreed a new and substantial sponsorship deal.

Once again, the entries to both competitions were truly international with fifty-four teams in the Thomas Cup and forty-four in the Uber Cup. Playing both competitions at the same time and in the same stadium continued to make sense, although, on this occasion, the Uber Cup found itself to be less exciting than what turned out to be an almost unique Thomas Cup, which provided the sport with one of its greatest occasions. In all three Olympic racket sports, it has been remarkable how often great sport has come from the doubles matches as opposed to the singles. For badminton, 1992 Kuala Lumpur was to prove that as never before.

China successfully defended its Uber Cup title, while elsewhere, women's badminton was making great strides. A young Swedish team— led by Christine Magnusson, who, despite her very Swedish name, was born in the Toro Kingdom in Uganda—won its matches in the group stage against both Japan and England but found the champions just too good in the semi-final. Korea won its group stage without losing and, having beaten Indonesia in the semi-final, won both doubles matches in the final and pushed the Chinese holders all the way.

Magnusson had an interesting background—her stepfather was Swedish, her mother, Ugandan. Her family had to flee Uganda during the rule of Idi Amin and moved to Sweden, where Christine took up badminton. By the age of sixteen, she was a Swedish international. In 1988, Associated Press began a story about her, 'Black Star Brings Prominence to Swedish Badminton', with the following anecdote:

> Christine Magnusson, Sweden's long-time badminton champion, sometimes hears her fans mistakenly cheering for the wrong side. Magnusson, who is originally from Uganda, is not the stereotype of the tall blonde Swede. But she has put Swedish badminton on the map. 'When I play international tournaments here at home, the audience often roots for my opponent. People take for granted that the white player is the Swede,' she said in a recent magazine interview.
>
> She doesn't take offence. 'People abroad are surprised to learn I'm Swedish, so I tell them "I just dyed my hair,"' she said.

As a sign of the battles to come in the Thomas Cup, the group stages were to produce both incidents and anxious moments. Malaysia lost to Korea, which was not in its pre-competition plans, but wins over Denmark and England were enough for it to reach the semi-finals. Indonesia lost to China in its group match by 5–0 and was accused of playing a weakened team to avoid meeting China in the semi-final. It was a charge upheld by the IBF committee of management and led to the withdrawal of the agreed travel grant, but the decision was overturned on appeal by the IBF Council. Playing preliminary rounds in a group format runs that type of risk.

Malaysia then rewarded its local supporters and the trust placed in it by the IBF, by beating China in a remarkable semi-final. Rashid Sidek was the star as he won the opening match 18/14, 10/15, 15/12 against the world champion, Zhao Jianhua who was assumed to be unbeatable. Razif and Jalani Sidek then won the top doubles match, beating Li Yongbo and

Tian Bingyi in three games. A score of 2–0 brought the packed crowd—all 12,000 of them—to a frenzy of excitement.

China then won the next two singles matches to square the contest. The tie left Malaysians Cheah Soon Kit and Soo Beng Kiang to recover from their previous poor form to win the deciding match 15/9, 18/14 amid scenes of huge excitement after five hours and thirty-six minutes of tension. Malaysia was delighted, with the story of success dominating the media, which was jubilant but then increased the tension by reminding everybody that a final had still to be played.

It is hard to imagine the pressures building on the Malaysian team, and the whole nation, over the four days before the final. We had encouraged David Miller, the leading sportswriter from *The Times* in London, to join us for the second week of play, and his article before the final exactly captured the mood:

> The semi-professional football programme has been cancelled here today in the interests of national priority: overwhelming public anxiety, reaching fever pitch, about the sport of badminton. More precisely, about winning the Thomas Cup. Even more precisely, doing so by beating Indonesia. Nowhere have I seen such national fervour since Argentina won the football World Cup in Buenos Aires and jammed the streets.
>
> Indonesia will be no pushover. Badminton is equally their national sport and the pride at stake is almost without parallel in the world of sport.

This final had history. Malaya had been the first winners in 1949 and on three later occasions, ending in 1967 when independent and renamed Malaysia beat Indonesia in Jakarta. Indonesia won its first Thomas Cup in 1956 and eight times thereafter.

Stadium Negara was full two hours before the start of the final. The official attendance was 12,000, but somehow, many more seemed to have managed to get in. The very modest air conditioning through the arms of the seats in the royal box made no impression on the humidity in the stadium. I was preparing to commentate for Singapore television and had been smart enough to have a tape machine installed beside my seat to take a series of TV quality tapes, with English commentary, for the IBF highlights programme. The king, Sultan Azlan Shah, and his queen, Raja Permaisuri Tuanku Bainun, took their seats with Madam Mahathir, wife of the prime minister, and Malaysian badminton's greatest supporter. We actually started two minutes early at 6.58 as the policeman in charge was concerned that the enormous and volatile crowd would wait no longer.

I suppose it was inevitable after the Malaysian triumph in the semi-final that we should see the unexpected. Rashid Sidek contrived to lose the second game in the first match to Ardy Wiranata but recovered to win 15/4 in the vital third game. Surprises continued when Razif and Jalani Sidek lost the top doubles to Gunawan and Hartono, a match which they were strong favourites to win.

Foo Kok Keong, an experienced singles player, put Malaysia back in front with a fairly easy two-game win over Alan Budikusuma. The second doubles was to be vital, and with ever louder noise and crowd involvement, Cheah Soon Kit and Soo Beng Kiang lost the first game, won the second, and brought the twenty-five year wait for return of the cup to a crescendo of excitement by winning the vital third game. It was stunning doubles play that had provided the great drama. The last singles match was a complete anti-climax; even so, the Malaysian crowd stayed in their thousands to see the king present the renowned Thomas Cup at 12.40 a.m.

After over six hours of commentary, I managed to extricate myself from a sodden chair and collected my precious tapes. Fortunately, the bar at the hotel was still open and the IBF group discussed the amazing evening they had just enjoyed. Merdeka Plaza in downtown Kuala Lumpur was full of delighted Malaysian supporters for many hours, and the media was busy producing the special editions for later that day. I can think of few sporting occasions that compared. The combination of venue, competing teams, wonderful play, excitement, history, and national pride have never been equalled. It was, without doubt, badminton's finest night.

14

Barcelona

It is unusual for any international federation to organise two major events close to each other in the same year, but that was precisely the badminton experience in 1992. After the excitement and success of the Thomas and Uber Cup finals in Kuala Lumpur in May, we renewed our organisational efforts and enjoyed many new experiences and made many new friends at the Games of the XXV Olympiad in Barcelona from 25 July to 9 August.

It had taken over twenty years of effort to become a full programme sport in the Olympic Games, and we were prepared to make our mark enthusiastically. We joined 169 nations, including the returning South Africa, twenty-five sports, with baseball and badminton as the two new sports, and the first ever professional basketball team, the 'Dream Team'— Jordan, Johnson, Bird, Barkley, *et al*, all destined to be the stars of the Games. Some 9,356 athletes were to take part in 257 events over fifteen days.

Our first Olympic home was the Pavelo de la Marr Bella, beside the Olympic Village in the Parc de Mar area of Barcelona. The construction and finishing of the Pavelo had been completed in time. The first of the detailed badminton preparations was a test event open to all the potential Olympic badminton athletes to be held at the end of May. It is normal in the build-up to Olympic Games that sports hold tests to ensure that the technical and playing conditions for the sport fall within their international federation rules and standards and that they are in ideal condition for the competitors.

In the case of badminton, the players appeared to be happy that the lighting was good, the air conditioning was effective and not intrusive, and that there was minimal drift in the hall. During the Games themselves, the badminton athletes would be able to travel on the internal Olympic Village transport system from the transport hub to the special gate in the village security fence just beside the Pavelo. This proved to be of great value to the national Olympic committees and their team managements.

The players taking part in the test tournament were widely international, but it was of some interest that players from Malaysia and Indonesia decided to stay at home or to play only a modest number of matches in the test tournament. The same situation appeared to apply to players from China, but there was a good entry from Europe and other parts of the world. The top European players gave the conditions a favourable vote and the local organisers were happy. We had been given great assistance over the previous years by Raphael Lucas, who was our local badminton manager. He was a PE teacher who played the game and worked very diligently to deliver for his city and country a high-quality competition venue. As a consequence, the inaugural badminton tournament in the Olympic Games would bring credit to him and to all his team of local volunteers.

The IBF, its officers, staff, and all the necessary officials gathered in Barcelona some days before the Games to ensure that everything was in order. The IOC accreditation system presented one small problem as the premier accreditations for the IBF were granted to the president and to the secretary general. The local organising committee came to me and thanked me for all my work and said that they had decided to provide for me a second accreditation as a technical delegate, which would allow me to fulfil my own duties during the Games.

It took just a short time for us to realise that on this occasion, we would have little responsibility for bringing the players to the actual tournament. This was the responsibility of their own national Olympic committees, which looked after travel, accommodation in the village, national team clothing, and all the other issues with which we would normally assist. My fellow technical delegate, Torsten Berg from Denmark, made sure that all the necessary shuttlecocks at the correct speed were safely in storage and all the court officials were prepared. It seemed that we were ready to go. However, there was no evidence of any television arrangements.

For Olympic Games in those days, it was the responsibility of organising committees to ensure the production of the television coverage. The IOC made a payment to the organising committee from the rights fees it had raised by selling the television rights to national broadcasters all around the globe.

To ensure successful delivery to the world, as well as to Spain, the Barcelona organising committee had appointed Manolo Romero to this very important position. Romero had begun his career in 1965 as an engineer with TVE, Spain's national television network, and had been involved in Olympic broadcasting since the Mexico Games of 1968. He was regarded as the leading expert in attracting different production teams from different countries with specialised skills in covering particular Olympic sports.

I had held several meetings with Romero over the previous years and had been encouraged by his assurance that some television coverage would be available from the centre court of the three badminton courts throughout the whole tournament. Each sport had a local television liaison officer, and the official allocated to badminton was a gentleman called Segundo. He did not appear to be full of the milk of human kindness and was clearly unhappy to have been allocated to badminton when he would have been happier with a major Spanish sport, like basketball. He was particularly unhelpful when asked to provide an answer to my very pertinent question, 'When is the television crew going to appear?'

The plan had been that the appointed crew from Danmarks Radio (DR) would turn up at the end of day two of the badminton event, practise for one day, and then provide the agreed coverage throughout the rest of the tournament. The early days' coverage would be provided by the local organisers. However, nothing was happening, and a combination of a language problem between Segundo and myself and a very busy Romero was presenting a crisis.

I found out that there was to be a meeting involving international federations on the morning of 26 July, just after the opening ceremony. I contacted Boris Stankovic, the secretary general of ASOIF and of the International Basketball Federation, and asked that the badminton television problem be put on the agenda. I turned up for the meeting to be held in the IOC's official hotel early in the morning of the 26th and found, to my horror, that this was not just a small meeting of international federations but a major meeting, led by Samaranch, containing all the important officials from the IOC, as well as the top people from Barcelona's organising committee.

I was in the wrong place at the wrong time. I could not reach Stankovic before the meeting started to withdraw my complaint and sat in increasing terror as Samaranch dealt with the coverage of the opening ceremony, one technical glitch, the first evidence of total world viewing figures and several other major issues for the organising committee. When the agenda reached international federation issues there were only two, and one was ours, regarding television and not occurring until two days hence. Samaranch was irritated and I just managed to reach a microphone and apologised by saying that there was not a problem, only a situation that would be resolved.

As the meeting finished and we all left the room, I was attacked—that is the right word—by a very angry Manolo Romero. He was obviously embarrassed by my action to raise in a major meeting what he regarded as an insignificant problem. I explained to him that I was very disappointed that he had not fulfilled his promise. If anything, that made him even angrier. The discussion became very heated, but I managed to ask him why he had changed the agreement and he replied that he had received no requests for international coverage.

By that stage, I probably lost my temper and told him that he must be blind, as his desk was probably covered by requests from Asian television stations all of which I had organised. There was no meeting of minds. Manolo stormed off, leaving me to think that I had probably destroyed years of work and possibly badminton's future in the Olympic movement. Somewhat forlorn, I slipped away, found a corner in the hotel coffee shop, and had a late, lonely breakfast.

The rest of the morning was filled with a relatively unimportant meeting with Un Yong Kim and the council of GAISF. It would be fair to say that my mind was elsewhere, and I may not have made a significant contribution, but unfortunately, as was common, the meeting was followed by lunch. Around 3.30 p.m., I took a call from Torsten Berg who said, 'I'm not sure what you did but we have a Spanish television crew wanting to start rigging in the badminton hall.' I headed back to the Pavelo as quickly as possible to find five rather pleasant Spanish television people with an outside broadcast truck that was roughly the size of a small ice cream van. They had taken some time to find the Pavelo, then admitted that they knew nothing about badminton, had never seen it played, did not know the rules, and suggested that this presented them with several basic television problems.

They told us that they had three cameras available, and we had to tell them where we wished them to be placed around the centre court, which would be the only court with television coverage. We then had three cameras in conventional positions, and they were able to experiment with court images but without players. So we arranged that they could attend the arranged practise sessions on the morning and evening of 27 July and start their live coverage on the morning of Tuesday the 28th. It was not the television coverage that we had hoped for, but it was a significant improvement on the situation with which I had been confronted some eight hours earlier. Segundo was also surprised, but not any happier. At that time, neither he nor I knew that television rights had been purchased by no less than twenty-five broadcasters in seven major badminton countries in Asia.

The very first day of Olympic badminton started at 10 a.m. on the morning of 28 July 1992. The first match on the television court was a men's singles involving Foo Kok Keong of Malaysia and Hans Sperre of Norway. I spoke to Kok Keong before the match and asked him that if he won the toss, he would opt to serve. I also asked that, at the end of the first rally, he would immediately change the shuttlecock so that I could collect it for historical purposes. To his credit, he did exactly what he had been asked to do. To this day, that very symbolic shuttlecock remains in the Olympic Museum in Lausanne.

Zhao Jianhua, the Chinese world champion, was also a television court player. It had been agreed that matches involving players from Asia on the television court would be in the morning session, which finished around 2 p.m. Similarly, the European players would be given preference on the television court for the evening session, which started around 6 p.m.

The last match chosen for the first morning session was a women's doubles match between Rosianna Tendean and Erma Sulistyaningsih of Indonesia against Gill Clark and Julie Bradbury of Great Britain. This turned into a classic, lasting around ninety minutes with the British pair beating the seeded Indonesians 15/10, 4/15, 17/15. The last few points involved long and exciting rallies; it was badminton at its best.

I had been called into action by the BBC which had decided to cover the match at the last minute and needed me to commentate. My own performance over the closing stages earned me a comment from Desmond Lynam, who was fronting the BBC coverage, 'And that was Craig Reedie getting a bit excited!' He was right—I was; Olympic badminton's journey had begun.

When I appeared at the Pavelo on the following morning, I was greeted by a smiling Segundo who proceeded to give me a kiss and then take me to his office. He went into a drawer in his desk and produced a bottle of Priorat, an excellent Catalan red wine, and two glasses, which he filled. At first, I was more than surprised at what seemed like a total character change until a combination of his pidgin English and my pidgin Spanish explained that he had only that morning seen the viewing figures for badminton. It came as a complete shock to him, and even to me, that the figures from the major Asian countries like Indonesia and China made badminton the most viewed sport on 28 July from the entire Olympic programme.

Even though it was a bit early in the day, the wine improved with every sip and Segundo became a helpful friend for the rest of our days in Barcelona. We thanked our Spanish crew for all their help, and I told Hans Groenfeldt, DR's badminton director, and his DR crew when they arrived that they did not have a day to practise but they would be live from 10 a.m. on 30 July. To finish what started as an unpleasant row, Manolo then sent me a fax with a generous apology. I responded in kind, and we became friends and met regularly at the Games for many years.

After the television traumas and the initial viewing figures congratulations, we all settled down to enjoy being at an Olympic Games. The IBF officials, our local organisers, and the players—now acknowledged athletes in their national teams—all enjoyed their first colourful opening ceremony. I had been lucky enough to be in the Seoul opening ceremony, which was held, to fit with the prime time needs of the major television markets, in daylight.

Barcelona held its ceremony in the wonderful warmth of a Spanish summer evening, and the organisers took full advantage of the opportunity to use special lighting effects, immortalised in the lighting of the Olympic flame by a flaming arrow shot from the middle of the stadium. The archer, Spanish Paralympian medallist Antonio Rebello, was one of over 200 archers considered for the onerous task. After days of practice using wind machines and many singed fingers, he was chosen just two hours before the ceremony. He must have had nerves of steel.

Another magical moment was the singing of the Games' anthem— 'Barcelona' by local opera legend Montserrat Caballé and rock superstar Freddie Mercury. Mercury wrote the song with composer and musician Mike Moran. Between them, they produced a memorable piece of music that, once heard, is never forgotten.

IOC accreditations allowed many of us to watch other sports, although Torsten Berg and I were fully committed to the arrangements for badminton in the Pavelo. We had been allocated a car with a driver called Oscar, who became best friends with our wives, Rosemary and Jette, as they enjoyed many of the events and the glories of the city of Barcelona. The Catalan capital is not short of wonders: the famous La Rambla, a tree-lined pedestrian street that stretches for three-quarters of a mile and is flanked by amazing markets, restaurants, cafes, and street artists; the amazing Picasso and Miro Museums; the Plaça Reial and its lovely fountain; and the many extraordinary buildings of visionary architect, Antonio Gaudi, whose crowning glory is his masterpiece, the Sagrada Familia, the most awe-inspiring basilica you will ever see.

Oscar was a volunteer from his day job as a supplier of cutlery to small restaurants in Catalonia, so we were very well advised on splendid places to eat. I managed to leave two evening sessions of badminton in favour of athletics and was delighted to watch two British gold medals for Linford Christie in the 100 m and Sally Gunnell in the 400 m hurdles. The excitement of watching Olympic medals being won by your fellow countrymen and women is amazing.

Our Danish television producers, delighted to be using their brand-new outside broadcast facilities, became good friends. The Pavelo delivered two outside areas set up with tables, chairs, and umbrellas that were well-used throughout the days of the Spanish summer, especially during the gap in play between the morning and evening sessions. After the close of play in the evening, Hans Groenfeldt and his crew would get together to share an evening beer—a popular Danish habit—and I became a regular participant as a friend and as a part-time BBC commentator. The brand-new equipment being used contained four special slots for slow-motion replays but only two were needed to enhance the coverage of badminton. An opportunity had presented itself.

The IOC was aware of the promotional efforts made over the past few years by the IBF to produce television-quality highlights from its major events, and I believed that the IOC would give permission for similar efforts from the Olympic Games. Hans agreed very quickly that for the finals of the Olympic tournament, he would use one of his free slow-motion slots to provide the IBF with the tapes they required. The result was that I left Barcelona after the Games with a pile of television-quality tapes, with which we made another highlights programme in London, with commentary by Barry Davies and me. Three months later, the IOC agreed that international federations could do just that. We were ahead of the game.

During those rather relaxed days in Barcelona, I took the opportunity to spend some time with the members of the IOC who came to watch the badminton event. Our main greeter was our president, Arthur Jones, who was a genial host, but I was able to enhance friendships made during the campaign for our sport's inclusion in the Games. On a couple of occasions, I joined other members and officials in the main IOC hotel, when friends and colleagues got together over a nightcap or two to discuss the day's happenings.

There was universal admiration for the famous picture produced by Spanish television of the high diving board at the outdoor pool on the Montjuïc hill. It showed the divers, as if they were high in the air against a background of Barcelona and the Sagrada Familia. It was rightly considered to be 'the image of the Games', indicative of the increasing importance of high-quality television imagery in reinforcing the magic of the Games for a worldwide audience.

A regular attendee at those late evening occasions was Charlie Battle from Atlanta, the city organising the next Summer Games in 1996. Charlie had played a huge part in the success of the Atlanta bid for the 'Centennial Games' and was the best 'presser of the flesh' anybody had ever met. He made friends everywhere and had an encyclopaedic memory for members of the IOC, their families, interests, and attitudes to Atlanta and the USA.

The Atlanta plans for swimming involved an upgrade of the outdoor pool in the grounds of a local university, a very different setting from Barcelona. 'How can Atlanta match the grandeur of Barcelona and their image of the Games?' Charlie was asked. 'Easy,' he said, 'In Atlanta we'll put the television camera on the top seat at one side of the pool with a perfect view of the high board, and on the other side we will put a great big picture of Barcelona.' Few asked him any more questions.

The badminton event ran smoothly during the early days, and we were pleased with the spectator attendance, especially when we were told that the semi-finals and finals were sold out. The first big upset on court was the defeat of Zhao Jianhua, the Chinese world champion and top seed, by Hermawan Susanto, the third-ranked Indonesian. It was a close and exciting contest with Susanto winning 15/2, 14/17, 17/14—a major surprise but greatly enhancing our Asian viewing figures. The Indonesian players had arrived in Barcelona in top form and Susanto was joined in the semi-finals by Ardy Wiranata and Alan Budikusuma.

In the women's singles event, Susi Susanti of Indonesia and Bang Soo-hyun of Korea won their semi-finals against Chinese opposition. The great days of Chinese domination in that event with Li Lingwei and Han Aiping, both retired, were clearly over. In men's doubles, the world's best pair, Park and Kim from Korea, dominated the event, and in women's doubles, the top Korean and Chinese pairings reached the finals.

The BBC had asked me to commentate on some matches in the earlier rounds but certainly for both semi-finals and finals. I had been working on my own with the microphone but was then joined by Barry Davies for the two important days. Probably without thinking, I was able to contribute some 'colour' to our first women's singles semi-final commentary by explaining that Susi Susanti came from a small town in Western Java called Tasik Malaya and was a Roman Catholic in the biggest Muslim country in the world. Barry leant forward and wrote down, 'only tactics from now on'—a clear line of demarcation for the next two days.

On finals day, I was delighted to hear that President Samaranch would fulfil a promise made to me—that he would come and present badminton's first ever Olympic medal. It was fitting that this was won by Susi Susanti, the Indonesian favourite, who became her country's first ever gold medallist. In all their previous Olympic Games, Indonesia had won only one bronze medal, in archery. The medal ceremony was an emotional experience, not only for Indonesia but for the many people from the sport who had worked long and hard to bring it about.

I must confess to a lump in my own throat as I left Barry Davies to put his own splendid words on the moment. The previous evening, I had asked Hans Groenfeldt to keep his cameras running after the medal ceremony as he would get some good crowd shots, a practice not completely in line with his instruction from the Spanish television organisers. He did just that and followed Susi Susanti into the large group of Indonesian supporters where she was embraced by a tall, good-looking, tearful official called General Try Sutrisno, president of the PBSI, the Indonesian Badminton Association. These pictures were seen in Indonesia by millions of supporters. Six months later, General Sutrisno was vice president of Indonesia.

To the delight of almost everybody, the following men's singles final was won by Susi's boyfriend, Alan Budikusuma, who beat his more highly seeded fellow countryman Ardy Wiranata 15/12, 18/13 to give Indonesia its second gold medal. In the men's doubles final, the gold medal was won by Park Joo-bong and Kim Moon-Soo of Korea, without doubt the best pair in the world. The silver medal was won by Eddy Hartono and Rudy Gunawan to complete a wonderful day for Indonesia. The bronze went to Razif and Jalani Sidek, the very first Olympic medallists from Malaysia.

Another all-Asian final in the women's doubles event was eventually won by Hwang Hye-yeung and Chung So-yuong of Korea, beating Guan Weizhen and Nong Qunhua of China in three long, close games—18/16, 12/15, 15/13. At the very end of a close third game, the service judge from England called a service fault on Guan Weizhen, which was controversial. Slow-motion replays indicated that the call was marginal at best, and the very public congratulations between the Korean girls was distasteful. The result ensured that Chinese players would leave the Games without a gold medal—a situation that no one could have predicted. The only European medallist was Thomas Stuer-Lauridsen of Denmark. Further success would have to wait until the next Games in Atlanta for Europe and Denmark.

As the hall slowly cleared of both players and spectators, and not wishing to break a habit, I joined the Danish television crew for a few relaxing beers at the end of play. We had enjoyed a happy and successful first Olympic appearance, a feeling reinforced by the reports sent back to the IOC by our two IOC members allocated to badminton, Walther Troeger, the former IOC sports director from Germany, and Nat Indrapana, a very supportive IOC member from Thailand.

We understood the benefit to the Olympic movement of having medals won by a range of different countries, although the degree of Asian success was not a surprise, and it did add spectacularly to our television viewing figures. We regretted the omission of mixed doubles, but that issue was to be resolved at an IOC meeting in Atlanta in 1994. President Samaranch was persuaded by a short video of a wonderful mixed doubles rally and subsequently gave his instructions to Gilbert Felli, the IOC sports director, that mixed doubles should be added to the programme for 1996.

We had had the benefit of a brand new, almost purpose-built venue, which was the closest venue to the Olympic village of any sport—a situation yet to be bettered in badminton's Olympic history. In singles events, over fifty players from over thirty-two countries, and in doubles events, over thirty pairs from over twenty-one countries took part, which met the principles of both standard of play and solidarity of entry requested by the IOC.

Eventually, I walked back up to the empty hall for a few moments of personal reflection and found that except for the lights, the hall had been completely cleared. Such is the organisational efficiency demanded by an Olympic Games, which are, after all, a multitude of world championships held in just over two weeks, you would not have known we had been there.

Rosemary and I then had five days to enjoy the Games and Barcelona. I started to make efforts to meet up with Dick Palmer, the secretary general and *chef de mission* of the BOA, to discuss his thoughts on the Games, which would inevitably dominate early discussion back in London. He proved almost impossible to contact, but we eventually met for lunch in one of Oscar the driver's recommended splendid small restaurants. It was then that I found out just why Dick had been so elusive. He had been dealing with the fallout from the BOA being advised that three British athletes—one from track and field and two from weightlifting—had tested positive for illegal substances. The information only reached the BOA in Barcelona when the athletes were already in the village.

Promising young sprinter Jason Livingston and weightlifters Andrew Davies and Andrew Saxton were sent home. Livingston subsequently served a four-year ban from competition, which effectively ended his career. The two weightlifters, both Commonwealth gold medallists, appealed and were later exonerated and allowed to return to competition, but not for Great Britain. Little did I know at the time that drugs and doping would one day become such an important part of my career in sport.

The timing of the news from Barcelona was unfortunate to say the least; it was an early lesson for me about just how damaging this type of incident can be during an Olympic Games. Despite the furore, Dick and I had a pleasant chat over our future, if, as planned, I took over the chairmanship of the BOA in the following October.

Those agreeable days at the end of the Games allowed for much-needed relaxation and a bit of reflection on almost twenty years of involvement in the IBF. To encourage this, I arranged a small farewell dinner with my IBF friends, but despite many visits to Barcelona, I had chosen a restaurant that did not open until fifteen minutes after we all arrived, around 8.30 p.m.—I was obviously a little better at sports administration than organising social events.

In retrospect, a combination of our Olympic inclusion and the delivery of substantial commercial revenue had been the main drivers of all the developments we had been able to achieve. Membership of the federation had increased; international play had developed; prize money had been introduced, but at a level the sport and its events could afford; the ruling council was much more internationally representative; and the original progressive voting structure based on size of membership had not been put under pressure.

The annual accounts for the year ended 31 December 1992 showed income of £1,649,771, of which the Olympic Games contributed £999,399. We had a surplus of £1,098,248 and balance sheet assets of £1,713,032. Nearly thirty years later, the annual accounts for what is now called the Badminton World Federation for the year ended 31 December 2019 showed assets of over $43 million.

I am delighted that I helped badminton along its very successful journey and will always be enormously proud that the sport and its international federation has grown in stature to become one of the best in the Olympic movement.

15

The BOA

The first time I heard of the British Olympic Association (BOA) was during a conversation with Mary Glen Haig at the Asian Games in Seoul in 1986. She suggested that after my success in getting badminton onto the Olympic programme, which would confer an automatic place for the sport on the BOA, I might consider a future position in the organisation.

In fact, this soon came to pass when British badminton joined its national Olympic committee in 1988 at the beginning of the four-year cycle leading to the 1992 Barcelona Games. I was the badminton representative but had no particular ambitions for high office. The subject must have been revisited as I was approached in early 1992 to see if I might be interested in assuming the position of chairman, always conditional, of course, on an election at the AGM in October. All my work with badminton, GAISF, and the IOC had given me an understanding of international sport and my connections at the IOC HQ in Lausanne was seen as a potential advantage to the BOA.

The current chairman was Sir Arthur Gold, a senior and very distinguished official from athletics. He had been president of the European Athletics Association and was a central figure in many British sports organisations. He had questioned the move to professionalism in sport and was a long-standing campaigner against the increasing prevalence of drugs in sport, leading to his proposal of the BOA by-law imposing a strict selection condition for British athletes. When asked if I would stand against him for the BOA chairmanship, I declined as I was not prepared to be a 'young Turk' who might end Arthur's distinguished career. In the event, Arthur decided to retire, and I allowed my name to go forward.

There was a degree of media attention on the BOA elections that year. Any new office bearers would enjoy a four-year term after the Barcelona Games with responsibility for the British team to compete in the 1994 Olympic Winter Games in Lillehammer and the 1996 Olympic Games in Atlanta. As well as the chairmanship, there would be potential changes in the other two official positions. Media comments seemed to indicate that this would be a minor revolution, which in general appeared to be welcomed. As things turned out, I was elected as chairman unopposed, with Neil Townshend taking over from Eileen Grey as vice president and Paul Pruszynski succeeding Robert Watson as treasurer.

If there was one common media view, it was that the BOA had elected as chairman, 'Craig who!' Although I was better known internationally through my positions with the IBF and GAISF, apart from my work in badminton, I had played no part in British sport. On the other hand, my new colleagues were both involved in winter sports.

Neil Townshend was a general practitioner from Broadway in Worcestershire, who had decided some years before that he wanted to be an Olympian. He studied the then list of Olympic sports and decided that he should take up the sport of luge, which had the clear advantage of not being a major sport in Britain, thus opening a distinctly uncluttered path to his ambition. Within a short time, he was the British luge record holder and was selected for the Winter Games in Lake Placid in 1980. Neil brought his medical knowledge to the BOA, which was a real asset. Paul Pruszynski was a management consultant with wide experience of London Transport and served on the British Bobsleigh Association.

At the AGM, Arthur Gold used his final remarks to urge the BOA to remain true to his ideals and the benefits of the amateur ethos of sport. While he urged the continuation of support for the Olympic movement, he was critical of the trend towards professionalism and television exposure, which he illustrated with the pithy comment that 'It was the amateurs who built the Noah's Ark, but the professionals who built the Titanic'. He was also of the view that the programme of the Games was becoming too large—a position I was unlikely to support, having spent the last ten years putting a new sport into the Games.

His views were, perhaps, representative of opinions held by many senior British sports officials. However, I allowed a statement that in my view, Olympic sport had emerged from the Barcelona Games in good heart, both from the quality of the sport, but also through the excellent delivery of the Games by the city and the country, which had, in turn, benefitted immensely by hosting the Games.

It was probably accurate to describe the election of a completely new team as a revolution. Indeed, perhaps a revolution was needed. We inherited a British sports system that appeared based on a plethora of different organisations, with little government co-ordination or support. There was no real emphasis on elite sport in any organised sense and the results from Barcelona indicated that other European countries were paying more attention and making more investment and changes in their structures.

British success at the Olympic Games could not be delivered without both technical and financial support for our athletes. The British results from Barcelona were only just acceptable as we finished thirteenth in the overall medal table. There was a clear need for one organisation to be responsible for elite sport and to unify British sport in that respect. The popular view was that the BOA would be ideal. An additional advantage I was able to bring to bear was my background from the IBF in encouraging athlete representation on decision-making bodies.

We would also need to find additional resources, probably commercial sponsorship, to fund our ambitions to introduce the services that we believed necessary for our athletes. A strategic review was prepared for submission to my first full BOA meeting, which was fully discussed and accepted.

In practical terms, our first change in staffing was to employ our own in-house lawyer. We had received excellent advice from Farrer's, a major firm of solicitors in London, and we retained them for strategic advice but, increasingly, there were legal issues in almost every part of our daily work. Bruce Mellstrom, a lawyer, joined us in early 1993 and became a key employee.

He had a difficult start. We were increasingly aware of the need to protect commercial partners and the word 'Olympic'. We were advised that a small London taxi company was presenting itself as 'Olympic Taxis'. Bruce agonised over a suitable warning letter and eventually sent it off. Almost by return, he received a faxed copy of his letter with a handwritten note at the top of the first page that read 'F.... you, BOA'—quite a welcome to the Olympic world.

We mulled over an appropriate response. Given the somewhat blunt Anglo-Saxon tone of the reply and given that 'Olympic Taxis' was relatively small beer in the scheme of things, along with, no doubt, a multitude of 'Olympic Launderettes' bakeries and kebab houses, we decided to back off and go after bigger fish.

Bruce was also involved in a potential case with the Inland Revenue, which threatened to raise a tax assessment on money raised by the BOA to fund the 1992 Olympic team as a trading organisation as opposed to a fundraising body. Fortunately, this claim was eventually unsuccessful but only after many months of argument

Another legal issue raised its ugly head in November 1992. At an IOC session held in Acapulco, the IOC came under pressure to resolve several issues on its drug-testing procedures and policies. It became clear that correct legal procedures should support the IOC strategy as several international federations and sports bodies were at risk from litigation raised by athletes. The problem applied specifically to the two weightlifters sent home by the BOA from the Barcelona games, Andrew Saxton and Andrew Davies, who were threatening to seek compensation.

Their offence, published by the Sports Council, was overturned by their national federation, the British Amateur Weightlifting Association. This was based on a disagreement between the IOC Medical Commission and Professor Arnold Beckett, its British member of twenty-five years standing, over the definition of clenbuterol, an anabolic steroid. The BOA bore no responsibility as it acted only as a consequence of decisions outside its control. The case was eventually closed, but proper international regulations were clearly required—it was a prophetic insight into the future.

We also became involved in the debate over the overall structure of British sport that had been energised by the report from Robert Atkins, the Sports Minister, on the creation of what he called a UK sports commission, possibly starting operations in 1993. We were faced with the reality that British sport administration was unnecessarily complicated by too many bodies, each with different remits, and by a clear lack of involvement from the government. There was also discussion about the possibility of a national lottery, its estimated proceeds, and how they could be distributed.

The somewhat academic discussions took time but did not distract us from the need to expand our commercial interests, change our governance with athlete representation, and identify the services that we would be best able to supply. I found it all very interesting, but it was a complete change from driving an international federation and its portfolio of worldwide events.

There was one clear priority. The decision to appoint Manchester as the British city to host the Olympic Games in 2000 presented the BOA in general, and me in particular, with a wide range of increased involvement. The final IOC decision would be taken at the 101st IOC session in Monte Carlo in September 1993, giving the winning city seven years to organise the Games. The previous Manchester bid presented in Tokyo in 1990 had been welcomed by the IOC but, at the end of the day, had been distinctly unsuccessful.

When we held a review of the BOA presence in the previous bid, it became clear that in the Olympic world, a totally committed and involved presence by the bidding city's national Olympic committee was crucial to success. In its own review, Manchester had reworked its plans and, after being selected by the BOA, had concentrated on three main projects. The first was to expand the base of the bid by getting more people involved. The second was to have facilities actually being built rather than just models. The third, and very important, was to have government involvement.

The most obvious change in Manchester's approach was the building of the new National Cycling Centre. The decision met the need to present modern facilities to the IOC, as well as providing a badly needed new venue for a popular sport in Britain. It is interesting to reflect that the Manchester velodrome was to bring huge Olympic success for athletes and in many ways to change the whole structure of cycling in the country. At the elite level, excellent facilities, a good coach (Peter Keen), and some modest money worked wonders.

The Manchester bid was formally announced on 18 February at 10 Downing Street by the prime minister, John Major, whose government not only funded some of the bid costs but gave an undertaking to involve the government in the provision of the necessary facilities and in the organisation of the Games. The partnership of Manchester, the government, and the BOA was formed. For me, this was an ideal vehicle to show that change in the status of the BOA, and my chairmanship, was a reality.

The Manchester structural plan was upgraded from the previous bid and concentrated on the development of East Manchester for the building of the main facilities. Along with the National Cycling Centre, the area would contain the new main stadium, a major indoor arena, for gymnastics, and the Olympic village. Other facilities would be sited or developed throughout and around the city with the allocation of boxing, volleyball, and one football venue to neighbouring Liverpool. The bid documents began by referencing Britain's Industrial Revolution, the partnership between Mr Rolls and Mr Royce in Manchester, and the dramatic effect hosting the Games would have on the infrastructure and development of the city, the north-west of the country, and British sport. All the points were entirely relevant, and frequent references were made to the success of Barcelona.

Visits by members of the IOC and to other bid events involved me in regular trips down to Manchester. I would catch a plane from Glasgow to arrive in Manchester around 5 p.m. and was met on the tarmac at Manchester Airport by Jim Taylor, one of the city staff drivers. I was always comforted in the journey into the city centre from the airport when we passed the sign that read, 'Manchester is a Nuclear Free Zone.' Living in the west of Scotland, close to the US Navy submarine base on the Gareloch, I had always believed that in any nuclear war, I would be fried around fifteen seconds before the people of Manchester.

The need to involve more people in the bid became clear during those visits as many different people and organisations were pleased to bring their knowledge and skills to the project. That was very clear in the visit of and presentations to the IOC Enquiry Commission in late March 1993. We worked them hard with presentations on the themes set out by the IOC, which were delivered by an impressive range of bodies from the city: police, BBC, universities, and commercial and cultural organisations. The visit culminated in a dinner with celebrities like Bobby Charlton, a national hero, and Colin Welland, a writer who won an Oscar for the screenplay for the 1981 film *Chariots of Fire*.

I took the opportunity to meet Welland to ask him about the opening sequences of *Chariots of Fire*:

> You know the opening sequence of British athletes training for the 1924 Paris Games were shot on the West Sands at St Andrews. The athletes ran along the sands, climbed over the white wooden railing, across the first fairway of the Old Course under the windows of the Royal and Ancient Golf Clubhouse and into a red brick building called Hamilton Hall on which you had hung a sign saying, 'Carlton Hotel Broadstairs' Has anyone mentioned that to you before?

To this, he replied, 'Every bloody Scotsman I have ever met!'

The report of the IOC Enquiry Commission was complimentary on the compact venue proposal and on the high level of technology available in Manchester, all of which was encouraging. We enjoyed a separate visit from President Samaranch, which, in addition to the more normal venues and civic tour, featured an hour with young children at a primary school.

The day started in glorious sunshine but by the end of a busy few hours it was raining heavily. We arranged a press conference and Samaranch made several positive remarks. The first question came from a journalist with the *Manchester Evening News*: 'How could you consider placing the Games in a city where it rains so often?' Samaranch replied, 'The more I travel around the world, the more I go to cities which would give their right arms for rain like this.' There were no more provocative questions. Samaranch returned via London, where he met with the prime minister in 10 Downing Street.

To reinforce the strong government support enjoyed by the bid, we took John Major to Lausanne for a formal meeting with the IOC and some members of its executive board. This made a good impression, and there was clear evidence that the Manchester bid was making progress. However, we were given a major cause for thought by the announcement from the Sydney bid team that if they were elected, they would meet the travel costs of all the athletes going to the Games.

A major negative in the Sydney bid was the high cost of travel and the major time change but the offer to meet travelling expenses was a real game changer. It also encouraged Beijing to make a similar offer and, in practice, forced Manchester to create a 'Millennium Foundation Fund' that would be used to meet a range of benefits for athletes, including training, equipment, competition facilities in Britain, sports science and medicine, and transport to and from the Games in Manchester.

What we did not to know at that time was that the Sydney bid would organise a tour of African national Olympic committees with the Australian prime minister, to make specific financial grants to NOCs to help them prepare for a Sydney Games. This piece of disconcerting information only emerged several years later during the Salt Lake City bidding scandal in 2001.

We enjoyed a particular opportunity to impress members of the IOC by inviting several of them to travel on from Lausanne, where they attended the opening of the new Olympic Museum, to Manchester to view our preparations. A party of fourteen members, with wives or husbands, gathered in Lausanne to be transported to Geneva airport on a special charter flight provided by British Airways.

After check-in, when the party was relaxing in an airport lounge, I decided to go down to the gate for the flight to find the British Airways staff in a heated argument with a couple from Aberdeen, who, by mistake, had been sold tickets on the flight to Manchester and then on to Aberdeen. I could see a crisis in the making. I spoke to the couple concerned, explained the unique circumstances, and told them that we would take them on the flight but that they should occupy the rear two seats in the cabin and effectively ignore all their fellow passengers.

This was happily agreed, and on the ninety-minute flight to Manchester, our unexpected passengers thoroughly enjoyed the champagne, lobster, and fillet steak on the menu. Before landing, I explained to them that we would be landing at the new Terminal 2 in Manchester Airport but would be grateful if they held back on leaving the plane to allow our guests to experience the warm public welcome that had been arranged for them. The couple did so, quietly offered me their thanks, and we parted company. The only sting in the tail for them was that one hour later, their luggage was in a VIP pile belonging to our Olympic guests in the middle of the Midland Hotel in Manchester.

Our IOC visitors enjoyed two days in Manchester with a brief tour of facilities and a visit to the splendid Tatton Park. To prove the high quality of our national transport system, accompanied by Robert Keys (our minister for transport), we then took them to London on a newly delivered express train. In London, they were welcomed by the prime minister, treated to a reception at 10 Downing Street, and then seated in the international box on the centre court at Wimbledon to watch some outstanding tennis. As you would expect, the whole exercise went down well with those we hoped to impress.

Efforts then moved to preparing the presentation that would be made to the full IOC session in Monte Carlo in September. There had been eight cities in the initial applications to host what would be the Millennium Games in the year 2000. Brasilia, Milan, and Tashkent had withdrawn during the host selection process, which left Sydney, Beijing, Berlin, and Istanbul as our competitors in the final stages of the race. We prepared well for the last round of lobbying in Monte Carlo and for the actual city presentation, which would be led by the prime minister. Unfortunately, a storm over the south of France closed the airport at Nice on the morning of the presentations, so we had a nervous wait until John Major, having been diverted to Marseille, was able to join us.

The presentation went well, and we joined the other four cities in a large auditorium in the Monte Carlo Sports Complex to hear the result. The general balance of opinion was that Beijing might just be the strongest candidate, and as we sat in blocks of seats allocated to each city, I could see that there was much excitement and many smiles throughout the Beijing delegation, which was placed in the next block. Not long before the formalities were to commence, a Chinese official rushed down to the senior members of the Beijing delegation and clearly delivered a message. Their smiles and excitement ended instantly. The reason became very clear when Samaranch announced that the 2000 Games would be hosted by Sydney, which won by only two votes—forty-five to forty-three. Manchester was eliminated in the third round of voting with eleven votes.

The stormy weather continued in Monte Carlo into the next day as we packed up and headed for home. I was surprised by the severity of my own reaction. Admittedly, I had spent a lot of time in Manchester and on the lobbying efforts and all the preparations for the final presentation, but I was not prepared for the feeling of intense disappointment the following morning. In many ways, it was a helpful experience as the Manchester bid taught me that the whole bidding process had to involve personal involvement at a minimum of 110 per cent and also that a combination of local, national, and government support was essential for an Olympic bid to be successful.

Manchester had succeeded in putting together many of the necessary attributes, but the hard message was that full national support had not been forthcoming, mainly because the south of Britain did not feel fully involved. My feeling of disappointment was made even stronger after a formal meeting of the House of Commons culture, media and sport select committee, which investigated the failure of the Manchester bid. To my surprise, at the end of his section of evidence, Bob Scott made the comment that in his view, the bid had not been strongly assisted by the two British members of the IOC—Mary Glen Haig and Princess Anne.

His comment prompted several adverse contributions from members of the committee and permitted by the chairman, Gerald Kaufman, a Manchester Labour MP, who then extended the debate into questions about the adequacy of British Olympic representation. I was given a rather difficult time by Mr Kaufman, who seemed to relish the opportunity. The episode stirred a debate on Olympic representation, covered in detail by a triumvirate of renowned British journalists—John Rodda at *The Guardian*, David Miller at *The Times*, and Iain McLeod at *The Daily Telegraph*. All in all, it did not make for a good outcome for a purportedly dispassionate review of an unsuccessful project.

Before attention returned to Olympic bids, I had my very first experience of winter sport, as we sent a team of thirty-two athletes to the Winter Olympic Games at Lillehammer in February 1994. Lillehammer was the first Winter Games to be organised in a town rather than a city and, despite all the projected difficulties of management, space, facilities and weather, turned out to be magical Games. The British team was thirty-two athletes strong, taking part in most sports, except for ice hockey and ski-jumping. It is recognised that we are not a winter sport nation but have enjoyed outstanding Olympic success in figure skating.

Lillehammer was to see the return of Jayne Torvill and Christopher Dean, who had become world celebrities in winning the gold medal for ice dancing in Sarajevo ten years before with their mesmerising performance to the music of Ravel's 'Bolero'. The figure-skating regulations had been changed and eligibility restored to previously professional athletes, so the return of such famous and popular competitors caused great expectation in Britain.

These were also the Games prefaced by the infamous assault with a police baton on the knee of US skater Nancy Kerrigan by the former husband of fellow US skater Tonya Harding. Kerrigan recovered from the attack and was able to skate in Lillehammer. With the world looking on as if watching a soap opera, Kerrigan won the silver medal, losing to Oksana Baiul in a controversial judges' decision. In floods of tears, Harding finished eighth and later admitted some guilt in the assault and was banned for life by her federation.

Several events were held in Lillehammer, with skating in Hamar, while other towns nearby hosted ice hockey and downhill skiing. The games were the first Winter Games to be held in a year without a Summer Games and attracted sixty-seven countries and 1,737 athletes.

Dick Palmer was our *chef de mission* in the village, Neil Townsend and I were in the NOC accommodation in the Birkebeiner lodges, and Simon Clegg ran our hospitality arrangements from our splendid, rented house just outside Lillehammer. The house was owned by Jens-Erik Ugland from an old Lillehammer family who had acted as our Olympic attaché in the host city.

We had decided to invest in a hospitality programme to enable us to entertain our government ministers, our sponsors and to host a series of corporate dinners for them and some selected Olympic friends. The house was ideal with sufficient bedrooms, lounges and a dining room to take twenty-four people. We brought out to Lillehammer two 'Sloane Rangers' who acted as chefs and chalet maids, as long as they got time off to watch Torvill and Dean.

The contrast with some other groups in Lillehammer was acute as the Lillehammer Hotel, the only large hotel in the town, was too small to accommodate everybody who wanted, or thought they deserved, a room. Such was the demand, the Lillehammer organising committee added a temporary building to the hotel with an additional supply of small, Scandinavian-style rooms. The US Olympic Committee erected its own temporary hotel, much to the annoyance of the representatives from the 1996 Atlanta organising committee, who stayed for only a very limited period as the room rate was $750 per day. This affected Charlie Battle and his wife, Lola, who were particularly unimpressed. An invitation to one of our corporate dinners may just have saved their marriage.

Our principal guests were the secretary of state for National Heritage, Peter Brooke, and his wife, Lindsay, to be followed by Sir Hector Monro, a former sports minister who had new environmental responsibilities. The Brookes were in the BOA party, which went to the first morning of slalom competition at Hafjell. Our small bus was directed up a hill by a volunteer soldier to what seemed like the back of the finish area, and we were shown to around 300 free seats in the Olympic family area.

This was not where we were supposed to be as our guests were not accredited but held tickets. It was the kind of thing that is inevitable and happens on the first day of any new venue at any Games. The young women in charge, whose name was Liv, understood the problem immediately and, as I told her the visit would be for only thirty minutes, simply allowed us to stay. It was freezing and the sun had not yet reached the seats. Liv then came back to us and asked if we would like to go over to the VIP tent for a warm drink. This was readily accepted and hugely enjoyed, which the Brookes thought was because of them.

I took Liv's accreditation details, and when I later went to hand the BOA's gift to Gerhard Heiberg, the Games chairman, I made a point of bringing her intelligent handling of this situation to the Games organisers. Hector Monro, a former sports minister and a former president of the Scottish Rugby Union, was an easy and pleasant guest. His only concern was a meeting after the Games with the Norwegian environmental minister, who, apparently was a young blonde woman with a theatrical background. His brief was to raise the issue of Norway off-loading its excess salmon and thus damaging the British market. He was very nervous. We wished him well but never heard the outcome of his meeting with the young blonde thespian minister. We ran our corporate dinners and chose our invited guests well so that our sponsors enjoyed another aspect of their visit to an Olympic Games. The programme was a real success.

My introduction to winter sport was complete when Lillehammer was blessed with a very heavy fall of snow, such that it lay almost one metre deep at the side of the roads. It was followed by the warmest day of the Games. The thermometer outside the window of our chalet read -16 degrees C. Amazingly, the hardy Norwegians seemed impervious to the cold weather. On one famous occasion, huge crowds, including young children, camped out overnight in temperatures as low as -25 degrees C so that they had prime positions to watch the cross-country skiing.

They cheered the athletes of rival countries almost as enthusiastically as they cheered their own heroes. Stein Gruben, a last-minute back-up, was a man brave enough to go down the Lysgårdsbakken ski-jump with the Olympic torch in hand, ablaze with the Olympic flame, during the opening ceremony. There was a heart-stopping wobble at the end, but he made it.

It was a great Games, made particularly memorable by the strong emphasis on the Games being a symbol of world peace and unity. Lillehammer was the first Games where the Greek tradition from the ancient Games of declaring an Olympic truce was revived by President Samaranch. The UN General Assembly urged the nations of the world to observe the truce at all future Games. Samaranch made a moving speech at the opening ceremony, where he reminded the audience—both in the stadium and on worldwide television—that the Bosnian city of Sarajevo, which had hosted the Winter Games just ten years earlier, was in the midst of a deadly siege. 'Our message is stronger than ever,' he said. 'Please stop the fighting. Please stop the killing. Please drop your guns.' It is at moments like those that one realises how powerful the Olympic ideals can be.

British results were mixed, but there were good placings for a young Stephen Cousins in figure skating (ninth), Mark Tout and the four-man bobsleigh (fifth), and then really good results from Nicky Gooch in short-track skating, culminating with a bronze medal in the 500 m event. All attention was focused on Jayne and Christopher in ice dancing, but their comeback produced a bronze medal behind two Russian pairs, although almost everybody in the stadium had the British pair as their personal favourites. We invited Jayne and Christopher to our BOA house for the evening of the women's figure skating just to help them escape the inevitable media frenzy.

The new experience in a part of the Olympic world that I did not know was a most enjoyable and successful interlude. Refreshed and in many ways encouraged, I returned to the debates on the structure and changes to British sport, then seen as increasingly necessary.

16

The IOC

The year 1994 brought two dates that changed my life. The first was at a relatively straightforward meeting of the BOA executive committee on 12 January. Among the normal items of business we discussed, calmly and almost routinely, was the consequences of the failed Manchester bid for the 2000 Olympic Games. There was a unanimous view that after three unsuccessful bids in succession—Birmingham in 1986 and Manchester in 1990 and 1993—it would wise to take stock and not to be rushed into another attempt for 2004.

It was decided however, that Mary Glen Haig and I would speak discreetly to a selected number of members of the IOC to seek their comments on which British city should be chosen by the BOA if we were to come back into a bidding competition. This was, in effect, a polite way of dealing with the equally unanimous view that, in future, any new British Olympic bid would be based on London.

I have always regarded this ordinary and judicious meeting as the start of the London campaign—a journey that would take nineteen and a half years until June 2013, when the limited company, the fiscal backbone of the 2012 London organising committee, was passed to the lawyers to be wound up. Bidding for and organising an Olympic Games are very long-term projects.

The second date was 5 September, the last day of the 103rd Session of the International Olympic Committee, which followed the XII Centennial Olympic congress in Paris. It was the memorable day when I was co-opted as a member of the IOC. Having reached the then age limit, Mary Glen Haig had retired in 1993, and there had been some media comment and several rumours about the identity of her successor. There had been a prolonged period of two years without any new members due, in the main, to some dispute in USA on who would fill the vacancy for a new member in that country. An article had appeared suggesting that three names had been submitted, probably by Mary Glen Haig: the hurdler David Hemery, the swimmer David Wilkie (both former gold medallists), and Chris Baillieu, the silver medallist rower and world champion.

There was also speculation that Sebastian Coe, one of our greatest athletes, was under consideration. It was known that he was a favourite of President Samaranch and had made a distinguished contribution on drugs in sport at the previous IOC congress in Baden-Baden in 1981. I had never discussed the position openly but asked Dick Palmer for advice. Dick then took some soundings and discreetly inserted my name into the process. I was also aware that my name had been supported by Jacques Rogge, the president of the European Olympic Committees and a future president of the IOC.

Olympic congresses are held only occasionally and are gatherings of representatives from all the different groups and organisations within the Olympic movement. They are consultative only, as any decisions they may take then require to be formally adopted by the IOC session. The themes for the 1994 Centennial Olympic congress, the Congress of Unity, were: 'The Olympic movement's contribution to modern society; The contemporary athlete: Sport in its social context: and Sport and the mass media'.

The congress was held in a huge auditorium at La Défense, in Paris, the home of the famous ancient university, the Sorbonne, where the Olympic movement was formed 100 years previously by Baron Pierre de Coubertin. While the various themes differed in content, they also differed in the level of interest they generated from the large audience. This was the first occasion at a Congress that representatives of the media were invited to speak and to contribute, which added to the debate, but sparse attendances after the opening day in such a large auditorium reduced the value of the discussions. As always, the most interesting element of such meetings was the amiable chat and stimulating exchange of views in the many hotel lobbies and bars in which all the delegates were based.

Neither the princess royal, the remaining IOC member in Britain, nor Sebastian Coe were able to attend the Congress. I was also aware that IOC membership would probably be an item on the agenda for the session but not for some days. So, as I did not want to be seen to be lobbying on my own behalf, I returned home to Glasgow, where, late on the morning of 5

September to my complete surprise, I took a call from a journalist to tell me that my name had been accepted.

A subsequent very kind letter of congratulations told me that of the ten new members approved at the session, mine was the only name accepted without question. Importantly and not widely understood, under the Olympic charter, members are 'in' their own countries rather than 'from' their countries. This is an important distinction because it means the members represent the IOC in their countries, not their countries on the IOC.

Even so, constitutionally, a member automatically becomes a member of his or her national Olympic committee, which deals with any potential conflict of interest. My being an IOC member would be a real benefit to the BOA, especially as the IOC was to develop a policy that the chairs of the leading NOCs should be members of the IOC. More opportunities beckoned.

With the 1996 Atlanta Games on the horizon, there was much work for the BOA to do in its efforts to improve the structure of British sport and to enhance its funding. The first draw of the new National Lottery—a pet project of the prime minister, John Major—took place in mid-1994. Sport was one of the 'good causes' to benefit from 20 per cent of that fund, and although initially, the distribution policy in sport was to invest in new facilities, the need for athlete revenue grants was another obvious need and very attractive to the BOA.

The suggestions made in the 1991 Atkins Report for the creation of a UK sport commission, which would have had a membership of up to 150 people, was struggling for acceptance. So, in 1993, Ian Sproat, the new sports minister, decided to change priorities. He announced the most logical—and certainly our favoured—option by creating a sports council for UK with responsibilities for elite sport, for all the services that entails and for attracting major events to the UK.

An independent chairman would have a board of ten people to include the chairs of the four home sports councils, a representative from the BOA, a representative from non-Olympic sport, a representative from professional sport and two independent members with strong sporting credentials. The home sports councils in England, Scotland, Wales, and Northern Ireland would then have responsibility for grassroots sport and more informal recreation.

A staff of twenty people would operate with a budget of £10 million. We were delighted and said so very readily as this huge but sensible structural change replicated in many ways what the BOA was trying to achieve. It is also worth stating the obvious—that in the Olympic Games, our athletes compete for Great Britain, not as in highly popular sports like football, cricket, and rugby as Home Nations.

Changing a political structure takes time, and the new royal charter for what is now known as 'UK Sport' could not be granted until 1 January 1996. Ian McLaurin, the chairman of Sainsburys, was named as the first independent chairman in March 1995 and began to shadow the work of the new body in advance of its formal start date. Membership was to include Rodney Walker, the new chairman of the English Sports Council, and Clive Lloyd, the distinguished West Indian cricketer, then living in Manchester.

Capital grants from lottery funds would stay with the home country councils but we made the case for revenue funding for elite athletes to be the responsibility of the UK body. The basic building blocks for what proved to be a unique future had been put in place, but it took many years for the results to be shown in Olympic and world championship medal tables.

Despite these structural improvements, there were inevitable developments which reflected previous confusion and arose before UK Sport was fully involved. The FA had decided to construct a new national stadium and allowed applications from cities to act as host. London (with Wembley), Manchester, Birmingham, and Bradford all expressed interest. However, at a full NOC meeting, the BOA announced that it would not bid for the 2004 Olympic Games as that decision would be taken by the IOC in 1997, and there was insufficient time to prepare all the necessary research and logistics. We suggested that any decision on a new national stadium should be deferred. Time was to tell that a final decision was taken to rebuild Wembley in London, and its future use as a national stadium with an Olympic dimension remained in question.

However, there were two pieces of very good news—the decision to amend the lottery distribution rules to allow for revenue-based applications and grants was eventually passed. Mind you, considerable time elapsed before significant money appeared in the banks of national governing bodies and then in the pockets of athletes.

Perhaps of equal importance, the application from Manchester to host the 2002 Commonwealth Games was accepted by the Commonwealth Games Federation. This was a wonderful reward for the city and reflected well on all the excellent planning and venue design involved in its recent 1993 Olympic bid. The planned legacy for East Manchester was assured, and the chance to stage a major multi-sport event was an opportunity not to be wasted. Not only that, it allowed the unfortunate memories from the

Commonwealth Games in Edinburgh in 1986 to pass into history. As had occurred on two previous occasions, there was only one bidder for 2002, which gave Sir Bob Scott, the Manchester chairman, the chance to say that even he could win a bid like that.

Throughout this busy period, we launched our plans for the services and organisation for the British team heading for Atlanta. We reviewed the current services we offered to athletes and used their input in planning a major change in how we added value to athletes.

In the mid-1980s, we had opened the British Olympic Medical Centre at Northwick Park Hospital in London under the direction of Dr Mark Harries, a sports medicine specialist. The centre played an increasingly important part in the preparation of athletes from the south of the country. We had also created a department in the BOA designed to help athletes in their post-sports careers; we employed careers specialist Scott Naden to deliver this very specific service. Prior to the Barcelona Games in 1992, we had arranged pre-games training camps, but these were based at sports centres within the UK. Atlanta would require a different approach.

Our research indicated that the weather in Atlanta in July would be warm and humid. Unless we made entirely different arrangements, it would be very challenging for British athletes to train at home, travel to Atlanta, and then complete their training just before competition. Simon Clegg, our deputy chief executive, and Kevin Hickey, our performance director, produced a list of seventeen cities within reasonable travelling distance of Atlanta that might provide a pre-games training base.

We invited all seventeen cities to consider hosting our training camp and eventually narrowed the list down to the cities of Athens (Georgia), Raleigh Durham (North Carolina), and Tallahassee (Florida). We then entered a formal bidding process and eventually decided that we would accept the offer from Tallahassee, Florida's state capital. On the morning that we presented our decision for approval to the BOA, to our considerable concern, we read the news from Tallahassee that two tourists had been shot in their car in the very city that we had chosen as our pre-games base. However, we concluded that all American cities have not insignificant levels of risk for visitors and citizens alike and decided to stick with our choice.

One of the most compelling reasons for the selection of Tallahassee was its stated willingness to appoint a project manager from the city to oversee and control all the necessary arrangements. It appointed Christopher Campbell, the regional director for AT&T, and he proved to be an outstanding operator with whom we built a very strong relationship.

Tallahassee also offered the facilities at Florida State University, one of Florida's regional universities with almost 40,000 students and a wealth of sports facilities, all supported by its very successful college football team, the Seminoles, which played its home matches in the 78,000-capacity Doak Campbell Stadium in the city. We would also have access to a range of student accommodation, which would provide an ideal base for a full pre-games training camp.

The university was prepared to purchase the necessary sports equipment, which was not already on site—judo mats, badminton posts, and nets, for example—and make available its athletics track and swimming pool. All in all, the prospect was highly appealing to the BOA and turned out to be very popular with our athletes. Atlanta Games medallists and future gold medallists Jonathan Edwards and Denise Lewis both made use of the facilities.

We were also able to solve one additional and important issue—travel to Tallahassee and ultimately to the Games themselves in Atlanta. At that time, British Airways had one daily flight from Gatwick to Atlanta. It was a busy route, so its ability to provide either sponsorship or the required number of seats was extremely limited.

Delta Airlines had recently introduced two daily flights to Atlanta and another daily flight to Cincinnati. Its UK marketing manager was Terrence Burns, who has since enjoyed a distinguished career in Olympic and sports marketing, and he was quick to see the potential benefit for the BOA and the airline. We entered a formal sponsorship contract that allowed us to offer very reduced travel costs to athletes if they wished to use the Tallahassee facilities over the next two years as well as the full travel arrangements for the Games for the British team.

Christopher Campbell set up a system of assistance to athletes who travelled to Florida, and some found this to be of great benefit. He also built a close relationship between the BOA and the city, even to the extent of creating a special area in the city centre which he called the 'Brickyard'. This would be a permanent memory of the BOA arrangement, where visiting athletes or officials could place their own named brick. To the best of my knowledge, the Brickyard remains to this day.

The BOA/American relationship grew in strength, and Christopher raised around $1 million for the BOA appeal. Relationships also became close with Florida State University, one of America's leading public universities with a strong academic and sporting record. The university achieved national fame through its college football team, which won three national championships during the 1990s under its famous coach Bobby

Bowden. To the fascination of its visiting sportsmen and women, it also held degree classes in circus acts.

We benefited from a further USA and Atlanta connection with the appointment of Brian Langton, president of Holiday Inns Worldwide, to be chairman of the BOA national appeal. I was informed that the BOA had enjoyed a major fundraising success in connection with the 1984 Los Angeles Games and that it would be appropriate to find another British citizen, but with US connections, to try to repeat the 1984 experience. Regrettably, we found it impossible to find another British fundraiser in USA. However, although Brian travelled widely, he had his head office in Atlanta so was able to direct the appeal effectively through his very able personal assistant Julia Fox.

Fundraising events in UK were enthusiastically supported by our president, the princess royal, who attended well-organised and successful dinners all around the country. For the Atlanta Games, we extended the reach of the dinners to a short tour to the United States. We managed to borrow an executive jet from Coca Cola to make stops in Atlanta, Boston, and Washington, when the princess was able to combine her BOA role with her British diplomatic duties. The generous agreement with Coca Cola provided twelve very comfortable seats and the ability to take-off and land without the normal airport processes of check-in and baggage collection. It was certainly a better way to travel, and much quicker.

The major event was a dinner in Brian Langton's main Holiday Inn at Buckhead in Atlanta with a full house of the local great and good. I decided to wear my kilt, a decision that the princess described as 'brave', but her own efforts and my modest contribution seemed to go down quite well. Perhaps it was my seat beside the wife of the managing director of the Coca Cola Company, or more likely some shrewd event planning by Mr Langton, but I saw little of the wine waiter.

After the dinner, a small group of new friends and I repaired to the bar in the foyer of the hotel for a welcome nightcap. After a second drink, I had to head across the foyer to an area marked as 'Restrooms', which were guarded by a large black woman in a white coat. She watched me appear across the foyer and with a huge smile on her face said, 'You sure exactly where you're going, boy?' Having survived the Atlanta event, we moved on to a rather quiet and formal dinner in Boston and then on to a splendid lunch at the ambassador's residence in the British embassy in Washington, a famous building designed by Sir Edwin Lutyens to resemble an English country house.

Our host was the ambassador, Sir Robin Renwick, and I was seated at the same table as a woman called Barbara Cassani, who ran the US business of British Airways. She was very pregnant, and in an attempt to break the ice and also to congratulate her, I asked the question often asked in the highlands of Scotland, 'Will it be a boy or a child?' Barbara's reaction was less warm than the restroom attendant in Atlanta, which probably explains why I missed an upgrade on the way home that evening. Nevertheless, we laughed about the moment some years later when I met with her before she took up her leading position with the London Olympic bid. It was all good fun and we raised good money.

Before the 1996 Games, we went back to Atlanta and Tallahassee and visited the team members still in the Florida State accommodation. They were relaxed and very appreciative of the facilities and the benefits of training in the same weather conditions as expected in Atlanta. Once again, the Coca Cola jet made the day possible as the princess and I had to be back in Atlanta before the air space was closed for the opening ceremony. A visit was arranged to the BOA Brickyard, and the princess placed her named brick to complete the project and then thanked all the Tallahassee helpers at a very pleasant reception.

We got back in time to attend the opening ceremony and join the rest of the British team members who had moved up to Atlanta for the occasion and would start their competitions over the next few days. As you might expect, the opening ceremony, in front of a crowd of over 85,000 and a TV audience of 3.5 billion, was big and bold. Hollywood legend, John Williams' stirring music—'Summon the Heroes'—set the tone in his unique way. A past master with emotive tunes, he had already done the music for Los Angeles in 1984 with his famous 'Olympic Fanfare'.

Celine Dion, Jessye Norman, and Gladys Knight sang and excerpts from Martin Luther King's, 'I Have a Dream' speech were played. Surrounded by several dozen princes, princesses, kings, presidents, and prime ministers, US President Bill Clinton opened the Games. Then, most movingly of all, the Olympic flame was lit by Muhammad Ali, whose presence, despite his clear struggles with Parkinson's disease, brought the house down. There could have been no other choice of course, but it was wonderful to witness.

As entry for non-accredited people to the athletes' village was very restricted, we had prepared a private athletes' lodge in a renovated old church to allow athletes to meet with their families or friends. All in all, we believed that the pre-Games arrangements had been as good as possible.

The team and many supporters had been entertained at the traditional government-funded team party a few days before the start of the Games. Our host, Chris Smith, the culture secretary, endeared himself to his audience by explaining that he was nervous about his presence on the international stage and did not want to make the kind of *faux pas* committed by a previous British ambassador, who, upon taking up his appointment in Washington in the autumn, had spoken to a journalist from *The Washington Post* who had asked him what he wanted for Christmas. The ambassador replied that he wanted a small jar of Harrods boiled sweets. On Christmas Eve that year, *The Washington Post* carried a lead story that for Christmas, the Russian ambassador wanted continuation of peace in the world, the Chinese ambassador wanted entry to the economic benefits of world co-operation, the German ambassador wanted complete progress towards European community agreement, and the British ambassador wanted a small jar of Harrods boiled sweets.

The Games themselves involved 10,000 athletes from 197 NOCs competing in twenty-six sports. Eleven former Soviet republics competed for the first time as independent nations and the host nation led the medal table. The British team was 300 strong competing in twenty-one of the sports but continuing the trend that only our hockey teams seemed able to qualify from Great Britain in team sports.

Dick Palmer was *chef de mission*, and public expectations in Britain were high. The athlete's village was mainly student accommodation at the University of Georgia, which was quite old, but the BOA had managed to negotiate rather better facilities at one of the village annexes. The athlete transport arrangements were something of a disaster as was Olympic transportation in general. Out-of-town drivers got lost, meaning that some athletes only got to their events with moments to spare. There was even an athlete sit-down protest at the transport mall. When US VIPs appeared, the transport arrangements seemed to change with each different arrival—an unnecessary added complication that caused yet more irritating confusion.

Away from the competition venues, the organising committee had allowed street traders to set up stalls on the pavements of several of the city's roads that rather spoiled the look of the city; in fact, parts of Atlanta more resembled a near eastern bazaar than an Olympic host city. The IOC was not amused.

I was aware that Atlanta were private sector Games, funded generously by sponsorship and television rights income. In an earlier visit to Atlanta, I had been invited to play golf one Sunday morning with Billy Payne, chairman of the organising committee, and two employees of Nations Bank—one of the early and important sponsors. As we waited for them to arrive, I asked Billy who they were and if he knew them, to which he replied, 'I don't know them, but I LOVE them.' The commercial approach delivered a surplus and some of the facilities provided good sporting and civic legacies.

Despite all the efforts to deliver British athletes in good spirits and good condition, the anticipated results were slow to appear. The athletics team won six medals with silver medals for Roger Black (400 m), Jonathan Edwards (triple jump), Steve Backley (javelin) and the 4 × 400 m relay team. Silver medals were also won by the sailors down at their venue in Savannah and another by the swimmers in the pool at Georgia State University. A delighted Tim Henman and Neil Broad won a silver in the tennis doubles event, but pride of place was to go to Steve Redgrave and Matthew Pinsent, who won another gold in rowing, while the Searle brothers, Rupert Obholzer, and Tim Foster won bronze in the coxless four.

A particularly disappointing day included the finals of the kayak canoeing event when Lynn Simpson, top of the world rankings, finished in twenty-third position and Linford Christie, the defending 100-m gold medallist from Barcelona, was disqualified for a false start. It was becoming clearer that we would have some questions to answer.

On the night of 27 July, a pipe bomb was detonated in Centennial Park, a busy centrepiece of the Games, killing two and injuring 111 people. The news broke in the early hours of the morning when Olympic sports fans in Britain were just about waking up. I took a call from Martin Hopkins, the BBC executive producer for the Games, but then could not reach him in his studio in the International Broadcast Centre which was locked down due to its proximity to the site of the explosion. The problem was to be able to inform the BBC that no British team members had been involved.

We picked up a rumour that the US team all carried pagers, allowing for a rapid head count. Without any such assistance, the British team headquarters staff, who had been enjoying an evening off, worked all night to try to provide the information that nobody had been involved. As the research developed, we seemed to be missing two team members, both grooms with the equestrian team. Eventually, around 11 a.m., Dick Palmer called me to tell me they had been found. They were in bed, not the beds they were supposed to be in, but safe all the same.

Towards the end of the Games, the questions that we expected began to appear thick and fast. One particularly provocative suggestion about the lack of medals came from one newspaper which claimed that it was all the fault of the BOA as it had created a slush fund of £7 million to fund a London Olympic bid—money that should have been spent on the athletes. More balanced criticism sought straightforward answers, but, as always in analysing athletic performance, answers are complicated.

On our return and after much consideration, the evidence was clear. International standards were increasing, and national expectation had been too high. However, many of our competitors enjoyed almost full-time support, in both money and services, which allowed them to live and train as full-time athletes. While results were disappointing, we believed that with the changes we had helped put in place for British sport, we were headed in the right direction.

Atlanta was my first Games as a member of the IOC. Having been elected in 1994, my first IOC session, the 104th, was in 1995 in Budapest, when I took my oath. Looking back, that session had two major decisions to take. One was the election of the city to host the 2002 Olympic Winter Games, with Salt Lake City, Östersund, Sion, and Quebec to make presentations. The ten new members appointed in 1994 in Paris were obvious candidates to be lobbied by the competing cities; as was allowed in those days, we were able visit the cities to look at their plans.

For me, the visits were highly illuminating as my only experience of winter sports had come in Lillehammer in early 1994. All four cities that hosted a visit produced interesting projects and offered me a whole range of experiences during which I may well have shown my naivety.

In Östersund—the Åre ski resort to be precise—when learning about the finish areas for alpine ski events, I was told that lunch would be served in the VIP tent. Just inside the door, I was introduced to his majesty, King Carl Gustav, and I asked him if he was in Åre to present medals to the winners of the alpine events in progress. 'Don't be silly,' he said. 'I am here to go skiing.' In Sion, I was given a special red anorak to wear, which had the word 'Coach' on the front as I, for the first and last time, tried cross country skiing.

As predicted by the local organisers, I fell at exactly the points on the course they had nominated—much to the amusement of a group of youngsters who were surprised that a 'coach' was so inept. In Quebec, the organisers gave me a generous, but mystifying gift, a green wooden decoy duck. To this day, I cannot fathom the connection between a decoy duck and winter sport.

Travel from Quebec to Salt Lake City was by two private executive jets. That seemed to be inordinately generous until we worked out that this was much easier than asking the party of guests to travel on a Sunday with a route involving three different commercial flights and two complicated changes. I was allocated to the jet belonging to a local Salt Lake supporter. It had gold fittings in the internal shower. For a wee lad from suburban Scotland, it was something to behold, if a little over the top.

The second issue in Budapest in 1995 was a debate on the age limit for members. Samaranch was to reach seventy-five that year, and there was a view that in recognition of his outstanding period of presidency, the age limit rules should be amended to allow him an additional five years. It would be fair to say that several members saw this as an opportunity to extend their own membership, and after a long, confused debate, complicated by different simple or two-thirds majorities required for different proposals, the age limited for all members was extended to eighty.

The voting system required written voting slips collected in special wooden boxes. They were carried around the voting members by the newest members and delivered to the scrutineers in their private room. This was both tiring and prolonged. For both reasons, the decision to elect Salt Lake City on the first round of voting was welcomed—Salt Lake City had lost narrowly to Nagano in Birmingham in the 1991 session.

The 105th session, held in Atlanta before the 1996 Centennial Games was much less controversial. It was marked in particular by the approval of the formal report from the Centennial Congress in Paris in 1994, the most prescient part of which was the IOC's adoption of the protection of the environment as an essential component of Olympism—the Olympic movement's overriding philosophy.

Having enjoyed the company and advice of two IOC members allocated to badminton in Barcelona in 1992, I found myself allocated to swimming on behalf of the IOC. It was another interesting challenge as my only experience of swimming was as a spectator—a distant perch from which the sport look reasonably simple. I duly turned up on the first morning at the swimming venue and found it extremely difficult to find the correct entry door.

I introduced myself to Ross Wales, the secretary of FINA (the international federation for the aquatic's disciplines), who was welcoming and helpful. I asked if he had any specific problems and he told me that there was a female Irish swimmer who had suddenly produced a list of surprising world-beating times. Clearly, I missed the nuances in his remarks until he told me that some officials suspected that she might have been 'popping the smarties!' The penny dropped, and I asked if I had to deal with that kind of problem, to which he replied, 'No. That will be decided by people who are much more intelligent than you!'

History would show that the young swimmer, Michelle Smith, who won three gold and one bronze medal, was later suspended for four years for drug offences. The ban ended her career, but there was a silver lining. A disgraced figure in her own country, the legal complications of her case led her to take an interest in the law. She is now a highly regarded barrister at law. The encounter with Ross Wales was another brush with a subject that would become an important part of my life in years to come.

Things improved in my new role when I was asked to try to speak to the stadium management and deal with issues, like mine in trying to gain entry to the venue. The venue manager was in a meeting, but his deputy was a helpful woman who had a broad Scottish accent. We were bound to get on. She denied that there were any problems because the signs were very clear. I told her that I could not find any signs, so we eventually agreed to have a joint expedition. To her surprise and embarrassment, no signs had been erected; to her subsequent credit, they were then put in place by the start time of the evening session. I duly completed my report to the IOC delegate with a moderate feeling of partial success.

The experience of having dual responsibilities involved long days but was an enjoyable combination of events and duties. The novelty of being allocated a car, driver, and a personal assistant from the IOC made life easier, although the regular transport blockages proved irritating at times. Our assistant was a delightful volunteer from Nations Bank called Tina Nasser, who was a splendid after-hours partner in the nightclubs of Buckhead, Atlanta's uptown district, with Colin and Catriona, my son and daughter, who were having a magical first Olympic experience. We all came home tired but happy, and ready to face the inevitable inquest, not about my nocturnal habits, but about the performance of the British team.

17

Complications

The fallout from the Atlanta Games continued for some time. There were many media comments; not too many were sympathetic. A good example was an article in *The Times* on 25 September 1996, which carried a headline, 'Britain in Danger of Being Left at the Starting Line'. The story featured a request to the Sports Council from British Athletics' executive chairman, Professor Peter Radford, formerly a world-class sprinter, for adequate funding for his sport to prepare for the Sydney Games in 2000.

The official response was that he should wait until the autumn and apply again for a distribution to be allocated in November 1997. Radford highlighted that despite the decision to allow revenue applications for lottery funds, the present amounts offered were derisory. He also shared the BOA view that the newly announced UK Sports Council needed to get up and running as soon as possible. Athletics made the clear point that proper funding of competitors would be a pre-condition of Olympic success, and the introduction of new and proper support systems was a relatively long-term process.

At the BOA annual general meeting, on precisely the same date, Dick Palmer presented his report on Atlanta, which he described as a hard, difficult Games, despite its many positive features. He made the call for increased support for athletes, support for coaches and team managers, including payment for time off work and financial rewards offered to all medallists in Sydney and Nagano.

This claim immediately produced the headlines 'Cash for Medals', but the point about financial support was made loud and clear. Support for money for athletes came in the report 'Athlete Performance Strategy to

2000', the results of a survey taken from athletes and coaches in Atlanta that was to be presented to all interested parties the following week at a special meeting held at Bisham Abbey.

The clear need for increased financial resources was reinforced by comparisons with performance systems in Australia, France, and Denmark, a country that produced athletes who delivered four gold medals in Atlanta from a population only 10 per cent of Great Britain's. All had benefitted from a performance system with the correct level of funding. To hammer home the point, in the meeting, I referred to the fifteen-month delay in bringing the new UK Sport Council up to an operational standard. We were in a form of limbo.

The pressures on us helped to introduce a significant change in personnel. Dick Palmer, our long-standing chief executive and secretary general, decided to stand down but to remain with the BOA and lead our efforts to secure ownership of the proposed new British Academy of Sport. He was replaced as secretary general by Simon Clegg, who had acted as his deputy for some years. I stood for re-election for a further four years and was happy to continue, as much work remained to be done.

The British Academy of Sport was a proposal made in conjunction with the new UK Sports Council and government assumed that major funding would be available from the National Lottery. This was a high-profile and very attractive proposition for different local authorities and, of course, for different sports. It was clear that many proposals would be made by different parts of the country, and once again, this was a project that would take considerable time to deliver.

In the event, twenty-five different bidders emerged, which were likely to be whittled down to no more than three or four for a final decision. The BOA view was clear. The proposed new academy would be the base to deliver all the services that we currently provided in Great Britain and would hugely enhance and improve the range of the services; all were to be funded from National Lottery proceeds. Few projects could have been more exciting. At the end of the first part of the bidding process, three solid and researched projects emerged to be considered for future discussion and a final decision.

The first was the Central Consortium, consisting of the existing sports facilities at Lilleshall, Holme Pierrepont, and would be based at Loughborough University. The second was a proposal from Don Valley in Sheffield. The third was the preferred BOA option, based on the former US Air Force base at Upper Heyford in Gloucestershire and supported by Oxfordshire County Council and Cherwell District Council. It would be built on a greenfield site of 145 acres close to the M40 motorway. We received the support of Douglas Hurd, the former foreign secretary, and our partners brought some major commercial players on board, including Wimpey, Taylor Woodrow, and Mars, in the hope that they would help raise the £75 million which would be added to the government's promised £100 million from lottery funds. The BOA would become the agreed 'in-house' management of the academy and would meet £1 million from its own funds towards the annual management charge.

As you might expect of facilities that had been used by servicemen from the United States Air Force, what had been left was of high quality. There was accommodation for up to 750 people in exiting dormitories, with additional accommodation in a selection of private houses. There was a large indoor hall, a bowling alley (likely to be demolished), a substantial mothballed hospital (which would provide offices for the academy), and, perhaps uniquely, a custom-built centre for sports medicine and sports science, both of which were central to any elite performance centre.

The site had all the space needed for an athletics track, a swimming pool, and other indoor facilities. The academy would be able to cooperate with Oxford and Oxford Brookes universities and with Eton College, which was planning to build an international rowing course. The BOA held discussions with the three major non-Olympic sports—football, rugby, and cricket—to investigate any sharing opportunities. I was aware of one discussion with the Football Association, with the proposition that unlimited space existed to create football pitches. It was also suggested that the FA could construct a high-quality accommodation block for its international players, who could base their preparations at Upper Heyford before matches at Wembley. Sadly, this did not come to pass.

There was no doubt in my mind that the partnership created by the BOA was the best option for the creation of a far-reaching centre for elite Olympic sport. The plans fitted well with the aspirations of the government as an ideal investment of National Lottery money. Bids were to be submitted by 31 January 1997, and the three bids above were short-listed.

It was inevitable that a project of such high value would attract widespread interest, and on 25 February, the Labour Party announced that it was not bound by the procedure to date; should it come to power, the whole process may have to start again. On 1 May, the Labour Party under Tony Blair won a huge majority in the general election, and Tony Banks was appointed as sports minister. We were aware that not everybody supported our suggested role in managing the academy, and inevitably, a new government would have a view. In October, Banks decided that the Central Consortium would not be allowed to proceed, so only Upper Heyford and Sheffield would make final presentations.

Sadly, after all the efforts made to produce an imaginative vision, and only a few weeks before the date of the final decision, we found out from a reliable source that the new government's view was that enough lottery money for sport had been allocated to the south of the country and that some should be invested in the north. This meant that the Don Valley bid in Sheffield would be successful. We appeared, of course, at the final selection meeting, which was predictably short, and after the expected decision, we politely congratulated Sheffield on its success as hosts of the newly titled 'Institute of Sport'. The whole process had been changed under political review. I am still convinced that a major opportunity had been missed. We had a new government to woo.

A more recurring complexity was highlighted at the 1997 BOA annual general meeting and on this occasion by our Winter Games sports. British athletes preparing for the 1998 Olympic Winter Games in Nagano had made application for financial support from the National Lottery, but no payments had been made. The distribution of lottery funds was a complex process. Applications were made to the UK Sports Council, which assessed them according to its own criteria.

However, the actual payments were still the responsibility of the home country sports councils, all of which had different payment systems. For the Winter Games sports, payments should have been made by the English Sports Council, but no funds had been received. The UK Sports Council was intended to become a lottery distributor in its own right, but the process was very slow. Headlines of 'Olympic lottery freeze' did not make for happy reading.

The year 1997 was also an Olympic bidding year, with the prize of hosting the 2004 Olympic Games. The original list of competing cities was very long, with eleven different NOCs presenting very different choices. To my surprise, the evaluation committee appointed by the IOC visited all eleven candidates, but the IOC decided to reduce the final number to five and removed Istanbul, Lille, Rio de Janeiro, Saint Petersburg, San Juan, and Seville from the original list. That left the cities of Athens, Rome, Cape Town, Stockholm, and Buenos Aires to prepare their bid books.

The BOA had decided not to submit a city for the 2004 race, but there was continued media interest in Great Britain about a future bid, almost certainly from London, which became a regular media item for comment. As an IOC member, the opportunity for me to visit the five candidate cities was of real interest, as it would, with potential benefits to a possible future decision by Britain, give me much greater knowledge of a bidding process in reality.

After the 1996 Games were allocated to Atlanta in North America, the chances were that strong candidates would emerge from Europe. This placed Rome in a favourable position and of course a second bid from Athens following its disappointment in not getting the 1996 Centennial Games. The presence on the list of Cape Town also generated much interest following the dramatic political changes that had happened in South Africa and the charismatic reputation of President Nelson Mandela. The five visits were to produce very different projects and some fascinating meetings.

Our first visit was to Buenos Aires. It was a completely new experience, and something of a surprise, as we made every effort to avoid any pre-conceived opinions from the Falklands War of fifteen years earlier. We found a city with a strong interest in sport but with a widely differing range in the quality of the available facilities. In all honesty, many of its sports venues needed major reconstruction, except for the venues for equestrian events, as the polo fields and racecourse were outstanding.

To our surprise, one of the welcoming officials had a perfect Welsh accent due entirely, as we were to discover, to the historical presence, over many years, of Welsh miners in Patagonia in Argentina's south. Our hosts arranged a short meeting with President Carlos Menem, but also a more informal gathering over dinner at a race meeting at the famous Hipódromo Argentino de Palermo racecourse with the country's minister for sport, Hugo Porta, one of the leading Argentinian rugby players and a world class fly-half.

During dinner, we noticed that the next race included a horse called Campese, the surname of an equally famous Australian rugby player. It seemed wise to make use of this unusual coincidence, so Porta and I both made a modest investment, which was pleasantly rewarded when the horse won at odds of 18 to 1. The Buenos Aires concept of a corridor of land containing most of the current facilities with two main roads and a rail line was a basis for a good bid, but significant investment in its sports facilities would have been needed.

Cape Town was an even more interesting visit, due entirely to a totally unexpected meeting. Our long journey involved Glasgow to London to Johannesburg to Cape Town, and slightly bleary eyed, we were met by Chris Ball, chief executive of the bid, with the request, 'Could you change quickly?' When I asked why, he replied, 'An opportunity has just arisen.

We are going to take you to see Mandela!' At that time, and still no doubt today, if anybody was asked to name any three people they would like to meet, almost everyone would have included the name Mandela.

Released from prison after twenty-seven years, he became the president of South Africa from 1994 to 1999, his country's first democratically elected president, and a Nobel Peace Prize winner. I joined my IOC colleagues—Vitaly Smirnov from Russia and Tony Bridge from Jamaica—for our meeting with Mandela, who spent time speaking to each of us individually. When talking at length to Smirnov, he was reminded by him that there were two other colleagues in the meeting. To this, Mandela replied politely, 'I am speaking to you at the moment. I will speak to them in a minute'.

Eventually, when it was my turn, he said, 'Welcome, Mr Reedie, and how is Tony?' I took my courage in both hands and replied, 'Thank you, President. The Prime Minister is fit and well!' Throughout the thirty minutes we were with him, Mandela made the effort to speak about us and our countries, rather than extol the virtues of the unbelievable changes he had inspired in his own country. We all left clutching a signed copy of his amazing book, *Long Walk to Freedom*, with memories of a memorable and unique occasion.

The four days in Cape Town included all the special places to visit. We were treated to helicopter flights over Table Mountain and out to Robben Island, a place where one can only look on in awe as you see the tiny cell in which Mandela spent so many years of remarkable life. The plans for Cape Town's potential Olympic Games involved the creation of many new sports facilities but would also feature the famous rugby ground, Newlands, where we were impressed by the existing work in sports medicine.

To give us a proper feel for the city, we made a visit to one of the new townships in the suburbs of Cape Town, an illustration of the efforts being made to develop and provide housing for the many still underprivileged members of society. In private conversation back in our hotel, we discussed the priority being given to a possible Olympic Games as opposed to the more basic social requirements in the city. It was a thought-provoking issue. Even so, the support of President Mandela would be a powerful asset to the bid.

In any visit to Athens, with the Panathenaic Stadium in the very centre of the city, it is impossible not to be enthralled by the history of the Modern Olympic Games. It is only a five-hour journey by road to the original site of the Ancient Olympic Games at Olympia where a modern Olympic

Academy has been developed. Like Athens, Olympia, with its evocative ruins and the stunning artefacts in its museum, offers a unique insight into the magic of the Olympic Games. It made me feel very privileged to be part of something that has a heritage of over 2,500 years and is so important to today's world.

Athens had bid for the Centennial Games in 1996, which had been awarded to Atlanta and the new bid committee had decided to present its case based on existing sports facilities and the very substantial legacy to be brought to the city by hosting the Games. This legacy would be concentrated on a new airport, extensive new road networks, a new light rail transport system, and the availability of the land occupied by the old airport as a potential site for the necessary new sports facilities.

The existing main stadium would be redeveloped, and an open-air swimming complex built beside it with land available to construct a completely new Olympic village complex. The bid was to be led by Gianna Angelopoulos-Daskalaki, who had been appointed as an ambassador at large for the Greek state. Married to Theodore Angelopoulos who was a Greek shipping and steel businessman, she was a formidable woman in her own right and able to bring a range of different skills to the bid. After the disappointment of Athens' defeat in 1996 and not a little bitterness thereafter, it was clear that a completely new approach was being taken to win the city the right to host the Games.

1997 was the first occasion that Sweden had bid to host a Summer Olympic Games and had nominated Stockholm as its candidate city. Stockholm had hosted the 1912 Olympic Games as the only bidder at that time and had, because of Australian quarantine issues, hosted the equestrian events in 1956 for the Melbourne Games. Sweden had also bid no less than six times to host the Olympic Winter Games but without success. There was considerable sympathy within the IOC for the bidding efforts of the Swedes and a lot of interest in their plans to bring what is the world's biggest sporting event to their capital city with a population of only 1 million.

With my Danish badminton experience, I knew all about the ability of Scandinavians to provide good sports facilities. It thus came as no surprise to find that almost all the necessary sports facilities for an Olympic Games had already been built in Stockholm and were operating successfully.

The geographical situation of Stockholm in northern Europe also provided long daylight hours so that a Summer Games could be handled very easily in a compact city but one with excellent transport arrangements. I had visited Stockholm on many occasions during my time in the International Badminton Federation when Swedish Stellan Mohlin had been president, so I was well aware of Swedish enthusiasm for sport and their abilities to organise excellent events.

The Stockholm visit was particularly easy as I met up with many old friends. The bid was run by Olof Stenhammer, who was CEO of the Stock Exchange, and, in an act of kindness, took Rosemary and me by helicopter to a small island in the Stockholm archipelago for lunch. We passed over a large herd of elks on one of the larger islands, and when I said I had never seen an elk before, he explained that they were found in large numbers in Sweden and that regular culls had to be organised. I stored this piece of information away for future use.

On our return later that evening to our room in the Grand Hotel, we almost died with fright as we opened the door. Someone had hung a large stuffed toy of an elk from the ceiling, presumably a reminder of our earlier conversation. Some jokes, although well intended, just do not work.

Stockholm's famous Olympic stadium from 1912 was still in use (as it is today), and facilities for twenty-five of the Olympic sports were in place. The city is attractive with water a central feature in the middle of the downtown area. A large multi-purpose stadium with unusual circular architecture was a new asset and the Swedish summer climate was ideal for sport. It was an interesting candidate.

Our last visit to a candidate city was to Rome, but we were unable to make the date for a group of IOC members, and so Rosemary and I made a short two-day visit at the insistence of Luciano Barra, the sports director of CONI, the Italian NOC, and an old friend. Italy was and is a major player in the Olympic world, and happy memories of the excellent 1960 Games in Rome still lingered in the world of sport.

Rome's bid was centred on the facilities in the famous Foro Italico with the main stadium, swimming complex, and tennis courts. Land had been made available for new facilities close to an industrial site beside the ring road, but that development would be a large project. Rome has always been my favourite city, and it was easy to agree to a special tour of some of the most famous historical sites. Unfortunately, the Sistine Chapel in the Vatican was closed; as a consolation, we were able to visit the underground crypt in St Peters Basilica The irony of Rosemary, an Ulster protestant, being given access to a sacred area under the most famous Catholic church in the world was not lost on me as we enjoyed our rare access.

As the IOC members gathered in Lausanne for their 106th session in 1997, it was becoming very clear that the impressive and dignified campaign run by Gianna Angelopoulos for Athens was making considerable headway. By comparison, the World Athletics Championships, held in Athens in August, seemingly successfully, received some critical comments from Primo Nebiolo, Italian president of the IAAF. The comments were seen to be directed against the Athens bid and, therefore, in favour of Rome. Nebiolo was a controversial figure, and his comments were unhelpful.

Decision day was 5 September, and the presentations were led by Stockholm with an emphasis on plans for athletes. Cape Town followed, and its presentation was led by President Mandela, his presence a moment of real significance for the Olympic movement. Athens followed, and unlike any of the other presentation, it was conducted almost entirely by Gianna Angelopoulos. Buenos Aires began the afternoon session, but President Menem rather missed his opportunity to promote his city and country. Rome was last to present with its charismatic mayor, Francesco Rutelli, and even included Luciano Pavarotti. The day had been totally gripping with city bids supported by presidents, prime ministers, mayors, famous personalities, and equally famous athletes.

Mandela's address had been measured and complimentary to the IOC for its own efforts against apartheid but, somehow, not historically memorable. My feeling was that his words had been written by a bid script writer, who had missed the most important point. The great man only needed to make one point—you helped me in the dark days of apartheid and helped my country emerge into the global family of nations, now, please help me consolidate all that you have done by granting us the honour to host the Olympic Games. In return, I promise to host Games that will never be forgotten. He did not say it, and a glorious opportunity slipped away. Perhaps such words may not have changed the outcome of the vote, but I am sure they would have made it much closer.

The presentation skills of Gianna Angelopoulos were outstanding. Stockholm's bid was technically excellent, but its hopes were damaged by the bomb explosions in its Olympic facilities in the run up to the session. As expected, the final decision took four rounds of voting. In the first round, Buenos Aires and Cape Town were tied, but Cape Town easily won the resulting vote-off. Stockholm was eliminated in the second round and Cape Town in the third. In the fourth round, Athens was the comfortable winner over Rome by sixty-six votes to forty-one.

The immediate reactions to the result, apart from much rejoicing in Greece, included a statement from Mario Pescante, the president of CONI, that now, the 2008 Games would definitely be held in Cape Town. There was also an interesting aside from Pavarotti, who said that if he had been allowed to sing, Rome would certainly have won. Perhaps he made a valid point: why put a dog on your team, then not let it bark?

One British newspaper identified that as the Angelopoulos family owned a luxurious house in London, this was the first time the Olympic Games had been won by a woman with the biggest garden in Chelsea. More considered comment in Britain was unanimous that the BOA plans to bid for the 2008 Games were now unrealistic. The IOC was unlikely to award a second Games in succession to Europe and that attention should now turn to a possible bid for 2012.

In many ways, those projections were accurate, but few knew my own view that the Athens decision would allow the extra time needed to bring British sport to a position which would give a London bid a chance. Unknown to many, but very significantly, the BOA had employed David Luckes, a recent hockey Olympian, to research the options to deliver just that outcome.

One interesting development in the long-running campaign to bring order to British sport, and to create a British Academy or Institute, was the announcement from the BOA that it had entered into an arrangement with Disney for access to its $100 million 200-acre Wide World of Sport Complex in Florida as a permanent warm-weather training centre. The inspiration came from the success of the Tallahassee training camp before the Atlanta Games and the introduction made to Simon Clegg of both Disney and the Orlando Regional Healthcare System which wished to enter a sponsorship arrangement in Britain.

The range and quality of the facilities would be ideal for visiting athletes and a charge of £50 per day, funded by lottery grants, would make visits to Florida eminently affordable. This price would cover food, accommodation, local transportation, medical insurance, and use of all the facilities. The sponsorship was valued at £550,000 *per annum*. The bobsleigh team had already used the centre for its pre-games training before the Nagano Winter Games. We read the several supportive media articles with a big smile at the comments about the references to 'Mickey Mouse' arrangements. The small print in the contract with Disney did allow free access to 'the Magic Kingdom'. A ministerial comment that this development would 'integrate with what we have planned' was treated with a sardonic smile.

Attention turned to delivering a British team to the Olympic Winter Games in Nagano in February 1998 with all the challenges imposed by the distances involved. The team of thirty-four athletes faced the long flight to Tokyo but was then faced with a further complicated journey to Nagano in the western mountains of Central Japan. The organising committee had been aware of this challenge and was greatly assisted by the Japanese government decision to extend the Shinkansen bullet train express service from Tokyo to Nagano. They were to be the biggest ever Winter Games, with 2176 athletes from seventy-two NOCs competing in seven sports and sixty-eight events.

New medal events included snowboarding, women's ice hockey, and, more interestingly, curling, with the two British teams both from Scotland, or north Britain to be more geographically and politically accurate. The curling rink was constructed in the neighbouring city of Karuizawa, 55 miles from Nagano, with the athletes accommodated in a satellite village. Conveniently, both venue and village were only thirty minutes from Nagano by bullet train. Although there was no British team, there was excitement at the first Olympic appearance of the elite level NHL ice-hockey players.

I met up with my Olympic family assistant (OFA), a specific volunteer allocated to each member of the IOC, presidents of international federations and of NOCs. Her name was Lin Watanabe, a student from Tokyo University who had been a university slalom champion and very familiar with snow sports. Lin spoke Japanese, English, Spanish, and Mandarin and was heading for a career with an American merchant bank. She became a vital member of the BOA team and even travelled back down to Narita Airport to collect Rosemary, who travelled out a few days behind me.

Lin also became involved in a specific problem in arranging rail travel for Tony Banks, our minister for sport, and his assistant, who were making their first visit to an Olympic Games. We received an urgent message from his department in London to inform us that they could not obtain two seats in the 'Green Car' (the business class carriage) in the bullet train from Tokyo. Lin solved this very easily by going down to the station in Nagano and buying the two tickets required and sending them down to the embassy in Tokyo.

Our principal guests arrived safely and then made a second request—could we find a bar in Nagano with international television coverage of the English Premier League so that the minister could watch his beloved Chelsea? Once again, Lin came up trumps. She worked wonders to find a location, but there was a limit to her miracles; Chelsea lost 2–0 away to Arsenal (its fierce London rivals).

In common with the Seoul Games in Korea in 1988, the Nagano opening ceremony was a daytime/daylight event and organised in an extended stadium developed from its use as a baseball park for only the official ceremonies. As we relaxed in the lounge before the opening ceremony, the minister confessed that he had left his ticket on his bedside table back at the hotel. This unexpected test for a helpful local official was resolved by him sending an available car back to central Nagano to retrieve the missing ticket. Thereafter, Tony enjoyed his short visit to Japan. The opening ceremony displayed much of the colourful history of Japan, but the highlight was a unique item when orchestras, situated in five different continents, played the final movement of Beethoven's 9th Symphony—'Ode to Joy'.

British performances featured our best-known skiers, Graham Bell and Alain Baxter, but the short-track skaters, led by Nicky Gooch, could not repeat their medal-winning performance from Lillehammer. Down in Karuizawa, the curling teams played through the very long round-robin system required by their sport. The women's team, skipped by Kirsty Hay, won through to the semi-final but lost very narrowly to the eventual gold medallists, Canada, by 6–5. In the bronze medal match, they lost to Sweden by 10–6. All in all, it was an encouraging debut for the sport and British interest. The highlight was the bronze medal, our only medal success, won by the British four-man bobsleigh team led by Sean Olsson, with Dean Ward, Courteney Rumbold, and Paul Attwood in a tie with the French but behind the German and Swiss teams.

One of the new snowboarding disciplines was won, narrowly, by the Canadian Ross Rebagliati, who was then disqualified by the IOC after testing positive for marijuana, the first time this had happened in Olympic history. The Canadian Olympic Committee lodged a protest, which was upheld by the Court of Arbitration for Sport ruling that marijuana was not classified as a prohibited substance. Rebagliati claimed he must have inhaled the drug at a party he had attended, which rather added to the discomfort of the IOC.

Much debate had taken place over previous years within the IOC as they struggled to agree a comprehensive policy on drug abuse. The Nagano incident served only to prove the potential danger to sport presented by this ever more complicated evil which was to become a persistent and major issue.

One of the learning experiences for a new IOC member is the realisation that there are different categories of accreditation that carry different benefits. Not everybody can be in the same place at the same time. In Nagano, there was a restaurant in the IOC hotel that was reserved for a certain level of accredited people. This did not cover the volunteer group of OFAs, and as the room was always 60 per cent empty, I decided to include Lin, our outstanding OFA, as our guest for lunch. I had discovered that Lin was lodged with all the other OFAs in a local dormitory and was given a very limited daily allowance for food, so I was sure a somewhat better lunch than her usual fare would be much appreciated.

Access to the restaurant was conferred on some IOC guests, including those from future Winter Games bidding cities. The city of Sion in Switzerland was considering a bid, and one of its delegates was a young, dark-haired, handsome Olympic skier called Lance Kelly. Rosemary and Lin had become good friends and they seemed to share an admiration for young Mr Kelly. I told Lin that I had noticed her interest and asked her if she had a weakness for skiers. When she admitted she did, I asked her to follow me.

We walked to a neighbouring table, and I tapped the shoulder of one of my IOC colleagues. When he stood up, I asked him if he would like to meet one of Japan's university slalom specialists. I then said to Lin, 'Please meet Jean Claude Killy'. To his undying credit, the extremely handsome French skiing legend treated Lin as if she was a princess. From that moment on, I had a very happy young OFA on my hands. The quality of good volunteers, at whatever level, can make a difference to the appreciation and success of an Olympic Games.

Between supporting the BOA team in action, which can be time-consuming at Winter Games, we organised some modest hospitality for friends and guests from the Olympic movement. Simon Clegg had a talent for hospitality events, and a lucky piece of local sponsorship allowed us access to an old sake factory where we were able to organise two evening dinners. Our sponsor brought a chef he knew up from Tokyo who produced outstanding food in a specially decorated Japanese room. Guests had to walk up an entry path lit by flaming torches and were welcomed by a group of Japanese drummers. Inside, a lucky few were invited to ceremonially break the lid of the waiting wooden barrel of sake. Good wine and a special atmosphere made the evenings the most prized invitation at the Games. In retrospect, occasions like those engender massive amounts of goodwill, which, over the years, can play a key part in more important projects.

On our return from Nagano, we found that little progress had been made to finalise the long-awaited UK Sport Council. The chairman, Ian McLaurin, and the chief executive, Howard Wells, had both resigned, presumably in frustration at the lack of progress. Our own annoyance spilled over at our AGM on 10 June when there was unanimity among all the sports that urgent action should be taken. Public comment, using terms like 'Shambles' and 'Calls for revolution', made the press.

It would be nice, but unrealistic, to claim instant success, but on 2 July, in the House of Commons, Chris Smith, the culture secretary, finally announced that the UK Sport Council was to become a lottery distributor in its own right and would receive around 5 per cent of the sports fund each year, plus a transfer to deliver the Institute of Sport in Sheffield. Rodney Walker was to move from his chairmanship of the English Sports Council and become the chairman of UK Sport, and I was invited to be his deputy chairman.

There was to be a new sports cabinet, bringing together the sports ministers of the four-home countries with the secretary of state, but I never heard any comment from any meeting, but some must have been held. Although results from the lottery investment would take some years to appear. At last, the correct pieces were to be in the correct places and with adequate funding. We could then turn to thoughts of a future 2012 bid.

18

The IOC in Peril

One morning in early 1998, my routine Olympic work was interrupted when I took a telephone call from an enthusiastic events' organiser. She told me that she had been asked to organise a dinner to celebrate the British Museum's relationship with the Olympic Museum in Lausanne, which had opened just five years earlier in June 1993. The British Museum's classical antiquities department had been very supportive of the Olympic Museum during its development, and it was time for a joint symbolic celebration. The organiser had a proposed guest list which contained the princess royal, IOC president Juan Antonio Samaranch, and the mayor of Athens. With such a high-profile list, I rather assumed that her plans would be difficult to deliver and simply noted the date.

Some months later, to my surprise, the organiser confirmed that her invitations had all been accepted and that she had added Gianna Angelopoulos, the president of the 2004 Athens Olympic organising committee, to a particularly good attendance list. Athens had won the right to organise the 2004 Games just a few months earlier, in September 1997, and the Greek Olympic world was buzzing with excitement. The celebration was clearly going to be an event of significant importance to the BOA.

On the evening of the dinner, 24 June, almost exactly the fifth birthday of the Olympic Museum, black-tie clad, I went to meet the IOC president and his wife, Bibis Samaranch, who was elegantly dressed as always, at their hotel. We then travelled to the museum, where we joined Her Royal Highness Gianna Angelopoulos and the mayor of Athens, Dimitris Avramopoulos. The location was the British Museum's most evocative space, the Duveen Gallery, also known as the Parthenon Room, where the stunning Elgin Marbles adorn the walls in all their splendour.

Although magnificent, their presence in London was and is highly controversial. Given that Greece was the home of the Ancient Games, and that Athens was the home of the first Modern Games in 1896 and host of the next Games in 2004, to use the Duveen Gallery for the dinner was an ideal choice. However, the room and its contents are also the symbolic centrepiece of an archaeological dispute decades old. Without going into too much detail, at the turn of the nineteenth century, Thomas Bruce, seventh earl of Elgin, 'rescued' about half of the marbles that had once decorated the Temple of the Parthenon on the Acropolis of Ancient Athens.

Elgin felt that the marbles, lying amid the ruins of a derelict Parthenon in Turkish-occupied Greece, were in need of a new home. Needless to say, many disagreed with him at the time, as do modern-day Greek governments. Not surprisingly, the Greeks would like their white marble masterpieces back. Equally unsurprisingly, the British Museum would prefer to keep their iconic collection.

So, the setting was perfect, but fraught with potential embarrassment, particularly as the Greek diaspora in Britain numbers over 300,000, that many of the wealthier ones were and are major donors to the British Museum, and that several of them had been invited to the dinner.

At my allocated table, I joined actor, raconteur, and 'quintessential English gentleman' Nigel Havers, who had been hired to enliven the evening with a few well-chosen words to inspire the distinguished audience. Havers had of course played Lord Andrew Lindsay, a character loosely based on British Olympic notable and 1928 gold medallist, Lord Burghley, sixth marquess of Exeter, in the 1981 multi-award-winning film *Chariots of Fire*. So, Havers was an excellent choice, the gathering was auspicious, the setting fabulous, and I settled down to enjoy a fine feast and a relaxed evening.

Havers had been briefed about the sensitivities, which, without putting too fine a point on it, boiled down to, 'Whatever you do, don't mention the marbles and steer clear of Elgin'. However, perhaps as a consequence of the ministering of an unusually attentive wine waiter or his inability to remember his lines, Havers went 'rogue'.

His first mistake was to eschew the microphone he was offered. With his highly-trained voice, he clearly felt no need of an audio aid. However, his table was in the middle of a long yet narrow rectangular room, so he proceeded to alternate his position to address both ends of the room in turn. His delivery was projected excellently, but the two sides of his linear audience only heard 50 per cent of it. Not only that, he proceeded to offer what he thought was an amusing insight into the contentious presence of the Elgin Marbles in the British Museum by beginning his tale with, 'You know, a few years ago, I played Lord Elgin in a film directed by my friend Christopher Miles, called *Lord Elgin and Some Stones of no Value*.' Chins dropped onto chests, honoured guests avoided one another's eyes, British faces flushed crimson, and Greek faces darkened like thunder.

The silence from the aghast audience, especially the Hellenic contingent, was deafening and produced a social and political disaster that caused no little embarrassment. The post-dinner discussions involved some of us poring much needed oil on very troubled waters. Thankfully, good relations between the two museums survived the furore, as did the Anglo–Greek relationship, but only just.

Anyway, at the sharp end of competitive sport, far removed from the marbled halls of the British Museum, serious issues would soon raise their ugly heads that would shake the very foundation of its existence and present those of us whose task it was to govern sport with profound moral and ethical questions.

The eighty-fifth Tour de France started in Dublin, Ireland, on 11 July 1998. Three days before the start, French police had found a car belonging to the Festina Team to be full of prohibited substances including erythropoietin (EPO), a hormone that the kidneys produce naturally to maintain crucial red blood cells, but which, if injected artificially, is a notorious performance-enhancing drug.

After the first stage of the French part of the tour, and following a raid on the Festina headquarters, arrests were made of the team's tour director and doctor, leading to the withdrawal of the team. The 'Festina Affair' extended its reach to the TVM Team, and this led to sit-down protests by the peloton riders. The whole affair revealed a total of forty-four positive samples for EPO, with many top riders accused of doping.

This was a major sports story but one that was regarded as a significant extension to the widely understood belief that cycling had a real drugs problem. However, on 27 July, IOC President Juan Antonio Samaranch gave an interview to *El Mundo* in Spain. He was quoted as saying that the list of banned substances should be 'drastically' reduced and drugs that do not damage an athlete's health should not be prohibited. The actual quotation said:

> Doping now is everything that, firstly, is harmful to an athlete's health, and secondly, artificially augments his performance. If it's just the second case, for me that's not doping. If it's the first case, it is.

This quotation coincided with the news that Randy Barnes of the USA, the Olympic shot put champion, and Dennis Mitchell, the bronze medallist in the 100 metres at the Barcelona Games, had both tested positive.

The reaction was swift and contradictory. On behalf of the BOA, I commented that we did not accept Samaranch's reported position, stating that any athlete found guilty of a doping offence would not be eligible for selection for the British Olympic team. This view was supported by the anti-doping officials of the Sports Council. Similarly, Samaranch's quoted position was questioned by the Prince Alexandre de Mérode, the Belgian chairman of the IOC Medical Commission, and the IOC director general, François Carrard, who suggested that the president might have been misquoted.

In fairness, the IOC had been struggling for some time to produce a policy, and its possible implementation, which would be suitable for sport in general as well as for the Olympic Games. The IOC invested in scientific research, approved laboratories, and published a list of prohibited substances, but without the power to make these regulations universal. In his defence, Samaranch had, for some years, been asking for someone to give him a 'definition of doping'—a question easier to ask than to answer. National governments also held very differing positions. Faced with obvious extensive abuse in the Tour de France and the need to face the doping problem head on, the IOC decided to call for and organise what was to become the first world conference on doping in sport.

It was organised for 2–4 February 1999 in Lausanne and attracted a large response from the world of sport: the IOC, NOCs, IFs, athletes, and many governments and governmental organisations. The conference and debates were conducted at the same time as the fallout from the Salt Lake City bidding scandal. I attended under the NOC heading and the British Government was represented by Tony Banks, the minister for sport. Along with some other government speakers, Banks took an aggressive position in complaints about the IOC, not all entirely relevant to the problems of doping.

His assistant asked if I would read the draft of his speech, which was very critical of the IOC and the IFs. I suggested that it should be modified as, if delivered in its original wording, it would have a damaging effect on the organisations in which British sport had an important membership. The minister asked me to justify my view, and I told him that one effect of his original draft would be to seriously damage the pending English Football Association's bid for the 2006 World Cup. He then agreed on the changes surprisingly quickly.

After three days of discussion, there was a balanced majority opinion that both governments and sport should find a way of cooperating to deal with the scourge of doping in sport. The conference produced the 'Lausanne Declaration on Doping in Sport', which dealt with a series of priorities, which included education, athletes' rights, acceptance of the Olympic movement's anti-doping code, sanctions, the creation of an independent international anti-doping agency, the necessary responsibilities of sports organisations, and collaboration with public authorities.

Under the heading of sanctions, there was agreement that the minimum-required sanction for major doping substances should be a suspension of the athlete from all competition for a period of two years for a first offence. There was not universal agreement on this but was supported by a majority of IFs. Sport organisations and governments would operate under their own powers until the new agency had been created and come into effect. Governments were united in their view that if an international agency was to be created, it should be 'independent: and, specifically, not run by the IOC'. Side meetings took place to investigate the shape of the new agency and it was agreed that this would be based on a fifty/fifty representation of sport and governments with the IOC providing the necessary funding for the first two years.

In many ways, it was a surprisingly good result from a meeting held in the middle of the worldwide criticism of the IOC over the selection of Salt Lake City. It took much work to finally establish the new agency which was created on 10 November 1999. I was asked to take on the sub-committee for finance and administration under the first president, Dick Pound. The World Anti-Doping Agency (WADA) was born, and at that time, I had no inkling of the effect it would have on my life.

As mentioned above, the drug scandals and the steps to a solution were intertwined with the biggest crisis faced by the IOC since its creation in 1894. It remains a salutary lesson to look back and examine the reaction to the publication of breaches in the regulations for the award to host an Olympic Games. The scandal grew into worldwide condemnation of the IOC, its constitution and membership, its processes, its president, its chosen cities, and the steps it took to deal with its crisis. Media in every form were full of the story for the best part of three months and then monitored in detail the improvements to IOC systems that had been demanded. A timetable might help explain the whole farrago.

During an executive board meeting in Lausanne in mid-December 1998, Marc Hodler, a senior IOC member and Swiss president of FIS (international skiing), disclosed to the gathered media that certain members of the IOC and the Salt Lake City organising committee appeared to have been involved in steps to 'arrange' votes for the host of the 2002 Olympic Winter Games. In simple terms, much used by an understandably ravenous media at the time, the Salt Lake organising committee had been attempting to 'buy votes', and in several instances, the offers appeared to have been accepted by members.

The resulting furore brought about resignations from the organising committee, the establishment of at least three committees of inquiry in the USA, and the further establishment of a special IOC inquiry commission to be led by senior IOC member, Dick Pound, a Montreal-based lawyer.

I first met Dick Pound when he visited Manchester during the city's first Olympic bid in 1989 and had served with him on IOC commissions since becoming a member in 1994. It was perhaps prophetic that we met at a marketing commission event in Berlin in late December the day after he had been in Lausanne and accepted the job to lead the IOC inquiry commission. During a late nightcap, he admitted to me that he was concerned that he was always asked to do 'the shitty jobs', an early realisation of what was likely to be in store.

As there was clear urgency, the IOC commission worked quickly and was able to report to the executive board by 24 January, by which time, more details had emerged and become public from journalistic efforts in Salt Lake City. The recommendations to the IOC, from the commission, included the suspension (and probable expulsion) of six members, with warnings to three others. In the meantime, three other members had already resigned. The publication of the report created another media frenzy. Every accusation, every rumoured wrongdoing, and the suggested penalties became front-page news in almost every newspaper and on many television stations.

Detailed historical bids for different Games were analysed and subsequent decisions questioned. Unending personal attacks were made on Samaranch, and many calls were made for the complete disbandment of the IOC. In an attempt to deflect some of the criticism in Britain, I proposed a revised city selection method, published this, and sent it to the IOC, suggesting an electoral college, transparency on bid expenditure and an enhanced evaluation process, which, roughly speaking, was decided for the imminent selection of the 2006 Winter Games city. The move had little effect on British opinion, and my duties as an IOC member 'in' Britain led me to a very difficult live interview on Channel 4 News with John Snow, its leading presenter.

I should stress before you read the end of this paragraph that IOC members are not chosen to represent their countries on the IOC, but the other way around; members are chosen by the IOC to represent the IOC in their countries. My attempts to present a more balanced view to Snow were unsuccessful as allegations of misconduct across many previous years were mentioned. Eventually, I had to claim that many of those earlier allegations covered events well before I became a member. I was then dismissed with the claim, 'We thought we elected you to deal with this kind of behaviour.' It was not a pleasant experience.

There had clearly been corruption instigated by at least one bidding city, Salt Lake, and several IOC members had succumbed to temptation. It was a very stressful time as the behaviour of perhaps 10 per cent of the membership was reprehensible. The details of the scale of corruption provided never-ending copy for journalists, including allegations of payments by the Salt Lake organising committee to cover the education of members' children, payments for private health care, and direct financial inducements.

Also, the possibility of previous wrongdoing in the bidding process was suggested by the admission from Australia that the Sydney 2000 bid had made large cash payments to the leaders of two African NOCs to encourage their votes. However, the Australians said that these payments were not bribes but funds designed to support the work of the NOCs concerned. As specific names appeared and excuses or explanations made, they only served to fuel the fire of criticism. The assumption that reform would be demanded by our major sponsors was a recurrent theme. Our marketing director, Michael Payne, travelled extensively to speak to and brief our major sponsors and to explain what the IOC would do.

The executive board made public its decision that a special session of the IOC would be held in Lausanne on 17 and 18 March, and that proposals would be made to the full membership that six accused members be expelled. There would also be a report on what steps the IOC would take to deal with the many accusations made and to put in place systems that would avoid any possible recurrence.

We met in Lausanne on 17 March and received a detailed report from Samaranch, who then stated that he sought a vote of confidence to deal with the problems as a first step in that process. He immediately stood up and left the meeting to reach its decision. My own reaction was that this was an acceptable way to deal with his own position as well as a skilful way to confirm his authority as president. It was not surprising to see that the resulting secret ballot gave him the support he needed, with only two dissenting votes.

Samaranch set the tone of the meeting in no uncertain terms:

We must clean our house. We must root out all forms of inappropriate or
unethical behaviour among our membership and expel those members
recommended by the Executive Board. No one thought that certain of
our members would act in a manner which would eventually bring the
IOC into disrepute—in fact into a crisis which has nearly destroyed the
reputation and credibility of all its members and the organisation itself.

We then received a verbal report from Dick Pound on the recommendations
made by the inquiry commission and the basis on which they had reached
their decisions. He also supported Samaranch's remarks on just how
important the decisions would be for the IOC. We then dealt formally,
and one by one, with each of the six members who were proposed for
expulsion. Slightly to my surprise, each member was allowed twenty
minutes to address the session and each one of the accused members
did so. A vote was taken at the end of each member's speech, and on all
six occasions, the proposals for expulsion were carried by substantial
majorities.

For the record, the expelled members were Agustin Arroyo of Ecuador,
Zein El-Abdin Ahmed Abdel Gadir of Sudan, Jean-Claude Ganga of the
Republic of Congo, Lamine Keita of Mali, Sergio Santander of Chile,
Charles Mukora of Kenya, and Paul Wallwork of Samoa. Sikhulumi
Sibandze of Swaziland, Bashir Mohamed of Libya, and Pirjo Häggman
of Finland resigned during the investigation. Dutch judo legend Anton
Geesink was warned, and there were ongoing investigations into two
other members, one of whom, Un Yong Kim of South Korea, eventually
fell foul of IOC ethics in 2005 and of Korea law when he was imprisoned
for two years for embezzlement.

Without doubt, the day was the most distasteful I had ever experienced
at a sports meeting. None of the expelled was a close friend, but we
were all colleagues in an organisation that had a philosophy committed
to promoting the best in humanity, so we had no choice but to publicly
disgrace and disown them as firmly and quickly as possible.

The second day of the session moved on to the range of changes
necessary to various IOC processes to give effect to the widespread
demand for change. An instant change was implemented for the choice of
the city to host the 2006 Olympic Winter Games, a decision which would
be taken at the next regular IOC session to be held in Seoul in June. A full
discussion took place to create a new ethics commission and to bring this

into effect at an early date. Further discussions took place on the creation of an IOC reform commission, which was to be called IOC 2000.

The terms of reference of the commission were to propose all the reforms considered appropriate to make improvements to the composition, structure, and organisation of the IOC; the role of the IOC; and the designation of the host of the Olympic Games. Divided among working groups to consider the three major topics, the commission would contain twenty-six athletes, forty-four IOC members, twelve IF presidents, twenty-four NOC presidents, people who had played an important role in organising Olympic Games, and personalities from the fields of diplomacy, politics, business and academics. I was allocated to Group 1 on structure and organisation and at one of the later meetings of the group was intrigued to find that one of the members was Henry Kissinger, the former US secretary of state.

Memorably, towards the end of a long day, Kissinger fell asleep during a discussion on membership and woke up just as I finished what I am sure was an eminently sensible proposal on the optimum number of future members. He leapt into the discussion and, in his famous gravelly voice said, 'I would like to agree with the last speaker!'

The task of the three working groups and the full IOC 2000 commission was to take up most of the year, and the final recommendations and the resulting changes to the Olympic charter were to be agreed at another session in December 1999. The result of all of these efforts was an entirely updated and more modern set of rules for the structure of the IOC and almost all its activities.

The change to membership and further involvement of athletes throughout the IOC and the Olympic movement was one of the more significant elements. The revised membership rules and an expansion to include IF and NOC representation, as well as athletes, together with the decision to discontinue visits to candidate cities were all approved. The whole package brought the IOC an effective, understandable, and transparent method of conducting its affairs. The structure has remained to this day with only minor changes.

One major practical and pressing change was to the selection process for the Olympic Winter Games of 2006, which would be conducted at the 109th session in Seoul in June. The system agreed in the March was, for the 2006 Games only, to create an electoral college who would be appointed after the presentations by the six candidate cities, and which would have the responsibility to nominate only two cities for final decision by the full session. After the trauma of the Salt Lake City crisis, this was seen as a safe and efficient way to proceed. The candidates were all European cities, reflecting the almost routine reality that the Winter Games are restricted to the northern parts of Europe, Asia, and North America.

We received a series of good presentations from Klagenfurt, Zakopane, Helsinki, Sion, Poprad-Tatry, and Turin and then the report from the evaluation commission. On the following morning, we elected the new selection college from eighteen members who had put their names forward. I was not chosen as my lack of experience in winter sports was a drawback. Four hours later, the selection college announced that Sion and Turin would contest the final vote.

Throughout the campaign, Sion and Turin had been the clear favourites, although Helsinki had made a case for using existing facilities in Lillehammer in neighbouring Norway. Sion represented the Valais area, just a few kilometres from Lausanne, and was seen as the best chance of a return of the Winter Games to Switzerland since St Moritz in 1948.

On the evening before the presentations, I had been chatting to a British journalist who believed that the contest was boring, 'As Sion is bound to win'. I told him to watch one of the Turin delegates, Mario Pescante from the Italian NOC, who was working the room in his experienced way. I told my media friend that he should not dismiss Turin lightly. In the event, Turin won the final vote by fifty-three to thirty-six. The scale of the winning margin was a surprise, and rumours abounded that it was caused by the 'Hodler factor'—a reaction to the part played by Swiss member Marc Hodler in exposing the Salt Lake City abuses.

I thought that was excessive, but when news broke of public protests in Lausanne and physical attacks on the IOC headquarters, the media reaction was, if anything, even more aggressive. The IOC had rather missed an opportunity to bring the Games back to its home country.

The slow burn towards a future London bid was subjected to a flare-up and unexpected heat at the end of the year. The Football Association had been overseeing a long-running project to decide on the final home for a new national stadium and had settled on rebuilding the existing site at Wembley in London. The original brief was to construct a stadium suitable for football, rugby league and other sports, specifically athletics, which were pre-conditions of Lottery funding. The BOA's provisional research on a West London Olympic bid would obviously use the new Wembley Stadium as a centrepiece.

The stadium project was intended to provide a suitable venue to allow bids for the World Athletics Championship in 2005, the Football World Cup in 2006, and a future Olympic Games. In a prolonged period of gestation, it became clear that football did not want a permanent athletics track. A lack of communication on that precise issue led to a possible compromise, where the building of a movable platform would reduce seating capacity but also involve high cost and an excessive time for construction and removal. However, this was exactly the solution found successfully in Glasgow's Hampden Park for the 2014 Commonwealth Games.

The FA position was strongly supported by the sports minister, Tony Banks, but he resigned in July 1999 and was replaced by Kate Hoey, a former Northern Ireland high jump champion, whose instincts were very different. Matters came to a head in October when it became very clear that the FA did not want to compromise, and a second architectural option was sought. Even this was unsatisfactory on issues like sightlines, and eventually, the narrow FA view was presented to the government, with the support of Ken Bates, a powerful FA official, on a take it or leave it basis.

To its obvious embarrassment, the government conceded and agreed a return of £40 million of lottery funding, which was to be earmarked for a proposed athletics stadium at Pickets Lock in London. Despite all previous agreements and a sensible case, I knew we could go no further when I received a polite letter dated 24 January 2000 from Tony Blair thanking me for the 'constructive contribution' of the BOA and quoting that, 'the Government remains firm in its Manifesto commitment to support a viable Olympic bid'. It was not a satisfactory, and rather cynical, response.

It was a pleasure to turn all our attention to the preparations for the British team at the Sydney Olympic Games. Our chosen venue for a pre-Games preparation camp was a variety of sites in and around the Gold Coast, south of Brisbane in Queensland. A visit became possible after the Kuala Lumpur Commonwealth Games in 1998. *En route*, I managed to arrange a three-day stopover at a Malaysian resort and, by chance, met Melinda Gainsford-Taylor, Australia's top sprinter, who was recuperating from a knee injury. She convinced me that the combination of good weather and good facilities would make the Gold Coast an ideal home for a visiting British team, along with a polite warning that the Australian team would be very strong at a home Olympic Games.

On arrival in the Gold Coast, we were met by the young woman in charge of sport for the local authority. She was very helpful but, famously, asked the question 'How many of our twenty-three 50-m pools would you like to use?' to which I had to reply, 'I'm sorry I don't know the answer to that question'. It was obvious immediately why Australia performs so well in the swimming pool. All of the 50-m pools had been built at schools.

We selected St Kilda School as the local BOA base and the swimming team used the 50-m pool just outside. We were able to arrange the use of the athletics track at Griffiths University along with a number of its existing indoor facilities. The neighbouring Hinze Dam would provide an ideal situation for excellent training facilities for the rowing team with the opportunity to create a course very similar to actual competition conditions. Over several following visits, Simon Clegg and his team were able to finalise contracts with the university, with a convenient and well-appointed Radisson Resort hotel and, with the government of Queensland and the Gold Coast council, would finance the additional equipment we would need for a proper multi-sport preparation camp.

Around the same time, we had been able to establish our own specific television programme entitled *Insider's Guide to the Olympics*. We asked most of the major sports production companies to bid for the contract, and after a long day of demanding interviews, awarded this to Brian Venner and his VTV Company. The programme was designed to allow the BOA to give prominence to Olympic athletes and in many cases to outstanding sportsmen and women from minority sports. I sold the programme to the BBC for its *Grandstand* programme on a Saturday afternoon, which attracted audiences of several million viewers.

We were able to arrange with the BBC that special reports would be made available for the programme from sports that were training in the Gold Coast. Unsurprisingly, these special reports tended to show pictures of sunshine, beaches, and happy young people. One morning, this resulted in an unexpected telephone call into my business office in Glasgow from an individual with a strong Australian accent. The caller turned out to be Peter Beattie who was the premier of Queensland. He apologised for the delay in thanking me, but he had just seen one of our special reports from the Gold Coast. He was very impressed and remarked that 'I can't buy advertising like this'.

Clearly our arrangements with the Queensland authorities had been successful as they used it as a model to develop the business of hosting sporting teams. Our experience of developing and using the Gold Coast camp meant that for the Games themselves we could fly the team members into Brisbane from the UK and then use the local airport at Coolangatta (now called the Gold Coast Airport) to fly them into the domestic terminal at Sydney, avoiding much of the international arrival pressures at the Games.

The build-up to the Sydney Games featured an interesting element of sports promotion. BBC television gave a handheld video recorder to each of Steve Redgrave, Matthew Pinsent, James Cracknell, and Tim Foster with instructions on how they might record their many months of preparation for the Games. It was the Games at which Redgrave would be competing in the coxless fours to try and win his fifth consecutive gold medal. Their experiences were edited down to three separate programmes called *Gold Fever*, which became compulsive viewing and presented the four outstanding rowers, but also the Team GB brand, in a very personal and compelling way. Having been overconfident in my medal predictions before the Atlanta Games, I was very careful to try to keep expectations for Sydney at a reasonable level.

Preparations for an Olympic Games, in particular when they are held many thousands of miles away, are always complicated. In August, only a few weeks before departure, the IAAF confirmed a doping penalty on Linford Christie, the former 100-m gold medallist from Barcelona. He was due to be included in the Team GB party as a coach to a team of athletics competitors, but his new penalty would cause his omission due to the BOA by-law that denied selection for anybody committing a doping offence. The problem was enhanced by the presence in the team of several athletes who were members of his particular coaching group, and we did not want to damage any of their prospects.

An elegant solution was found by agreeing that this small group of athletes would be based at a training camp at Couran Cove, in Queensland, run by Ron Clarke, the Australian former distance runner and medallist, from where they would be permitted to train at the Griffiths University track in the Gold Coast. I happened to be at the Gold Coast training camp before the Games on the first day that the athletes came to the track, including the group from Couran Cave. The next arrival was a team of drug-testers from the Australian Drug Agency, closely followed by an ITV television crew. Fortunately, I knew the presenter, Mark Austin, and he made sure that his report was factual rather than sensational.

There was much pressure on the Sydney Games from a range of different directions. The IOC was anxious that the Games would repair some of the damage caused to the movement by the over-commercialisation of the Atlanta Games and help erase the bitter memories of the crisis over the selection of Salt Lake City, which had dominated most of the preceding year. The BOA was also concerned to recover from the poor results in Atlanta and to prove that its expertise in preparing Team GB athletes for the Games would pay off in performances.

Team GB was 310 strong with another 150 coaches and support staff and all had to be transported to Sydney, complete with myriad piles of

Kelvin Hall Arena.

World Invitation Tournament guests.

Towards our own hall.

Joint meeting with WBF officials.

The unification meeting.

Deng Xiaoping.
Rival WBF has Chinese top leader for presentations.

Left: Tom Bacher.

Below: Queen Elizabeth at Thomas Cup finals.

Meeting teams in the Albert Hall.

China's First Thomas Cup.

With Samaranch in Copenhagen.

Li Lingwei and Han Aiping, World's 1983.

Above: With Wan Li,
Great Hall of the People.

Right: The kilted
president.

The great Erland Kops speaks for the athletes.

The new Thomas/Uber Cups, Kuala Lumpur.

Stadium Negara.

The business committee with Richard Avory.

Palasthotel, East Berlin.

The Olympic flag—at last.

Above: With Yoshio Sakarauchi, Japanese foreign minister.

Right: The treasured Samaranch letter.

COMITÉ INTERNATIONAL OLYMPIQUE
CHÂTEAU DE VIDY, 1007 LAUSANNE, SUISSE

CITIUS · ALTIUS · FORTIUS

LE PRÉSIDENT

Mr. C. C. REEDIE,
127 St. Vincent Street,
GLASGOW G2 5JF / Scotland

Lausanne, 13th June 1985
Ref. No. 0702 /85

Re : Badminton

Dear Mr. Reedie,

Thank you very much for your letter of 7th June 1985.

I am convinced that the demonstration of badminton will be a great success at the Games of the XXIVth Olympiad in 1988 and we look forward to welcoming your sport on the Olympic Programme for 1992.

Yours sincerely,

Juan Antonio SAMARANCH

I know that olympic-badminton owes you very, very much

Milo, an unusual sponsor.

Capital Indoor Arena, Beijing.

With Gerry Williams at work in Beijing.

Barcelona's former fish market.

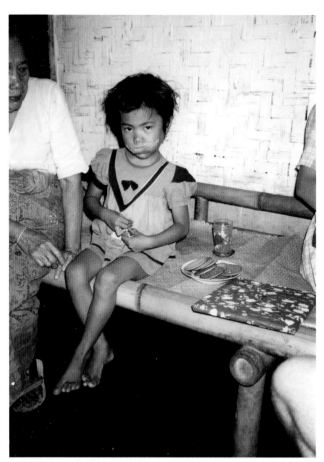

Left: Saripah.

Below: She shows me the village badminton court under a tree.

First Manchester bid.

Manchester's model plan.

No. 10 supporting Manchester.

An unusual start to a birthday party.

The Pavello del Mar—eventually.

Hans Grønfeldt, Danish television producer.

HRH congratulates British winners.

The first ever gold medal point.

 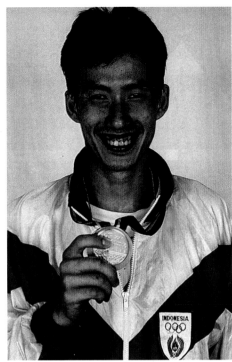

Above left: Susi Susanto.

Above right: Alan Budikusuma.

BBC TV Team, Barcelona.

Above left: Charlie Battle.

Above right: Torvill and Dean.

Bobby Charlton, Manchester ambassador.

BOA House, Lillehammar.

Above: John Major at the IOC.

Below: Paying court to the IOC president.

Florida State Seminoles.

The Brickyard.

Above: With Francesco Rutelli, mayor of Rome.

Right: Gianna Angelopoulos.

Samaranch and Tony Banks at Theodore P. Angelopoulos's garden party at the Old Rectory, Chelsea.

BOA Nagano dinner venue.

Gold Coast Home.

Training at Hinze Dam.

Our selected 50-metre pool.

Mens' Four—Redgrave's fifth gold.

Jonathan Edwards' gold.

With Jacques Chirac in Paris.

Curling gold in Salt Lake City.

Government say 'Yes': 15 May 2003.

Pre-games camp in Cyprus.

Tony Blair and our ambassador in Athens.

Team GB HQ Athens.

Seb and Keith driving the dream—somewhere.

The trial evaluation team.

Above: The evaluation team visits the prime minister at No. 10.

Below: Daly Thomson to charm Nawal el Moutawakel.

Above: BOA centenary dinner.

Left: Greeting our president.

Evaluation team at Wimbledon.

Tony Blair in Singapore.

Rosemary with Cherie Blair.

The BOA presence at the London presentation.

London triumphs: a happy Jacques Rogge.

Work starts on the London Olympic Park.

Birds Nest stadium, Beijing.

© Getty 2008 / Shaun Botterill, 17.08.2008

Distraught British silver medalists.

London bus at closing ceremony.

IOC coordination commission in London.

Huge model of Tokyo.

2009.04.18

With former Prime Minister Mori in Tokyo.

Above: With Pele in Rio.

Below left: Amy Williams' skeleton gold.

Below right: First torch run in Vancouver.

Left: Wedding of Prince Albert in Monaco.

Below: The London board model the volunteer jackets.

Above: The London stadium.

Below: Cocom, one year to go.

Above: In Olympia for the lighting of the torch.

Below left: With my torch in St Andrews.

Below right: Last visit with Seb to the finished stadium.

Above: President Jacques Rogge arrives.

Below: Opening Ceremony: England's green and pleasant land.

Left: Chris Hoy with the Team GB flag.

Below: Equestrian at Greenwich.

Above: Andy Murray.

Below left: With Chris Hoy.

Below right: Gold for Jess Ennis on Super Saturday.

Closing Ceremony: the Spice Girls on their London taxis.

Renewing friendship with Noriko Takagi (Nakayama) in Tokyo.

Alfredo di Stefano, Hon. president of Real Madrid.

Queen Sofia of Spain.

Tokyo wins: a happy Prime Minister Shinzo Abbe.

The WADA booth at Olympic Games.

equipment and teams of horses. No effort had been spared and the pre-games camp had worked well. From a very personal point of view, I remembered all the efforts to present the second Manchester bid, which lost to Sydney in Monte Carlo in 1993, and gave me a good reason to wish the Australian organisers well.

At the opening ceremony of the Games, 199 NOCs were ready to take part in 300 events in twenty-eight sports. Of note was the presence of a unified team from both South and North Korea and the inclusion of wheelchair racing in the athletics programme. The increase in the interest in and the scale of the Games could be measured by a total of 195,000 accreditations, compared with 140,000 in Barcelona. The ceremony was colourful and stressed the reconciliation with the original inhabitants of the continent.

The evening was spoiled for the IOC and its members when it became known that Bibis Samaranch, the elegant and popular wife of President Samaranch, was seriously ill in hospital in Barcelona and that immediately, after the ceremony, he had returned to Spain. Sadly, his arrival was just a few hours too late as Bibis had died before he could reach her. He returned to Sydney four days later, and along with many others, I attended a special church service in her memory.

We entertained Chris Smith (the culture secretary) and Kate Hoey (the sports minister) as our principal guests. Several sports wished to complete their preparations up on the Gold Coast, and we managed to arrange with the BBC that its feed would be installed in the Radisson Resort so that British athletes could see the Games via the same pictures as all their friends and families at home, rather than the Australian view from its domestic broadcasters.

Swimming is the first of the major sports in the Games' programme, and both the USA and Australia won an abundance of medals. British success began in the velodrome. I was about to entertain Rodney Walker, chairman of UK Sport, and his wife, to dinner when Simon Clegg, *chef de mission*, called me to tell me that Jason Queally had just broken the Olympic record in the kilometre event but there were four more athletes to compete, and he did not think he would win a medal. Just as we drew up at the restaurant, Simon phoned back with the news that Jason had won the gold.

Rodney was responsible for the distribution of lottery money to athletes, and I said to him, 'I am relieved at that!' He replied in his deep Yorkshire twang: 'You're effin relieved!' We were off and running. Triple-jumper Jonathan Edwards, still up on the Gold Coast, told me later that Jason's win was the best thing that could have happened to enthuse those athletes still training for their events.

The first Saturday of the Games began with rowing and the much-heralded entry of the men in the coxless fours after their very public exposure. The obvious delight in Steve Redgrave's amazing fifth consecutive gold medal proved to be inspirational for the whole team. If proof were needed, the British women's quadruple skulls then won the first ever Olympic rowing medal by a British women's crew. The crew featured Katherine Grainger in her first Olympics—the start of an amazing career. To put the icing on the rowing cake, the men's eight then won our second gold of the regatta, beating the home crew from Australia. Rowing's customary delivery of Olympic medals was maintained.

Although you might be able to find different sailing conditions, if you were an Olympic sailor, I imagine that it would be difficult to find a better backdrop for your competition than Sydney Harbour with its legendary bridge and Opera House, one of the truly great buildings in the world.

At the invitation of Paul Henderson, president of International Sailing, I had spent quite a long time on his official boat on the first day of sailing, with no wind and diminishing hope that the event would ever start. Conditions improved and British sailors then delivered three gold and two silver medals.

At an Olympic Games, members of the IOC are invited to make medal presentations, which, while very different from actually winning them, still bring great personal pleasure. On the evening of the first of the sailing ceremonies, I was out in the main stadium waiting for Paula Radcliffe to compete in the 10,000 metres, when I took a call from the IOC. The caller asked if I could possibly make it to the sailing ceremony to present medals, 'as Britain has done very well!'

It involved a dash back to the hotel to smarten up and then a rush through the crowds to the place for the ceremony—the steps of the Opera House, in floodlight, with an orchestra and a crowd of many thousands of people. It was a uniquely wonderful venue. The first three medal ceremonies involved British success with gold medals for Ian Percy and Shirley Robertson and silver for Ian Walker and Mark Covell. Shirley and I remain friends to this day. To follow in the second ceremony, we had Ben Ainslie, who became possibly the best sailor in the world, and Ian Barker and Simon Hiscocks. Sailing was our top sport in Sydney.

We knew from our colleagues in the BBC and from our own communications department that success was very popular at home in Britain. The BBC's sports rights portfolio was weak at the time, and it was delighted to be able to show British medal success, and lots of other Olympic moments in its many hours of coverage. The flow of medals continued in badminton, canoeing, equestrian, judo, and shooting, with Richard Faulds gold medal in the double-trap event.

The athletics team then appeared for the second week, both fresh and rested, and delivered much success in the huge Olympic stadium. Denise Lewis won gold in the heptathlon and Jonathan Edwards followed his 1995 world record in triple jump (18.29 m, which still stands) with a gold medal to follow his silver in Atlanta. He was my second medal presentation and when we met in the call room before the ceremony, he telephoned his two sons in Newcastle and I heard him say, 'What do you mean you are playing a football video game about England in Euro 2000, your father has just won a gold medal!'

Jonathan was to play a major role as a director of London 2012, and we are still golfing friends. Medals in athletics get huge attention, and silver medals for Darren Campbell and Steve Backley, followed by bronze medals for Kelly Holmes and Katherine Merry, which earned much credit for UK Athletics, were won on the great Australian night when Aussie heroine, Cathy Freeman, in her iconic green and gold 'swift suit' replete with hood, won the women's 400 metres. Needless to say, the sports-mad Australian crowd went nuts.

The good news followed all the way to the last day, when Steph Cook and Kate Allenby won gold and bronze in the first ever women's modern pentathlon. Then, in the final bout in the boxing tournament, Audley Harrison won gold in the super-heavyweight division—a suitable and popular reward for his enthusiastic membership of Team GB. The final tally was eleven gold, ten silver, and seven bronze in a massive improvement from Atlanta. The media response was encouraging, and we returned home to celebrate our tenth place in the unofficial medal table.

As soon as we arrived home, we resumed our research for a future Games bid. After being allowed much time off as a member of the GB hockey team in Sydney, David Luckes continued his detailed background work, spurred by the fact that the IOC decision on the host for the 2012 Olympic Games would be taken in just five years' time.

19

Rocky Road to London

The reaction to Team GB's success in Sydney was a little mixed, but mainly complimentary. One article by Michael Parkinson claimed that medals were won 'in spite of the system and not because of it', which allowed me to respond with, 'the system is worth its weight in gold'. The long-awaited lottery funding of national governing bodies and athletes themselves, when combined with the private investment from the BOA and especially the success of the Gold Coast preparation camp, resulted in wonderful results much enjoyed by the British public.

Another letter from the prime minister dated 3 October contained the words 'outstanding achievement' and was headed 'Dear Craig'. We must have done something right. After being re-elected again for four years, it was clear to me that a London bid would have to be much higher up the BOA agenda.

Over the previous years, we had become players in the bidding debate but never quite at the centre of discussions as required by the IOC. However, much work had been done, extensively but discreetly. Three years before the Sydney Games in early 1997, we had employed David Luckes, an Olympian from the sport of hockey, initially for a three-month period to examine the technical requirements of a possible London bid, for the next theoretical possibility: the 2004 Games.

Wisely in my view, no pressure to bid had emerged for 2004 as we needed more time to bring the structure and delivery of elite sport in Britain to a much-improved level. However, the initial work done by David exposed just how valuable this work would be in our thinking and the requirements that we would need to present at a future date.

This date could be 2001 for the Games of 2008. David's contract was extended.

Over the previous few years, the BOA had been a supporter of the decision to build a national stadium to include sports like football, rugby league, and athletics. The decision to re-build the existing Wembley Stadium, with its 1948 Olympic history, ensured that our original planning should be based on Wembley as the main stadium. The village would be the next challenge and early thinking centred on Northolt Airport or land at Southall Gasworks. Finding potential sites for twenty-six sports is a very difficult exercise as, inevitably, their creation would involve serious funding challenges. The necessary partnership with local and national government was obvious but only a theoretical exercise.

London itself was changing. The Greater London Council (GLC) had been abolished in 1986 and replaced with power in thirty-two London borough councils. The new Labour government legislated for the Greater London Authority (GLA) in 1999, and this was fully established on 3 July 2000. Ken Livingstone was elected, as an independent candidate, to the position of the first elected mayor in March that year. Ken was passionate about East London, and it was clear that a West London Games was not a political fit. The decision to remove athletics from the Wembley plans served to reinforce the position that we should look east, not west.

The new focus became sharper when opportunities emerged with buildings like ExCel and the Millennium Dome. We also identified a large area of land in the Hackney area that was badly in need of redevelopment and the political will to deliver it. David Luckes took me to look at the whole area on a wet and grey afternoon. As we stood next to the abandoned Hackney Wick Greyhound Stadium on Hackney Marshes and stared at the bleak and run-down vista, complete with evocative places like Fish Island and Pudding Mill Lane, we agreed that one needed a vivid imagination to envisage just how a massive Olympic development might be achieved.

The need for such an ingenious development was to be reinforced by the decision taken by the government, ultimately finalised in October 2001, to abandon the plans to construct a National Athletics Centre at Pickets Lock in north London to host the 2005 World Athletics Championship. By withdrawing from the athletics' commitment, the British reputation for hosting major events was further damaged. The original plans would have delivered a stadium for 43,000 spectators at a cost of £87 million, with £40 million returned by the Football Association after the disagreement over Wembley. To walk away from a decision to host the world championships of the biggest Olympic sport did not go down well in Olympic circles.

A further complication, with adverse publicity on sports events bidding, arose from the disappointing outcome of the Football Association bid for the 2006 World Cup. The underlying problem appeared to be the existence of a private agreement and guarantee given by the English FA chairman to his counterpart in Germany that if Germany supported England in its bid for the 1996 European Championships, England would then support Germany in its bid for the World Cup.

As matters progressed, the English FA decided to mount its own bid for the World Cup but by doing so caused much irritation in UEFA (the governing body of European football) and lost its support. I had met the UEFA president, Lennart Johansson, at a dinner in Stockholm and he confirmed that the agreement had been reached and subsequently broken, with further political problems. The English FA bid received only minor support and was eliminated in the second round of voting. The resulting publicity only added to media scepticism about British sporting bids.

In this troubled atmosphere, David Luckes continued his research into the possibility of fitting a main stadium, athletes' village, and other major sport venues into what would eventually become the London Olympic Park. He also examined how other sports could fit into existing London venues. When added to the West London research, the resulting document reached 395 pages and became the BOA's starting position in the many discussions that were to follow. We had always understood that any successful bid would involve the cooperation and support of both London and the government, and we were able to arrange a meeting to present our thoughts to the new mayor.

The BOA team was led by Simon Clegg and David Luckes, and the London party was led by Ken Livingstone and, interestingly, included Glenda Jackson, an Oscar-winning actress who had moved to a political career in both Westminster and thereafter in London City Hall. Simon was told to avoid PowerPoint presentations, which caused a few problems in reducing 395 pages to an effective level. After only a short presentation, Ken interrupted and said:

> I have no interest in sport, and care about it even less, but if you want to run London for the Olympic Games you will have my complete and absolute support and you will never have to come back and ask me for anything twice.

He was not interested in our West London option and would only support the eastern option as this would give him the opportunity to redevelop the most deprived part of 'his' capital city, at someone else's cost. Ken Livingstone was to become a crucial supporter and player in everything else that was achieved. We were hugely encouraged. Ken is and was not everyone's cup of tea, but to have a canny politician like him as an ally was invaluable.

During this convoluted domestic scenario, I had made my first visits to Athens as a member of the IOC coordination commission for the 2004 Games. Originally, the commission was under the chairmanship of Jacques Rogge and then, after his election as IOC president, of Denis Oswald. I had known Denis for many years from GAISF days when he was the young secretary of the International Rowing Association. An Olympian and a Swiss lawyer, he was to become a successful member of the IOC and, eventually, president of his own sport's international federation.

My appointment to the coordination commission was a form of promotion but it also provided much insight into the day-to-day work of an organising committee. Athens won the right to host the 2004 Games in 1997, but its preparations had started badly with political influences preventing progress for much of its first three years. This led President Samaranch to warn the organisers about the lack of progress and alert them with a 'yellow card'—a stark warning that clearly suggested that any further delays would be a 'red', and the withdrawal of the right to host the Games.

Dynamic Greek businesswoman Gianna Angelopoulos, who had been an inspiring leader of the Athens' bid, was persuaded to return as the new president of the organising committee and the efforts to complete seven years' work in the remaining four years began in earnest. The lessons were clear. Supportive governments were essential for a successful Olympic bid, but the delivery of the Games should not be their responsibility. Not only that, it was vital that politicians played a role, but at arm's length, as enablers, not as meddlers.

During February and March 2001, I was made a member of the IOC evaluation commission for the bids for the 2008 Olympic Games. This appointment was particularly helpful in planning for any future British involvement. The IOC had changed its own regulations so that the bidding process had two distinct parts. No less than ten cities had expressed interest in hosting the 2008 Games and answered the original questionnaire supplied by the IOC. At that stage, the cities of Bangkok, Cairo, Havana, Kuala Lumpur, and Seville were not shortlisted, so the cities of Beijing, Toronto, Paris, Istanbul, and Osaka proceeded to the second round.

Having seen the results of the original questionnaire, a small evaluation commission then travelled to the cities. We visited Beijing first and found a well-organised bid committee, although a visit to Beijing in the middle of a Chinese winter did not show the city in its best possible light. The weather was grey and the air polluted, but the plans submitted showed the construction of a range of new sports facilities which would be a major legacy as well as an excellent base for hosting the Games.

We travelled on from Beijing to Osaka and found a modern and organised city with ambitions to use the hosting of the Games for legacy projects. To my surprise, I was invited to join Shun Ichiro Okano, one of the Japanese IOC members, for a private meeting that he had arranged in a local Japanese bar. In true Japanese style, the meeting consisted of the opening of and consumption of a good bottle of Scotch whisky, until Okano revealed the point of the meeting.

He explained that the Japanese Olympic Committee, having nominated Osaka, was having second thoughts as it was nervous about running Osaka against Beijing. However, at the commission meeting the following day, the Osaka team presented a financial plan that appeared to include very large structural costs in its Olympic Games budget. We questioned this financial presentation, but Osaka was determined to support its original estimates. This was a significant problem for the bid.

Our next city visit was to Toronto, a vibrant city beside Lake Ontario with an attractive waterfront. The very first presentation made to us came from the city mayor, Mal Lastman. He was small of stature, probably only 5 feet 6 inches tall, and almost disappeared behind a lectern that was roughly the same height. To our enormous amusement, he opened his remarks with the words, 'I have been told to be short'. The technical side of the bid was attractive and strongly featured the SkyDome, a baseball venue that had the world's first retractable roof and contained its own hotel.

The commission became involved in an incident after its final meeting when the lift, containing 90 per cent of its membership, got stuck on its final downward journey. The cramped inhabitants survived an hour of claustrophobic discomfort until they were released. Apparently, the commission meeting had not been planned for and the lift engineer had gone home—one more note for the future.

The final visits were to Istanbul and Paris. In Istanbul, we found a sprawling but fascinating city, with a questionnaire that appeared to be the weakest of the five final candidates. In particular, although it was clear that the city would become an attractive candidate for the future, there were weaknesses in the general infrastructure necessary for a successful bid. We travelled on from Istanbul to Paris and arrived, conveniently, just seven days after Bertrand Delanoe had been elected mayor of the city.

To celebrate the occasion, Monsieur Delanoë invited the commission to lunch in the Hotel de Ville the following morning, where we enjoyed good food and a selection of accompanying wines from an outstanding wine cellar. If the selection process was to be an eating and drinking contest, Paris was the clear favourite.

The Paris organising committee was well-organised and showed the commission the Stade de France and other existing sports venues. One difficulty arose when the French sports minister, committed communist Madame Marie-George Buffet, insisted that if the Games were to be held in Paris, the anti-doping rules would be the existing French rules and not the IOC rules. This apparent difficulty took two days to resolve and avoided what could have been a major issue.

The commission held its final meeting to complete its report in Lausanne, and the report was submitted to the executive board and finally to all the IOC members. During the final discussions, there was a debate about whether the report should include any reference to the issue of human rights in China. I argued that since there had been much media comment on this potential problem for a Beijing bid, the evaluation commission report should mention that human rights had been considered, otherwise the report could be criticised for such an omission. The wording I supported was contained in the first page of the final report. The commission recommended the bids from Beijing, Paris, and Toronto at a higher level than those from Istanbul and Osaka.

The 112th session of the IOC was held in Moscow in 2001 and dealt with two major items on its agenda—the host city of the 2008 Games and the election of a new president of the IOC to replace Juan Antonio Samaranch. The city presentations included prime ministers, senior political representatives, mayors, distinguished athletes, NOC officials, and IOC members. Assurances were given on the use of the IOC anti-doping rules and comments on transport and pollution issues.

The Toronto delegation dealt with unfortunate remarks containing racial slurs attributed to the mayor of Toronto prior to a visit to Kenya. His comments were the last thing a hardworking organising committee needed. His extraordinarily crass and offensive words were reported by *The Guardian*:

The loud-mouthed mayor of Toronto may have cost Canada's largest city the chance to host the 2008 summer Olympic Games with an ill-timed and racist remark about his fear of going to Africa in case of 'natives' boiling him in a pot. 'Why the hell would I want to go to a place like Mombasa?' Mayor Mel Lastman said to a freelance journalist before leaving for a trip to Kenya to pitch the Toronto Olympic bid. 'I just see myself in a pot of boiling water with all these natives dancing around me'.

Needless to say, his humorous remark about his stature at the start of his Toronto presentation suddenly took on an entirely different meaning.

In the first round of voting, Osaka was eliminated with only six votes, and in the second round, Beijing attracted fifty-six votes to win the right to host the 2008 Games. Toronto won twenty-two votes, Paris eighteen, and Istanbul nine. It seemed clear that with the 2004 Games to be held in Athens, there would be little support for another European Games.

I had been asked by the British government whether London should bid for 2008 and offered the advice that this could only be justified by the theory that more than one bid would be necessary to win the Games and that the costs would be considerable. I was also on record as saying that the only city that London could not beat was Beijing, a comment that was not particularly popular in London but very well-received in Beijing. The capital city of the biggest country in the world, with a population of over 20 million people and total political and government support, would have been formidable competition. The final vindication of that position by Beijing's emphatic victory brought certainty to the timing of a future London bid. The relatively disappointing result from the efforts of Paris was also noted with interest.

As part of the rule changes from the IOC 2000 commission, the term of an IOC president would be for a period of eight years, with a period of possible re-election of a further four years. This extended period of service had the effect of encouraging five members to submit their names as successors to Samaranch. The members had a choice between Anita de Frantz of America, Un Yong Kim of South Korea, Richard Pound of Canada, Jacques Rogge of Belgium, and Pal Schmitt of Hungary.

Kim had been forced to respond to an inquiry from the IOC ethics commission over an element in his manifesto proposing an annual subsidy to members of $50,000—a controversial idea that met with little favour among the members. The general view was that the choice lay between Rogge and Pound with much speculation on whether Samaranch favoured a particular candidate. In the first round of voting, Anita de Frantz was eliminated, and in the second round, there was a winner, but his identity was delayed until we all moved to the Column Hall of Moscow's House of Unions, the same venue for the announcement of Samaranch's election in 1980.

Rogge had polled fifty-nine votes, Kim twenty-three, Pound twenty-two, and Schmitt six. Rogge had been the favourite, but the surprise was that Kim had beaten Pound into third place. Pound was crestfallen, and there was little doubt that his track record as chair of several high-profile *ad hoc* committees, in which he had done much of Samaranch's 'dirty work', had counted against him. Similarly, his formidable intellect and tendency to speak forcefully had led many members to see him as a threat. For Britain, Rogge's election meant we would now have to deal with a rugby-playing former Olympic sailor, but one with noticeable anglophile tendencies.

Jacques' campaign and likely success in becoming the new president of the IOC brought to mind a private meeting held with Italian IOC member, Mario Pescante, during the Sydney Games in 2000. We discussed the possible implications for the European Olympic Committees (EOC) if Jacques was to be successful in his presidency bid. The end result of our discussions was that if Jacques won the IOC, Mario Pescante would stand for the presidency of the EOC, and I would stand as the EOC vice president.

We thought that a new EOC secretary general could come from a central European country. In an attempt to back-up those theories, I decided to stand for election to the IOC executive board at the Moscow session. There were two seats available, one for four years and one for a very limited period of under a year, but with the option of re-election. Lambis Nikolaou of Greece was awarded the first seat in recognition of the Athens Games, and I stood for the second seat against Tony Khoury of Libya, who won a close but slightly unusual election by fifty-four votes to fifty-one.

When Tony stood for re-election six months later, in February 2002 at the session in Salt Lake City I did not put my name forward. Some months after his election in Moscow, I took a call from Jacques, who asked me if I would be happy to stay as an ordinary member of the EOC executive, rather than a vice president as he was under great pressure from Russia to make a space available for a Russian candidate. I agreed immediately and Alexander Kozlovsky, a member of the Russian Olympic Committee, became the EOC vice president. I have sometimes wondered what might have been my different career path if those elections had been fallen in my favour. However, that is only of minor academic interest as I left the EOC soon after when the London bid was successful.

The terrorist attacks on the United States on 11 September 2001 changed the world of sport as dramatically as it changed everything else. In Olympic terms, it raised huge question marks over the security plans for the 2002 Olympic Winter Games in Salt Lake City, which had a knock-on effect on all the participating NOCs. We had arranged a pre-Games training camp in Calgary, host of the 1988 Games. Team GB was forty-nine strong in a total of 2,399 athletes from seventy-eight NOCs competing in seventy-eight events.

With added security in place, the Salt Lake opening ceremony was memorable for many reasons. They included the wonderfully poignant moment when the Mormon Tabernacle Choir sang the national anthem as a tattered Stars and Stripes, recovered from the from the rubble of the World Trade Centre, was delivered by New York City firefighters so that eight American athletes could carry it into the stadium. The Games were opened by President Bush while standing in the middle of the US team. Despite the fallout from the bidding scandal and its effect on the organising committee, the Games were a great success.

From a British point of view, Salt Lake was one of our most successful Winter Games for a number of years. Skeleton returned to the bobsleigh programme, and Alex Coomber won a bronze medal, the first of a series of British successes in the discipline, which was to be a feature of future Winter Games. Both curling teams were competitive, but the men's results faded at the end of the round-robin series. The women reversed that process and won through to the semi-final where they beat the Canadian world champions.

Curling was staged at the Ice Sheet in Ogden, around 60 miles from Salt Lake City. We were aware of increasing interest at home for the final, and the BBC asked me if I could approach Manolo Romero, the man in charge of international television, to see if an additional transmission circuit for the BBC could be provided.

Manolo agreed on grounds that this may well help increase the potential audience. The final, against the Swiss team, built to the perfect climax. With her last stone in the final end, Rhona Martin, the British skip, won the gold medal to the great delight of her team—Debbie Knox, Janice Rankin, and Fiona MacDonald. At breakfast in the IOC hotel the following morning, Manolo Romero stopped to chat as I was getting viewing figures from Martin Hopkins of the BBC. At midnight in Britain, over 50 per cent of viewers were watching the women's team, a figure which delighted the nation and the helpful television officials in the USA.

There was further cause for celebration on the last day of competition in the alpine skiing events. Alain Baxter from Aviemore in Scotland performed well in difficult conditions but was well outside the medals when he crossed the finish line. A succession of athletes then fell or skied out and, with rising excitement, we watched Alain win Britain's first ever alpine ski medal—bronze—at an Olympic Games. This result produced the best team performance for sixty-six years and good news for the BOA exactly when we needed it.

I travelled home on Monday 26 February after an unacceptably slow exit from Salt Lake City and helped welcome the Scottish curling heroines on the 28th. On the evening of 1 March, around 7 p.m., the phone rang. A voice said, 'Good evening, Craig. This is Jacques.' I knew instantly that we had a problem as the drug test on Alain Baxter was the only one outstanding from Team GB.

The news that he had tested positive for an amphetamine was a complete shock as we had been very careful to emphasise to all team members the dangers in taking any substance, no matter how apparently innocuous. I called Simon Clegg and we agreed a plan of action. Simon found Alain in a bar in Aviemore in the middle of his celebration. We arranged that he left for London on the first available method of transport.

In London, he was debriefed by Michael Beloff, a leading barrister, and we arranged that Alain leave for Norway to spend time with a friend until we could plan a course of action. This worked well for around two weeks until a call came from the Dundee *Courier* asking us to comment on a story they were about to run regarding a positive test from Alain Baxter. Apparently, a family member had spoken out of turn and the news broke.

We had discovered that Alain had been suffering from a minor nose infection and used a standard British Vicks inhaler. When in the USA, his inhaler had run out and he had found what he thought was an exact replacement that looked identical to his old one and began to use it. Had he read the very small print on the back of the inhaler, he would have seen that the US version contained amphetamine. The British one did not.

There was much media sympathy for him, and we decided to make every reasonable effort to explain to the IOC the detailed circumstances of his case. I came under media pressure as a conflict of interest existed between my role as a member of the board of the World Anti-Doping Agency and my position as chairman of the British NOC. I explained that I was conscious of this potential conflict but argued that I could support my athlete in such special circumstances, and this was just about accepted.

We appeared before the initial commission of inquiry which took much time to consider the case but decided that an offence had been committed. We appealed this to the IOC and appeared at a further hearing in Lausanne.

Predictably, the final judgement was that the bronze medal would be withdrawn and returned to the IOC with the sanction to be referred to the International Ski Federation. The FIS decided that a sanction of three months was appropriate, which brought the matter to a close. In essence we managed to save Alain's reputation—he was not a dope cheat—but we could not save his medal.

The second multi-sport event of 2002 was the Commonwealth Games, hosted in Manchester in July. After losing to Sydney in 1993, Manchester applied for the Commonwealth Games and were awarded hosting rights in 1995, its prospectus based on the plans prepared for the Olympic bid. I joined the board of Manchester 2002 and admired the planning to create a main stadium, which would be partly finished for 2002 but then fully developed as a football stadium with Manchester City as a tenant. The University of Manchester would host the games village and the MEN arena, the G-Mex arena, and the National Cycling Centre were all brought into full use.

The chairman of the board was Charles Allen of Granada Television with a membership containing a balance of opinion between the responsible local authority, sport, and the Commonwealth Games officials. The BBC undertook to be host broadcaster and paid for the local rights. Over 9,000 volunteers were engaged and became the stars of the show. Despite all the enthusiasm and hard work invested by Manchester, the financial projections proved to be disappointing, and finance was provided by the government in London at a level to allow the games to proceed.

A combination of Lancashire sunshine; sporting stars Ian Thorpe, Jonathan Edwards, and Paula Radcliffe to name only three; the traditional medal contest between England and Australia; and wall-to-wall coverage by the BBC made the Games a real success. Even a typical Manchester downpour during the closing ceremony did nothing to undermine the view that the successful delivery of the Games helped restore some of the reputation for Britain's ability to organise sport. This was enhanced greatly by some well-considered comments from Jacques Rogge, the IOC president, who had been an interested spectator.

It was inevitable that the reaction in Manchester would be to suggest that it should be chosen as the city for any future Olympic bid. I had developed a warm feeling for the city over many years but had to overcome that as I was firmly of the view that the next British bid should be based on London. *The Times* produced the most significant quotation:

Britain owes the city and particularly its workers a debt of thanks for restoring this country's prestige by presenting a competition with style and efficiency. After the debacles of Wembley and Pickett's Lock and the failure to stage the 2005 World Athletics Championships, these Games were important for international prestige. Manchester demonstrated how the birthplace of so many sports can successfully put on a multi-event competition such as this.

The Commonwealth Games Federation was delighted. Several IOC members who visited the Gamers were all impressed, and very significantly, the prime minister and some of his government were impressed.

Tessa Jowell became culture secretary in 2001 and, in that position, became involved with sport along with her sports minister, Richard Caborn. She was first exposed to the problems of bidding for major events through the Picketts Lock experience. However, she added sporting interest to her large portfolio, and she became the senior politician in government who would have responsibility for a London bid. Greatly to her advantage was a close friendship and total political support of the prime minister, Tony Blair.

The 395 pages of the Luckes report had been with government for the best part of a year, and eventually, it decided to seek independent advice. Arup and Partners won a contract to prepare an analysis of the underlying costs for a London Games and an executive summary of its report became public at the beginning of November; a flurry of media speculation followed.

It was clear that the chosen site would be in East London where a new Olympic village could be built close to the new main stadium and the new aquatics centre. It was an ideal configuration to place the village as close as possible to the main venues in order to restrict travel times for the athletes in the biggest sports. The full Arup report was encouraging and estimated that the costs would be close to the figures known from the Sydney Games.

We knew that discussions in government were progressing and made efforts to present the case from the BOA as fully as possible. David Welch, sports editor of *The Daily Telegraph*, decided to run a very public campaign in support of the bid, which picked up media traction and provided us with an ideal vehicle to promote the concept.

We received public support from a variety of sources: Michael Knight, the Sydney sports minister; Gianna Angelopoulos, as she confirmed her progress for the upcoming Athens games; and Dick Pound and Alex Gilady from the IOC. A full meeting of all thirty-five Olympic national governing bodies met and formally endorsed the bid. One very significant result from *The Telegraph* campaign was a poll indicating that 75 per cent of the public favoured the bid.

On the government side, Tessa Jowell visited Barcelona with David Luckes to look at the benefits to the city from the 1992 Games. Richard Caborn visited Athens and Sydney on similar missions. However, there was no unanimity within the government with distinct reservations over the finances as set out in the Arup report. The government commissioned a further in-house review and revealed a serious underestimate of the costs, reinforcing the original scepticism held by the Treasury.

Both the BOA and the government had to appear before a meeting of the select committee from the department of culture, media and sport in early January 2003, and Tessa Jowell then had to lead a debate in the House of Commons, both on the benefits, or otherwise, of an Olympic bid. Gerald Kaufman, chairman of the select committee, said that a bid would be 'madness'. He was a long-term critic.

At the same time, the need to have an agreed commitment from both the government and London led to an understanding that additional finance would be made available from London via an increase in council tax and further funding from the National Lottery. We hoped that a final decision would be announced, but this was further delayed as Blair and his government were fully engaged with decisions on the Iraq War. In those most serious of circumstances, we simply had to sit and wait. Under the new IOC system of presenting the response to an initial questionnaire, we were very conscious of a real timing problem.

Potential dates for a final decision in February and March 2003 passed as Britain's involvement in Iraq dominated all political discussion. After all the efforts, we were beginning to think that the enthusiasm within the government from January might be waning.

On 14 May, I was due to travel to Riga in Latvia for an EOC executive meeting but was asked if I could cancel and meet with officials at the department of culture, media and sport in London. It turned out to be a long evening as discussions with officials were followed by a meeting with Richard Caborn and, finally, a long session with Tessa Jowell. She confirmed the information that the London bid was on the agenda for the meeting of the cabinet the next day, but that as the agenda was long, she was not certain that it would be discussed.

Ominously, because of the Whitsunday break, the next Cabinet meeting after that would not take place for another three weeks. This further potential delay was a real problem, as we may not have had sufficient time to establish a proper bid committee to prepare the necessary information required by the IOC initial questionnaire, which had to be in Lausanne by 31 December.

I told Tessa that if the potential delay actually happened, we would have to cancel the whole project due to lack of time, so we were in her hands to ensure a decision the following day. We then discussed my request that if the decision was favourable, the prime minister should call Jacques Rogge, who was attending a separate sports meeting in Madrid. When I asked if she had the correct contact number, she confirmed that she had, and I guessed that even she was nervous about the timing issue.

On the following morning, Simon Clegg and I sat waiting in the BOA office in Wandsworth and eventually, around 11.45, Jacques called in delight. 'Congratulations,' he said, 'that is marvellous news. Now we have all the great cities involved in the race for 2012!' His initial reaction was accurate. The final five cities—London, Madrid, Moscow, New York, and Paris—went through to the second candidature phase to become the best bidding race in Olympic history.

We completed the hasty arrangements for an afternoon press conference in City Hall with Tessa and Ken Livingstone. This long-running campaign proved to have been the most complicated element. The future was set precisely by the IOC with the dates: 31 December 2003, the date for submission of the initial questionnaire; 15 May 2004, the date for the selection of the candidate cities; 5 July 2005, the date of the final IOC decision; and hopefully, July 2012, when the London Olympic Games would open. We had much to do.

20

More Bumps in the Road

Having finally created the partnership we needed—government, London, and BOA—we were faced with two realities. The first was that, inevitably, we would become the junior partner. The second was that, despite almost ten years of effort since the second unsuccessful Manchester bid in 1993, we were starting a very difficult campaign with some good original research, but nothing else. We had much goodwill, but no bid committee, no offices, no staff, and no money. One example of the goodwill had been, at his request, a meeting with Patrick Carter, chairman of Sport England.

We met for lunch at the East India Club, my London home and, as we had never met, made polite introductions. He asked, 'What kind of meeting would you like to have?' I replied, 'Well, it was your invitation, so it's your choice.' He said he preferred a cards on the table meeting, which was fine with me. 'Are you sure about a London Olympic bid?' he asked. 'If you are, I have around £75 million of lottery money to invest in facilities. In the possible chance that I might agree, what would be your first request?' I replied, 'I want the national sailing centre at Weymouth'. 'Done!' he said. In two seconds, we agreed the new centre for our most successful sport at the Sydney Games. It took another two years to complete all the necessary building plans and bureaucracy, but the decision was hugely encouraging—who said there is no such thing as a free lunch?

The reactions to the government commitment to get behind the bid produced a wide range of views. Many were supportive, not least *The Daily Telegraph*, which had run its own helpful campaign; others questioned our ability to pull together the necessary combination of people and finance, and many told us what we should and should not do. Several made comparisons with other likely bidding cities and issued warnings about how difficult it would be to maintain the alliances we had just created.

Inevitably, a long list of names of who should be considered as leaders of the bid emerged. The government appointed headhunters to produce lists of appropriate personalities, which were assumed to contain some of the great and good of British industry. The occasional unlikely name appeared, but it was never realistic that Cherie Blair or the young Prince William would have applied.

I had my own view that someone with business experience and, perhaps, political connections would be ideal and had researched the name of Lord Simon, a previous chief executive and chairman of BP and a former government minister. He had undertaken a major fundraising role for Cambridge University, which rather added to his attraction. However, as far as I know, he was never approached.

When the shortlist was produced for consideration by the three partners, the following names appeared—Charles Allen of Manchester Commonwealth Games fame; Sir Christopher Meyer, our former ambassador to the USA; Gerry Robinson, businessman and chairman of the Arts Council; Kevin Roberts from the advertising world; and Barbara Cassani, the American entrepreneur who had established the airline Go.

Each of the three partners were to interview the candidates, which for me was a demanding exercise. I met Sir Christopher Meyer in London. He was a multi-linguist with a wife adding several other languages, but he had just taken on the leadership of the press complaints commission and could not spare the time. A telephone call to Gerry Robinson confirmed that he really wanted more time to return to his homeland in Ireland, and Charles Allen was in the middle of a Granada takeover campaign. I interviewed Kevin Roberts over breakfast in his London hotel, but his busy commitments and travel between Auckland, London, and New York would limit his available time. I also interviewed Barbara Cassani and renewed a short friendship from lunch in New York at a fundraiser in our embassy for the BOA before the Atlanta Games.

Barbara, born and bred in the USA, had lived in London for many years. She had been appointed by British Airways to set up the budget airline Go and given £25 million as seed capital. The airline started operating in 1998 and made profits by 2000. She led the management buyout of the company in 2001 and became its first chief executive until the business was sold to EasyJet, a move she strongly opposed. I was aware that with her successful business career, she was supported by Ken Livingstone, who had experience of the appointment of the American Bob Kiley to a senior position in London Underground. Barbara was an enthusiast of equestrian sport and had the great advantage that she could start the following day. She was confirmed as chairman of the bid on 18 June 2003. To introduce her to the complexities of the IOC, I invited her and Guy, her husband, to come north to our home in Bridge of Weir, where a pleasant evening ensued.

By this time, we had an office. A few days after the press conference on 15 May, we were offered, rent free, one half of the fiftieth floor of No. 1 Canada Square in Canary Wharf. This was a large open-floor area with some small glass offices at each end. Situated in East London, it seemed a perfect situation. I said yes almost immediately and asked for a chair, desk, telephone, and computer link as a young man called David Luckes would be knocking on the door the following morning. The financial deal seemed perfect but less so when I was later informed that the service charges would be £80,000 *per annum*.

Barbara's first Olympic involvement came the following month when she joined me at the 115th IOC session in Prague—an ideal opportunity for her to meet and talk to voting members and to observe the decision on host city of the 2010 Olympic Winter Games. Her presence as the American woman appointed to run the London bid made her a celebrated attendee, and there was much media interest as she was introduced to as many members as possible in the coffee and lunch breaks. As a further introduction to the bidding duties, we also spent some time with the group of British journalists covering the session, who were treated with respect.

One particular meeting was five minutes with Samaranch, by then the former IOC president, who, based on his vast experience, offered the extremely helpful advice of a very wise old Olympic owl:

> Many people are very important: the international federations are very important; the national Olympic committees are very important; the mass media are very important ... but only the IOC members vote!

The session dealt with its normal agenda and received good reports on strong and marketing and TV revenues. The main interest, however, was the selection of the city to host the 2010 Olympic Winter Games—a contest involving Vancouver, Salzburg, and Pyeongchang, a relatively small winter sports resort in Korea. The rumours in advance of the meeting were that Vancouver and Salzburg seemed to be stronger candidates, but the presentation from Pyeongchang, highlighting the opportunity to ease tensions between South and North Korea, made a real impact.

There was an underlying feeling that most European votes might go to Vancouver as this would be likely to prevent a future bid from Toronto for the 2012 Summer Games in which there was great interest in London and several other European cities. In the first round of voting, Salzburg was eliminated, and a second round, held with the details made public only after the announcement ceremony, declared Vancouver to be the winner.

The voting details were sensational. In the first round, Salzburg was eliminated with sixteen votes, but Pyeongchang led with fifty-one—only three short of the necessary majority, with Vancouver on forty votes. In the second round, Vancouver won with fifty-six votes to Pyeongchang's fifty-three, a result only one vote above the necessary majority of fifty-five. The performance of Pyeongchang, with a combination of excellent technical preparations and strong political support, had made an impression.

There was one other election during the session that appeared to have some effect on the final host city selection. Un Yong Kim of Korea stood as a vice president of the IOC and was elected. After the Vancouver decision was announced, there was much debate and concern among Korean officials and journalists that the success of Kim had some effect on the disappointment of Pyeongchang. This public debate was to count heavily against Kim in future years. Barbara Cassani watched the whole process with interest, and her visit to Prague was an ideal introduction to the Olympic bidding process and, in some ways, to the vagaries of Olympic politics.

Our next Olympic date was much more conventional. Barbara and I joined Jacques Rogge, president of the IOC, along with politicians Ken Livingstone and Tessa Jowell, Olympic rowing champion Matthew Pinsent, and Phil Craven, president of the International Paralympic Committee and a new IOC member, in a visit to number 10 Downing Street for a meeting with the prime minister, Tony Blair. Jacques had been able to attend the finals of the Wimbledon Championships and took the opportunity of visiting London, where he expressed his excitement over London becoming a bidding city. In his short meeting with the media, Jacques made clear that his preferences in the merits of any bidding city were the provisions for athletes and the need for excellent security. His comments were not unhelpful as we began to prepare the details of the London proposals.

Given Barbara's business connections, it was no surprise that she brought with her to the start-up London bid several of her former colleagues from the airline. One of these, Jane Willacy, had previously worked for Keith Mills and gave his name to Barbara, and subsequently to London and the government, as an ideal candidate for the position of chief executive. I interviewed Keith in a headhunter's office in London for over two and a half hours. His sporting interest was sailing, and he had been very successful in the business of rewards cards, having invented the air miles programme for British Airways and subsequently the Nectar cards programme. I found him to be everything anybody would want in a chief executive, and he joined the team on 26 September. He was to become one of the absolutely key players in everything that followed.

Original funding for the bid came from both the Greater London Authority and the department of culture, media and sport, with subsequent funding to be raised from commercial sponsorship. We also recruited former Olympic gold medallist in rowing and renowned sports physiologist Professor Roger Jackson from Canada to add to the technical expertise of David Luckes and Charlie Wijeratna, who would lead on commercial matters. The bid team grew over the following months with a concentration on preparing the initial questionnaire required by the IOC, which would be the basis of its final selection of candidate cities.

Nine cities had indicated their intention and London was joined by Paris, Madrid, New York, Moscow, Leipzig, Rio de Janeiro, Istanbul, and Havana. The questionnaire required answers to questions under headings like accommodation, finance, general infrastructure, village, security, sports venues, and transport. With such a strong list of initial applicants and the range of questions to be answered, there was much work to be done.

With the bid offices in Canary Wharf in London, I was relatively uninvolved for the first time in the previous ten years. The BOA was in touch with developments, but apart from the presence of David Luckes, we were not preparing the document to be sent to the IOC. Every now and again, I would take a telephone call regarding the speed of progress or the occasional disagreement but, in general, preparation of the questionnaire was proceeding at a pace which would allow delivery before the final date. Everything seemed to be in order.

Perhaps inevitably, the sense of well-being brought by making progress was interrupted in late December by a letter from the IOC suggesting that Prime Minister Tony Blair may have broken the bidding regulations. He had been lobbying for London during a meeting of the Commonwealth heads of government in Nigeria. His comments were made at a sports breakfast in the country's capital, Abuja, which dealt specifically with the successful Commonwealth Games in Manchester and the effect it had had on his own feelings about sport and his encouragement of a subsequent London bid.

I contacted the relevant IOC official and, in a formal letter, suggested that the prime minister had simply been expressing his passion for sport and how he was very enthusiastic about the Games coming to his home country. At the same time, Downing Street released its own similar statement. Both were accepted by the IOC, but the incident, and the publicity which it encouraged, were a clear illustration of the need to ensure that the promotion of London should be restricted until its selection as a candidate city and carefully planned thereafter.

For the previous three years, I had added to my BOA and IOC responsibilities with my appointment as a board member of the World Anti-Doping Agency (WADA), which had been formed following the first world conference on doping in sport. I had attended its first board meeting on 10 November 1999 with twenty-five other representatives from the IOC, IFs, NOCs, national governments, and representatives of Olympic athletes. The expectations of the different groups were very diverse and often very, so much so, that it was obvious that it would take time to discuss and resolve them before WADA became a practical proposition. I had agreed to take on the chairmanship of the finance and administration sub-committee and Suvi Lundén, Finland's minister of culture, had arranged that one of her staff, Harri Syväsalmi, would serve as chief executive.

We were to be funded for the first two years by the IOC and, in practice, operated from Lausanne with meetings in the Olympic Headquarters. It was agreed that WADA should be independent from the IOC and that it needed separate office premises, especially as its CEO would move to Lausanne. With some local help, I found a small suite of offices at Avenue du Tribunal-Fédéral with five rooms—rather more than our instant needs. To save our limited funds, I arranged a sub-lease to a new company called Olympic Games Knowledge Services, formed by Craig McLatchey, a former secretary of the Australian NOC. It was the most modest of beginnings.

WADA's future agenda included demands for action on a whole range of requirements—out of competition testing (we were close to the Sydney Games), an athlete's passport, results management, and multiple meetings with IFs—all before we had completed the organisation and strategy of a brand-new body. In almost every case, the progress demanded was delivered as we created sub-committees to deal with ethics and education, medical health and research, standards, and harmonisation, legal, finance, and general administration; all were developed with new staff by an effective executive committee.

It was clear that the continued use of the Olympic movement's anti-doping code should be replaced by a new and more extensive world anti-doping code, together with a full and improved list of prohibited substances, the creation of accredited laboratories, and more investment in research.

We grew out of our modest Lausanne offices very quickly, and in 2001, as our new headquarters city, we selected Montreal, beating Bonn, Stockholm, Vienna, and (to their irritation) Lausanne. Governments also decided the detailed breakdown of the commitment they had made to meet 50 per cent of the WADA budget. This was a remarkable breakthrough, but one which was to raise almost constant arguments over a budget process which did not suit the preferred five-year projections systems much beloved by governments.

The second World Conference on Doping was held in Copenhagen in 2003 and the first world anti-doping code was approved. Among many changes was a clause that introduced a sanction of two years for serious offences. That was contentious for some IFs—in particular for football and cycling, which preferred their own freedom to set their own sanctions. The debate in Copenhagen was ironic as WADA was almost a direct descendant of the Festina cycling affair in 1998. In cycling it was possible for an athlete to be banned in Denmark, but free to compete in France. Similarly, a sanction for an offence in one IF could extend to three months whereas in another sport, for the same offence, the sanction could be a lifetime ban. The harmonisation of sanctions was a crucial in the acceptance of the new code.

Governments were pleased with the results of the conference and many of them signed the Copenhagen declaration, indicating their acceptance of the decisions taken. Unfortunately, that simple process was not sufficient for several governments, which had to transfer the decisions taken to their own legislatures and into their own legislation. They needed a more formal vehicle to allow them to do this, and the suggestion was made to seek a UNESCO convention. Work was started immediately, and the UNESCO anti-doping convention came into being in February 2007, to become the fastest such convention in history and one that is now ratified by 191 countries.

The requirement to promote the convention and the rest of WADA's work led to the opening of regional offices in Tokyo, Cape Town, and

Montevideo, in addition to Lausanne, where much of the governmental connection and development work was undertaken. All of the above was delivered by WADA under the chairmanship of Dick Pound, the senior IOC member; the necessity to create a truly responsible and independent international organisation had begun.

In the meantime, the London bid's answers to the IOC's initial questionnaire had been completed and the document submitted within the time limit of 31 December 2003. It then became essential that the promotion of the bid should then begin in earnest, leaving the biggest part of the bid team to concentrate on further developing the underlying technical arrangements. I was confident that from the results of the initial questionnaire, London would be successful in moving to candidate city status, but part of the progress of the bid would involve retaining or even increasing public support.

Our new communications director, Mike Lee, had undertaken the arrangements for a formal presentation of the bid on 16 January 2004, which was held at the Royal Opera House. Speeches would be made by Barbara Cassani, Ken Livingstone, and—most importantly—Prime Minister Tony Blair. He delivered a very passionate speech in favour of a London Games, which did much to deliver government support and sent out the public message that we had hoped for.

BBC television helped with video presentations and interviews with many famous British Olympic athletes. One of these, and perhaps the most enthusiastic, was given by Seb Coe, who had agreed to become first a bid ambassador and then the bid vice president. The evening was a great success, and our communications team made sure that it was well publicised, including in Madrid and Paris, which were about to have their own bid announcements.

In mid-February, a big black cloud appeared on the horizon. I was warned by Giselle Davies, the communications director of the IOC, that she had become aware of a possible *Panorama* programme based on undercover reporters, posing as businessmen from London approaching IOC members in Eastern Europe and offering to purchase votes for London. The memories of the Salt Lake City scandal were still fresh in IOC minds, and there was little doubt that if the rumour was proved to be true, it would be very embarrassing for London and the bid.

I questioned the reality of the rumours and got confirmation that the *Panorama* investigative team was considering just such a programme. As a first attempt to prevent the programme, I spoke privately to Russian IOC member Vitaly Smirnov, one of the most senior members of the IOC, and sought his advice on the best way to proceed. He told me that he had not personally been approached but had heard the rumours, thanked me for giving him the information, and suggested that I should speak to all of our colleagues in Eastern Europe to warn them of the possible approaches that might be made to them. This had to be done discreetly and it took some time to ensure that the necessary conversations were both clear and confidential. Advice to me from the IOC was that if members could be warned of the dangers and therefore not speak to any investigative journalist, then the programme would have difficulty in finding people to confirm its accusations.

Over the next several weeks, I made a succession of telephone calls and was left with the clear impression that my efforts might just have been successful. The rumours stopped and no further information came from any member of the IOC.

On 17 May, in Lausanne, the IOC presented the results of its expert study of the initial questionnaires submitted by all nine of the interested cities for the 2012 Olympic Games. The rankings were based on eleven different categories for the organisation of the games with different weightings applied to them. London received the top score of ten for accommodation, which also had a high weighting. However, the report was critical of infrastructure, transport facilities, a lack of sports venues, and inexperience in holding major events. It also questioned finance and our legacy strategy, as well as posing questions over public support.

The IOC had awarded scores to each city on the eleven categories, producing a total average score. Paris was given 8.5, Madrid 8.3, London 7.6, New York 7.5, and Moscow 6.5. The remaining cities, Leipzig, Istanbul, Havana, and Rio de Janeiro were not supported as future candidate cities. My personal reaction was one of satisfaction to have 'Made the cut' but also that Rio had not; I had seen it as a troublesome outsider.

The more considered reaction from the London bid team and its supporters was both enthusiastic and realistic. The timing of the initial questionnaire had not allowed the bid team to fully develop the venue strategy and the resulting legacy provision. They were also perfectly clear that much work needed to be done on infrastructure and in particular on how improvements could be brought to the problems of transport throughout a busy city like London.

There was considerable satisfaction that London had moved to the status of candidate city as this would allow the use of the Olympic rings in any future promotional material, and thus the potential for enhanced marketing and financial support. While accepting that the decision had placed us in third place, the IOC report had at least made very explicit the areas in which we should concentrate our efforts. That evening, the London team headed to a special celebration set up by the River Thames, close to the London Eye, at which our new logo with the Olympic rings would be revealed.

Around 500 people had accepted invitations to join what was a happy celebration in warm evening sunshine. Barbara Cassani had stayed in Lausanne to allow additional time to speak to the media after the IOC meeting and was the last to arrive. She received a warm welcome and made a happy and gracious speech that was very well received. Some weeks before, Barbara had let it be known to a very small group of people, of which I was one, that she had decided that she was not the sort of person who would be able to take the bid all the way through to decision day in Singapore. During Barbara's speech, I happened to be standing beside Tessa Jowell and leant down to whisper in her ear, 'This may not go down well next Monday'. Tessa replied, 'Shut up'.

In particular, Barbara was not comfortable with the inevitable requirement to travel and promote the bid to the constituency of around 100 members of the IOC. Her skills had been to organise the start-up of the bid and to bring it to the stage where London was accepted as a candidate city. It had been agreed that any announcement about Barbara should be deferred until after the IOC report, when it was hoped that London would move into the second round of the process. In the discreet discussions that had been taking place, I had been aware of the occasional moment of tension over the last year as the technical bid was developed. Also, with the benefit of the experience of being with Barbara in Prague at the IOC session, it was clear to me that she was an uncertain lobbyist.

In the discussions about her replacement, Keith Mills had been involved in the initial conversations with Barbara and did much to manage the process. One of the obvious candidates to replace Barbara was Seb Coe, who had been involved with the bid as a vice president but without any day-to-day responsibility. Discussions had to take place with the government as they were the principal funders of the whole process, and the ultimate decision would certainly need political support. Fortunately, Tessa Jowell was firmly of the view that Seb Coe would be the best option. I took a telephone call from Tessa while at our holiday home in St Andrews during which I asked if any consideration had been given to promote Keith Mills who had provided stability and organisation ever since he was appointed.

I first met Seb Coe many years before when he was fronting the unsuccessful attempt to produce a London bid for the 1993 decision, which went to Manchester, and had followed his outstanding athletic career and his subsequent political career. We met infrequently but always enjoyed our discussions and had become friends. He had many skills and was well-known in Olympic circles. After open and helpful discussions, a unanimous view emerged that Seb should take the position of chairman, but in recognition of his abilities, additional responsibility should be given to Keith, who would become 'president international'.

A press conference was arranged at the DCMS offices for the following Monday. Barbara made a short speech indicating clearly why she believed a change in leadership was required and spoke warmly about the time she had spent with the bid and her efforts to create a team that had been able to get London declared a candidate city. I had the opportunity to speak with Seb before the conference, and he gave a compelling account of his own reaction to becoming chairman and how he would commit to the bid, its organisation, and its promotion for the benefit of London and Olympic sport.

There were relatively few questions, other than to ask just how it had been possible to keep this change of leadership quiet for several days. Media reaction was modest, although a small number of people working in the bid expressed disappointment that Barbara had decided to resign as chairman. She agreed to continue her involvement with the bid but on a much-restricted basis.

After the press conference, Seb and I walked across the road to the hotel and shared a late afternoon beer. He asked what his first bid action should be, and I suggested that he should instantly travel to Barcelona to meet Juan Antonio Samaranch, past president of the IOC and a declared Coe admirer, or at least announce that he would do just that. The purpose was to put Seb instantly in the correct position as far as influence with the IOC was concerned.

The next big sporting event that would allow for major promotion of the bid was the Athens Olympic Games. In addition to the bid involvement, at the BOA, I oversaw all the preparations being made for Team GB. There had been concerns over many years about the readiness of the city, which had led to a complete change in the leadership of the organising committee.

The impressive businesswoman Gianna Angelopoulos had assumed responsibility for the Games after political interference had led her to step down after leading the Athens bid. However, she experienced frequent delays in building facilities and delivering the promised legacy. She also had to face growing concerns about security as preparations for the Games extended over the crisis of the Iraq War. All of the issues had been at the front of great concern to the IOC coordination commission, which I attended as a member. Witnessing the way in which those challenges were addressed and dealt with was a great help to BOA's Athens planning.

A contract with Helios Airways greatly assisted the BOA pre-Games training camp established at Pathos in Cyprus, where our hotel partners had constructed a nine-lane 50-m pool for the swimming team. It also created some subsidiary accommodation available to the distance runners above the golf course at Aphrodite Hills. During a prior site visit, I had been invited to open the new swimming pool, along with Bill Sweetenham, our new national swimming coach from Australia.

It was to be a simple ceremony to unveil a discreet plaque placed at the entrance to the pool. To everybody's surprise, a delegation, including a priest from the Greek Orthodox Church, arrived to bless the pool. The senior religious official, formally dressed, held a small bouquet of twigs from an olive tree and a large bowl of water, from an unknown source. His blessing took around twenty minutes in the heat of a very warm day.

Eventually, he reached the significant moment and dipped his olive branch twigs in the water, withdrew them, and threw the collected water straight over the lens of the adjacent BBC camera. The resulting short but sharp expletive provided an unusual climax to the ceremony. The subsequent unveiling of the plaque took around thirty-five seconds.

The Athens Games were to be very different from any previous Games I had attended. On arrival at Athens airport, Rosemary and I were asked to wait for some time until 'our police protection group' arrived. I had no prior knowledge of any such arrangement but was told that special arrangements had been made for the chairmen/presidents of the British and USA national Olympic committees due to perceived threats arising from the Iraq War.

I explained that having no fewer than five policemen involved in travel around Athens, and the sporting venues would make life impossible when trying to run an NOC team. It was explained that these arrangements had been negotiated between the Greek government and the British ambassador, and I was asked to try to make them work, otherwise they might be reviewed. As matters progressed, we found that having protection from five local policemen who became good friends was very helpful. They were all from the vice squad, who, I am happy to report, guarded us, without incident of any kind, including steering us away from traffic hazards and chance encounters with ladies of the night.

Before the opening ceremony, I had to attend the annual IOC session. We had become aware that, despite several months of efforts earlier in the year, the BBC would, after all, be transmitting a *Panorama* programme showing so-called 'businessmen' from London approaching members of the IOC posing as 'agents' to purchase votes for London in its campaign to host the 2012 Olympic Games.

The programme was, in many ways, less damaging than we had feared. However, it did feature an interview with Ivan Slavkov, a member of the IOC from Bulgaria, who was recorded as saying that he would be able to assist the businessmen from London. To my intense annoyance, I realised that I must have missed Slavkov in my series of telephone calls warning my IOC colleagues of the intended programme.

The existence of the programme and its broadcast created a major problem in the eyes of the IOC constituency. I agreed with President Jacques Rogge that the programme would not be shown at the IOC session unless specifically requested by members. Just such a request was made by Spanish IOC member, Juan Antonio Samaranch, son of the previous president, whose request could only be interpreted as being linked to the rival 2012 bid from Madrid. The programme was shown in a private viewing room before the second day of the session, and a large number of the members were in attendance.

I had called Seb Coe in London and suggested that he should get down to Athens at the earliest possible opportunity. We had little time to speak to members after their viewing of the programme as they made their way to the session room, but in an attempt to be seen to be taking a strong reaction, I composed a letter of complaint to Mark Thompson, the director general of the BBC. It was an effort to explain our position to the members of the IOC, most of whom believed that as the BBC was the national broadcaster in Britain and had recently purchased television rights to show the Games, they could not believe that it would then deliberately transmit the *Panorama* programme. However, this was not the time to explain the system of royal charters and independent investigative journalism underlying the BBC.

The letter to the BBC was only marginally helpful, and I was criticised in Britain for writing it. The mood in the London camp was low. Incidentally, the ethics commission of the IOC subsequently reported that Slavkov's actions were contrary to the ethical principles of the IOC and recommended his expulsion, which was carried out at the session in Singapore.

That afternoon, totally unexpectedly, a report became public that Konstantinos Kenteris and Ekaterini Thanou, two Greek sprinters holding gold and silver medals from the Sydney Games and who were strong favourites to deliver Greek success in their home Games, had missed a drug test in very confusing circumstances. It was a sensational announcement and produced a reaction similar to the Ben Johnson situation in Korea in 1988. To our amazement and delight, the issue of the *Panorama* programme all but disappeared from world media and criticism from IOC members in Athens. After the session finished, Seb and I enjoyed a quiet beer and yet another huge sigh of relief.

21

Driving the Dream

The much-troubled Athens Olympic Games opened on time on 13 August 2004. It was a miracle wrought by a last-gasp building frenzy and not inconsiderable spending. ATHOC (the Games' organising committee) had lost almost all of its first three years of progress and had delivered seven years of work in only the last four years of its existence. Many seasoned Olympic observers who had visited Athens in the weeks prior to the Games returned home convinced that they would not happen, or that if they did, the athletes and spectators would have to deal with half-finished venues and piles of builders' rubble. In fact, everything was ready, and the city and the venues looked wonderful—a potential Greek tragedy had become an Athenian triumph.

In the May before the Games, the IOC coordination commission was very concerned. The plans for the main stadium involved a new roof designed by the Spanish architect Santiago Calatrava, which was a substantial engineering project as the large structure had to be lifted into place. At our last meeting before the Games, we all went out to see the structure move—and it did, about 2 metres. The planned roof over the main swimming pool would not, after all, be installed, and during our meeting, we heard a presentation from the gentleman in charge of the general secretariat of sports with responsibility for delivery of all venues. At one stage, the translator said, 'What is this word "Overlay"? We do not have a word in Greek for Overlay'. This turned out to be a large budget item that had yet to be decided.

Nevertheless, it is greatly to the credit of the Greek organisers that by the time of the opening ceremony, all the venues were ready and the main structural changes to the city—new roads, airport, and 'Proastiakos Athens', the Athens Suburban Railway—were all operational. In fact, Proastiakos opened just two weeks before the opening ceremony.

The Games welcomed 10,625 athletes from 201 NOCs competing in 301 events in twenty-eight sports. This was an increase in athlete numbers of over 600 from the Sydney Games. There was a real feeling of history as these were the first official Games in Greece since the inaugural Games of the modern era in 1896. Strictly speaking, there was a 'second' Games in Athens in 1906, the 'Intercalated' Games, which did much to boost the faltering growth of the Games. Although regarded as 'Olympic' at the time, the IOC no longer recognises them as such.

The 2004 opening ceremony was a splendid occasion marked by a memorable display of Greek culture and history with outstanding music and lighting. Team GB athletes, fresh from their pre-Games training camp in Cyprus, entered the ceremony much later than normal as the first initials of each team were those from the Greek alphabet, rather than the more usual Latin alphabet. This confusion caused our distinguished rower Matthew Pinsent, who was waiting outside the arena, to text Demetra Koutsoukos, his Greek fiancée (now wife), asking, 'How many letters are actually in your alphabet?'

Again, somewhat unusually, some of the British athletes had taken part in the torch relay when the Greek organisers decided to take the torch to previous Olympic cities around the world. The torch was in London on the middle Saturday of the Wimbledon Tennis Championships and was to start its journey from the Centre Court, with the first torchbearer to be Sir Roger Bannister. Roger, in accepting the role, had asked two questions: 'Would you mind if I did not run as I have just had a hip replacement; and do I have to wear the pyjamas?' I replied that it would be fine if he only walked round the court and that, for him only, 'pyjamas', by which he meant the runners' standard uniform, would not be required.

Unfortunately, the day produced heavy rain and the first torch was lit from the royal box by Sir Roger, before Tim Henman carried it around the Wimbledon grounds. He then passed it to Virginia Wade and many other celebrated athletes and personalities on a 30-mile route into Central London. When Sir Steve Redgrave completed the London leg of the international relay by running along the Mall to light a temporary cauldron, he made a very prescient remark—'unbelievable. It was ten deep, all the way along—absolutely amazing. If we get the chance to do it again in 2012 this country will not know what's hit it!'

Team GB numbered 264 athletes, plus their support staff, taking part in twenty-one of the twenty-eight sports. The benefits from pre-Games training in Mediterranean heat, and some humidity, paid dividends as medals were won in eleven different sports. The final medal tally was nine gold, nine silver, and twelve bronze to finish tenth in the medal table, but hopes for the future lay in the number of fourth places—thirteen in all. All British successes were enthusiastically received by a large contingent of British supporters who had travelled to Athens and helped to enhance the atmosphere. The BOA ticket and tour agency was much busier than for Atlanta or Sydney.

One new visitor to the Games was Tim Phillips, chairman of the All-England Club at Wimbledon. He was accredited by the International Tennis Federation and arrived to join his tennis colleagues for the Olympic tennis event. Unfortunately, British Airways lost his luggage, which must have been particularly irritating as he used to be the airline's regional general manager, Europe. We helped him out with a series of polo shirts from the Team GB store and included him in our small van along with our, by then, friendly police bodyguards.

For three days, on every occasion we visited what were for him new sports, Britain won a medal. So we were very reluctant to lose his company when his suitcase eventually appeared and the tennis event started. The subsequent decision of his committee at Wimbledon to allow a London Games tennis event to be held on its legendary grass courts was of huge benefit to the London bid.

Our sailors repeated their successes from Sydney when Ben Ainslie won his second finn gold medal and Shirley Robertson, then competing in the yngling class with Sarah Webb and Sarah Ayton (the 'Three Blondes in a Boat'), won her second successive gold medal. A few days later, at the first of the sailing medal ceremonies, Jacques Rogge made a special effort to come to the Agios Kosmas Sailing Centre to present Ben's medal. Ben asked me why Rogge had done that and was delighted to hear that Jacques had also been an Olympic Finn sailor.

In the Olympic velodrome, the names of Hoy and Wiggins made their first of many appearances in the medal rankings by winning the 1,000-m time trial and the 4,000-m individual pursuit, respectively. In the Markopoulo Equestrian Centre, the three-day event was dominated by British athletes, with Leslie Law winning individual gold, Pippa Funnell winning the individual bronze, and the British team winning the silver medal in the team event.

At the Schinias Olympic Rowing and Canoeing Centre, the spectators were treated to one of the closest races in the history of the rowing. In the men's coxless fours, the British team of Steve Williams, James Cracknell, Ed Coode, and Matthew Pinsent won the gold medal by 0.06 seconds from their Canadian opponents. The crowd had to wait almost thirty minutes for the official result. The victory reinforced British domination in this event at the Olympic Games. Apart from four golds in succession from London 1908 to Los Angeles 1932, Britain has also won five in a row from Sydney 2000 to Rio 2016.

Later in the regatta in the women's coxless pairs, Katherine Grainger and Cath Bishop won the silver medal. It was the second silver in succession for Katherine, adding to a treasure trove that she would eventually turn into four silvers and a gold before being appointed to the chair of UK Sport. In athletics, in the Spyros Louis main stadium, to the delight of her many supporters and friends, Kelly Holmes won both the 800 and 1,500 metres gold medals in one of the outstanding performances in British athletics history. On the very last day of the athletics event in the 4 × 100-m relay, the British squad of Jason Gardner, Darren Campbell, Marlon Devonish, and Mark Lewis Francis won gold by defeating the seemingly unbeatable United States relay team. The margin of victory was 0.01—the tip of Mark Lewis-Francis' nose; it was certainly the icing on the Team GB cake.

One interesting diversion was the need to present a case at an appeal before the Court of Arbitration for Sport for results at the equestrian team event. In her final leg of the three-day, event competition, the show jumping, Bettina Hoy of Germany missed her starting time and was awarded fourteen time faults, enough to take her out of the medals. She claimed that she had not heard the bell to start her round and the decision was reversed. The British team appealed the result. At the CAS hearing, Sarah Sutcliffe, the BOA lawyer, won an easy decision as Bettina's defence seemed to involve her apologising in tears at her mistake.

The result of the case meant that the medal ceremony, which had not been held in Athens, had to be staged elsewhere. We agreed with the IOC that the ceremony could be held at the Team GB post-Games reception at Buckingham Palace in the presence of her majesty the queen. The ceremony was staged in the palace ballroom before the entire British team, who cheered as medals were presented by the princess royal, the senior IOC member in Britain, silver to Leslie Law, Pippa Funnel, Mary King, and William Fox-Pitt, the three-day event team. Law also won the individual gold and Funnel the bronze. Medals were also awarded to the cycling team pursuit quartet—Steve Cummings, Paul Manning, Rob Hayles, and Bradley Wiggins, who had also overcome a doubtful decision by the International Cycling Federation. After the ceremony, our most distinguished royal host confided that all other investitures she had conducted in that room had been held in almost total silence.

The Athens Games were the first opportunity for the London bid team, now representing a candidate city, to speak with and promote their ideas to members of the IOC. The British ambassador's residence in Athens is a distinguished neoclassical building with, not unlike a classical Roman villa, a large and attractive garden at the side. Conveniently, it was situated within easy distance of the Hilton Hotel, the official IOC hotel. On the night before the opening ceremony, we had been able to arrange a cocktail party in the company of Tony Blair. Obviously, we invited our guests carefully.

The evening turned out to be relaxed and happy and seemed to be enjoyed by all. Different members of the BOA and the London bid team introduced Blair to our IOC guests. My first such introduction helped to create an atmosphere of relaxed enjoyment when I presented him to Dick Pound, my IOC colleague and president of WADA. Dick had a large, appropriately iced gin and tonic in his hand at just the wrong moment. He quickly switched the drink to his other hand and shook the hand of the prime minister with the words, 'I apologise for my very cold hand, but I am a lawyer.' After the trauma of the BBC *Panorama* revelation, this was a very different occasion and served its purpose extremely well.

At the opening ceremony the following evening, the crowds gathered in a warm and evocative atmosphere—this was Athens, the Mediterranean, the cradle of civilisation. Tony Blair appeared to be the most senior politician present and was seated in the front row of the VIP area. Behind and on either side were the seats for the IOC, other guests, and the rest of the Olympic family.

Unusually, there was a moment, roughly ten minutes before the start of the Ceremony, when everybody was seated. I have never been overenthusiastic about pushing myself forward, but in an instant decision, I decided to get up, in full public view, and walk down to the front of the VIP area to greet my prime minister and his wife, Cherie. I know that this simple gesture was seen and understood in the eyes of several of the IOC members, who appreciated its significance; it served to indicate a close relationship between sport and politics in our country, not always a feature of political life in Britain.

As the Games started the following day, Simon Clegg took Blair to the Olympic Village in Parnitha, adjacent to the main Games venues at Marousi, so that he could meet some of the British athletes. It was a newly built development of over 2,300 apartments, which is now home to over

10,000 people. He then paid a visit to the rowing course for the same purpose. The Blairs left Athens encouraged by what they had seen from both the British and Greek points of view.

I picked up on my BOA responsibilities and also with the arrangements that we had put in place to assist the London bid team. In most previous Games, the BOA had concentrated on the provision of an athlete's lounge, rather than hospitality arrangements for guests or sponsors. The athletes lodge for Athens was situated in the prestigious research institute, the British School at Athens. However, not all NOCs can compete with CONI, the Italian NOC, which always creates '*Casa Italia*'—a huge undertaking to provide hospitality for athletes, media, guests, and anyone else who is lucky enough to get in. It is such an elaborate offering that the organisation of the building and its services is put out to tender in Italy.

The London team needed some modestly comparable arrangements, and we had arranged to rent a very attractive house with an equally attractive garden, plus swimming pool, in an exclusive residential area of Athens. The London team arranged two very capable girls as chefs and invited voting members, their spouses and friends, to join them at lunch each day with good food in the sunshine and the opportunity to relax, or even dip into the pool.

IOC duties at Olympic Games can involve long days, with a particular emphasis on events in the evening, during finals at the swimming pool or in the main stadium. The decision to concentrate on lunchtime hospitality turned out to be astute as we attracted many of the people we were most anxious to meet. After they were fed, watered, and completely relaxed, they were invited to join one of the team to look at the models we had prepared of the proposed new Olympic Park in London and a first chance to see the expanded list of London venues. This was carefully arranged and designed to begin the process of answering the criticisms made by the IOC responses to the initial questionnaire. Personally, I was delighted after only ten minutes with Mario Pescante, the Italian NOC president, who said 'Great. I had no idea.' His was exactly the reaction we were looking for.

Our happy house was clearly a success and attracted warm expressions of approval. One of those came from Cherie Blair, who intended to come back to Athens for the second week to watch athletics and asked if it would be possible for her to use the accommodation in the hospitality house. While we did not want to cause any friction with the wife of our prime minister, we were aware that allowing her to make these arrangements would cause distinct security problems, in addition to more traffic around the pleasant residential area.

The solution was found to provide accommodation for Cherie, family, and friends in the embassy, which would provide all the necessary security. Unfortunately, it would also subject her to the attention of Ambassador Simon Gass' small collection of cats. Cherie was not a great feline lover.

The Athens Games were to be my last Games as chairman of the BOA. Having been elected for the first time in 1992, it had been my long-held view that three terms of four years would be quite sufficient. The development of the London bid presented an unexpected issue, and I took discreet advice on whether resignation after the Athens games was wise or not. I spoke at some length to Kevan Gosper, a senior IOC member form Australia, who advised that, if I resigned, two things would happen. The first was that people would say, 'I wonder what Reedie knows that nobody else knows?' and secondly, 'If London loses, you'll get blamed!'

I thought the first of these was, perhaps, arguable, but the second was entirely compelling. I had decided that as the date of the BOA annual general meeting was, traditionally, in October, that I would write to all thirty-five national governing federations in Britain to set out the situation and to say that I would stand for re-election in October 2004 for another term of four years, but if elected, I would resign in October 2005 whether London won the 2012 Games or not. This compromise avoided the inevitable problems for the bid committee and satisfied the NOC as I was subsequently elected unanimously but under those conditions.

The London team worked conscientiously throughout the Games, meeting with IOC members on every possible occasion, almost all of which took place in the official lounges at each sport venue. It was clear that the experience from two weeks of intense effort would require a full debrief so that a proper, considered, and feasible process of dealing with voting members could be prepared. As an opener to what might be possible, I decided to take Robin Mitchell, IOC member from Fiji, to dinner in Athens.

Robin and I had joined the IOC at roughly the same time. He had a wife called Rosemary; I also had a wife called Rosemary. His wife was a general medical practitioner; my wife was also a general medical practitioner. They had family living in Manchester, so if I could not get Robin Mitchell to vote for London, we would obviously be barking up the wrong tree. We chose a good fish restaurant beside the harbour in Piraeus and after good food and a nice bottle of wine, Robin said to me, 'Ok, Here's the deal. If I guarantee to vote for London, will you leave me alone?' They were not all as easy as that.

One final happy memory of Athens involved the traditional habit of an IOC member entertaining their driver and the splendid Olympic family assistant who had both served them so well throughout the Games. On this occasion, the number at dinner was increased by my daughter and son-in-law, who had spent the second week with us, but also our five friendly policemen. We filled a long table at a splendid taverna in Plaka, the 'Neighbourhood of the Gods', a labyrinthine cluster of streets sitting above the city's ancient agora, now a favourite area for bars and restaurants.

The local advice from our policemen included the choice of restaurant, food, and, significantly, wine. I had no idea how many bottles were consumed, but our guests from the local constabulary, who had drunk 90 per cent of them, then kindly drove us home, with the motorbike outrider at the front doing 'wheelies' through the streets of Athens. Fortunately, the rest of us had had enough Greek vino to enjoy the hair-raising ride rather than be terrified by it.

Both the BOA and the London bid team left Athens much encouraged. Results from the Games, placing Team GB in tenth place in the unofficial medal table, was warmly received at home and produced yet more confirmation that the investment by UK Sport of lottery and exchequer money was bearing fruit. Moreover, even after the complications presented before the Games by the BBC *Panorama* programme, the response from IOC members to the potential of a well-organised London bid was equally encouraging. My own position became very clear—I needed to spend almost all my available time on London bid matters as well as IOC responsibilities.

The post-Salt Lake scandal had led to the IOC revising its host city bidding rules, which prevented members from visiting bidding cities, and also set instructions to bidding cities on how they could approach and engage with members. Under those restrictions, the most important opportunities involved attending official meetings of regional associations of NOCs and formal meetings of groups of international federations.

Before we began to do that, the bid committee had to make firm the siting of our sports venues and thereafter establish a transport system and a portfolio of legacies from hosting the Games that would be persuasive to the audiences we would be meeting. The IOC rules were rather less restrictive to members, which allowed me to plan to attend other meetings to which a formal delegation from London might cause eyes to be raised in Lausanne.

As the technical work on planning venues continued, the communications team gave much thought to how we would plan the London presentations to the various assemblies within the Olympic movement. Perhaps due to his recognition of the BOA efforts to take a British team to Moscow in 1980, despite serious government opposition, Seb Coe was always sympathetic to the position of the BOA within the London bid and fully understood our efforts over many years to try to win the Games for Britain.

A broad outline began to appear of how we might arrange the presentations we were to make around the world. It was a format involving the BOA, the bid leadership, and always an athlete. In general, for our foreign meetings of sports people, we did not include any political involvement in presentations—an instinctive position that was to have an ever-increasing effect. So that the video part of the presentations was relevant, we watched with interest the development of the necessary bid book that would go to every voting member, in both English and French.

Most people in Britain knew that the centre of a London Olympic Games would be in East London, but it was important that we explained to the voting members, and to the international media, that the investment in a new Olympic park in that location made sense for all concerned, not least the athletes who would be based in the Olympic village. The plans were to take an area of industrial devastation and completely rebuild it to contain the village, main stadium, swimming complex, cycling velodrome, an indoor hall for a selected indoor sport, a hockey centre, and an international broadcast and media centre.

Very close to the park, we would place gymnastics in the Millennium Dome in North Greenwich, equestrian events in Greenwich Park, four indoor sports in the Excel Centre, and shooting at the Royal Artillery Barracks. In the city centre, we would use Lord's Cricket Ground for archery, Horse Guards Parade for beach volleyball, Hyde Park for triathlon, Earls Court Exhibition Centre for volleyball, Wimbledon for tennis, and the main hotels in Park Lane for Olympic accommodation. To the north-west of London, we had the new Wembley Stadium for football; further to the west, the Eton College Rowing Centre at Dorney Lake, Windsor, and the sailing at Weymouth in Dorset.

The distribution of venues around new and existing sites and by making use of famous landmarks would allow us to focus on London's well-known attractions, while emphasising its status as the world's most cosmopolitan major cities with over 300 communities speaking over 200 languages. Spreading venues also allowed us to highlight the inspired use of the Channel Tunnel rail link to the Olympic Park and the huge improvements in the Underground and other areas of the much-criticised London transport network. The emphasis would be on ease of travel and access for athletes, placing as many of the new facilities in close proximity to the village, but with easy access to events in the centre of the city and to the West End.

The plans were the basis of our presentations around the world and also of our bid book, some 600 pages in English and French, which was delivered to the IOC in November 2004 by Amber Charles, a fourteen-year-old basketball player from East Ham in Newham. The idea of promoting the bid by using young people was at a very preliminary stage, but it would prove to be invaluable. Just as important was the venue layout with as many venues as possible in or close to the Olympic Park—something of vital importance to international federations.

After all the meetings in Athens, we had a reasonably accurate view of the possible voting intentions of the members of the IOC. The problem facing us, and all bid cities, was how to gauge, as the bid progressed, whether any of the improvements made or media exposure of them might increase or decrease a member's opinion and hence their voting intentions. Like all previous organised bids, we created and maintained a record of voting intentions, but to update them, we needed constant sources of information.

Andrew Craig, a Brit based in Detroit and an expert in Olympic marketing programmes, came on board to monitor the lobbying efforts. He was joined by John Boulter, a former Olympic 800-m runner and employee of Adidas. John was based in France and had a wide experience of the Olympic movement, so that he could monitor and report on French-speaking members and countries. To help with Central and South America, we were joined by a former journalist, Carlos Garcia, originally from Uruguay but resident in Canada.

It would have been counterproductive to expect anybody, other than a very senior bid official, to approach and try to persuade any member to be supportive of London. In reality, all the direct contact and lobbying, if that is the correct word, was done by Seb, Keith Mills, or me. However, a regular flow of news, rumour, and opinion could be very valuable, and Andrew, John, and Carlos became regular contributors.

We were informed that whatever information we received should be dealt with in total secrecy. As a consequence, we were instructed on the use of a very secure computer system, designed to keep all such 'useful' information completely secret. Access to the system was based on a device with a changing combination of revolving numbers which proved so complicated that it was hardly ever used. On one occasion when I was able to get access, I found that the quality of the information logged on the system was so poor that it was rendered useless. We then returned to the tried and tested system of speaking to one another, and when either Seb or Keith was able to meet a member, they would call, and I would bring them up to date with as much information as I could.

Our targeted London presentations were taken to the continental meetings of NOCs in Doha, Accra, Dubrovnik, and Brisbane with varied degrees of success. We found that these meetings were not always particularly well-organised, and that sufficient time was not, on occasions, made available to the five bidding cities. The most spectacular occasion was at the meeting of African NOCs in Accra. The organisers got the recommended order of presentations wrong, and after we finished our London performance, an officious chairman announced that he was moving on to the next item on his agenda and did not want to hear from the bid from New York. Michael Bloomberg, the multi-billionaire New York chairman, had flown in specially on his private jet to make the presentation and, to his enormous credit, simply went back to the airport and flew home. While providing information to the individual NOCs was always useful, the main opportunity at those gatherings was to hold individual meetings with the IOC members from that continent.

Inevitably, we would watch the presentations from our rival bidding cities and a whole range of increased intelligence could be obtained by watching their presentations or speaking to people who had viewed them. We also got to know the senior officials from the other bids and to get a feel for any progress they may have made. From the IOC ranking of the initial questionnaires, Paris and Madrid were the obvious competition; media opinion, including much in Britain, placed Paris as favourite.

We noticed that whenever a formal Paris presentation had to be made, Phillipe Baudillon and Armand de Rendinger, the people who were actually running the Paris bid, were replaced by a political figure from the French government or from the city of Paris. On occasions, even the French NOC was not represented. Conversely, our contacts clearly liked the way we structured our presentations involving our NOC, our bid team and our athletes.

As part of these long trips, it was sometimes possible to arrange a short side visit to meet up with a particular member of the IOC. I made such a trip to Manila in the Philippines to visit Francisco Elizalde, whom I had known for many years since joining the IOC. Francisco had an interesting Olympic Games history. He was educated in the United States, but his studies had to be prolonged at the end of the Second World War and his parents offered him a visit to the 1948 London Olympic Games if his school results were satisfactory. The resulting exam success meant that Francisco did indeed visit the 1948 Games.

When I found out that he was coming to London on a private visit well before the London bid, I arranged to meet with him and said I could organise a visit to Henley Royal Regatta or to the Wimbledon Championships. He told me that he had been to Henley in 1948, so if it was alright with me, he would like to go to Wimbledon.

My visit to the Elizalde family in Manila was a delight, and among other attractions, Francisco took me to see two of the most attractive churches in the city. At one, it was possible to climb up behind the end wall of the main part of the church, put your hand through a small hole, and touch the foot of Christ (a large statue behind the high altar). Outside that church, there was a large local market with many stalls selling gifts and mementos. To mark the occasion, I bought a small golden foot that I carried as a good luck charm in my jacket pocket for the next few months.

On a similar visit to Helsinki, I arranged to meet and to stay with Finnish member Peter Tallberg and his wife, Nina. Peter had been the first chairman of the IOC athletes' commission, and we had worked together on different technical commissions for some years. Our intelligence told us that Nina loved London and tried to make at least one shopping trip each year. As Peter opened a second bottle of good red wine, Nina joined the conversation and addressed her husband, 'Now Peter, you know why Craig has come to see us. Let me be clear. If you don't not vote for London and if London doesn't win, don't bother coming home'. Evenings of such conviviality and comments like Nina's were, to say the least, very encouraging.

The early task in February 2005 was to prepare for and welcome the IOC evaluation commission on its visit to London under the chairmanship of Moroccan member Nawal El Moutawakel. Nawal had been the first Arab woman to win an Olympic gold medal—in the 400-m hurdles at Los Angeles in 1984—and, crucially, was a very good friend of Seb. Our preparations were extensive, including inventing a 'trial evaluation commission'.

Having been a member of the IOC evaluation commission before the award of the 2008 Beijing Games, I was asked to chair a group of nine experts, covering all the subject areas dealt with in our bid book. The group would replicate exactly the programme in London of the real evaluation commission, which we did only ten days before the commissioners were due to arrive. We used the same hotel in Canary Wharf, the same presentation room, and the same bus transport; we visited the same sports venues and we received presentations from all the experts on transport, finance, security, legal affairs, and legacy that London was asked to make.

We started badly. Two of our trial evaluation guests came from Australia to help with the technical parts of the bid. When they arrived at Heathrow, we forgot to meet one of them and the other managed to lose his luggage. Clearly, improvement was required.

That the exercise was important became very clear. We found gaps between the travel arrangements and the venue presentations. We tested the timings of the presentations and found they varied. We tried to ask our presenters the types of questions which we thought the IOC would ask. We also found that by using a new traffic management system called 'Greenway'—a method of controlling traffic lights by keeping them 'green'—allowed buses to travel without ever being stopped. In fact, it was so successful that we thought the IOC commission would be unlikely to believe the transport times it produced.

Our last day was timed to finish at lunchtime with a final speech by Seb. As a friendly gesture, we invited everyone who was working in the bid offices to join that last session and to listen to their chairman.

Seb was at his most eloquent best and finished his speech with some real emotion, which encouraged a long ovation. I just sat without comment, until he eventually said, 'Any comments?' I replied, 'Seb, it was magnificent, but it was 19 minutes too long.' My comment was intended to make the London presenters understand that our IOC guests would be working long hours, with many presentations and much writing to do, and many of them would be working in a foreign language.

Ten days later, we did it all again, this time for real. The visit went almost without a hitch. We already knew the commission members and built up a good relationship. IOC rules allow the bidding city to arrange just one evening of entertainment. Our choice was to invite the commission to dinner at Buckingham Palace with her majesty the queen, other members of the royal family, and some senior British politicians. We took the commissioners from their hotel in Canary Wharf to the palace by boat up the Thames, where special lighting had been set up on many of the famous buildings along the route.

With many royals, dignitaries, and status-conscious politicians, the table plan was not easy, but the evening turned out to be a success. The princess royal made the introductions to the commission members, and they all got a copy of a special group photograph as they left the palace. Two of the guests were Australians, Bob Elphinstone and Simon Balderstone. As they opened their envelope and looked at the photograph, Balderstone was heard to say; 'Jeez. How is this going to go down at the next meeting of the Australian Republican Association?'

The only slight hitch we experienced was at the royal suite at Heathrow, which had been made available for the commission's departure to New York. We were not ready for some members to ask if they could go to the duty-free shops. There were none at the royal suite—presumably the royal family has no need of them—but cars were promptly arranged for the short trip to Terminal 4 for a bit of tourist shopping.

BA pulled its New York aircraft to a position right outside the royal suite so that the commissioners could depart through a corridor of cheering children. We then found out that BA had managed to leave an ordinary passenger in a wheelchair back in Terminal 4 and that the stairs up to the re-positioned plane would be a problem. Cool and calm management by a senior BA manager produced a vehicle with a lifting platform, and the problem was solved so that the choreographed departure was only seven minutes late. Somewhat pleased with ourselves and mightily relieved, we all went home for a good night's sleep.

22

Last Push to Singapore

Having survived the evaluation commission visit, we took stock of where we thought we were in the developing race for the Games. Our communications team followed the evaluation visits to the other four cities and tried to understand the reactions in their local media.

In Britain, it was clear that the success of the visit had a real impact on the attitudes of our own media. The efforts made by the bid to sell the London project to the commission and the treatment offered to the sizeable foreign media attendance in London convinced our domestic media that the bid was serious and making substantial progress.

The IOC had also become aware that it had a real contest on its hands, as IOC president, Jacques Rogge, had made a call to bid leaders asking them to treat their competitors with more respect. We asked government agencies and our politicians to use their own opportunities to promote London. Everything was becoming serious.

A presentation to the annual joint meeting of the international federations was arranged and prepared with particular care as the venue, Berlin in April, would also host a meeting of the IOC executive board. After much internal discussion, we prepared to announce a willingness to make special support grants to both IFs and NOCs coming to London to help defray costs of their pre-Games' arrangements and pre-Games training camps if held in Britain. The grants would be of a maximum of $50,000, with the total cost estimated at £15 million.

Despite some initial reluctance on my part, I went along with the suggestion on the grounds that if any support schemes were to emerge, it would be better to be first. I was conscious of the Sydney organisers' offer in 1993 to meet all travelling costs, the late announcement of which made a real difference to their ultimately successful campaign for the 2000 Games. Our announcement of the grants brought a swift reaction from other cities and complaints from them to the IOC which began to seek assurances that the offers were all included in our bid book. As often happens at meetings where there is a large attendance of interested parties, opposition developed quickly, and we decided that the potential damage to the bid had to be removed. The offers were withdrawn.

A purely domestic opportunity for promotion arose on 24 May 2005, the 100th anniversary of the founding of the British Olympic Association. To celebrate the centenary, the BOA had researched and published a book entitled *Chasing Gold: A Unique Collection of Photographs Charting the Achievements of the Men and Women who brought Olympic Glory to Great Britain.*

We arranged a reception for all medallists at Buckingham Palace. We hosted a party for all Olympians. With another 170 guests, we entertained President Jacques Rogge and leading members from the European Olympic Committees and their wives to a centenary dinner in the Banqueting House in Whitehall. In true British style, our guests were entertained by the orchestra of the Scots Guards, a renowned regiment first formed by King Charles I in 1642. Among the gold medallists present were Richard Meade, Jayne Torvill, Christopher Deane, Stephanie Cook, Sarah Webb, Mike McIntyre, and from athletics Seb, David Hemery, Jonathan Edwards, Mary Peters, and Denise Lewis, with a large group of the rowers led by Steve Redgrave and Matthew Pinsent.

The toast list was short but distinguished. The princess royal, as usual very well briefed, set the tone by recording just a few of the significant moments and people from the BOA in its first 100 years. They included the remarkable career of Lord Desborough, our first chairman; the contribution of Philip Noel Baker, who was awarded the Nobel Peace Prize in 1959 for his work on sport and peace; and British support of the Olympic charter, notably in 1980 when a British team competed at the boycotted Games of Moscow.

Of course, it was the Moscow debate which produced the memorable quote from Sir Denis Follows, BOA chairman at the time, 'In our country we prefer to follow Magna Carta, rather than Jimmy Carter'. Jacques Rogge responded to the toast to the IOC with his excellent command of the English language and, equally well briefed, proposed a toast to the BOA to which I had to reply.

I had found it quite difficult to prepare some relevant material for such an auspicious occasion without repeating what had already been said. In such circumstances, statistics can be helpful, and I was able to start by saying:

> In this room this evening there are 37 Olympic Gold Medallists, 51
> Olympians, 72 members of the NOC and sports administrators,
> eight members of the IOC, eight representatives from our sponsoring
> companies, three representatives from our good friends at BBC sport,
> the two senior political figures at the Department of Culture, Media and
> Sport; but only one past winner of the Glasgow Open Men's Doubles
> Badminton Championship.

I tried to make brief mention of our success, and only occasional failure, at the Olympic Games but in the knowledge that we would make a fourth bid to host the Games in only forty-three days' time, and that there were several votes in the audience, I finished:

> If the IOC grant us what would be the perfect birthday present to host
> the Games in London in the Diamond Jubilee Year of our Patron Her
> Majesty the Queen, they would place into our hands the Olympic spirit.
> Mr President, as we have done on two previous occasions, we will guard
> that spirit, we will cherish it and we will proudly hand it on.

As we chatted with friends and colleagues at the end of the evening, Seb came up to me and said, 'That was a marvellous closing phrase. We will use that in Singapore.'

The reports of the IOC evaluation commission were published in June and eagerly read by all five cities. They do not rank cities but provide detailed comments on the answers given by the candidate cities to all seventeen themes presented in their bid books. Close comparison of the answers is vital to allow each IOC member to determine how they might vote in the IOC session.

The London report was encouraging. Under the heading of Olympic Games concept and legacy, the report added:

> Whilst the development of the Olympic Park as part of the Lower
> Lea Valley regeneration is to take place irrespective of the outcome of
> the bid, the Olympic Games would accelerate the process and ensure
> that sport would be the major focus of the project. The location of the
> Olympic village within the Olympic Park (which includes the proposed
> Olympic Stadium) would be very convenient, as 49% of athletes would

be competing in close proximity to the village. Whilst the Olympic Park would undoubtedly leave a strong sporting and environmental legacy for London, the magnitude of the project, including the planned upgrade and expansion of transport infrastructure, would require careful planning to ensure all facilities and rehabilitation projects were completed on time.

Under the heading of Olympic transport, the report stated specifically:

During the bid process substantial London rail transport infrastructure investments have been clearly confirmed, guaranteed and accelerated. Provided that this proposed programme of public transport improvements is fully delivered on schedule before 2012 and the extensive Olympic route network is implemented, the Commission believes that London would be capable of coping with games time traffic and that Olympic and Paralympic transport requirements would be met.

When added to strong comments on accommodation, environment and sustainability, sports experience, and the Paralympic movement, the report did much to answer the questions which were identified as problems by the IOC in its initial questionnaire. Everybody was happy with the result.

Our communications team had also been working to encourage government promotion of the benefits of the bid as there was clear political advantage in well-organised and hopefully successful Olympic bids. The overall political picture among the bids was of some concern and was noted by members of the IOC.

In June 2005, to considerable surprise, the referendum in France to approve the new European Union constitution was lost by a noticeable majority, putting the future of the constitution in doubt. On the other hand, Spain had accepted the change by a large majority. That was not an ideal situation for the Paris bid when there was a good chance that a European city would be elected to host the Games.

On a separate issue, I had enjoyed a long discussion with a respected senior IOC member who insisted that internationally, the Iraq War was seen as US President George's Bush's war, not Tony Blair's war. When added to the evaluation commission report and the political differences in France, I was beginning to think that if Paris was seen as favourite, London could not be far behind. The Singapore session and presentations would be vital.

The London team arrived in Singapore on 28 June and settled into a specially selected hotel, the Beaufort, a lovely resort on Sentosa Island, just south of Singapore. Our early arrival was designed to allow us to finalise and polish the London presentation to be made on 6 July. The team spent five days recovering from the journey and working in great detail under the control of Sara Donaldson, whose company 'Live' was charged with all the creation and editing of the London presentation.

We would rehearse each of the agreed speeches and build into them our specially produced bid film called 'Inspiration', produced by Daryl Goodrich and Caroline Rowland, whose earlier videos for the bid drew critical acclaim. If anybody thought this would be easy, they were proved wrong. On the first morning, when Seb, as sometimes he did, turned up ten minutes after the agreed start time, Sara addressed his error with a few well-chosen, but powerful words. Nobody was late again.

Speeches were timed, and redrafted if necessary, to fit in with the segments of the new video. My own opening remarks in French were rehearsed repeatedly to try to ensure that the accent was perfectly *'Parisienne'* rather than pure Glasgow-Gallic. More like a boot camp than a jolly, to my great disappointment, I was not allowed to hire clubs and play some golf on one of Sentosa's several golf courses, but Rosemary interrupted her sunbathing to play with Jacques Rogge's wife, Anne, much to their mutual enjoyment.

A brave decision had been taken some months before to include in the permitted London delegation of 100 supporters an allocation of thirty places to young people from East London as opposed to the normal count of supporters, politicians, and sponsors. The original idea had come from our Canadian expert, Roger Jackson, and developed into a central theme of the London project. The youngsters in Singapore included Amber Charles, the young girl who had presented the London bid book to the IOC the previous November.

My contribution to the idea was to insist that the presence of the young people should be made very public as part of the London presentation. It was no surprise that the theme of bringing young people into sport would become a powerful tool in persuading voting members to vote in favour of London. Not only would our young people be seated in the presentation room, but they would also be subjects in our video.

We had to design and rehearse the necessary contributions from Tony Blair (on video), Denise Lewis, Ken Livingstone. and Tessa Jowell, all to fit in to the stipulated forty-five-minute time limit from the IOC. I can only remember one real hiccup. Tessa Jowell rewrote her speech when on the plane to Singapore to say what she wanted to say, as opposed to what the bid team wanted her to say, all of which had been carefully planned and collated. There was a period of tension and disagreement, which I carefully avoided, until normal service was resumed.

Fully rehearsed and well rested, the team moved into its downtown hotels. I was delighted to be moved into the legend that is Raffles, the IOC's hotel, to try to 'bump into' as many members as possible and to join up with all my colleagues before the opening of the session. We were invited to a reception hosted by the president of Singapore, S. R. Nathan, to be held at the Presidential Palace.

To my surprise, President Nathan had also invited Prime Minister Tony Blair and his wife to join what was otherwise an exclusively IOC event. Without making the opportunity too obvious, I was able to use the two hours of the reception to introduce Tony Blair to as many members as I could, and at the same time, Rosemary made the same efforts with Cherie Blair. I was, of course, aware that the prime minister was joining us after meetings he had held in the Middle East, but his presence at the presidential reception was a complete surprise and an unexpected bonus. Blair is an outstanding personality when meeting with people, and his early presence in Singapore was to prove of major benefit to the London effort.

The two days before the actual presentation became a blur of media interviews as the famous supporters of all five bids arrived in Singapore. Their presence provided unlimited opportunities for both the local and international media to comment and speculate about the outcome of the vote. From the London point of view, we held the almost statutory formal press conference with the bid leadership and in addition a second conference with our leading athletes who were joined by David Beckham.

David was particularly well-known in Asia, and his presence caused some organisational problems. Many young people in Singapore wanted to see him at any hour of the day and, in the case of the young girls, probably to propose to him. This was all productive as far as London was concerned as we seemed to dominate the local media, especially when Beckham, in his East London vernacular, announced that he would like to see the Games held 'in his manor'.

The more serious lobbying took place in the reception areas of the two hotels. We had arranged separate suites for the prime minister, Ken Livingston, and Tessa Jowell, all of whom would spend time in one-on-one meetings with IOC members. To help coordinate these arrangements, we had brought to Singapore a young woman called Sarah Ordonyo, who used to work for the IOC and was known to all the members.

For those members who were carefully selected to meet with Tony Blair, we had prepared short, three-point briefing notes for the prime minister, and at the end of a very long day, he had met with around thirty individual members, and those of us who were making introductions or simply sitting-in could not remember one of the bullet points being missed.

One member in particular, perhaps a speculative choice, told me some months later that his discussion with Blair did not cover the Olympic Games. The member asked, 'What was your biggest problem when you became Prime Minister?' To this, Blair replied, 'Controlling the Civil Service!' They then spent the rest of the allocated twenty minutes discussing the management of large organisations. He was so impressed by Blair that he decided to change his intention to support Paris and move to supporting London if that was to be the final vote.

We were also invited to a separate reception hosted by the high commissioner at his residence, when we were joined by what appeared to be the entire British community in Singapore. They very much enjoyed the presence of the princess royal, the bid team, and athletes. Rosemary and I had been involved in a separate IOC event but managed to join the high commissioner's party but only for about ten minutes. On arrival at the bottom of the drive up to the venue, we were told by a large assembly of photographers to move quickly, get out the way, or even piss off as, apparently, we were going to block their view of the arrival of Mr and Mrs Beckham.

Our early departure was caused by a dinner date at the top of the Stamford Hotel with four 'certain' votes. Nobody at the high commissioner's party had a vote, so the dinner was important. That very pleasant dinner produced a moment of great significance. Towards the end, we were interrupted by Adam Boulton of Sky News fame, who showed me a quote from French President Jacques Chirac on British food, which read, 'You can't trust people who cook as badly as that. After Finland it's the country with the worst food.'

If nothing else, Chirac's intemperate remark would cost Paris the vote of Finland's Peter Tallberg. Mind you, I was certain, thanks to the shopping habits of Peter Tallberg's wife, Nina, that we already had his vote. Of course, I asked Adam to make sure this got as much international attention as possible.

The very last occasion for lobbying, and in a very public situation, is the cocktail party held after the official opening of the IOC session when the host country has an opportunity to show its culture and history, listen to a State of the Union address by the IOC president and have the head of state officially open the session. Thereafter, everybody involved—IOC members and the whole audience—move to a huge room for snacks and drinks.

On the way, passing through the inevitable security gate, I turned to speak to whoever was following me and found I was sharing the queue with Hilary Clinton. As the senator for New York, she had made the long journey to Singapore to represent and speak on behalf of her city. I introduced myself and we chatted for a few moments, during which I told her that as members could only vote when a city from their country was eliminated, my burning ambition was not to have to vote at all, as this would mean that London would win. She was charming and wished London well.

On this occasion, Seb was in charge of introducing members to the Blairs, and all three were working hard. After roughly forty-five minutes, there was some commotion at the door and in came President Chirac, surrounded by Singapore policemen. He had just arrived in Singapore, only a few hours before the Paris presentation, the first of the five presentations the following morning. The contrast between a somewhat aloof Chirac and the relaxed, involved, and smiling Tony Blair was clear for all to see. When the two actually met, there was a brief handshake and Blair said, '*á demain*, Jacques' and moved on.

Unknown to me, Blair had decided to hold a further short, informal gathering in his suite before leaving to catch his flight back to UK, where he was due to chair a meeting of the G8 countries at the Gleneagles Hotel the following day. We had invited a small number of members, mainly from Commonwealth countries, who were likely to be London supporters. It was a nice gesture after a long day.

Just before leaving, Blair asked if I could have a quiet word with him in the room next door, and he said, 'Tell me. Do we have enough votes to get through the first-round tomorrow?' I replied, 'Yes. I am confident of at least 20.' 'Good,' he said, 'That means that you won't be joining me on a desert island.' He thanked the team and left for London, having given generously of his time and made huge efforts to help. There is no doubt that his presence in Singapore was crucial to everything that was achieved.

On the following day, I joined all the other members in the large session room to watch the presentations of the five candidate cities. First into bat was Paris, which focused on a long, glamorous, and expensive video produced by Luc Besson, the famous film producer. Both Chirac and Mayor Bertrand Delanoe made conventional speeches, but the overall impression was that they missed an opportunity to show more emotion.

Paris was followed by New York, which was a much livelier presentation, but serious damage had been done to the New York case by a very public disagreement over the building of what would have been the main stadium for the city. The Moscow presentation was rather conventional but featured President Putin, who spoke in excellent English. Coffee breaks were built in after each presentation, which allowed for discreet discussion. London was next after lunch.

The presentation team met in the allocated 'waiting room' well in advance of the starting time, and I spent a relaxing twenty minutes with David Beckham, who had been invited to join us as this room was some distance away from anybody desperate to meet him. Perhaps fifteen minutes before time, I realised that I had forgotten my little gold foot, my good luck charm, and rushed back to my room to put it in my pocket. That having been achieved, London entered the room along with our 100 supporters, including our thirty youngsters from East London.

The princess royal opened the presentation with an invitation to the members from her majesty the queen to come to London. I followed on behalf of the BOA and delivered my opening remarks in my very well-rehearsed French, then expanded to the British commitment to the Olympic movement since 1896, reminding the members that this was our fourth bid in the last twenty years and that we were the cradle of the Paralympic movement. The phrase from my BOA centenary speech on the Olympic spirit—'We will guard it; we will cherish it and we will proudly hand it on'—was the introduction to the theme of young people in the first part of our brilliant 'Inspiration' video.

The video begins with a black sprinter on his blocks at the start of a 100-m final. It then cuts to a scene in a poor and dusty African street with kids idly throwing stones as a police car passes. One of them catches sight of a future Olympic final on a television in a nearby bar. He becomes inspired as he hears the commentary and watches as a Nigerian sprinter wins the 100-m race in London 2012.

Similar scenes follow: a little Japanese girl is fascinated by the gymnastics, as is a Brazilian boy watching the cycling, and a Russian girl watching the swimming—all in London 2012. The children were adorable, the *Gladiator*-inspired choral music was powerful, and the script, delivered wonderfully by Ian McKellen, was evocative. It was a tear-jerkingly marvellous little film and made the vital point that we understood the magical power of the Games to inspire young people.

It was the perfect introduction to Seb, who spoke next. He began his speech with the words, 'Mr President, members of the IOC, to make an Olympic champion takes millions of young people around the world to be inspired to choose Olympic sport'. At one point, Seb introduced Amber Charles and the thirty youngsters in the audience, who all stood and waved. The picture told the story. The theme of the London presentation was clear—London would inspire young people around the world.

Seb then led on the technical parts of the bid and introduced Denise Lewis, our gold medallist from the heptathlon in Sydney, who presented the views of British athletes and emphasised that the Olympic village would be constructed at the very heart of the Olympic park. A short video, 'Magic of London', introduced Ken Livingstone, who developed the main theme using the words, 'If you wish to mobilise the youth of the world, start in London.'

A video from Tony Blair followed, in flawless French, with a further commitment from the government. 'Our vision is for millions more young people in Britain and around the world to participate in sport and improve their lives. London has the power to make that happen.' Tessa Jowell followed with a guarantee that the construction and use of the Olympic park would provide benefits for generations to come, which led perfectly into Seb's closing remarks. His words were perfect, powerfully delivered:

> When I was 12 about the same age as Amber, I was marched into a large school hall with my classmates. We sat in front of an ancient, black and white TV and watched grainy pictures from the Mexico Olympic Games. Two athletes from our hometown were competing. John Sherwood won a bronze medal in the 400 m hurdles. His wife Sheila just narrowly missed gold in the long jump. That day a window to a new world opened for me. By the time I was back in my classroom, I knew what I wanted to do and what I wanted to be.

He concluded with the following lines:

> Your decision today is critical. It is a decision about which bid offers the vision and sporting legacy to best promote the Olympic cause. It is a decision about which city will help us show a new generation why sport matters; in a world of many distractions, why Olympic sport matters; and in the 21st century why the Olympic Ideals still matter so much. On behalf of the youth of today, the athletes of tomorrow and the Olympians of the future, we humbly submit the bid of London 2012.

If ever there was a moment when Seb led us to overtake our rivals on the crest of the home straight, as he so often did in his races with a burst of stunning acceleration, his words, so carefully crafted by our team, were that moment.

It was a *tour de force*, full of emotion, and the perfect conclusion to a very different style of Olympic bid. The three British members—the princess royal, Matthew Pinsent, and yours truly—could not have been prouder and began to believe that they may never need to vote. However, reality dawned very quickly. We had to answer questions.

Only two were asked, both by Prince Albert of Monaco, who had a history of asking questions of bidding cities. Seb had only just sat down and had yet to put on his earphones when Albert asked, 'Why are you holding the Games in late August?' I told Seb to answer firmly that the opening ceremony would be on 27 July 2012.

The second question was to check the time to get to the sailing venue at Weymouth, which allowed him to call on Debbie Jevans, our sports technical expert, who delivered the correct time—two hours, fifty minutes. Thirty minutes later, when I returned to the session and my seat, just behind Prince Albert, he turned around and said to me, 'I am sorry about those questions, I was looking at the Paralympic dates.' Fortunately, he missed my sigh of relief.

Immediately after the presentation, the London leadership held a brief press conference that involved them walking through a delighted group of the London supporters, all very much affected by what they had just seen. I was approached by Bobby Charlton, with tears running down his cheeks, and I told him that reaction might be a bit strong. 'I never cry when we lose,' he said, 'I only cry when we win!' Bobby is an emotional man and we had become friends during the two unsuccessful Manchester bids, but again, I had a feeling that his emotional reaction to the London presentation might just be prophetic.

There was certainly something in the ether in Singapore—a strange sense that the wind had changed and was blowing in our direction. On the eve of the vote, an old friend of mine, Olympic filmmaker, Stewart Binns, had bumped into French skiing legend Jean-Claude Killy, IOC member and part of the Paris bid, who said to him, 'Congratulations, I think you have won.' My adrenalin started to flow; my heart thumped. Surely, Bobby and Jean-Claude could not both be wrong.

I slipped away from the press conference and took my seat, behind a contrite Prince Albert, to watch the Madrid presentation. This was well produced but concentrated on pictures of the city and of Spanish dance and customs with an appeal to its international standing as a capital city. There were no surprises. The session then prepared to vote, and as had become the rule, only members could remain. The electronic voting system and procedures were clearly explained, and we were informed that no detailed figures would be announced as these would follow the announcement ceremony in around twenty minutes.

After the first round of voting, it was announced that Moscow had been eliminated. After the second round, New York had gone. Neither decision was a great surprise, but tension grew as we waited for the third-round decision. When Jacques Rogge announced that Madrid had been removed, it was clear that the predictions of a London *v.* Paris final vote had come to pass. Only a few moments later, after the fourth round, the president announced, 'We have a decision.'

Members were not allowed to leave the room and were effectively locked in until the start of the announcement ceremony. This was an unusual experience, certainly for the members who had been involved with their own city, and even more difficult for the members in France and Great Britain. I tried to pass the time with very mundane conversations until the seating arrangements on the stage had been completed and we were asked to take our places.

As we walked to the stage, I found myself beside Francisco Elizaldi, my colleague from the Philippines, who had been one of the three members appointed as scrutineers to supervise the voting process. This meant that he was one of the very few people who knew the result and I made sure I did not embarrass him in our short discussion. I took out the little golden foot, my good luck charm, purchased in Manila, showed it to Francisco and said, 'Do you remember this?' He smiled and patted me firmly on the back three times and said, 'Yes and I am the man with the result.'

Almost instantly, I knew he had just been very clever, very kind, and had told me very discreetly that London had won. On the stage, I found myself sitting beside Swedish IOC member Arne Ljungqvist, a trained medical and scientific expert, who took my pulse and said, 'This is surprising, you are very calm'. In reply, I said to him, 'Well, I have done this twice before, and lost'.

We had to sit through a made-for-television programme showing a segment of the presentations from each city as well as an attractive promotion for Singapore, which had organised the event so well. I sat quietly watching Seb, Keith, and the whole London team sitting patiently at the front of their section. Only London and Paris were represented, and worryingly, all the photographers were situated in front of the Paris delegation. It would have been very wrong to even think of indicating what I thought might be the result to the assembled audience. So, we all waited for the envelope containing the result to be handed to Jacques Rogge. He took an age to open it, before saying, 'the Games of the Thirtieth Olympiad are awarded to the city of London!'

In the presentation room, the photographers had to make a quick change of position. The London team exploded. Back in London, a huge crowd of 35,000 watching on a big screen in Trafalgar Square erupted. Barry Davies, live on BBC, was apoplectic: 'We've done it; we've won it!'

The celebrations began. It took some time to get off the stage after warm handshakes with so many members and a quiet but warm greeting with Princess Anne. Then came the extraordinarily emotional time with all the team, all besides themselves with joy. After a while, I noticed a pall hanging over the Paris team and quietly went across to try to speak to some of them. I spotted Jean Claude Killy and embraced him. It was difficult to find the correct words, but to his great credit, he solved that problem by saying, 'Well done. Congratulations. You deserved to win. We did a few things to help you, but I am a sportsman, so I know how to lose as well as how to win.'

There was lots of media work to be done, and Philip Pope, the BOA communications director, took charge with a list of interviews and dragged me away as I was speaking in a group with Princess Anne. I asked her if she would like to join me, and at once, she said, 'Yes,' so we delivered the thanks, congratulations, and reactions from the BOA together. After thirty minutes of huge excitement, we had to return to the room to perform a public signing of the host city contract. Simon Clegg and I signed on behalf of the BOA and, with a big smile on his face, Ken Livingstone on behalf of London.

In fact, we had already signed the contract three days earlier. The IOC insists that all candidate cities make a legal commitment by signing ahead of the vote in order to ensure that the winning city does not try to re-negotiate its delivery of the Games after winning. Ken being Ken, and a canny politician, had tried not to understand the IOC requirement of having the contract signed before the presentations and decision as he preferred to wait until after London had won. He only relented when told that if he insisted on that, London would not be allowed to present at all. We were able to arrange a photo of Seb and Tessa Jowell with the contract who, understandably, were happy to oblige.

I was given a copy of the signed scrutineer's results sheets, which made very interesting reading. My first-round estimate of twenty votes proved correct with a London total of twenty-two. The second round showed an increase to twenty-seven, but Madrid leapt ahead with thirty-two. In the vital third round, Madrid dropped to thirty-one, Paris increased from twenty-five to thirty-three, and London jumped ahead with thirty-nine. In the fourth and final round, London won with fifty-four votes to Paris with fifty, the winning margin only one vote above the necessary majority of fifty-three. It was close, very close, but the figures revealed that London had been ahead of Paris in each of the four rounds.

After a few moments to celebrate quietly with Rosemary, we both attended the post vote reception hosted by the IOC and enjoyed even more kind words of congratulations. I arranged a very short formal letter to all members, thanking them for their decision, then had it signed by Princess Anne and Phil Craven as well as myself, so that it could be placed on every member's desk the following morning when the session started. We then made efforts to join the London team and our supporters at a bar and restaurant called 'Indochine', a perfect spot with a large outdoor area on Singapore's waterfront. The amazing euphoria after the announcement was a feeling never to be forgotten.

Well into the evening, I had a short, and personal, chat with a delighted Ken Livingstone, perhaps our longest and best supporter. He was still in his official suit, prepared for us by Ted Baker, and his dark blue shirt. The attire and colour were not ideal for a hot night in the tropics and Ken was perspiring freely. He also had red wine pouring from every pore of his body as he whispered to me confidentially, 'Do you know, I've just worked out what really happened. If it hadn't been for your French, we would've won by a f******g landslide.'

During an evening that can only be described as, to put it mildly, bacchanalian, Rosemary lost her jacket; I lost Rosemary and, somehow, managed to get back to the hotel and bed without her. As I clambered into what I am pretty sure was our bed, the little red light on the alarm clock said 5.38 a.m.

23

Lifestyle Changes

The morning after the night before was a very slow morning. Unlike the rest of the bid team, I was in my place in the IOC session with the agenda for the remaining three days in front of me. I suppose you could call it 'jock grit'; whatever it was, I did regret my resolve several times as the minutes passed. The special short letter of thanks for choosing London was on the table in front of each member, but attention turned almost immediately to more normal business. Needless to say, after only two hours sleep, the first coffee break could not come soon enough.

It was during the afternoon coffee break that we saw pictures on the television screens in the secure area behind the session room—that there appeared to have been some form of disturbance on the London Underground. Former President Samaranch asked me if I knew what had happened, but all I could report was a comment from the television coverage that there had been a power surge. Along with all the other members, I returned to the work of the session.

We broke up for the day around 6.15 p.m., and I walked up the slope towards the hotel foyer. When I turned the last corner, I faced a bombardment of television cameras and reporters asking whether any decisions had been taken to confirm the hosting of the Olympic Games. I had no idea what they were talking about and fought my way through into the IOC offices. There, watching television was a stunned group of staff, who broke the terrible news of the 7 July 2005 terrorist attacks in London, where the bombing of public transport resulted in many fatalities.

Even now, it is difficult to explain the instant reaction to the tragedy. I had two married families and one grandchild in London and was very relieved when Rosemary told me that she had been able to get through to them and find that they were safe. Four Islamist terrorist attacks had taken the lives of fifty-two Londoners, from eighteen different nationalities, and injured 700 others. Contact with London became very difficult as the mobile telephone networks went down, but I was sure that the bid team would be making the necessary statements and arrangements.

I missed the excellent statement made by Ken Livingstone as he left his hotel to head for the airport. I also missed the problems at the airport as the BA plane on which the team, and many supporters, were booked had a technical problem. Fortunately, seats on another plane were found for Ken, Tessa, Seb, and Keith, as it was vital that they should return to London.

Even in the IOC hotel, there were security issues. I could not get through to the princess royal, even by using the hotel switchboard to her room, and had to walk the corridors to meet her. I had arranged a small private dinner back at the Beaufort Hotel on Sentosa Island and was unsure whether we should go ahead. We discussed the London situation and our reaction and decided that, as the table was very discreetly placed, we should go ahead and join Rosemary, Dick Pound, and David Howman, of WADA, who had also been invited. We managed to maintain a varied and neutral conversation throughout.

At the start of the IOC session on the following morning, I made a short statement on behalf of the BOA, assuring the IOC that Britain would deliver on the obligations it had accepted two days before to organise the 2012 Olympic Games in London.

For the early part of that evening, I attended a small reception as a guest of CONI, the Italian Olympic Committee, which, almost inevitably, was a sombre occasion, although it was the first opportunity to discuss in some detail the London atrocities and the potential effect on the 2012 Games. There was the not unexpected discussion on the dates of the London decision on 6 July and the subsequent terrorist attacks on the 7th. I was told that the president of the French Olympic Committee, Henri Sérandour, had reacted to a question about French views on the unfortunate accident of dates and the implication that Paris might have benefitted, had they been different, by saying; 'Never speak to me like that again. Today we are all Londoners!' His was the first letter I wrote when I got home.

We flew home on 9 July, arriving in Glasgow mid-morning on the 10th. After unpacking, filling the washing machine and cutting the grass, we re-packed the car and headed to St Andrews and our holiday home to enjoy a week of relaxation at the 134th Open Championships to be played on the Old Course. After such a long journey, it was not a surprise that we 'crashed' around 8 p.m. The result of such early sleep is an equally early awakening, around 6 a.m. to be precise. Not surprisingly, there was nothing in the house for breakfast. The half-bottle of whisky was not required, and I was despatched to an early opening store for luxuries like bread, milk, butter, and cereal.

Driving home, I stopped at the junction of Greyfriars Gardens and North Street and reacted to a knock on the car window. To my surprise, it was Bob Marshall, the senior porter in the Royal and Ancient Golf Club clubhouse who said, referring to my speech in French in Singapore, 'Congratulations Craig. Terrific result. Couldn't understand a bloody word you said!' There is nothing quite like a warm welcome home.

The week was relaxing, but full of happy congratulations and reminiscences with friends old and new. We were invited to a special graduation ceremony at St Andrews University, the oldest University in Scotland, when honorary degrees of doctor of laws were conferred on Peter Alliss (the celebrated BBC golf commentator), Nick Faldo (winner of six major championships), and Peter Thomson (the great Australian champion, winner of five Opens, including three in a row). He was my first sporting hero whom I had met some years before in Melbourne. Faldo, in particular, was very enthusiastic about the London bid success.

I knew that another spectator that week would be Phillipe Baudillon, the chief executive of the Paris bid, whose wife had won a trip to St Andrews for the Open Championship. I managed to find them and invited them to join Rosemary and me in Forgan House, the R&A's second clubhouse overlooking the eighteenth green, where we enjoyed a glass or two of light wine.

At one stage, as Phillipe and I were sitting on the balcony, an enterprising BBC cameraman got us in shot, and an even more enterprising producer gave our names to the commentator, who described the moment the renewal of the *'entente cordiale'* between London and Paris. I think Phillipe enjoyed the occasion, but he was still in shock at the result and all he would say, tellingly in my view, was, 'You could control your politicians much better than we could control ours!' The golf was outstanding, with Tiger Woods winning the Claret Jug and Jack Niklaus making an emotional farewell to the Open on the Swilcan Bridge while finishing his final round.

The week allowed me to come down to earth after Singapore and to think through why London had been successful. I was very aware of the London bid efforts, history and achievements and particularly the intense promotion, lobbying and presentation in Singapore. In addition, the wide-ranging media campaign run by London was much more extensive than any of our competitors, although the subject of a later complaint from Paris. I was less certain of our four opposing cities.

In retrospect, even after only ten days, it was clear that Moscow had decided to bid as it saw benefit in being involved in the 2012 race, but its thinking and attitudes were still old Soviet style. Interestingly, Jon Tibbs, a British communications expert who had worked for Paris, was engaged by Sochi for its bid for the 2014 Olympic Winter Games and persuaded his clients to change completely their methods of bidding and presenting from those used by Moscow for 2012—successfully as it turned out.

New York was damaged by the very public row over the development of a new stadium on the west side of Manhattan to be the home of the New York Jets football team. The Jets were to contribute $800 million to the costs, with $300 million coming from the city and $300 million from New York State for the retractable roof. The city withdrew its offer in June 2005, which created doubt on the proposed main stadium for the Games. The result was a great disappointment to Mayor Michael Bloomberg and his bid leader, Dan Doctoroff. It would also be fair to say that there was a certain anti-USA attitude within the IOC after the Salt Lake City scandal, which may also have helped to explain the removal of baseball/softball from the ports programme, a move that saved London noticeable staging costs.

Madrid was more difficult to evaluate. The voting patterns revealed that almost all of the Moscow votes moved to Madrid, presumably under some influence from former IOC President Samaranch. There were several examples of Spanish reluctance regarding Paris, which resulted in the vital third-round vote that eliminated Madrid. I was also aware of elements of complacency throughout their bid.

Paris was the greatest puzzle. It had been clear favourite for many months before Singapore. Even Kate Hoey, our former minister for sport, was quoted as saying 'I hope Paris wins, because they deserve it!' Paris received a very strong report from the evaluation commission, even though France was crippled by national strikes at the time. As mentioned before, the bid was always of great interest to politicians, and their involvement was very public.

On Olympic day in June 2005, around one month before the vote, they promoted the bid with an exhibition of all Olympic sports on the Champs-Élyées. It was brilliantly done and received worldwide publicity, producing a feeling that this was a springboard to winning. However, they then sat back in their position as favourites and made little further effort to promote the bid. There is anecdotal evidence that their international intelligence was poor, which led to a lack of lobbying, acutely obvious in Singapore. The very late arrival of President Chirac was also an obvious mistake.

The combination of all these circumstances made the London efforts over the last week in Singapore critical to the recovery of any lost ground and to the presentation of what was an ever-improving case in the best possible way. The combination of good lobbying, good media communications, a good presentation with a very relevant and different theme, and the presence and efforts of Tony Blair produced a unique opportunity for sport in Britain, which was long awaited and turned out to be wonderfully successful.

Having decided to retire from the chairmanship of the BOA in October 2005, I found myself for the first time in forty-four years without a senior position in either an international federation or a national Olympic committee. I enjoyed the work in the IOC and WADA but the decision to move on from the BOA was reinforced by a short discussion with a member of the BOA in late July when he said, 'Do we have to wait until October?' My instant reaction was that his question could only be described as a little tactless. However, there was just a hint of common sense in it. Even so, leaving the position presented its own problems.

In August, Matthew Pinsent, who had been a possible candidate as my successor as chairman, announced that he would not stand for election. His ambition, following his distinguished rowing career, was to develop a career in the media, and he announced a possible position with the BBC, which would present potential conflicts of interest with the directorship of the London organising committee, a role to be fulfilled by the chairman of the BOA.

Two other names entered into consideration—David Hemery, the 400-m hurdles gold medallist from the Mexico Games, and Lord Colin Moynihan, the cox of the silver medal-winning rowing eight in Moscow and a former minister for sport. Just before the date of the BOA AGM, media reports emerged that Richard Caborn, the current minister for sport, had been lobbying for Hemery as the election of Moynihan would place two conservative lords on the London Olympic Board—a situation not appreciated by the Labour government.

I had been invited to Downing Street by Tony Blair two days before the BOA meeting, and my retirement, to chat about what, in his words, was 'one of the best things that happened this year!' I greatly appreciated the invitation and was able to thank him personally for the time and effort he had been able to commit to the Singapore presentation.

The prime minister raised the voting issue with me, and I responded by quoting the IOC regulation supporting the complete independence of the national Olympic committee in any country. In any event, Colin Moynihan was elected by twenty-eight votes to fifteen—perhaps a precursor of events to come.

One slightly unusual reaction to the London success was an announcement from the Scottish Football Association that they would not object to a British football team taking part in London in 2012, men or women, but that no Scottish players would participate. This reflected its long-held view, but was still a little disappointing as I had made efforts to persuade them of the unique opportunity a London Olympic Games would present to all sport in our islands. Their fear was that any such decision might lead FIFA to change its membership rules to insist on one 'British' member, instead of the four it had always enjoyed. Its stance was in spite of my insistence from a discussion with Sepp Blatter, the president of FIFA, that he had no intention of reducing FIFA's members in that way.

The year-end became a real thrill when the announcement came that I was to join Seb and Keith Mills as knights of the realm, distinctions conferred, presumably, by a grateful nation in recognition of the efforts to win the right to host the Olympic Games. Rosemary, who became Lady Reedie, was delighted, as her late father, Professor Sir John Biggart, was knighted two months before we got married all those years ago. I remembered asking him what difference his title made to his life, to which he replied, 'I think I was expected to leave a bigger tip!'

In February 2006, it was quite an unusual experience to go to the Turin Olympic Winter Games without any specific responsibility for Team GB or as part of a bidding process. Eighty NOCs competed in eighty-four events in seven sports in a city that benefited greatly from hosting the Games as it moved from its industrial past to a more modern economy with a new emphasis on tourism. The organising committee was faced with a substantial overrun on costs of around $4.4 billion, but succeeded in overcoming some typical winter sport problems when an excess of snow made transport difficult and driver training almost impossible. There was a resulting problem in some low spectator attendances at some sports.

Team GB was thirty-nine athletes strong but came home with only one medal—Shelly Rudman's silver medal in the skeleton event. The two curling teams were ranked fourth and fifth respectively, only just outside the medal placings. The Turin Games became unique when Italian police raided the accommodation occupied by the Austrian team, where doping materials were discovered. Ultimately, six athletes were banned. The involvement of the local police and its success was to produce a range of further discussions in the World Anti-Doping Agency, with respect to its relationships with law enforcement.

With, at least in theory, more time on my hands, I had ever-increasing responsibilities as the *de facto* treasurer of WADA. In many ways, the agency was developing its ever more demanded range of services to both sport and governments under its hybrid charter. The main financial pressures were the payment of contributions by governments at the amounts decided by governments themselves, which were then matched dollar for dollar by the IOC.

In some ways, this was associated with the ratification of the UNESCO convention, the creation of which was completed at record speed, but its ratification was slow, to the annoyance of the sports movement. The IOC and the sports movement had made adoption of the WADA rules compulsory, especially for Olympic Games, and expected governments to act with the same speed. Much time and effort were spent on encouraging contributions from governments as these, matched by the IOC, were our only source of revenue.

Governments also preferred a budgeting system that covered several years as this fitted in with their own domestic budgeting processes. For WADA, and its finance committee, this presented an almost impossible situation as we were faced with requests to enhance the range of services, which were appearing at almost every meeting. Examples of the pressures were the increased costs of litigation, as decisions taken by signatories under the world anti-doping code were regularly challenged in courts all round the world.

WADA had also developed its own Anti-Doping Administration and Management System (ADAMS) and encouraged its signatories to make use of it, as this would ease the transfer of information and produce a common system designed to offer uniformity. It came as no surprise to us to find that several major signatories had their own proprietary systems and were reluctant to change.

Developing ADAMS also introduced me to what eventually became an impossibility—agreeing a computer-based system that could be described as complete and settled. The inevitable improvements requested by different users provided constant challenges on system development and control as well as the costs of the whole exercise. It took years of trial and error to develop a proper balance between outside providers or an in-house department.

The WADA code was always designed to be a living document, and at this time, we were starting the first process of revising the code and agreeing a proper system of consultation among the many interested parties in the anti-doping community. The code had enjoyed wide acceptance, and it was important to maintain this degree of recognition and use.

To help with this process, we renewed our contact with Richard Young, an experienced lawyer from Colorado Springs in USA who, over the years, was to develop into the 'father figure' of the code. The discussions on these issues of principle took much time at the twice-yearly meetings of the WADA board and the three meetings of the executive committee. The end result of the consultation process was to be presented to the third world conference to be held in Madrid in 2007.

Practical applications of the code and its acceptance brought challenges, and much media attention, when FIFA, the international federation for football, the world's biggest sport, operated under its own anti-doping rules, which were not compliant with the code. At this time, it appeared that a stand-off would develop between WADA and FIFA at the 2006 World Cup to be held in Germany. Fortunately, wise heads agreed to take a voluntary opinion from the Court of Arbitration for Sport (CAS), which allowed for a resolution of the legal difficulties. This was a satisfactory outcome, as FIFA had been one of the two major IFs that had been reluctant to accept the new code at the 2003 World Conference in Copenhagen.

The second IF in that position was the Union Cycliste Internationale (UCI)—the world governing body for cycling. The sport struggled with the public impression that doping in cycling was widespread and that the UCI lacked adequate rules to combat it. Emanating from a research project on EPO undertaken by the French Anti-Doping Laboratory, sensational revelations appeared in public of possible offences committed during the *Tour de France* by its seven-time winner Lance Armstrong.

Any such research should not have involved any possibility of identifying the name of the athlete, but this information was leaked to *L'Équipe*, the influential French sports newspaper. The result of this breach caused severe problems for the UCI and for its former president, Hein Verbruggen, who instigated inquiries into the affair—the second such inquiry headed by a Dutch lawyer, Emile Vrijman, whose report, controversially, cleared Armstrong and contained criticism of WADA and its then president, Dick Pound.

The WADA view was that the Vrijman Report contained many inaccuracies that had to be refuted, but in such a way that legal consequences, already in the public domain, would not be inflamed. Regrettably, the resolution of the whole affair, including an attempt at arbitration by the IOC, encouraged a personal disagreement between Pound and Verbruggen, which became a bitter war of words, and was to last for many years. It was eventually settled only after a case in the Swiss courts. The affair caused much public and unfortunate debate.

While my responsibilities continued across both my IOC and WADA positions, it became clear rather quickly that my automatic position on the board of the London organising committee would continue to dominate my sporting time and interest. For London, the transition from bidder to organiser had to take place. Even though around 60 per cent of the guests would be losing their jobs, being good employers, a celebratory party was arranged at a pub on the south side of Trafalgar Square when everybody attending was invited to wear something gold.

The challenges of bidding are very different from the challenges of organising. I was not sure how we could make it work. I should not have been concerned. In welcoming all the guests, Seb cleverly announced that he had to record some apologies for absence:

> I have apologies from Mike Lee, who is finishing his book, 'How I won the Games single handed' [Mike was our brilliant communications director, who was also very adept at blowing his own trumpet]. Kate Hoey cannot be here as she is still in Lausanne demanding a recount. And President Chirac has announced that he cannot come, as our food is shit!

The evening was an uproarious success.

Of course, the direct result of the London Bid success in Singapore was quite clear, we would now have to organise one of the world's greatest technical, financial and political challenges and deliver an Olympic Games in London in 2012. Not only that, we would have to make real our promise that they would be stunning and memorable for London, Britain, and sport—no problem then.

We had told the IOC that both Seb Coe and Keith Mills would hold senior positions on the organising committee, and on 7 October 2005, what was basically the bid board became the interim organising committee board. Seb took the chairmanship with Keith as his deputy, with the statutory representation from the IOC, BOA, and the British Paralympic Association (BPA); joined by Neale Colman (Greater London Authority), Mary Reilly (London Development Agency), Howard Bernstein

(Manchester City Council), Patrick Carter (Sport England), and Jonathan Edwards (athlete representative). Jonathan had been nominated by the British athletes' committee and would have been a popular choice from Seb, although his nomination might not have been completely popular among the rowing fraternity. He was to become a key player over the next seven years.

It was not widely known at the time, but the responsible authorities in London had begun work on the proposed Olympic park even before the Singapore success. The available land contained many acres of disused, very old, or temporary structures that made up an area of almost total industrial devastation, all criss-crossed by several power cables that would have to be removed.

A decision was taken to bury the cables underground—an expensive operation, but one which meant that the new development could continue without interruption. I was impressed, as I had memories of the pressing point made by US broadcast rightsholder, NBC, before the Athens Games— that the cables over the Olympic facilities would greatly detract from the quality of the television presentation of the Games, leaving the organising committee with the cost of a late and unwelcome engineering challenge.

In addition, owners of the businesses situated in the area of the Olympic Park had been compensated for the closure and removal of their businesses to allow the necessary ground clearance to proceed. Most people assumed that this would be a relatively easy and inexpensive exercise due to the quality of the buildings involved.

However, there was one exception. H. Forman and Son, a well-known and long-standing business producing smoked salmon, proved to have unexpected skills in negotiation. Very shrewdly, the owners took some time to agree a package with the authorities, which ultimately provided them with a brand-new smokehouse, which was developed into a restaurant on a site just next door to the proposed new Olympic Park. The business survived and continues to flourish to this day.

On clearing the site, the first stage of the development involved the construction of three huge soil-cleaning plants, which remained fully occupied for months as they cleaned and then replaced all the soil, some of it chemically contaminated, in the huge area of the new development.

The new interim board could not continue to use the old bid offices in Canary Wharf and required new premises. It also needed to ensure sufficient funding to allow it to expand its numbers and to employ the many talented people who would be needed to organise the Games. Using his highly developed commercial skills and his foresight, Keith Mills had agreed with Gordon Brown, the chancellor of the exchequer, a future funding arrangement satisfactory to the government during the bid.

When the board began to arrange its first funding arrangement—a £50 million agreement with Barclays Bank—the government offered to lend a similar amount, but at a lower interest rate. This kind offer was politely declined, as Keith knew only too well the conditions that would have applied to such a government loan. Barclays was happy to agree the facility and provided accommodation in its own building. I am sure it was assumed that the deal with Barclays would develop into a full sponsorship agreement, but Barclays decided that its sponsorship of the Premier League in England was more important. Even so, the London organising committee for the Olympic Games (LOCOG) was to occupy the Barclays building but with a future sponsorship arrangement with Lloyds TSB.

Those early days also saw one crucial decision made. As we developed the new full board of directors, we also advertised—one advert only— for a chief executive. Two applicants made the final interview, and on 19 December 2005, we appointed Paul Deighton, who came to LOCOG from the investment bank Goldman Sachs where he had been the head of its European operations, a partner, and chief operating officer, Europe. If there was one crucial decision that the early organisers got right, it was this appointment as Paul was to become the vital linchpin of the organisation right through to the Games in 2012.

It was also necessary to complete the membership of the fully representative board of directors. Some of these were part of the host city contract, which insisted that members of the IOC in Britain would automatically serve on the organising committee. The princess royal, Phillip Craven, myself, and—at a later date—skeleton bobsleigher and IOC athlete member Adam Pengilly all served in this capacity.

The board would also contain representatives from the BOA and the British Paralympic Association (BPA). Chosen as independent members were Charles Allen and Tony Hall, who would lead the Cultural Olympiad; Justin King, chief executive of Sainsbury's; Stephen Lovegrove, nominated by the government; Martin Stewart, audit committee chair; and Robin Wales, mayor of the borough of Newham—they all joined the board, with Neil Wood retained as finance director.

Another major decision was to locate in the Barclays building the Olympic delivery authority (ODA). It was established by act of parliament in 2006 as a non-departmental public body of the department for culture, media and sport to ensure the delivery of the venues, their infrastructure, and the legacy of the Games.

Its original chairman was Jack Lemley, an American construction expert who had led the Anglo–French group that had built the channel tunnel. Regrettably, differences of opinion appeared between the ODA and government ministers over cost issues, and Lemley resigned in October 2006. He was replaced by renowned civil engineer John Armitt, but day-to-day control was in the hands of David Higgins, an Australian expert, with whom LOCOG and Paul Deighton built a very close relationship.

A second non-departmental public body to be established was the Olympic lottery distributor to deal with funds raised by the National Lottery for the Games. I was asked to join this small group, which eventually distributed just under £2 billion almost entirely to the ODA.

For me, the combination of the LOCOG board and the Olympic lottery distributor meant a large number of documents to be a read along with regular visits to London almost exclusively for work in preparation for the Games. I made use of the sponsorship arrangements with British Airways by catching the 6.30 a.m. flight from Glasgow to London City Airport, arriving around 7.45 a.m. A quick transition to the Docklands Light Railway and the Jubilee Line meant that I was regularly second into the LOCOG offices.

On every occasion, first in was Paul Deighton, and we would spend not much more than fifteen minutes together dealing with any international issues which were likely to emerge. The second visitor to Paul's small glass office was David Higgins of the ODA; together, they would identify the crisis of the day and then resolve it. I am not sure where this system appears in the many expert management handbooks, but it worked beautifully.

On rare occasions, it was a pleasure for Rosemary and me to welcome our London-based colleagues to our home in Bridge of Weir. We had brief visits from Paul and Alison Deighton, just like our previous visits from Barbara Cassani and her husband Guy and Keith and Maureen Mills. During the Deighton's visit, I tried to take Paul through the complex IOC structures and requirements. Towards the end of a pleasant dinner and discussion, he asked me if I had to offer him only one word of advice, what would it be. I said, 'I think you should develop the ability to say no, without upsetting anybody'. He developed that skill to great effect.

We also entertained Seb Coe when he fulfilled a promise made to Rosemary to thank her for her work during the London bid by coming up to speak at her annual social evening as lady captain of Ranfurly Castle Golf Club. His audience was a clubhouse packed with seventy-three middle-aged women—an audience that, apparently, he handled with no great difficulty.

Having completed the new board, we found that Paul Deighton had a real ability to employ and fit into his management structure a group of people who were experts in each of their individual areas. The abilities of James Bulley (venues and infrastructure), Richard George (transport), Debbie Jevans (sport director), Nigel Garfitt (villages and games services), Jean Tomlin (HR director), Jackie Brock-Doyle (communications), and Chris Townsend (commercial director), with several others to follow, produced a senior management team of many talents. There was a real buzz in LOCOG as preparations began and many different pressures became obvious.

One of those was the requests by the national governing bodies of sport in Britain to persuade LOCOG to change the bids original plans to locate particular sports in venues close to the Olympic village. One particular example came from British shooting. It hoped that any investment in shooting facilities would be made at its longstanding headquarters at Bisley, unfortunately, over 40 miles from the Olympic village. The debate continued for some time and involved LOCOG considering a potential change of venue to Dartford. However, a detailed examination of the proposed site revealed ground that they would be unavailable for construction. The original bid plan to create a temporary venue at the historical Royal Artillery Barracks in Woolwich, just 9 miles away, was confirmed.

Every Olympic organising committee creates its own operating logo. LOCOG spent almost a full year and employed design consultants to announce the Wolff Olins' final design on 5 June 2007. To say that the reaction was less than supportive would be a major understatement. Unlike previous Olympic logos, or more standard commercial logos, with some form of artwork above the Olympic rings, the London proposal was to use the four numbers—2 0 1 2—and to place the Olympic rings in the number zero. Howls of protest filled the newspapers and dominated radio and television. A petition with 30,000 signatures and a suggested parliamentary motion that would insist that LOCOG scrapped the emblem was raised.

The logo was launched at the Roundhouse in Camden and explanations given that it was designed to be attractive to a younger generation and to be sufficiently flexible for different uses. The occasional more balanced view pointed out that there had been objections to the logo selected for the Barcelona games in 1992, but it had turned out to be a great success. In practise, as the logo was developed, it was also used, for the first time, by the Paralympic movement; by removing the Olympic rings or the

Paralympic agitos, the logo could then be used as part of a very extensive cultural programme.

Interestingly, the radical logo grew on people, especially through its flexibility, and it soon became one of the most widely used and recognisable of all Games logos. Even so, the furore provided a pointed lesson for LOCOG; for the remaining five years, everything it did would be very public and regular criticism would become a fact of life.

24

From Beijing to London

In any Olympic city, or country, sports news increases exponentially. London and Britain were to be no different. For the national governing bodies of Britain's Olympic sports, there was almost unbelievably good news. The creation of UK Sport, its independence, structure, and funding had taken too many years, but its funding package was beginning to make a real difference to the services and support offered to our elite athletes.

The IOC decision to award the organisation of the 2012 Olympic Games to London concentrated government minds on the importance of Team GB producing good results in a home Games. A combination of exchequer and lottery funding was identified, and the increase over the six years to 2012 in the UK Sport funding package was announced as £200 million with further increases to come. This huge increase allowed all the British Olympic sports to develop their own performance programmes, to employ top coaches and to deliver for their athletes everything they had only previously been able to dream of.

The first opportunity to check on the benefits of the new funding would be the Beijing Games in 2008. I was able to keep the BOA up to date with plans in the host city as I travelled to Beijing at least twice a year as a member of the IOC coordination commission. This was a fascinating opportunity to see the progress made by China since my very first visit in 1978. At that time, there was very little vehicle traffic and small houses with coal fires on one of the main boulevard's close to Tiananmen Square.

The first coordination commission visit is traditionally held around one year after the award of the games to a city. The 2008 commission, chaired by Dutch IOC member Hein Verbruggen, made its first visit towards the end of 2002. It was our first introduction to the traffic problems of a major city with a population in excess of 20 million people. There was a very obvious cloud of pollution over most of the city, which meant that our examination of the venue and transportation plans was seen through a grey smog.

However, what was clear from the very beginning was that the Beijing organising committee (BOCOG) received total financial and political support from both the national and Beijing regional governments. This was to continue for the period up to the Games, and it was very helpful to be dealing with the same people on each visit. We made friends with the various department heads in BOCOG, which created a positive working relationship.

During each visit, we were entertained at dinner, and on the first such occasion, we were taken to a hotel that provided a classic European dinner with delicacies like foie gras and fillet steaks on the menu. While we appreciated their thoughtfulness, we suggested that on future visits to Beijing, we would prefer to eat Chinese food. They did just that with splendid regular dinners in the excellent Chinese restaurant at the top of the Beijing Hotel.

These were warm and friendly occasions with good food washed down with red wine and, of course, Chinese maotai, a very strong Chinese spirit used for endless toasts and dispensed liberally in shot glasses. Maotai appeared to have an influence on our Chinese hosts, but rather less on the mainly European visitors. One particular Chinese official—Mr Zhang, I think—would frequently break into song as the self-appointed leader of the local entertainment. I was amused on one occasion when my neighbour at dinner described him as 'the best drinker inside the 5th ring road.'

It was clear from the start that Beijing would prepare for and present exceptional Games with a combination of new and spectacular stadia, along with remodelled and improved existing facilities like the Capital Indoor Stadium in which I had organised the World Badminton Championships in 1988. With the same philosophy we had adopted in London, Beijing's biggest facilities, and hence most athletes, would be close to the planned Olympic Village. The original plans for the Birds Nest Stadium and the neighbouring Water Cube were outstanding in their design. We were impressed by the legacy plans for many of the new facilities as they were to be placed in several of the Beijing universities. That made great sense in a city with a huge and expanding population.

After one Beijing visit, I was able to arrange a side trip on the return journey to Macau, as this was the preferred base for the BOA pre-Games training camp. The required facilities were good, the climate and weather conditions were similar to those expected in Beijing, and there were regular direct flights from Macau to Beijing, which would suit the athletes using the Macau camp. The visit was designed to encourage the authorities in Macao as we had gained much experience from our similar arrangements before the Sydney Games.

I had arranged to meet the senior sports official in Macau, Manuel Silverio, and the meeting was timed for early afternoon. Mr Silverio was around forty minutes late and had clearly enjoyed a very good lunch. He was in a particularly benign mood, and it became very easy to agree the use of the facilities we required and at approximately the price we wanted to pay.

Winter sports were not forgotten as beneficiaries of the strong flow of money from UK Sport in Britain, as the summer sports geared up for what were likely to be special Games in Beijing. At the 119th IOC session in Guatemala in July 2007, three candidate cities made presentations for the 2014 Olympic Winter Games—Pyeongchang, Salzburg, and Sochi.

Pyeongchang was regarded as having a good chance, as they had lost only very narrowly to Vancouver for the 2010 Winter Games at the session in Prague in 2003. The unknown quantity was the southern Russian city of Sochi, which was relatively unknown for winter sport, but which had been strongly promoted by its bid committee and friends in Russia.

It appeared to me that all three cities had studied in detail the 2005 Olympic bidding process, which had been won by London. There was considerable interest from all three candidates in the benefit to London of having our prime minister, Tony Blair, as a leading member of our bid team at the final presentations. That must have been the reason I was asked to hold separate private meetings in Guatemala with President Fischer of Austria, President Roh of South Korea, and President Putin of Russia.

The first meeting was with President Heinz Fischer, a shrewd politician and former academic who was Austria's president until 2016. I had considerable sympathy for the Salzburg bid, having spent part of my honeymoon in that beautiful city many years before. Austria was a strong winter sports country, although there were tensions between the Austrian NOC and the president of its national skiing federation. Salzburg seemed to be the right size of city for a Winter Games and its history, beauty, and existing facilities seemed attractive. President Fischer was also an attractive personality, even allowing for his unusual habit of enjoying a cigar with his breakfast.

Korea's President Roh Moo-hyon was an interesting man who was born into a poor family and never received a college education. Unfortunately, only a few years after our meeting, it was alleged that he had taken bribes while in office, leading to him committing suicide by throwing himself of a cliff near his home. A rather stern-looking man, but with a warm smile, he reminded me of the success of the 1988 Seoul Olympic Games and made all the necessary commitments to be expected from a Korean president.

I was unsure about the meeting with the formidable President Vladimir Putin, although impressed that he had made the effort to join the Sochi team in Guatemala. Even so, his reputation as ex-KGB and a man not to be trifled with went before him. The Sochi team had built a temporary ice rink in Guatemala City, where some of Russia's most famous skaters performed for the fascinated spectators from the session's host city deep in the tropics. Putin opened our meeting in fluent English, but explained that, as ours was a formal meeting, he would speak Russian, with excellent translation, but that he would understand every word I said.

He explained at some length the reasons behind his support of Sochi. He wanted to create a winter sports centre in Russia which would provide training facilities for the Russian winter teams and provide new winter facilities for the local population and all other Russian enthusiasts—facilities that should be available in a country with such an excellent tradition in winter sports. He did not mention the level of investment and I doubt he would have answered if I had asked him.

At the end of almost thirty minutes, he changed back into English and said, 'Mr Reedie, this is off the record, but could you tell me if Scotland is going to become independent?' I was amazed that the second most powerful man in the world seemed so aware of what was then a modest political argument in a distant country. I explained that the Scottish National Party had won in local elections but did not have an overall majority.

All three heads of government received the same advice from me: during their stay in Guatemala City, they should speak to as many members of the IOC as possible and, certainly, at the reception for all members, hosted by the local organisers on the evening after the official opening of the session, they should be mixing with and speaking to members. I told them that this was a very successful exercise for Blair in Singapore. There was nothing new or unusual in that advice and I think all three presidents were active along those lines.

The report of the evaluation commission showed large variations in the estimated financial arrangements of the three cities. The estimated operating budgets were not dissimilar, with all three cities indicating a modest surplus after including the IOC contribution of $435 million.

What was very different was the estimated non-organising committee capital budget of $2.1 billion for Salzburg, $7.1 billion for Pyeongchang, and an extraordinary $18 billion for Sochi.

In a close vote, Pyeongchang led in the first round with thirty-six votes, just ahead of Sochi with thirty-four, and Salzburg narrowly lost out with twenty-five votes. In the second round, Sochi increased its vote to fifty-one, narrowly beating Pyeongchang with forty-seven. A big Russian party ensued as a very subdued Pyeongchang group digested a second close defeat in consecutive Winter Games votes. Most of the Salzburg votes moved to Sochi, perhaps because of a European preference and the promises of a new winter sport development in Russia.

On reflection, this decision was to cause huge and unfortunate effects on the IOC. The Sochi bid book and the IOC's evaluation report gave the necessary guarantees on compliance with the WADA code, the UNESCO convention, and the construction of a new anti-doping laboratory in Sochi. Sadly, nobody was able to predict the massive doping programme that was to emerge, with specific rule breaches and unacceptable behaviour during the Sochi Games.

In addition, media reports of unpredicted and unexplained increases in spending in the non-organising committee budget in Sochi, which escalated to the astronomical figure of $51 billion, had a devastating effect on other mainly European cities that were considering bids for future Winter Games. While these huge, extra costs for massive infrastructure projects were not the responsibility of the IOC, they proved almost impossible to justify when associated with an Olympic Games.

The slightly unusual issue of a Scottish Olympic team had already been raised just before the Guatemala session. In the Scottish elections, the Scottish National Party, led by Alex Salmond, became the governing party in the devolved parliament in Edinburgh; although it did not have an overall majority, Salmond began a provocative campaign to have a Scottish Olympic team, reflecting quite a lot of the media mischief around the London preparations. Inevitably, as a Scot, but a former chairman of the British Olympic Association, I was involved in explaining the IOC rules on recognition of a new national Olympic committee from an independent nation, which did not apply to the Scottish situation as in Olympic competition, athletes competed for Great Britain.

It was helpful that several successful Scottish athletes explained that their presence in Team GB and the generous funding support from UK Sport were essential to their sports careers and there was no possibility of similar levels of services and support likely from a Scottish alternative.

Sadly, this initial political argument resurfaced regularly over the years, but without any success.

In Madrid in November 2007, WADA held the third world conference on doping in sport. My responsibility, over the previous years and at the conference, was to deal with the challenges of raising contributions from governments, which were then matched by the IOC, to a level to meet the ever-expanding workload requested of WADA. The conference dealt with presentations from the major WADA departments, but its main purpose was to approve the next version of the world anti-doping code.

Revisions of the code had settled into a six-yearly pattern, but the need to hold a full period of consultation on the code had presented the agency with a hugely increased administrative commitment. The appointed code review team had, over the previous eighteen months, held three rounds of consultation, sent out two completely new drafts of amendments, and received submissions from 200 stakeholders.

The major changes in the proposed new code were as follows:

1. The requirement for all anti-doping organisations to have an anti-doping education programme.
2. Revised regulations on missed tests.
3. Increased flexibility on sanctions to allow reduction below two years in cases with no intention to enhance performance and increases to four years in aggravating circumstances.
4. Rules on provisional suspensions
5. A requirement for a country to have ratified the UNESCO Convention before hosting any world championship or major events.

The extensive changes to the code demanded wide consultation before approval so that its acceptance, which had been strongly appreciated by the sporting world, could be continued. When approved, the new code would come into effect on 1 January 2009, and the transition period would allow all stakeholders to change their own regulations so that they were in line with the code.

Another very important item on the agenda of the WADA board meeting at the conference was the retirement of Dick Pound as the first chairman of WADA and the election of his successor. The meeting was given a detailed explanation of the intentions under WADA rules and the processes that had been agreed to ensure that the second president of WADA would represent the public authorities. The rules enshrined the intention that there should be a rotation of the two senior positions in WADA and should alternate between the sports movement and the public authorities. For some time in the previous eighteen months, there was discussion and an emerging opinion that the likely candidate for the WADA presidency from governments would be Jean Francois Lamour, the French sports minister, who was also a former Olympic gold medallist in fencing.

Nominations for the positions of president and vice president had to be made by 20 September. Two nominations were received for the position of president, one from Europe and one from Oceania. One nomination had been received from the Olympic movement for the position of vice president with the decisions to be made at the conference in Madrid. Since that date, the presidential candidate from Europe had withdrawn. This decision was a great disappointment for the European governments, which had made representations that the rules of candidate selection might be amended; Dick Pound, as chairman of the meeting, resisted that suggestion.

About one month before the date of the Madrid conference, I had met Jean-Francois Lamour in Paris and spent some time trying to persuade him not to resign. He made rather wild comments that the appearance of the candidate from Oceania was 'an Anglo-Saxon plot'. I told him this was nonsense but failed to persuade him. I found out only later that he announced his withdrawal by a statement made to the French sports newspaper *L'Équipe*.

At the time of the decision, there were strong statements made by Madame Maud de Boer-Buquicchio, deputy secretary general of the Council of Europe, representing European governments, stating that they disagreed with the process and suggesting that the elections should be deferred for six months. The European governments then said that they could not support the remaining candidate being presented and would, therefore, abstain. This was opposed by other government representatives and Dick Pound had to rule that the election would proceed, without any secret ballot. This unfortunate situation had been the subject of a whole range of rumours throughout the conference about the possible appearance of other late candidates, which had fuelled the antagonistic attitudes of different government groups.

Richard Caborn from Britain, who had just stepped down as minister for sport, had asked me whether he should put his own name forward. My response was to say that it would have to be his decision, but he was unlikely to be successful. He took no further action. At the end of the day, with only four abstentions, John Fahey from Australia was elected to the position of president of WADA from 1 January 2008. Prof. Arne

Ljunqvist was elected as vice president. Fahey was a former Australian politician who had been an influential member of the Sydney 2000 bid committee. Arne Ljunqvist was the senior scientific expert from the IAAF, with long experience in WADA. Despite all the final difficulties, the new team leadership and the new code were in place.

The early part of 2008 was dominated by the preparations for the Beijing Games with pressures emerging for the BOA, the London organisers, and the Beijing organising committee itself. In its preparations for the Games, there was much work to be done by the BOA to organise the pre-Games training camp in Macao. It emerged that the almost standard wording in the BOA athletes' team agreement—to maintain team confidentiality—was being interpreted as an attempt to introduce a 'gagging order'.

This became an issue in those parts of the media that were critical of the original IOC decision to take the games to Beijing and China in the first place. It was also revealed that in preparing the British athletes, some thought had been given that they be offered masks to wear in the event of high levels of air pollution in Beijing. Both issues were quickly resolved, and no further publicity ensued. The Beijing organising committee had decided to follow the policy introduced by the Athens organising committee in 2004—that the torch relay would have an international element, a 'Journey of Harmony', and would visit some previous host cities, of which London would be one.

A recommendation was announced by the Greater London Authority that Linford Christie should be a torchbearer if the Beijing torch came to London. The decision, which was not discussed with the IOC, upset Lausanne and offended the BOA bylaw, which prevented any athlete convicted of a doping offence being selected for Team GB. After this invitation became public, it was subsequently withdrawn. However, the decision to have an international element in the torch relay would soon turn out to be far less successful than intended and became something of a PR disaster.

The IOC had to deal with regular media comments that China had a poor record on human rights and that there was a lack of access to the internet, all leading to the not unsurprising request that NOCs should boycott the Games. We responded with our well-proven statement that boycotts do not work and only penalise the athletes. We maintained the argument that by hosting the Olympic Games in Beijing, we would help to expose Chinese society to outside scrutiny and promote sport in the biggest country of the world. We also said that by hosting the subsequent Paralympic Games, there would be a major improvement in services for disabled people within China. We were surprised to see the relative openness from China in reaction to the major earthquake in Sichuan Province before the Games. Pictures of the political leadership from Beijing in their shirt sleeves in the middle of the rubble presented a rather positive image of its society.

All of the above does of course beg the question, one that hindsight always raises—did in fact the Beijing Games create more openness within China, or alter the policies of the regime in any way? The answer, I suspect, is probably not. Even so, I still hold the view that it was worth the try. Not only that, if the world of sport adopted a policy of only competing against teams from countries it liked, there would not be much international competition at all.

During the London sector of the torch relay on 6 April, there were significant anti-Chinese protests, focused on issues including Tibetan independence, animal rights, and human rights abuses. What was already a volatile situation was not helped when it became all too apparent that those running with the torch, eighty British personalities like Steve Redgrave, were surrounded by a posse of large Chinese gentlemen recruited from Beijing's security services.

On that particular day, I happened to be at a meeting in Beijing and was having dinner with John Fahey, the new president of WADA, who was making a special visit to the Chinese anti-doping committee. During the dinner, Rosemary was sending me texts describing the degree of protests in London, which, of course, received wide and repetitive television coverage.

I knew that IOC president, Jacques Rogge, was arriving in Beijing that evening and I managed to speak to Seb Coe in London and then present to Jacques what we thought was a balanced view of the scale and extent of the protests. Similar protests took place in Paris and during the US leg of the relay. These events reinforced the advice we had given the Beijing organising committee—that the international portion of the torch relay would present risks of precisely the sort that had taken place. Needless to say, the IOC soon banned 'international' elements in future Olympic torch relays.

At the IOC session just before the Games, I put my name forward for election to the executive board and did a fair bit of discreet lobbying. There were two seats available for election as Gunilla Lindberg from Sweden, the general secretary of the Association of National Olympic Committees (ANOC), was retiring, having served her allotted time; Puerto Rico's Richard Carrión, chairman of the finance committee, was standing for re-election, having been voted on in 2004.

In addition, Nawal el Moutawakel of Morocco was also standing. Importantly, if Nawal was not elected, the executive board would be all male; she represented strong competition, especially as she was also a highly renowned Olympic gold medallist and a well-known symbol of female success in the Islamic world.

Just before the item on elections, I had joined Seb and Paul Deighton on stage as they reported to the session on London 2012's progress. On returning to my seat, I found a handwritten note marked, 'Sir Craig Reedie, Personal'. It was a note from Richard Carrión, telling me that he had decided not to stand against Nawal as the executive board should not be an all-male institution. As I looked up, Richard was speaking; as the election process had started, he was making his announcement publicly.

I had about thirty seconds to make up my mind about whether I should also defer in favour of Nawal, and then contest the second seat against Richard, already the chair of an important IOC commission, who would be sure of the president's support. I decided to take the second option and lost to Richard by fifty-six votes to thirty-nine. I received some nice comments from members, but the reality was that this was my second failure to join the executive board—a position regarded as important by the British media.

The Beijing Games welcomed 10,942 athletes from 204 NOCs taking part in twenty-eight sports with 302 events. The opening ceremony in the huge Birds Nest Stadium on 8 August at 8 p.m. was timed to coincide with the number '8', a lucky number in Chinese society. From the very first appearance of 2,008 drummers to various tableaux based on the Silk Road, the ceremony was a wonderful exhibition of Chinese history and culture.

What became clear only after the ceremony was the design of the stadium contained a full-sized motorway underneath the field of play that made possible a series of lifts to bring up different displays, which added greatly to the range and quality of the ceremony.

On the coaches back to the IOC hotel, I was asked many times 'How will London match that?' The response we developed was to say that nobody would expect London even to try to match the scale and grandeur of the Beijing opening ceremony. We would do our own thing—prophetic in every sense, as it turned out.

Relaxed from its training camp in Macau, Team GB totalled 308 athletes. I had no particular duties with the BOA, only indirect duties as a member of the IOC coordination commission and no more than a watching brief from London 2012, so I could easily prioritise the efforts and successes of British athletes. My London 'watching brief' involved a lot of work in making sure that the 'London House', established in the city, catered well for members of the Olympic family as well as guests and sponsors. It would have made no sense not to invite members of the IOC to a pleasant, relaxed, and welcoming venue established by the next organising city.

From day two, Team GB began a series of outstanding medal performances when Nicole Cooke won gold in the cycling road race in a close sprint finish. On day three, Becky Addlington won her first gold medal in the 400-m freestyle event in the huge Water Cube, with her teammate, Jo Jackson, winning bronze. Over the years, British swimming had not been a major success in Olympic Games and Becky's second gold medal a few days later in the 800 m was a turning point in the re-establishment of the sport in Britain.

The spectacular results by members of the Team GB cycling squad in the spectacular Laoshan Velodrome were to change the sporting habits of the nation watching at home. To win seven gold, three silver, and one bronze medal was a level of performance and success unique in British Olympic records. Three gold medals were won by Chris Hoy, in the individual sprint, team sprint, and keirin events, results which were to make him one of the most distinguished Olympians in British sporting history. A message soon appeared from Glasgow City Council to announce that a new velodrome, to be built in the major new sports centre in the east end of the city, would be named the Chris Hoy Velodrome.

By accident, I met Chris after his keirin success during a visit to the Olympic Village and was able to tell him that he had made significant history. He was almost certain to be the first resident of Edinburgh to have a building named after him in Glasgow. Two gold medals for Bradley Wiggins, one in the 4,000-m pursuit team and one in the individual pursuit over the same distance, and more gold won by Vicki Pendleton and Rebecca Romero in their events did more to encourage people to take up cycling—a slightly unusual consequence as the natural place for cycling is on the road, not in expensive velodrome affordable only by affluent countries.

As is often the case with Olympic Games, the sailing events had to be organised some distance from the host city. For Beijing, the choice of venue was the coastal city of Qingdao, over 400 miles south-east of Beijing and famous for 'Tsingtao', the country's most famous beer. Yet again, the British sailing team was hugely successful, bringing back four gold, one silver, and one bronze medal. Ben Ainslie won his (by now almost to be expected) gold medal in the finn class. Ian Percy and Andrew Simpson won gold in the star class, as did Sarah Ayton, Sarah Webb, and, on this occasion, Pippa Wilson, when they retained their yngling class gold medal.

The other sport located at a distance from Beijing was the equestrian events. Due to concerns about equine disease and quarantine issues in mainland China, they were held in Hong Kong with great assistance from the Hong Kong Jockey Club, where the British three-day event team won two bronze medals, Kristina Cook in the individual and Sharon Hunt, Daisy Dick, William Fox-Pitt, Mary King, and Kristina Cook in the team event.

In any British Olympic team, there is always a big contingent of rowers who have over the years delivered much success. In Beijing, the long run of success in the men's coxless four was continued when Tom James, Steve Williams, Pete Reed, and Andy Triggs-Hodge won gold. The lightweight double sculls pair of Zac Purchase and Mark Hunter won Britain's second gold and the men's eight and the women's coxless quadruple sculls both won silver medals. The four British women—Frances Houghton, Katherine Grainger, Debbie Flood, and Annabel Vernon—had enjoyed a long series of wins at regattas over the season and were world champions. They led comfortably throughout the final but were caught by the fast-finishing Chinese crew, losing by just a second and a half. The result meant a third successive silver medal for Katherine Grainger. Famously, she would go one better four years later, before adding another silver in Rio in 2016.

I had selected Katherine's and the girls' event as one of my medal presentations and found myself in some difficulty as my Chinese was all but non-existent in congratulating the winning crew. I had even more trouble in trying to think of just a few words for the devastated British crew. So, I chickened out—with just a smile for the winners and a very brief peck on the cheek of each of our silver medallists. In the small committee room later, Matt Smith, secretary of the World Rowing Federation, said 'Very elegant, Craig.'

Some days later, when they had just about recovered from their disappointment, I persuaded Katherine and two of her crew to join me for a drink in the London House. There they met up with a relaxed Bradley Wiggins and admired the ability of the barman to mix excellent glasses of mojitos for them.

In the main stadium, Christine Ohuruogu won the 400 m; in the boxing venue, James Degale won the middleweight division; Tim Brabants won gold and silver in flatwater canoeing; and medals were also won in modern pentathlon and Taekwondo. The bronze medal won by Louis Smith in the pommel horse event in gymnastics was a forerunner of the improvement in British results in that sport.

Having watched Goldie Sayers narrowly beaten into fourth place in her javelin event, I was even more delighted to present her with the bronze medal eleven years later at the London 2012 Anniversary Games. The Russian competitor, Mariya Abakumova, who had finished second, was eventually disqualified by the IOC after her conviction for a doping offence and at the end of a prolonged legal process. The final medal tally of nineteen gold, thirteen silver, and fifteen bronze medals—coming in fourth place in the unofficial medal table behind China, United States, and Russia—was the best British performance for 100 years.

There was real satisfaction that the results elevated Team GB to a much higher Olympic status. They also delivered much admiration for the achievements of the athletes and increased the status of the London 2012 preparations significantly. In some ways, we also shared in the glow of the huge media appreciation for the outstanding results from Michael Phelps in the pool with eight gold medals and seven world records, and Usain Bolt on the track with three gold medals and two world records.

The results were also very timely as a warm sporting welcome to Gordon Brown, our new prime minister. Major political figures tend to want to appear at Opening Ceremonies of Olympic Games, but we managed to persuade Brown to visit Beijing and spend some time with the team in the second week of the Games and to be in the stadium when London was handed the Olympic flag in the traditional handover. The recipient was Boris Johnson, the new mayor of London, who took one look at the scale of the Beijing Games and the success of the British team then became an immediate convert to the Olympic cause (although the less said about some of his intemperate remarks the better).

We were heavily restricted in our request to use the stadium technical facilities for the London segment of the closing ceremony. Our presentation was based on a bright red London double decker bus carrying Jimmy Page of Led Zeppelin, singer/songwriter Leona Lewis, and footballer David Beckham, who kicked a football into the crowd of athletes. Johnson accepted the flag, with just a moment of difficulty, while, 5,000 miles away on a big screen, outside Buckingham Palace, 40,000 people, including the famous Michael Phelps, celebrated the moment. It was our turn next.

Several months after our return from Beijing, London hosted the 'IOC Beijing debrief' led by the IOC and the previous host city as part of the IOC's transfer of knowledge programme. Presentations and discussions covered a range of subjects from sport, transport, technology, logistics and the Games time experience of athletes, spectators, workforce, and media. We were able to show the meeting that three and a half years after the award of the Games, our Olympic stadium was taking shape—the aquatics centre and the village were rising out of the ground and 3,500 workers of an estimated final total of 30,000 were at work in the Olympic Park. A guide for NOCs had been prepared to show potential sites for up to 641 pre-Games training camps. The commercial team had announced another six new sponsors. The message was clear that the London preparations were on time and proceeding well.

25

Mixed Progress to London

By the end of 2008, we were roughly halfway towards the London Olympic Games with a much clearer view of the size and complexity of the project. Our main focus was concentrated on the Olympic Park in East London, where the main facilities were under construction. One of the advantages of regularly flying into London City Airport was the opportunity it gave me for a bird's eye view of the site and the sheer size of the area we were dealing with.

The Olympic delivery authority (ODA) had established an independent consultancy group called CLM, the first letter of the names of the major construction companies contracted to build different parts of the park (CH2MHill, Laing O'Rourke, and MACE) and was to monitor the overall development. CLM's skills were to lead to a substantial reduction in the overall costs of the development. Further encouragement came from the decision by the Westfield retail group to develop on the fringe of the park what was to become the biggest shopping centre in Europe.

When linked to the improvements in London underground's Jubilee Line and the complete re-development of Stratford station, it meant that almost all spectators would travel by rail using a route through the shopping centre to enter the park. The further development of a second station, Stratford International, providing a direct fast link to Kings Cross in the city centre, made a huge contribution to solving the problem of moving tens of thousands of spectators without them having to use cars.

We developed good relationships with the IOC coordination commission (COCOM), which made half-yearly visits to London to check on our progress. The chairman was Denis Oswald, an old friend of many years standing as the president of International Rowing and an experienced Swiss lawyer. Denis, who had been chairman of the same commission for the Athens Games, was helped by several IOC members who really understood sport and were experienced in attending, or even organising, Olympic Games: John Coates from Australia, a senior organiser of the Sydney Games; Gunilla Lindberg from Sweden, an expert on national Olympic committees, villages, and NOC services; Ng Ser Miang from Singapore, sound on marketing and finance; Alex Gilady, a former vice president of US network NBC and a world authority on broadcasting and media; Nawal el Moutawakel, who had chaired the IOC evaluation commission for the 2012 Games; Austin Sealey, who had been the Barbados ambassador to the UK; and Namibian sprinter Frankie Fredericks, representing the athletes, who knew Britain well as he had trained in Britain and competed in British events for many years.

IOC protocol allowed the IOC members in Britain to attend the COCOM meetings, and Princess Anne and I were diligent in our attendance, although we were both members of the board of the London organising committee (LOCOG). Having served on both evaluation and coordination commissions for the IOC for different Games, it was an unusual feeling to have completely changed sides. The meetings normally took around four days and gave us the opportunity, on one evening of their stay in London, to entertain the members.

For the very first COCOM meeting, we took its members to dinner in the stunning great hall of Inigo Jones Queen's House in Greenwich, where the dimensions of which form a perfect 40-foot cube. During the Games, the house would be used as a VIP centre and its grounds for the equestrian events and modern pentathlon. During the dinner, we were also amused by what appeared to be a lack of complete agreement on policy from the IOC concerning the village, athletes, and NOC services. Gunilla Lindberg was the clear expert, and we were very glad to have her advice, but this was regularly contradicted by Frankie Fredericks, representing the athletes, which served to take just a little pressure off the London officials dealing with this wide area of responsibility.

With that exception, we were happy to have the guidance of the COCOM experts and particularly good relationships developed between Seb and Paul from LOCOG and Denis Oswald and Gilbert Felli, the IOC Olympic Games executive director. The meetings also involved all the LOCOG directors and their staff, to such an extent that Seb looked forward to the COCOM visits as these were the only days on which he knew where everybody was.

While the early pressures were on the construction of the major facilities situated around the village, plans for a multi-event arena at the north end of the park, originally called the Handball Arena, but later, because of its distinctive appearance, renamed, the Copper Box, and the Velodrome were under way. Unless there was clear evidence of a demand for regular future use, we planned to use what we called 'demountable' buildings as an effective way of providing sports facilities without building long-term 'white elephants' of little value. The buildings could be 'demounted' after the Games, moved, and re-erected where there was need. The theory was attractive, and the best example was the 25,000-seat basketball hall. Similar construction was planned for smaller venues for the sports of badminton and weightlifting, and because international federations like their sports to be hosted close to the centre of the action, both close to the Olympic Park.

In addition to venue development and the new and improved transport links, the initial planning was underway to recruit volunteers, develop a ticketing strategy, plan the Cultural Olympiad and, crucially, the never-ending campaign to raise the sponsorship and marketing revenue needed to run the Games. The major banking crisis and its economic impact did not make this particular task any easier. We also appointed Bill Morris, from the BBC, to start the planning for the opening and closing ceremonies.

At every sports event I was able to attend which had a formal opening ceremony, I made it my responsibility to bring back to London a DVD or tape of the ceremony, so that we had a cache of different ideas. What was clear was that the most successful ceremonies were held in darkness, which allowed clever technicians to deliver exhilarating light shows and powerful audio-visual effects. If we wanted to achieve similar effects in London, it would involve discussions about the design of the main stadium. As a result of these discussions, the technical wizardry that ensued was extraordinary.

The stadium was rigged with a 1-million-watt sound system with more than 500 speakers, 3.7 acres of staging, and 13,000 props. Some 25-centimetre pixel panels were placed around the stadium, including between every seat. Each panel was connected to a central computer and was fitted with nine full-colour LED pixels, which enabled images to be broadcast during the performance, like a 1960s go-go dancer, a London Underground train, and a representation of the birth of the internet. The end result meant that the London opening ceremony became the finest 'light show' ever produced.

However, the awarding of rights to host future Olympic Games seemed a never-ending process. The 2009 contest for the 2016 Games was to create much interest and, in its final decision, much controversy. At the outset of the process, seven cities had presented their initial questionnaires to the IOC: Baku, Chicago, Doha, Madrid, Prague, Rio de Janeiro, and Tokyo. The IOC internal working group that studied the questionnaires awarded weighted average scores to each city as follows: 8.3 to Tokyo, 8.1 to Madrid, 7 to Chicago, 6.92 to Doha, 6.42 to Rio, 5.3 to Prague, and 4.3 to Baku. The weighted average scores were based on the results of the questionnaire on a whole range of issues, including accommodation, finance, government support, Olympic village, sports venues, and transport.

In April 2008, the IOC decided to make Tokyo, Madrid, Chicago, and Rio candidate cities, which, after the results of the questionnaire, caused friction among the supporters of Doha. The normal window in the sporting calendar for on Olympic Games is July and August in the northern hemisphere and the IOC was concerned over the high temperatures in Doha at that time of the year. Doha and Qatar were also candidates for the 2022 FIFA World Cup and the media focus on that bidding process was obviously of some concern to the IOC.

I was asked to serve on the evaluation commission for the 2016 Games and would have the pleasant experience of advising each of the four cities that they should include $675 million as the IOC contribution to the Games, with an additional $335 million from TOP (the Olympic Partners) sponsorship revenues. In addition, the IOC would once again provide the host broadcaster through its fully owned subsidiary, Olympic Broadcasting Services (OBS). Thanks to the very large increase in both its television and sponsorship revenues, the level of this support was a clear indication of the ability of the IOC to assist its organising cities.

The first city we visited was Chicago in early April 2009 when one of its local newspapers published pen pictures of the members of the evaluation commission, chaired once again by Nawal el Moutawakel. Our environmental expert was Simon Balderstone from Australia, and his pen picture contained the phrase 'Member of the last Australian Everest expedition. Did not reach the summit'—a perfect example of damning with faint praise.

Chicago offered a compact bid proposal with eight venues to be constructed in the very large McCormick Place Convention Center. There was ample hotel accommodation, and the city presented an attractive waterfront situation on Lake Michigan. The accommodation presentation was made by a member of the Pritzker family who owned the 1,500-room Park Hyatt Hotel in Chicago, clearly thought to be the main IOC hotel if

Chicago was successful. I politely pointed out that this was a decision for the IOC and not for the organising committee.

During the coffee break I spoke to Mr Pritzker and explained my intervention as 'only for the record'. 'Do not worry,' he said. 'If you decide to go to the Hilton, I will give you the private number of their Managing Director and you can call him up any morning your f****** breakfast is cold'.

However, there was one clear difficulty—the United States Olympic Committee wanted to amend the standard host city contract, which was not acceptable to the IOC. The bid was unable to provide a full guarantee covering a potential economic shortfall but suggested a complex insurance-based solution with a total provision of $750 million. Rather like the situation in London, the main stadium would be a temporary stadium, and in one light-hearted moment, I offered them the option of purchasing up to 55,000 seats from the temporary parts of our stadium after the London Games.

Our second visit was to Tokyo, during its 'Sakura' (cherry blossom) time, which is the ideal time of year for any visit. The Tokyo plan was based on further developments of the positive legacy of the 1964 Games by using some of the legacy facilities from those Games to provide a '100 year' Olympic legacy for the city. I was familiar with the territory as I had once run a major badminton event in the Yoyogi Gymnasium, one of the splendid facilities from the 1964 Games.

The plan was a compact one and a combination of national and city government provided ample guarantees and the finance necessary for any infrastructure to deliver the games. We had some concern over the relatively low level of public support and the inevitable transport challenges in such a busy urban city. Some of the facilities that had been listed as existing facilities would in fact have been needed to be built.

The commission visit to Rio was the first occasion I had been to Brazil. The bid was driven by the Brazilian government, which had an extensive urban regeneration programme that appeared attractive. Three different levels of government—national, regional, and city—guaranteed to finance the necessary infrastructure and to cover any shortfall, but careful monitoring would be required of three different political institutions. The bid plan showed the construction of facilities in four different zones in the city, but these would impact on travel distances so that careful planning of transport infrastructure would be necessary.

To my surprise, I found that Rio was short of suitable hotels to meet the IOC Games requirements, which planned to include four different

Olympic villages and six cruise ships after development of the port area. Significantly, the commission received a very high-level presentation on government support and the overall financial picture of the country from Henrique Meirelles, chairman of the Central Bank of Brazil, and Dilma Rousseff, the senior adviser to the president of Brazil. The bid committee also presented detailed information on the city's police structure and capabilities, acknowledging Rio's endemic domestic crime and violence problems.

We travelled on directly from Rio to Madrid, where we found a very compact presentation of the planned sports facilities. They fitted in with the overall bid philosophy, combining a hard legacy of new sports facilities and a soft legacy of sports development initiatives to encourage community participation. The bid showed strong support from the public in Madrid and throughout Spain. The concept of compact sports venues, plus the location of the Olympic village and the media and broadcasting centres, would result in short travel times for athletes and other client groups.

We received presentations from the three levels of government involved—national, regional, and city—which would combine to cover any potential shortfall in the budget. However, it became clear that the presence of three different government stakeholders would present problems of control to a potential organising committee. At the time of the visit, there was some doubt whether Spanish anti-doping legislation complied with the world anti-doping code—an issue that needed to be resolved.

The final decision on the 2016 host city took place at the IOC session at the start of the 13th Olympic congress held in Copenhagen in October 2009. The general opinion was that Chicago and Rio might just be favourites in a very close contest. Rio had employed Mike Lee, the former communications director of the London bid, and his company presented a stylised map of the world showing stars on the cities of all countries which had previously held games. The map showed the large area of South America with not a single star on it. The visual argument turned out to be very effective.

The Chicago bid was supported by both President Barack Obama and his wife, Michelle. In a last-minute decision, the president flew into Copenhagen early on the morning of 2 October, when Chicago was the first city to make its presentation. The president's arrival requirements resulted in increased control of local traffic; security arrangements of such an important guest meant a very early start of the meeting. There was some discussion that those minor inconveniences counted against Chicago.

Personally, I was not aware of any inconvenience but was certainly not best pleased by the closure of one of the elevators in the IOC hotel for the exclusive use of Chicago bid supporter, Oprah Winfrey. It was a celebrity indulgence that did little to promote her city. Chicago had also struggled with the underlying guarantee issue and the prospect of the United States Olympic Committee organising its own television station.

Accompanied by American volleyball gold medallist, Robert Ctvrtlik, an athlete IOC member, Michelle Obama held a series of private meetings with members of the IOC. During the short meeting to which Rosemary and I were invited, the first lady tried to explain the positioning of the proposed sports venues on a large map of Chicago. Ctvrtlik intervened and asked if I was prepared to advise on how Mrs Obama should conduct her meetings with members. I suggested that she did not need to speak in any detail about the proposed Chicago arrangements. All members had received a copy of the Chicago bid book and should know all about the detailed venue arrangements. She would be much more effective if she got the members to speak about themselves.

In a series of close votes, Madrid led in the first round with twenty-eight votes, with twenty-six for Rio and twenty-two for Tokyo. It was a major surprise that despite the last-minute arrival of the president of the United States, and to the dismay of the US broadcasters that had gathered in numbers, Chicago was eliminated with eighteen votes. When the results were announced, Obama was already in mid-Atlantic on Air Force One and later arrived back in Washington with his tail tucked somewhat firmly between his legs.

In the second round, Tokyo lost two votes and Rio led comfortably with forty-six votes, winning in the third round with sixty-six votes to the Madrid total of thirty-two. There were some members who expressed concern at the perceived 'insult' to the president of the United States.

There were others who were disappointed at the defeat of Madrid after its strong showing against London in 2005, although the presence of Rio would inevitably have threatened a possible Spanish area of influence in South America as a whole. Rio had been organiser of the 2007 Pan American Games; it had been an enthusiastic bidder and made full use of Mike Lee's very selective promotional map. Winning the Olympic Games in 2016, to follow the FIFA World Cup in 2014, added to Brazil's increasing economic growth and confirmed its status as one the most important new powerhouses in the world. Everything seemed to be set fair and few foresaw the troubles to come.

On its final day, the session had to decide on the sports to be brought into the Olympic programme. Baseball/softball, roller sports, squash, golf, karate, and rugby sevens had all made the appropriate request. The executive board decided to put the sports of rugby sevens and golf before the session, and both were invited to make presentations.

It was never any secret that I was in favour of golf re-joining the Olympic programme after its last appearance in 1904—a very long time ago. As in other sports, much has changed in golf since then. The winner of the individual tournament was George Lyon from Canada. He was a somewhat eccentric but very talented man and highly proficient in several sports, including cricket, baseball, and pole vault. At forty-six years old, he was relatively new to golf, having only picked up a club eight years earlier. He sang and told jokes during his rounds and collected his winner's trophy by walking to the podium on his hands. The team event medals in 1904 were won by three American teams: the Western Golf Association (gold), the Mississippi Golf Association (silver), and the US Professional Golf Association (bronze).

I had tried to support golf's reinstatement campaign, which was led by Peter Dawson, the secretary of the Royal and Ancient Golf Club of St Andrews and president of the International Golf Federation. Not long before the date of the presentation, I took a call from Peter who explained a clash of dates between the presentation and the organisation of the Presidents Cup competition to be held in San Francisco. The clash had the potential to remove some of the top players who might have been available to present to the IOC in Copenhagen.

He told me that arrangements were in place to bring Padraig Harrington, an Open champion; Suzanne Peterson, the second-ranked women in the world; and Michelle Wie, the talented and very promising American/ Korean star as part of the presentation team. With one place left to fill, he asked me if he should bring golfing legend Jack Nicklaus. I suggested that since the IOC was keen to encourage young people into sport, he should bring Mateo Manassero, the young Italian golfer who was the number one amateur in the world.

With the glamourous Michelle Wei as the star, the presentation went well, particularly when she asked the IOC to admit golf so that she could do 'something that Arnold Palmer and Jack Niklaus had never done— win an Olympic gold medal'. Both golf and rugby sevens were admitted, decisions which were to add much excitement to Team GB performances in Rio and to bring about the construction of a brand-new championship golf course in the city. It was what is known as 'a result'.

In pursuit of a second 'result', I was involved in one of the final decisions in the session, the elections to the executive board. It was my third attempt. On this occasion, there was a range of places to be filled. The first of these was to re-elect Jacques Rogge as president on the expiry of his first eight years in the position. He was re-elected almost unanimously for a further term of four years. Two vacancies appeared for the position of vice president; those were filled by Mario Pescante of Italy and Ng Ser Miang of Singapore.

There were two places available for ordinary members of the executive board, and five names had been submitted—Patrick Hickey of Ireland, John Coates of Australia, C. K. Wu of Chinese Taipei, Samih Moudallal of Syria, and me. In a series of votes, where the member with the lowest number of votes was eliminated, I was elected in the fourth round by fifty-two votes against Patrick Hickey with thirty-nine. For the second seat, the remaining four members enjoyed a further voting process with John Coates being elected in the third round of voting by forty-eight votes to C. K. Wu with forty-three.

In those days, the elections to the executive board produced multiple rumours, fervent discussions, and lots of interest from the media. As the session was longer than usual due to that year's Olympic congress, there was even more time for unofficial lobbying and media interest. I had asked good friends Jon Tibbs and Marcus Kecht, who were intimately involved in several separate bidding processes and with IOC elections, to keep me up to date with opinions and rumours from the many seemingly discreet meetings between members. To my surprise, I was told that Colin Moynihan, my successor as chairman of the BOA, was said to be acting against my interests and was sympathetic to the efforts of John Coates, his friend and fellow rowing cox from Australia.

Patrick Hickey came to the elections as president of the European Olympic Committees (EOC), and I had spent several months speaking to my own European colleagues as, for some years, I had been a member of the EOC executive committee. I was also much helped by a friend and colleague from the WADA board, who was very well connected in Eastern Europe. I was told after the election that Patrick had been almost certain of success, and not to be elected to either of the two available seats was a blow to his political ambitions. At the end of seven long days, I became the first British member of the executive board since the marquis of Exeter in 1961 and only the third ever member from Britain.

The name of Colin Moynihan appeared again in Britain as all the preparations for the 2012 Games picked up even more pace. Although I retained a seat on the BOA by virtue of my IOC position, I had not been a regular attender at BOA meetings due to my other commitments. I had been aware for some time that his management style was very different from mine, but that should not have been a surprise with his own political and commercial experience.

One of his first decisions was to invest in a management and commercial review of the BOA by instructing Bain and Company, well-known consultants. From memory, a large publication was produced with many graphs and photographs, which probably cost a lot of money, but which seemed to comment only on what the BOA was currently doing and was distinctly short on suggestions for any new activities.

I was also aware that after the Beijing Games in 2008, there had been major changes in personnel, one of which was to lose the services of Simon Clegg as chief executive, which meant that Simon also lost his involvement with LOCOG. This was regrettable after all the many and lengthy efforts that Simon had made to establish the winning London bid.

The BOA had operated for many years from a row of modest Georgian houses in Wandsworth and those had been sold for on acceptable price. I am not sure whether the funds were reinvested or were used for general revenue projects. However, a new and very modern suite of offices in the fashionable Charlotte Street in Fitzrovia, Central London, was rented, and new senior staff appointed with a corresponding increase in salaries. Colin had become increasingly critical of the joint marketing agreement (JMPA) between the BOA and LOCOG as, in his view, it did not provide sufficient funds for the level of activity he planned.

The JMPA was signed in early 2005 and became an integral part of the host city contract. It was negotiated under IOC guidelines and was based on recent declared accounts of the BOA. It was designed to replace commercial income which the BOA would have normally received over the period up to the Games, as all its commercial rights were then held by the organising committee. The JMPA was not designed to support any additional responsibilities that the BOA may have aspired to take on over and above the requirements of arranging the host nation's team for the Olympic Games. The IOC was also very aware of the incident under the JMPA for the Sydney Games, when the Australian Olympic Committee had been able to extract large sums of money out of the organising committee by means of a buyout of a veto that the Australian Olympic Committee had inserted on all matters to do with sport.

For that reason, the IOC took a very careful view of future marketing agreements. For the London Games the agreement reached was a fair amount, with £19 million of cash and £8 million of value in kind, totalling £27 million. A final negotiation between the BOA's Simon Clegg and Keith

Mills of LOCOG resulted in an additional bonus of $8 million, with $4 million to the British Paralympic Association (BPA) in the event of LOCOG exceeding projected revenues. Such a calculation would only be undertaken after the Games and would be top-sliced for the BOA and BPA before the distribution of any other surplus.

The agreement delivered to the BOA the appropriate guaranteed compensation for its commercial rights, which, when coupled with the extensive additional fund-raising activities available to a well-organised BOA, would have provided more than sufficient funds to meet its obligations. The BOA board was informed of all the details and the organisation should have budgeted accordingly.

At the end of 2010, Colin Moynihan and the BOA intensified their opposition to the JMPA agreement by instigating a legal case against LOCOG, based on the definition of 'surplus' contained in the host city contract. Depending on the surplus to be delivered by LOCOG, the BOA argued that the additional payment of an estimated $8 million should be paid to the BOA at an early date as the further condition of LOCOG exceeding its domestic sponsorship revenue had already been made. The BOA had signed—by me—a joint venture agreement with the mayor of London and the secretary of state for culture, media and sport on 18 February 2005, setting out the accounting practises for the organising committee based on the Olympic and Paralympic Games being treated as one project, and the definition of 'surplus'.

LOCOG joined this joint venture agreement after it was established in October 2005. The BOA case appeared to be based on the phrase in the host city contract that the Olympic Games were 'The Games of the XXX Olympiad in 2012', which they claimed referred only to the Olympic Games and would exclude the Paralympic Games. If this were to be the case, and the costs of the Paralympic Games were to be dealt with separately, there would be a substantial surplus from the Olympic Games and a corresponding deficit from the Paralympic Games, which would influence the overall distribution of the surplus under the host city contract greatly in favour of the BOA. It was a somewhat stretched semantic argument, but nonetheless clever, or devious, depending on how you look at it.

LOCOG responded by saying that it could only agree to the payment of any additional funds to the BOA after both Games were completed and the LOCOG accounts finalised. The JMPA contained a dispute resolution clause giving the IOC the right to determine any disagreement. After much correspondence and the organisation of a joint meeting of the parties, the BOA was unable to accept any informal arrangement to resolve the dispute and decided to seek a ruling from the Court of Arbitration for Sport (CAS). Both parties prepared their submissions, and these were filed with CAS on 9 March 2011.

Despite the opposition of the BOA, the IOC decided that it would exercise its right to determine a dispute under the JMPA and asked both parties to submit any additional papers. It published its final decision on 18 March 2011, which examined its past practice, previous interpretations of the word 'surplus' and its assessment of it. The final decision from the IOC read:

> The IOC has no hesitation to determine that the word 'surplus' in the JMPA has to be interpreted as the financial result of staging the Olympic and Paralympic Games combined. The IOC feels comfortable to do so as the parties and their leaders at the time, which were familiar with the organisation of previous Olympic Games and Paralympic Games, cannot have understood it differently.

On the following day, the BOA and LOCOG announced an agreed settlement of the dispute. This contained confirmations that any payments due to the BOA and the BPA would be paid after the final accounts and before the IOC distribution of surplus came into effect. LOCOG would assist the BOA in its attempt to find sponsors for the next quadrennium (2013–2016), assist with sales of two iconic Team GB items, assist with tickets, and assist with BOA requirements for access to the Olympic park.

One of the regrettable effects of the dispute was to cause major conflict of interest problems for those members of the LOCOG board who were the IOC members and were denied access to BOA meetings. It also created similar issues for Colin Moynihan and Andy Hunt (the new BOA secretary), who were members of the LOCOG board. At the end of the saga, both Moynihan and Hunt retained their board positions but no longer attended any meetings of the LOCOG audit committee.

The dispute became very public, and apart from the additional management, time, and expense involved, it was a source of real irritation to both LOCOG and the IOC, which had been pleased with the almost seamless progress towards good Games in London. The reputation of the BOA was greatly damaged. Few could understand the unique situation where the local NOC took a dispute to CAS over a host city contract, which caused significant damage to the whole London project.

There was one further major potential issue. I took a call one morning from Nick Wright, private secretary to the princess royal, telling me that she may have to consider her position as president of the BOA if the stand-off continued. I was aware that she did not take kindly to being excluded from BOA meetings and to be declared conflicted over the surplus argument.

A telephone call was arranged for the following evening, when it became clear that she was exasperated by the claims being driven by Colin Moynihan. I set out my own views that her resignation would not only have serious implications for the BOA, but also for LOCOG, the IOC, and her own personal position within the whole London project. It was also obvious that unfortunate and persistent media comments would only add fuel to the fire.

My own situation with the two organisations was exactly the same, and we discussed how we could best deal with the embarrassing position in which we were being placed. The best outcome was to think over the possible solutions, but to take no immediate action.

Around seven days later, I spoke with Tim Laurence, her husband, who suggested that there should be a middle view and a compromise. I assured him that that was unlikely, but that legal advice to LOCOG was very robust and, in my view, would overcome the legal advice given to the BOA. Of even more regret was the situation of being conflicted at LOCOG meetings, which was an embarrassment to all the other LOCOG board members. Although the four IOC members could continue their board membership, they would have to leave any part of a meeting when the 'surplus' issue was being discussed.

The princess and I had a full and frank private discussion at a LOCOG meeting, and we decided that on the balance of probabilities, the BOA would lose the argument and that we would both restrict ourselves in any involvement with the BOA, but no resignation would be announced. This incident was a further blow to the BOA, which was the organisation that had originated the London bid and had developed the whole project. The steps taken by Colin Moynihan made relationships with the board and the senior management of LOCOG tense and difficult throughout the remaining months to the Games.

A much more modest issue brought me, wearing my WADA hat, to the project group established by the government to consider the future of anti-doping in Britain. For many years, the conduct of anti-doping and the prosecution of offences was the responsibility of the Sports Council. There was an acknowledged conflict of interest in any organisation which financed and promoted sport and had a responsibility for sanctioning athletes who had committed a doping offence.

There was a clear case for the establishment of a separate UK body, but the final decision would be made easier if there was a separate financial arrangement put in place. The logic behind the suggestion and almost all the details had been progressed, but the government was reluctant to commit any money. The project group had listened for several successive meetings to a civil servant from the department of culture, media and sport who seemed unable to make any commitment. Most of the other members of the group had held some position in either government or public sector life, but I was the only member from the private sector.

I pressed our civil servant hard by saying that we did not want to meet again only to give him another opportunity not to take a decision. This rather direct approach to the problem appeared to work when he returned two weeks later with an offer of a guaranteed £8 million to establish what was to become UK Anti-Doping. The moral was clear. If you want to make changes to your own institution within a major project, there is no project better than organising an Olympic Games. I was to become an 'adviser' to the new UKAD.

Back in the ever-expanding LOCOG offices, the sports department, led by Sports Director Debbie Jevans, was negotiating the final arrangements with each of the twenty-eight Olympic international sports federations (IFs). One of the more difficult of these negotiations was with the federation for my own sport of badminton. The Badminton World Federation (BWF) had been very satisfied with our original plans to hold its event in a new demountable stadium close to the Olympic Park.

It had become clear that demountable buildings were more expensive than at first thought, and as the large indoor venue at Wembley had been remodelled and was now available, we suggested to the BWF that its event should move there. The Wembley arena was the spiritual home of English badminton, but it was forty minutes from the Olympic Village. The negotiations were long and complex, but the BWF finally agreed to the move and ultimately enjoyed a splendid event at Wembley, As a test event, it also, very skilfully, held its 2011 world championships at Wembley.

We were faced with similar discussions with the International Equestrian Federation over the ground for the jumping events to be staged in Greenwich Park. This was after several months of work reacting to a small but well-organised protest group that did not want the equestrian events there in any shape or form. The design of the cross-country course in particular involved the removal of a small number of trees.

Led by Chairman Seb Coe, a senior group of LOCOG experts attended the final planning meeting for the equestrian facilities at the London borough of Greenwich. To his great credit, Seb told me afterwards that he knew it was going to be a difficult meeting when outside the venue, a woman protester hit him with her handbag and said, 'I always preferred Steve Ovett anyway!' Planning permission was granted.

26

Final Steps to London

The final Olympic diversion in the all-encompassing efforts to get London ready in time was the February 2010 Olympic Winter Games in Vancouver—2,600 athletes from eighty-two countries took part in eighty-six events covering fifteen different disciplines.

I had a close relationship with the Vancouver people, which began some years earlier with a dinner at the Morningside Country Club in Rancho Mirage, California. Rosemary and I were members of a neighbouring golf club, which we used for an annual visit in January of each year to relieve us of the miseries of a west of Scotland winter. We were invited to meet Mr and Mrs Jack Poole at Morningside, Jack being the chairman of VANOC, the company underwriting the Vancouver Olympic Games. To make sure that no Olympic voting rules were broken, Jack and I slipped away to the other side of the bar for a quiet whisky. We had also entertained at home John Furlong, chief executive of the Vancouver bid, on his very first trip outside Canada at the beginning of the bidding process.

Vancouver built a large new oval in the suburb of Richmond to host speed skating, which became a real legacy of the Games, and invested in improvements to the 'Sea to Sky Highway' to the ski resort of Whistler. The Canadian Olympic Association had financed its team well and the whole of Canada was ready to support them. On the day before the opening ceremony, a Georgian luge competitor called Nodar Kumaritashvili died in an accident during a training run which cast a pall over the Games. In Vancouver's huge BC Arena, after an unfortunate hitch in the opening ceremony when a mechanical failure caused one of four pillars used to raise the flame to the cauldron to stall, the Canadians enjoyed a very successful Games. The organising committee struggled with unusually warm weather, which involved them in flying in new snow by helicopter but allowed me to play golf at Shaughnessy Golf Club in downtown Vancouver.

Team GB was fifty-two athletes strong, and the two curling teams were medal contenders, although the men finished in fifth place and the women in seventh place. To everyone's delight, Amy Williams won the gold medal in the skeleton event, maintaining British success in the discipline, However, an accurate assessment of Team GB's results still showed our relative lack of success in winter sports.

The final event at Vancouver was the gold medal match in the ice-hockey competition between Canada and the United States. Hockey is a national obsession in Canada, and the Olympic final between the hosts and its near neighbour and partner in the National Hockey League (NHL) demanded the attention of the whole country. The home team won the gold medal in extra time with the national hero, Sidney Crosby, scoring the winning goal to provide the perfect end to the Games.

We were invited to a cocktail party before the closing ceremony, where I met Stephen Harper, the Canadian prime minister, and suggested that the hockey result and the national euphoria it created should make him consider a snap general election. He declined politely, but probably wrongly.

After Vancouver, London became the 'host city in waiting'. The work in the Olympic Park was progressing well and fell ever more regularly into the hands of Alison Nimmo, the design and registration director. Alison joined the ODA from her experience in rebuilding Manchester after the IRA bombings in 1966 and was to inherit the finishing of the park after the departure of David Higgins to Network Rail in 2010. David always liked a challenge and said that he could move on after doing a lot of the 'heavy lifting' in the park.

An aerial view of the park showed the Olympic Village, Aquatics Centre, Orbiter, Olympic Stadium, Copper Box, International Broadcast Centre, Media Centre, Velodrome, BMX Track, Basketball Hall, and Riverbank Arena for hockey. The park would have 250 acres of new green space, embellished by 300,000 wetlands plants and 4,000 semi-mature trees. All the vision and imagination required when we looked at the disused Hackney Greyhound Stadium a decade earlier was becoming a wonderful reality.

In May, we found that we had a new government. The long-standing Labour government, which had been in power since 1997, and been very supportive of all the BOA and London bid efforts, lost power. David Cameron and Nick Clegg took over in a Conservative/Liberal Democrat coalition. Jeremy Hunt became secretary of state for culture, media and sport, with Hugh Robertson as sports minister.

It was a tribute to all concerned that political unity, which had existed throughout the bid and in all the major organising developments, was retained. Both new government appointees defended the increase in costs to develop the park and its infrastructure; very wisely, they were happy to keep Tessa Jowell on the Olympic board in respect of her long involvement and experience.

LOCOG (the London organising committee) and the first user of the park's sporting venues were now flat out as it prepared to move from all the necessary strategic planning to a complete operational role across all the activities to present a great Games. Chris Townsend and the marketing team were able to announce that contracts for 90 per cent of their target of £700 million were in place.

Planning was underway for the recruitment of the necessary 70,000 volunteers and we were to interview around 260,000 applicants. Transport and security were regular and important items of discussion with our partners. Sport and venues, communications, the Cultural Olympiad, and development of the Paralympic Games all moved ahead. For the Paralympics, we appointed Chris Holmes, a distinguished Paralympian, as director of Paralympic integration. All this was undertaken within the constraints imposed on LOCOG as a responsible limited company with all the normal auditing, legal, and financial responsibilities.

The board met regularly within our offices on the twenty-third floor of One Churchill Place in Canary Wharf and full and transparent reporting gave all the members the information they required in well organised meetings. The atmosphere was conducive to good discussions, with only one momentary surprise. One board member, probably Tony Hall, suddenly caught Seb Coe's attention and asked, 'Mr Chairman. You are a Chelsea supporter. Your Deputy Chairman is on the Board of Tottenham Hotspur. Your Chief Executive has a box at Arsenal. How on earth do we get anything done here?' There were few discordant notes and lots of good humour as above.

Bill Morris, our director in charge of ceremonies, began an informal consultation with many colleagues on what they thought should be included in the opening ceremony. The artistic team, led by distinguished film producer Danny Boyle, would have its own responsibility to develop the shape and scope of the ceremonies, but the Morris initiative was unexpected and intriguing.

I had not given any thought to a possible answer to the question, but perhaps reflecting my own confusion, I suggested that at some time during the ceremony, which was titled 'Isles of Wonder', the music should contain Nimrod, the ninth of Elgar's fourteen *Enigma Variations*, which although Elgar may never have attended one, I thought was perfect for an Olympic ceremony. As a more general comment, I suggested that during the ceremony we should try to make people laugh as humour was such an important part of British culture.

I can claim no responsibility for the two subsequent, very funny moments inserted into the ceremony—the legendary cameo parachute appearance by the Queen and Rowan Atkinson's hilarious rendition of the theme from *Chariots of Fire*—but Nimrod was featured towards the start.

Having lost an election earlier in the year, Tony Blair was able to publish his memoir entitled *Tony Blair: A Journey*. I bought a copy and turned to see how he had recorded his efforts for the London bid. There was some surprise when I found that this part of his record was very short, but on page 546 there was, for me, a spectacular spelling mistake—Craig Reedie had mysteriously become Craig Tweedie.

I wrote a prompt letter to Hutchison's, the publisher, saying that in the unlikely event that they would re-publish the book, they should address this glaring error. Around three weeks later, a package arrived with a second copy of the book and a personal handwritten letter from Tony Blair:

Dear Craig, A million apologies. A misspelling of your name (in the typing from my execrable longhand) resulted in the book getting your name wrong. The next edition is correcting! Sorry. Very best wishes, Yours ever, Tony.

The inside front cover of the corrected book was also inscribed: 'To Craig, with my best wishes and thanks for the great work you did for us all. Tony Blair'. It takes a big man.

To our great surprise and delight, an invitation arrived one morning to attend the wedding of His Serene Highness Prince Albert of Monaco to Princess Charlene and a host of associated celebrations. The dates were just before the IOC session in Durban, so this made the trip a bit longer, but the different dress codes for the different events risked excess baggage charges—morning coat, dinner jacket, and lounge suit were all compulsory and that was just for me, while different and new dresses and hats were obligatory for Rosemary.

The occasion was splendid in every way. We enjoyed the welcome cocktails and dinner, followed the next day by the wedding ceremony and the dinner and dance after that, all taking place in the splendour of Monte Carlo at its best. The large turnout by the members of the IOC made it a relaxed and enjoyable experience, and, in all honesty, we have never looked better.

However, as you might expect with sport, there were signs of problems to come for London. In 2008, the IOC had approved its 'Osaka rule', first discussed the previous year at the World Athletics Championships held in that city. Under the rule, any athlete receiving a suspension related to doping that lasted longer than six months was prohibited from participating in the next Olympic Games. This had great similarity to the then existing BOA by-law, which stated that any athlete properly convicted of a doping offence would lose the right to be a member of Team GB for all future Games.

The Osaka rule had been challenged in an American arbitration by a famous athlete called Lashawn Merritt. He had served a sanction for a doping offence for a period of twenty-one months which would expire before the London Olympic Games. His further sanction of six months under the Osaka rule would have meant that he would miss the games entirely. The IOC had obtained a ruling from the Court of Arbitration for Sport (CAS) that the Osaka rule dealt with the eligibility to compete rather than a sanction. The case in the American arbitration overturned that opinion and declared clearly that the further six months of a ban from the Olympics was in fact a sanction and not an eligibility punishment.

The case would clearly be sent to CAS again and its final decision would have an effect on several athletes who were currently banned from the London Games. The WADA rules, which were adopted by the IOC and applied to all sports, were also in opposition to the Osaka rule, and the legal confusion gave early warning of the debate to come, which, inevitably, would challenge the BOA in a law that I had helped institute and my position on the WADA board. I had always supported the BOA rule as long it was good law; the risk now existed that it might be declared bad law.

The Americans' appeal to CAS was upheld, and the IOC had to remove its Osaka rule. Colin Moynihan and the BOA then fought a public—and ultimately expensive and unsuccessful—campaign to protect the BOA by-law, but their appeal to CAS was heard by the same CAS panel, who inevitably reached the same result. The BOA by-law was removed.

As the contractors continued their work on the Olympic Stadium in the Park, a debate arose on the post-Games use of the main stadium with public statements on the potential for either West Ham United or Tottenham Hotspur to become future tenants. An Olympic Park legacy company had been formed, and three members of the board were revealed as having links to West Ham. Tottenham Hotspur were advised by Mike Lee, the former London bid communications chief, and, if successful, would demolish the stadium, build a new stadium designed exclusively for football, and meet redevelopment costs at the Crystal Palace centre with its existing athletics track.

The nub of the disturbing issue only fifteen months from the Games was the promise made to retain the athletics track as part of the legacy of a successful London bid. When we were planning the venues and the Olympic Park, the sport of football had not expressed any serious interest with most of their attention on the new Wembley stadium.

Football's attitude at that time almost certainly resulted in the final planning for the Olympic stadium as a permanent bowl, running track, and 25,000 seats with a further 55,000 temporary seats, to be removed after the Games. This would have provided the promised athletics' legacy with room to build additional seating for future possible European or world championships. While this rather distracting issue did not stop construction, it rather diminished the popular view that excellent progress was underway.

In contrast, we were able to announce exciting progress in the International Inspiration Programme. This was established to deliver the promise made in Singapore: 'London's vision is to reach young people all around the world. To connect them with the inspirational power of the Games, so they are inspired to choose sport.'

Established in partnership with UNESCO and UK Sport, but driven by Keith Mills, 12 million young people in twenty countries—from Azerbaijan to Zambia—had experienced sport through this first-ever host city international sports development programme. It was to be one of the great successes of the London Games. We had hoped that Rio might be prepared to continue with the programme, but regrettably, they could not. It was further developed within the UK after the Games.

As we headed for the 'one year to go' celebrations, both the ODA and LOCOG were close to full employment levels. The regular half-yearly COCOM meetings with the IOC examined progress in every detail, and presentations had to be made to specialist interest groups. These included the world broadcasters, the international written media, and, crucially, the full presentations at the meeting of all the *chefs de mission* of the 204 national Olympic committees.

This final, large, international meeting was held during the August riots in Tottenham following the shooting of a young black man called Mark Duggan. The riots expanded to cover other parts of London and other cities in Britain and were very disturbing. I can recall during the days of the chefs' meeting, sitting at the back of one of the LOCOG meeting rooms in Canary Wharf, watching anxiously as the ominous smoke slowly rose into the sky from the riot-torn area in North London. Despite the unfortunate domestic backdrop, we had prepared well for the NOCs and their chefs, headed by James McLeod, so were presented with very few questions; the NOC part of the Olympic world went home in the knowledge that preparations for their athletes were well in hand.

When fully staffed, LOCOG had around 7,000 employees, every one fully involved in the myriad preparations: volunteering, marketing, ticket sales, transport, sport, accommodation, Games services, venue management, technology, test events, city operations, Paralympic Games, and bringing the whole organisation together into one coordinated whole.

The success of our ability to do this is best described in the dashboard agreed with the IOC coordination commission at its last official meeting with LOCOG from 28–30 March 2012. There were sixty-five individual work areas over seven general headings, and each work area was marked green for low risk, yellow for medium risk, and red for high risk. When examined, not one single high risk was identified, and detailed completion reports on every aspect of each of the sixty-five work areas were presented. The skills and enthusiasm shown by LOCOG were remarkable and appreciated.

At this last COCOM meeting, our traditional dinner was downgraded to a cocktail party as almost everybody in the IOC party had other items on their agendas in London. The host of the cocktail party was to be Jeremy Hunt, the secretary of state, but he was on paternity leave, so our host was Boris Johnson, mayor of London, who was facing a re-election campaign two months hence. In his opening remarks and dealing with his election, Boris drifted into a 'rocket' analogy. I looked at Keith Mills and we shared our amazement. Boris explained by saying, 'But of course I fully understand that I might be electorally ejected from the command module!' This served only to prove that he must write his own speeches as no professional speech writer would ever write words like that.

A whole department in LOCOG had made all the necessary but complicated arrangements for the London torch relay. On 10 May, Seb,

Keith, Paul, and I travelled to Olympia to see the torch lit in the Temple of Hera and watched it start its traditional route through Greece to the Panathenaic Stadium in Athens.

On 16 May, the torch and the Olympic flame arrived at Royal Naval Air Station Culdrose in Cornwall. On the following morning, the flame was taken to Land's End, where an Olympic cauldron was lit, and multigold medallist Ben Ainslie ran the first leg of the relay. Over the next two months, more than 8,000 torchbearers carried the torch over 8,000 miles around the country through enormous crowds and increasing excitement. An estimate of 12 million people coming out to watch the torch relay was almost certainly an understatement.

I had volunteered to run with the torch up the eighteenth fairway of the Old Course at St Andrews for two reasons: one was that the hole is almost completely flat and the second is that it is only just over 300 metres in length. This excellent idea turned out to be impossible as the security convoy was not allowed onto the golf course. So, I rose very early and waited to enjoy the torch exchange at the end of Hepburn Gardens in St Andrews.

To my amazement, I found that my son had brought my granddaughter Anna up from London on the overnight sleeper, and both were waiting to watch grandad's somewhat ponderous but hugely proud run with the torch. I ended up having to run 600 metres as one of the selected torchbearers had withdrawn, which made the pace much easier for me and probably also for the special accompanying team from the Metropolitan Police.

We had also agreed that we would take the torch to Dublin in Ireland for a short visit during its planned stay in Northern Ireland. Rosemary is Belfast born and bred and this was a great excuse for a short visit to her home city. We met up on the evening before the selected day with Seb and Patrick Hickey, chairman of the Olympic Council of Ireland. On the following morning, we took a series of fast cars and two special torchbearers to make a ceremonial crossing of the Irish border. Michael Carruth and Wayne McCullough, two Irish boxers, carried the torch at this special moment.

We drove south to Howth, just north of Dublin, to a stage set up outside the offices of the Olympic Council of Ireland where the president of Ireland, Michael Higgins, made one of the best Olympic speeches I have ever heard, in both English and the Gaelic language of Ireland. His speech included the following telling words:

> Sport builds bridges between people and the making of friendships is
> a fundamental part of sporting endeavour. At the heart of the Olympic

ideal is the concept of dedicated athletes from different nations meeting in a spirit of mutual understanding, friendship and fair play to determine who will excel on the day.

His understanding of the Olympic emblem visiting his country and its presence in helping a historically troubled relationships made it a memorable event. The torch was then run through Dublin and driven back to Belfast after a hugely significant day.

It is difficult to overestimate the effect of the torch relay on the build-up to the London Games. The selection of torchbearers allowed organisations around the country to nominate special people for their 'Moment to Shine'. The relay took seventy days, and the route was designed to bring the torch within 10 miles of 95 per cent of the British population. The communications effort behind the relay brought daily reports into every household, and the crowds were large and enthusiastic along every part of the route. As the torch came close to London, the crowds were huge with people standing thirteen deep in Oxford Street; 60,000 people attended the London torch event in Hyde Park.

Security was a major topic for both LOCOG and the IOC, with the ultimate responsibility lying with the British government. It set the 'security level', but in practice, LOCOG coordinated and organised all the necessary venue security under a large contract with G4S, the major private security company. The manpower required had been increased some months before the Games, but with only a few weeks to go, G4S announced that due in the main to a major fault in their own systems, it would be unable to provide the numbers of security personnel required.

The news was greeted with understandable consternation in the media as the reputation of G4S was, quite rightly, dragged through the mud, but within a few days, Paul Deighton and his team managed to solve the problem by arranging to bring in a large contingent from the army. The military personnel were trained quickly and deployed effectively; they became one of the most instantly recognisable and popular parts of the whole London team.

As athletes and officials arrived and moved into the Olympic Village, they were welcomed in a short ceremony by Charles Allan and Tessa Jowell, who were the mayor and deputy mayor of the village. I spent more than a little time on the arrival of Jacques Rogge, the IOC president, and several of my IOC colleagues. Dick Pound had been a long-time critic of Heathrow Airport, but our arrivals team excelled themselves when he found that the time from landing to being in his room at the Hilton Hotel was just over one hour. I met a number of IOC members personally, a courtesy which I had enjoyed at previous Games, and which is always appreciated. There appeared to be no problems, until the arrival of Ung Chang, IOC member in the Democratic People's Republic of Korea.

Against all prior instructions, he was detained on arrival at Heathrow, when the only contact telephone number he had was my mobile. I assured him that he would wait only a few minutes and that I would deal with the problem. A few minutes became thirty minutes, but to my relief, I was then told that the problem was solved. On inquiring just what had happened, a rather humble immigration official at Heathrow explained that the woman on the Olympic passport desk had to ask for advice as she had never seen a North Korean passport before.

The official IOC hotel was the Hilton on Park Lane, selected as it was easier to secure than a number of alternatives. The IOC session was to be held in the Great Room at Grosvenor House, which involved a couple of short walks up and down Park Lane in the sunny weather. Traditionally for IOC sessions, the host city is invited to organise the opening ceremony of the session. This was done on 23 July in the Royal Opera House. The ceremony allows the host city and country to present a showcase of its history and culture; our evening featured the orchestra of the Royal Opera House, the Royal Ballet, and performances from, among others, Placido Domingo, Bryn Terfel, and Renee Fleming. Master of ceremonies was Jonathan Edwards, chair of the LOCOG athletes' committee.

The one really unusual feature was the reading by newly re-elected mayor, Boris Johnson, of a Pindaric ode for the London Olympic Games, in the original Greek language. Fortunately, given Boris' tendency to go off piste with his speeches, the ode was written by Oxford classicist Professor Armand D'Angour and included (in English) the very apt lines, 'This new Olympic flame behold,/that once burned bright in Greece of old;/with happy hearts receive once more/these Games revived on London's shore.'

Earlier that evening, the IOC had been welcomed and entertained by her majesty the queen at Buckingham Palace, where each guest had been personally greeted with the moment recorded by a cleverly placed camera, providing a special memento of the occasion. During the following cocktail party, Jacques Rogge was able to introduce informally more members to a very relaxed and gracious host and other members of our royal family.

In making the arrangements, the officials at Buckingham Palace explained that they had organised more cocktail parties than we could ever imagine and made the offer that they would repeat the celebration before the opening ceremony of the Games with invitations to the many (over 100) heads of state who would be attending and then arrange special bus transport to the stadium. This solved a major logistical problem.

The session dealt with all the normal business of the IOC, including a report from LOCOG on the seven years of preparation for the Games. This was followed by reports and presentations from the future organising committees from Sochi (2014), Rio (2016), and Pyeongchang (2018), along with the Youth Olympic Games cities, Innsbruck (2012), Nanjing (2014), and Lillehammer (2018). The meeting heard confirmation of the new agreement on marketing rights with the United States Olympic Committee and reports from all the IOC commissions.

At the end of the session, I was elected as a vice president but deferred in favour of Nawal el Moutawakel for the first of the two vice president positions. The second elected position made me the first IOC vice president from Britain since Lord Burghley in 1952. Among the newly elected members was Li Lingwei from China, a much-admired friend and one of the best badminton players of all time.

On 27 July, we set off to the Olympic Stadium to enjoy Danny Boyle's opening ceremony. I made sure that all my colleagues on the executive committee left the bus first and everyone was greeted at the door of the stadium by Seb Coe and Paul Deighton. About to watch one of the biggest moments of their lives, the two London organisers were smart enough to spare just a few minutes to offer personal welcomes. Almost immediately, I had a warm feeling. The ceremony delighted from its opening tableau— the Green and Pleasant Land, through the pandemonium of the Industrial Revolution, to a tribute to the National Health Service.

Shorter segments celebrated the arrival of the queen and a short interlude with Sir Simon Rattle conducting the London Symphony Orchestra in the theme from *Chariots of Fire*. It was during these two shorter sections that the queen was seen to arrive by parachuting from a helicopter accompanied by James Bond (played by Daniel Craig), and the introduction of the orchestra by Rowan Atkinson as he contributed his memorable rendering of a single note. Without doubt, the two moments provided never-to-be-forgotten laughter and were greatly appreciated by the huge worldwide audience.

Before the entry of the competing teams and the Olympic ceremonials, the work of Tim Berners-Lee, who invented the worldwide web, was celebrated and included a poignant moment with the singing of 'Abide with Me' by Emeli Sandé. Her majesty the queen formally opened the Games. Under the watchful eye of England football legend David Beckham, the torch came down the Thames in a speedboat to be handed on to our great

Olympian Sir Steve Redgrave, who passed it to seven young athletes, each nominated by a previous British gold medallist. Rather than the traditional single cauldron, London had prepared 204 metal petals representing each of the participating NOCs, who carried their petal into the opening ceremony; these were raised from the floor and converged to complete the cauldron. Paul McCartney and his band brought the ceremony to an end with 'Hey Jude' followed by a spectacular fireworks display.

The ceremony combined an unusual mixture of famous artists: Daniel Craig, Kenneth Branagh, Evelyn Glennie, Mike Oldfield, J. K. Rowling, and the Arctic Monkeys, assisted by 7,500 volunteers. Despite the inevitable prior British scepticism, the ceremony was regarded as an enormous success, watched by a worldwide television audience of 900 million. All the efforts to provide lighting and sound excellence were completely repaid as the whole spectacle of the stadium enhanced the originality of the content. It was precisely what was needed after the amazing and immense ceremony in Beijing four years earlier.

After the ceremony, we even managed to get all the IOC members on their buses quickly and many were complimentary. Not all of them had bothered to read the excellent programme notes with their explanations of the various scenes. One of my colleagues asked me to explain why we had used so many beds as trampolines—the tribute to the National Health Service and Great Ormond Street Hospital had passed him by. Most importantly, the athletes all walked back to their village with smiles on their faces and their spirits uplifted. It was time for them to play their part the next morning.

Team GB was 530 strong and joined a total of 10,768 athletes from 204 NOCs competing in 302 events in twenty-six sports. The BOA had been able to establish a performance centre beside its accommodation in the village, and with the benefit of large amounts of financial support, for athletes and their national federations, from UK Sport, proceeded to produce results that were the best since the Games of 1908. Mind you, 1908 is probably the wrong comparison as those Games lasted for eight months and most of the competitors were British. However, great results from the home team added hugely to the overall success of the Games.

The almost-packed stadiums were delighted to cheer British success, and the troubled ticket-selling process and distribution rapidly became a thing of the past. The transport system to the park and to all other events worked well, and a warm atmosphere developed throughout the city and the country. My own roles were to support the LOCOG team wherever I could, deal with requests from my IOC colleagues, and support British athletes as often as I could. I had no role with the BOA that had developed its own BOA house in a building in the Westfield Centre, and I preferred to avoid contact with the leadership of my old organisation after the damage and embarrassment done by Colin Moynihan's financial dispute. I was able to arrange accreditations for my son, daughter, and their respective wife and husband, and, on two occasions, for my oldest grandkids, Johnnie and Anna.

The Games were a never-ending extravaganza of ecstatic athletes and delighted organisers, with gold medal successes across the whole range of sport. We had to watch success for the USA and China in the swimming pool and the gymnastics in the Dome Arena for the first four days of the Games. It was predictable that cycling and rowing would start the British gold rush on day five, with Bradley Wiggins winning the individual time trial and Heather Stanning and Helen Glover the coxless pairs.

Day six saw another cycling gold when Philip Hindes, Chris Hoy, and Jason Kenny won the team sprint. In the judo arena in the Excel Centre, Tagir Khaybulaev won the 100-kg gold in front of his own President Putin, and the International Judo Federation asked that Putin should present his medal. The answer was 'No!' Peter Wilson added to the Team GB golds with a win in the shooting double trap, and Etienne Stott and Tim Baillie won the Canadian doubles in canoeing.

Day seven was a day to remember with the famous pursuit team of Clancy, Thomas, Burke, and Kennaugh winning gold, to be followed by Victoria Pendleton in the keirin. Out at the rowing course at Eton Dorney, I turned up in good time as I had chosen the women's double skulls as my first medal presentation event. Katherine Grainger had won silver medals at the previous three games and had enjoyed a record season as world champion with Anna Watkins in the event. They won handsomely in front of the huge crowd, and I was proud to join them in what was an emotional presentation ceremony.

A few nights later, I invited them to dinner at the IOC marketing club and told them to bring their medals. They were, by then, relaxed and happy. and we chatted about their future careers. Katherine was studying for her PhD in criminology, and Anna told me she was also working towards a PhD, but in advanced mathematics, which she hoped to apply to weather forecasting. 'You might not understand, Craig,' she said. I replied, 'Would you like another glass of wine?' They were two very smart ladies.

Saturday 4 August was day eight, and the first day of track and field athletics. It was to become a special day for Britain and will always be remembered as 'Super Saturday', which would bring us a haul of six gold medals. With the exception of some seats in the Olympic Family area, the Olympic Stadium was packed by 10 a.m. Jessica Ennis started her heptathlon event with a wonderful 100-m hurdles to give her an early lead. At Eton Dorney, Kat Copeland and Sophie Hosking won their lightweight double skulls gold, to be followed by Alex Gregory, Pete Reed, Tom James, and Andy Triggs-Hodge in the men's four. I happened to watch that particular gold medal on a television set in a hotel near Wimbledon as a guest of the International Tennis Federation. The champagne tasted even nicer.

Never to be outdone by the boys, the women's team pursuit in the velodrome was won by Dani King, Laura Trott, and Joanna Rowsell. In the evening in the stadium, Greg Rutherford won gold in the long jump, Jess Ennis won gold in the heptathlon, and Mo Farah won gold in the 10,000 metres—three athletics golds in twenty-six minutes, making it Britain's best Olympic day in 104 years. Seb and I had managed to arrange that we could present Jess's medal together, and as we waited for that ceremony, he took me up the ramp towards the track and gave me an individual commentary on how to win a 10,000-m race. It was quite a day. I do not think I have ever experienced anything like it.

For me, day nine produced a clash of events. The men's singles finals in both badminton and tennis were to be played that day. At Wembley, Lin Dan of China won the badminton gold medal, beating Lee Chong Wei of Malaysia in probably the best match I have ever seen. It was outstanding in every way. I left Wembley and headed for Wimbledon, expecting to be in time as tennis finals can be long matches. In the car, I took a call from Jane Fraser, secretary to the president of the ITF, who said, 'Where are you? We are keeping two seats for you but hurry up as Andy Murray is winning easily!' Many years before I had played badminton against Andy's grandparents in the Victoria Hall in Dunblane, so I was keen to see him in his Olympic final. We just made it and watched the moment when he won his first really significant title on Centre Court at Wimbledon, one of the world's great sporting arenas. News then came through that Ben Ainslie had won another finn-class gold medal at Weymouth—my cup runneth over.

Regrettably, however, from that moment, the day went a little downhill. I headed for the stadium, hoping to finish an evening watching the extraordinary Usain Bolt in the 100 metres. Then the IOC called me and asked if I could help out by presenting medals at a team final in the fencing arena in Excel. The timing should have allowed me to get back from Excel to see what is always one of the highlights of any Games—the 100 metres final. Unfortunately, the fencing competition then ran late, there was a petition to the jury of appeal, and it was clear we would not get back to the stadium in time. I apologised to Rosemary, and then headed back into town to watch it on television. To our initial annoyance but eventually to our amusement, the television set in our hotel room had broken down.

While the daily priority was to visit different sports and, hopefully, to watch British success, we varied our programme in a number of ways. On some days, we travelled out to the park on the Jubilee Line, just to see how the transport arrangements were working, and walked through the Westfield Shopping Centre along with everyone else. We met up with our daughter, Catriona, and two grandsons, Johnnie and Henry, so that they could share some of the Olympic experience. On one day, we took all three of them back to the hotel, having arranged the necessary hotel accreditation. Young Henry was very proud to wear his accreditation, after he had spent some time in our room jumping on the bed, and then told his mother that he did not know that Grandad had such a big house.

I kept in touch with Dave Gordon, who was in charge of production for BBC television. He asked if I would go into their studio in the middle of the park, which was a collection of adapted containers, and speak to Sue Barker, one of their leading presenters. He wanted to arrange an interview going back to the start of the bid and the subsequent preparations, in which Sue had played an important part. The interview was quite long but relaxed between two friends and was able to show the changes from the original draft plans to the reality of the final Olympic Park.

At the end of the interview, we discussed the future, including the effect of the Games on British sport, and I made the point that the job of the organising committee was to stage the Games, not organise the future of sport, but that I was sure that many people would 'pick up the ball and run with it'. That evening, in the room behind the VIP box in the stadium, David Cameron spoke to me and complimented me on how well I had spoken on television that afternoon because, he said, 'You're the only person who hasn't told me what to do!'

Two more gold medals appeared on day ten for Jason Kenny in the cycling sprint event and the team equestrian jumping event. The huge temporary stands at Greenwich for equestrian events were packed with enthusiastic spectators, but I was delighted to be able to chat with a most unexpected London volunteer, Richard Meade, eventing gold medallist from the Mexico Games in 1968 and Munich in 1972. He was now proudly wearing his purple volunteer anorak and controlling the crowds in the stands.

Day eleven continued the wonderful litany of successes with Laura Trott and Chris Hoy in the velodrome, and another emotional medal ceremony for both Chris and me after the keirin event. It was followed by Alistair Brownlee in the triathlon, held in Hyde Park and the surrounding city centre streets, which allowed tens of thousands of spectators a free view of an Olympic event. Those who went out to Greenwich were rewarded with gold in the team dressage.

Britain's gold medal treasure hunt had a day off on day twelve, but the following day could only be called 'Ladies' Day'. Nicola Adams won gold in the very first women's boxing tournament, Charlotte Dujardin won the individual dressage, and Jade Jones won the 57-kg weight event in Taekwondo. Day fourteen was another day without gold, although lots of Brits qualified for finals. The haul of gold grew again on day fifteen with Luke Campbell in boxing and Ed McKeever in canoe sprint. Mo Farah then produced the first of his incredible double wins when he took gold in the 5,000 metres. On day sixteen, Anthony Joshua won our last gold in the heavyweight boxing event. The final medal tally for Team GB was twenty-nine gold, seventeen silver, and nineteen bronze—way above expectations and in third place in the unofficial medal table behind the United States and China.

Over the sixteen days of the Games, I managed to visit twenty-three of the twenty-eight sports and watched never-ending British success, which greatly encouraged the venue management teams from LOCOG and everyone else engaged in the organisation of the Games. There was next to no attrition among the 70,000 volunteers, which was remarkable, and the atmosphere in the stadia and in the city was outstanding.

While it is easy to record the winners of the twenty-nine gold medals, further examination of the results reveals four medals in gymnastics, one of the big sports in the Olympic programme, which delighted the huge audiences in the dome arena. The hockey teams were at the top of their competitions with a bronze medal for the women and a fourth place for the men. In judo, there were two medals in a very competitive world sport and four silver medals at Weymouth in sailing. Swimming is the second biggest sport in the Games, and a total of three medals and one in diving showed that the sport had challenges going forward. The very strong results from cycling and rowing justified all the investment made, and Team GB finished the Games with memories of an outstanding sixteen days.

The last day of the Games turned out to be a very special one. Our son and daughter-in-law, Colin and Kathie, invited us to an early lunch at

Scott's, the famous fish restaurant, and presented us with three Olympic medals, one from the 1908 Games, one from the 1948 Games, and one from the 2012 Games. The 1908 medal must have been very hard to find. To the medals, they added a few special words:

> 12th August 2012. The day has arrived to celebrate a momentous occasion, not just in British history, but also in that of global sport. Whilst today marks the end, it also marks the beginning. A line has been drawn in the sand ... Thank you for letting us share it with you.
>   Colin and Kathie

The medals and the words hang proudly on our wall at home.

Later, we headed for the closing ceremony, which became known as 'A Symphony of British Music'. British pop acts appeared and tributes to John Lennon and Freddie Mercury were featured, followed by Annie Lennox, Ed Sheeran, and the Spice Girls, singing on the top of five London black cabs. Some 4,100 volunteers appeared in the show, and as the next host of the Games in 2016, Rio de Janeiro presented an eight-minute segment displaying Brazilian culture. Jacques Rogge closed the Games by describing them as 'happy and glorious'. In his closing remarks, Seb thanked his team and all who had contributed to the success of the Games and concluded his remarks with the words, 'When our time came, Britain, we did it right!'

After a spectacular lowering of the cauldron and the firework display, most of the guests left, and a small group of the senior management of LOCOG and some directors enjoyed a quiet final drink together. There was a feeling of satisfaction but no excess of emotion, mainly gratitude that the Games and the show had all gone so well. Seb came over to me and asked me if I would go outside and sit for a few moments in the VIP box. When I asked why, he said, 'Please, just for a moment.' So, I went outside and sat down in the back row and watched some people begin the task of cleaning the stadium. After a few moments, he came and sat down beside me and said, 'I just wanted you to know, that none of this was possible without you.'

27

Moving On

The night after an Olympic closing ceremony is a short one. There is much to celebrate, and the adrenalin has to subside. Then, the final IOC event—the farewell breakfast—starts at 8 a.m., when the IOC invites the organisers of the Games to come for a relaxed presentation ceremony of commemorative Olympic pins to those of the LOCOG team who had special responsibilities during the Games.

For the BOA, its chairman, Colin Moynihan, received an Olympic order, a traditional award made to the chairman of the NOC of the host country. The London breakfast broke up around 9 a.m. and within twenty minutes, Colin issued a press release, acknowledging his Olympic Order and announcing his resignation as chairman of the BOA. The resignation, but particularly the timing of it, caused considerable surprise as Team GB had performed so well at the Games. However, his resignation just after the closing ceremony rather confirmed the feeling of unhappiness within the ranks of the BOA, the organisation which had started the whole project eighteen years before. The special additional payment from LOCOG to the BOA under the joint marketing agreement of $8,000, negotiated by Simon Clegg, was to be of great benefit to the BOA.

However, after only sixteen days, and a complete transformation from Olympic rings to Paralympic agitos, smoothly conducted by LOCOG, we all returned to the stadium for the opening ceremony of the fourteenth Summer Paralympic Games with the title of 'Enlightenment', inspired by the Shakespeare play *The Tempest*. The official programme for the evening set the scene:

Tonight, the Paralympics returned to Britain and this opening ceremony therefore marks an emotional homecoming. The original 1948 Stoke Mandeville Games was the creation of Sir Ludwig Guttmann, an extraordinary scientist, who, during the Second World War introduced a whole new approach to treating and empowering people with spinal cord injuries. Guttmann's science and humanity ignited the global Paralympic movement and in this same spirit we wanted to create a ceremony celebrating the transformational possibilities of ideas, science and human endeavour.

They were to be the largest Paralympic Games ever staged, with 4,302 athletes from 164 National Paralympic Committees competing in 503 events in twenty sports. Once again, crowds of spectators filled the venues, and it became clear that for London 2012, if you failed in any attempts to buy Olympic tickets, then you bought Paralympic tickets.

The atmosphere in and around the stadia was just the same as during the Olympic Games. LOCOG became the organisation responsible for providing television coverage of the event as the Paralympic movement did not have a comparable organisation to Olympic Broadcasting Services. The International Paralympic Committee (IPC) was probably more interested in television exposure, while LOCOG was at least as interested in television revenue. The spiritual father of broadcasting for disability sport in Britain had been Dave Gordon, who headed the BBC efforts during the Olympic Games. LOCOG decided, after a bidding process, to award the rights to Channel 4. Although Dave Gordon was disappointed, he quickly appreciated that the scale and professionalism of the Channel 4 production added greatly to the success of the Games.

A repeat of packed stadiums, wall-to-wall television coverage, and home team success made the London Paralympic Games the best of all time. Even allowing for the larger number of events, the British team performance of thirty-four gold medals, forty-three silver, and forty-three bronze—120 in total, third behind China and Russia in the unofficial medal table, which was a remarkable achievement and made stars of many of the athletes who took part.

In their splendid *Official Commemorative Book*, Tom Knight and Sybil Roscoe quoted a spectator as saying, 'It was incredibly uplifting, and I felt proud to be British. I have never seen the Paralympic Games before, and I didn't see disability. I just saw sport.' The closing ceremony, entitled 'The Festival of the Flame', had Coldplay, the celebrated British group, as the main stars. They led a cast of disabled performers in another memorable ceremony with the highlight being the Coldplay hit 'Yellow' leading to a display of the famous stadium light effects in that colour. The Paralympic flag was passed to Rio.

Any appreciation of the London Games must include the Cultural Olympiad. Its director, Ruth Mackenzie, said:

> We're trying to put art back into the heart of the Games ... Pierre de Coubertin wanted art, education and sport to be the three pillars of the Games. I hope that our artistic commissions will rest in people's hearts and souls, as well as remaining as a physical legacy.

During the four years leading up to the Games, a huge number of events were held, many concentrating on young people, to involve them and to encourage their creative energies. Music and exhibitions were encouraged throughout the entire four years. I went back to my hometown of Stirling one day to watch a concert by young musicians from the notorious Raploch Estate, once described as one of Britain's worst 'sink' housing estates.

The Raploch area had undergone a great deal of physical regeneration, and in 2008, the area became the home of the UK's first El Sistema children's orchestra, called Big Noise Raploch. On 21 June 2012, the orchestra with, over 100 members, joined Gustavo Dudamel's Simón Bolivar Symphony Orchestra of Venezuela, whose musicians came from the country's shanty towns in Venezuela.

By way of a complete contrast, the World Shakespeare Festival saw seventy productions at its home in Stratford-upon-Avon and across the UK, in thirty-seven different languages. All thirty-seven Shakespeare plays were presented at the Globe Theatre in London.

The climax of the Cultural Olympiad came with the London Festival from 21 June to 9 September 2012, when more than 19.5 million attended. It was the largest display of art and culture seen in the UK since the Festival of Britain in 1951.

After an extraordinary summer, on returning home, it was time for me to slow down and try to put into perspective the emotions, excitements, and successes of the previous eighteen years. For sport, the process of research, planning, and bringing the bid together had been unfailingly good news. Winning the right to host the Games had delivered for sport almost everything that Britain's national sports federations and their athletes could have wished for and placed Olympic sport and the BOA at the very centre of the project.

The seven years of LOCOG had proved to be the ultimate benchmark in the creation of a team to deliver an Olympic Games. It was led by a charismatic chairman from sport with a huge Olympic pedigree. In turn, he was supported by a supreme businessman and an even more talented chief executive who recruited a host of gifted people to a rather strange business which doubled in size each year for seven years, then went into liquidation.

For London, the process was equally beneficial. Political leadership in the city and in government overcame any initial reluctance and bravely invested in a project with many risks and the potential for embarrassing failure. The maintenance of political unity throughout was both unusual and critical. The conversion of a scene of industrial devastation into a large new modern park with a host of new sports and residential facilities was a great achievement.

To do so on time, and within the final cost estimate, did much to change the popular belief that Britain could not deliver major structural projects. When allied to the improvements in transport and the provision of employment, Britain's decision to support a bid for the Games was repaid handsomely. The physical legacy was there for all to see and enjoy, while the employment benefits in the seven years after the Games, across the six boroughs involved, brought a total of 125,000 new jobs, with many more to come.

For the country, the Games reaffirmed Britain's passion for sport, especially when its athletes won medals. The television viewing figures were outstanding; the whole country came together behind Team GB and again for the Paralympics. London and Londoners accepted that their city had been invaded and taken over for six weeks and welcomed all their guests.

Staging the Paralympics provided huge benefits for those with disabilities, and they enjoyed the limelight in venues packed with spectators. The Beijing Paralympics had been the catalyst for changing attitudes towards the 95 million Chinese people with disabilities. The London Paras strengthened the idea that a disabled athlete is just the same as any other athlete.

For months after the Games, British embassies and consulates around the world were to send messages back to London that the success of the Games in London had enhanced the view of Britain for people everywhere. In November, Seb Coe took over the chairmanship of the BOA and we turned our attention to the future.

The prospect of me moving on became clear very quickly when Jacques Rogge asked me to be chair of the IOC evaluation commission for the

2020 Games, with the final decision to be taken by the session at Buenos Aires in September 2013. The evaluation commission would consist of Gilbert Felli, the IOC Olympic Games executive director, IOC members, Nat Indrapana, Guy Drut, Frank Fredericks, Claudia Bokel (athletes' rep), Patrick Baumann (IFs), Eduardo Palomo (NOCs), and Andrew Parsons (IPC).

The IF representative should have been Pat McQuaid, president of cycling's Union Cycliste Internationale (UCI), but he could not commit to the agreed dates of city visits and was replaced by Patrick Baumann, general secretary of the International Basketball Federation, and also a lawyer.

The process for the selection of host for the 2020 Games had been modified by the IOC. A special working group would examine the files of the applicant cities, which had been submitted by five cities by the closing date of 15 February 2013. Sadly, an expected bid from Rome was blocked by Prime Minister Mario Monti on financial grounds, but the decision was not taken until 14 February, only hours before the documentation was due in Lausanne. Monti's decision, and its timing, brought about the resignation from his vice presidency of the IOC of Mario Pescante, a former president of the Italian NOC and former sports minister.

The selection working group's role was, based on the concept proposed by each city, to assess the current conditions in each applicant city and country and to determine the potential of each city and its country to organise a successful Olympic Games in 2020. Crucially, it had to assess the feasibility of completing each city's proposed projects within the time available and to measure the risks associated with each project. The working group was to base its analysis on the information provided by the cities in their application files and through video conferences with each city. It was also required to consult with some external experts.

In its subsequent report, the working group recommended that Madrid, Istanbul, and Tokyo be considered as candidate cities, but that Baku should not. The report on Doha raised a number of questions about the ability of the city to organise an Olympic Games given the massive infrastructure yet to be built and new cooling technology yet to be invented, by dates which were within the required period set out by the IOC. Consequently, the executive board decided not to make Doha a candidate city.

Visit dates were confirmed as 4–7 March for Tokyo, 18–21 March for Madrid, and 24–27 March for Istanbul. I held several planning discussions with Jacqueline Barrett, the excellent head of candidate relations at the

IOC, and her staff, and on 3 March 2013, with the responsibility to produce a final report that would be helpful to the members making their decision, set off on what was to be a fascinating exercise. It also proved to be a unique opportunity to promote the Olympic Games and the whole Olympic movement.

The commission was to have its own working room with its own restaurant in our hotel where we wrote our reports, ate, socialised together, and then tried to sleep soundly for the following equally busy day. Our three days in each city followed the same pattern of presentations on the fourteen themes in the candidate files in the morning and visits to existing or planned sites of new facilities in the afternoon.

On arrival at Narita Airport, Tokyo, I was met by Noriko Nakayama, who, under her maiden name, Noriko Takagi, was the first of a generation of great Japanese badminton players and the winner of the ladies' singles at the badminton demonstration tournament before the Munich Olympic Games in 1972. We had been, and still are, close friends. The bouquet of flowers she carried was almost bigger than Noriko, but it was a special moment.

The visit started with a disagreement on protocol with our Japanese hosts. They told us that on the opening session the following morning, we would enter the room to be greeted by the prime minister, Shinzo Abe, who would be waiting for us. We pointed out that protocol rather insisted that we should wait for the prime minister, but this caused much discussion. Eventually, I gave up and headed for bed.

The next morning, through an organised group of hotel employees, smiling and clapping, we walked towards the specially set up meeting room, which we entered to find the prime minister standing waiting for us. He opened the meeting by saying, 'Good morning. My name is Shinzo Abe, Prime Minister of Japan. I remember the 1964 Olympic Games in Tokyo very well. It had a very popular song. I am going to sing it for you.' He did. The choral greeting, perhaps not as melodious as it should have been, seemed to me to be so bizarre, given the status of the performer, that I pinched myself to make sure that I was not still in bed and dreaming.

The detailed presentations were all coherent and well-prepared, and this bid was much more compact. The commission was impressed by the strong support from the government of Japan and similar support from the newly elected mayor of Tokyo, Naoki Inose. There were also additional commitments from representatives of Japanese industry, including the president of Toyota, who spoke in fluent English, which he had learned specially for the occasion.

We also commented on the increase in public support revealed by our own polling, which was much greater than for the previous Tokyo bid in 2009. The bid committee made mention of the encouragement it had received from the huge crowd of spectators who had gathered to welcome home the successful Japanese team from the London Games. During our many visits to different sports venues and facilities in the compact planned area in Tokyo, to our surprise, we disturbed the city's governor, Naoki Inose, playing tennis, allowing him to demonstrate his own involvement in sport. Perhaps it was cleverly planned that way.

Each bidding city is permitted one evening to entertain the evaluation commission. In Tokyo, we were taken to the National Guest House, which seemed an unusual combination of classical European architecture outside and Japanese art and culture inside. Our hosts were Prime Minister Abe and Princess Takamado, whose father was industrialist Shigejiro Tottori and who had married Norihito, Prince Takamado in 1984. She had been a student at Girton College, Cambridge, where she read anthropology and archaeology and spoke better English than I do. Sadly, her husband had died of a heart attack during a game of squash in Canada in 2002. He was only forty-seven years old.

A city visit always ends with a press conference, which has to be handled with discretion in fairness to all the other cities in the process. The Tokyo conference was attended by over 900 journalists, who, thankfully, did not ask too many difficult questions. The one unusual feature was the presence of a journalist from Madrid, who tried to get me to talk about the Spanish economy. Eventually, I told her that if I had been an expert on that particular subject, I was unlikely to be in Tokyo doing what I was doing. We left impressed that Tokyo would be a strong candidate city.

After a few days at home, the next visit was to Madrid, a city which had lost to Munich for the 1972 Games and which was presenting its third consecutive bid, having lost to London for 2012 and Rio for 2016. We expected to find a continuation of the compact bid that had been presented for the 2016 Games and we were not surprised.

Any sporting visit to Madrid will soon focus on the hugely impressive Santiago Bernabeu, the football home of Real Madrid, the world's most famous and successful team. Its trophy room is perhaps its greatest asset. It currently houses thirteen European/Champions League titles, thirty-four La Liga titles, and seven world club titles—an unprecedented treasure trove.

After a welcome meeting with Prime Minister Mariano Rajoy, Mayor Ana Botella, and the bid leader, Alejandro Blanco, president of the Spanish

Olympic Committee, we were on our guided tour. It was a nostalgic moment for me as Madrid had twice won the European Cup in finals staged at Glasgow's Hampden Park.

The first was in 1960, when 'Los Blancos' won 7–3 against German champions Eintracht Frankfurt in front of a crowd of 127,621, of which I was one. The Madrid team contained many famous stars, including Ferenc Puskas from Hungary, Argentinian émigré Alfredo Di Stéfano, and home-grown legends including Luis Del Sol and Francisco Gento. Many aficionados of football still regard Madrid's performance as the greatest ever by a club team.

Its second victory in Glasgow was in 2002, when I had been able to meet Juan Antonio Samaranch for lunch on the day of the final, during which he introduced me to an eighty-seven-year-old Di Stéfano, who was part of the official Madrid party. In 2013, Di Stéfano was the honorary president of Real Madrid. Sport is good at throwing up happy coincidences like that.

The evaluation commission was allowed to gather on the perfect surface of the pitch and to take penalty kicks against Madrid's famous goalkeeper, Iker Casillas. My effort made it to the goal line but presented no problem to the legendary goalkeeper. The Bernabeu would have been the perfect venue for 2020's football, but for the commission, the club's training ground was, in many ways, more impressive, with a number of football pitches that could easily accommodate hockey with space to spare for other sports.

Our travel around the city—from the proposed new Madrid Stadium to the IFEMA Conference Centre and on to the multi-sport Club de Campo country club—proved just how compact the city's plans were. The relatively new Olympic sport of golf would feature at the very central golf course in Club de Campo. The organisers took a risk by inviting me to hit a shot at one of the short holes, but thankfully, miracles still happen, and I managed to put the ball on the green.

Madrid's night for entertaining was a dinner at Madrid's imposing Royal Palace hosted by Felipe, prince of Asturias, heir apparent to the throne and in the presence of his mother, Her Majesty Queen Sofia, to whom I had often given a British Olympic pin as she built her impressive Olympic collection. The table seated over fifty guests on each side, which may have prompted Queen Sofia's remark that they did not do this every evening.

We finished our visit with a closing commission meeting to deal with the economic issues and the issue of industrial disputes current in Spain at the time. The city's plans were excellent and the budget modest, but it was admitted that the benefits enjoyed by Barcelona during and after the successful 1992 Games were a real driving force for Madrid.

Our flight to Istanbul involved travel on a Turkish Airline plane marked 'Istanbul 2020'. The enthusiasm and support for the bid was clear throughout our visit. As the city presented its slogan—'Bridge Together' as the first Muslim/Secular city on two continents—it could be argued that Istanbul had the best answer to the question, 'Why do you want to bid?'

The bid made use of facilities planned on both sides of the Bosporus, the extraordinary and historically potent stretch of water through the middle of the city, which marks the boundary between Europe and Asia. Istanbul had strong support from both national and city governments presented to us by the president of Turkey, Abdullah Gül, who was a graduate of Exeter University before beginning his political career.

We prepared for the formal presentations of the three cities we visited, but we but did not expect the very regular contacts with Turkish athletes as we visited the sports facilities that would be used for the Games. On these occasions, Patrick Baumann was to come into his own as an accomplished basketball expert who could easily convert to being an authority on volleyball or table tennis. Tragically, Patrick was to die from a heart attack during the Youth Olympics in Buenos Aires in 2018. He was just fifty-one years old.

Istanbul is a passionate football city, and I am sure we visited the stadiums of all its major clubs. Turkish people are also great builders, and we received presentations on the speed and scope with which they could handle the construction of the several facilities they would need and their surrounding infrastructure. The plans for a new six-runway airport were shown, with an anticipated opening date of 2018.

The city's chosen entertainment night was a visit to a restaurant overlooking the Bosporus where a very special fireworks display was planned. Our host was to be Recep Tayyip Erdoğan, the prime minister. In a crowded room, he seemed to be the target of at least 50 per cent of the guests, who wanted a discreet word with him. I tried to engage him about the excellent plans we had seen from the Istanbul Bid Committee, but he was totally distracted by a political scenario, of which I knew nothing. Apparently, in 2010, a flotilla of Turkish ships, the 'Gaza Freedom Flotilla', organised by the 'Free Gaza Movement', had been attacked by Israeli naval commandos in international waters near the Gaza Strip. Nine Turkish activists had been killed and ten Israelis wounded.

For reasons that are not altogether clear, perhaps just a coincidence, the Israeli prime minister, Benjamin Netanyahu, had chosen the days we were in Istanbul to call Prime Minister Erdoğan and apologise. Erdoğan was very animated at dinner and recounted many different telephone calls, including one to President Obama. However, the prospect of organising an Olympic Games was clearly not at the forefront of his mind.

We left Istanbul with a host of memories, not least a change of travel plans on our last day of visits. I knew that the road into the city from the area in the south-west would be a test of traffic congestion. To my surprise, we were told that the organisers had changed their plans and would take us by boat. Very cleverly thought through, the journey up the Bosporus to our waterside hotel in a modern motor yacht, on a sunny evening, with an ample supply of very acceptable wine was memorable in every way. After a few weeks of rest, we returned to Lausanne to write our report.

Domestic British issues soon provided an interesting diversion from international travel and Olympic bids. Alex Salmond, the new first minister of Scotland, leading a Scottish National Party government, revisited the provocative claim that Scotland should have its own Olympic team. Salmond had been very congratulatory in London when I had just become an IOC vice president, but his warm feelings cooled when a Scottish Sunday newspaper reported an interview with me when I doubted publicly that IOC regulations would allow an independent Scottish team as Scotland was not an independent nation and thus would not meet the most basic of IOC requirements.

I had been invited to join the board of the organising committee of the 2014 Commonwealth Games, the hosting of which had been won by Glasgow, an exercise that I had helped modestly. However, my joining the board would require the agreement of the new Scottish government, which was to be denied. Clearly in Scotland, it was wise not to disagree with Mr Salmond. In the event, it was easy to devise a pragmatic alternative to formal membership through a series of regular private visits to the chief executive of the Glasgow Games, David Grevemberg, at which I was able to pass on my experience with LOCOG, by then successfully dissolved.

Glasgow had also decided to bid for the 2018 Olympic Youth Games. Seb Coe and I joined the bid team as it finalised its plans for the project. The team had been able to involve and excite literally thousands of young people all over the west of Scotland and would be able to draw on the facilities provided for the 2014 Commonwealth Games. The other bidders were Buenos Aires and Medellin in Colombia. The bidding process was modelled on the process for the full Olympic Games, but having submitted its candidate file, each city was then invited to make a presentation to the IOC evaluation commission, chaired by Claudia Bokel, chair of the IOC athletes' commission, who had been a member of my 2020 evaluation commission. However, on this occasion, the presentations would be by videoconference.

On 10 April, we all lined up in our multi-coloured polo shirts and presented for an hour to the IOC evaluators in Lausanne. Our realistic impression was that Glasgow had done well. The final decision would be taken at the IOC extraordinary session in July.

The full report from the 2020 Games evaluation commission, on which I served, had been written in April, but it was distributed to members and the media in June. Since the completion of the report, two of the cities had made announcements of 'benefits' not included in their candidate files—Tokyo had offered to meet the IOC cargo costs and Istanbul had revealed an 'Innovation Fund' of $250 million. To avoid any misunderstanding, this fund was to support the creation of legacies for Turkey's youth agenda. Both items were to be removed from the electronic versions of the bid books.

The final report covered the two questions—why the city wished to organise the Games and how it would deliver the Games. They also had to provide answers to the fourteen themes, from vision, concept, and legacy to marketing and finance. Cities were invited to include in their budgets $790 million for the IOC contribution and $335 million for the IOC TOP sponsorship programme contribution, at 2020 values, and to discount those figures to approximate 2012 figures.

The cities had used different discounting assumptions, which explained different 2012 figures in each city's budget. In general, the report acknowledged that the plans for all three cities were of high quality but included an appeal that cities should meet the IOC requirements and avoid any additional 'nice to have' costs that would go beyond those requirements.

The report was welcomed by each city and appeared to reflect their views that it contained an accurate report of the visit of the commission. Some media comment was made on the (perhaps inevitable) much higher requirement of Istanbul with its plan to hold events on both sides of the Bosporus, and for the costs of new sports facilities and the surrounding transport infrastructure. Tokyo appeared to be presenting a compact, city-centre Games, but the costs of hotel accommodation seemed high, and attention was paid to physical security in the event of seismic disturbances and the ability of Tokyo Bay to avoid the risk of any tsunami.

In Madrid, the main observations involved the economic cycle with the resulting pressures on Spain and the long-running issue of Spanish doping legislation yet to be passed. The three cities had been invited to present to the IOC in Lausanne in July.

The report had been written before the social protests around Taksim Square in Istanbul. The area was to be the host of rugby sevens and weightlifting at the Games, and a proposal to demolish Taksim's Gezi Park was strongly resisted. Police tried to disperse protesters with tear gas and water cannon, and the images beamed worldwide through television exposure were a great disappointment for the members of the Istanbul bid team. They also had reservations about controversial Prime Minister Erdoğan leading its presentation at the IOC session in Buenos Aires. I spent some time in Lausanne on this very topic with Hassan Arrat, one of the bid leaders. After the city presentations in Lausanne, there appeared to be notable admiration for Istanbul's aspirations and high marks for the changes in the Tokyo bid from previous bidding attempts.

The real city election at the Lausanne meeting was the decision on the host of the Youth Games in 2018. Glasgow faced stiff competition from Buenos Aires and Medellin. Seb and I helped the Glasgow team with its presentation, and it seemed to be well-received. The two South American cities were also impressive with the president of Colombia, Juan Manuel Santos, speaking in support of his city. In answering one question, his response caused more than a few raised eyebrows when he spoke of peace negotiations between his negotiators and FARC, Colombia's main guerrilla group. I am not sure that his remarks lost Medellin any votes, but they were unusually candid.

Unfortunately, Glasgow was eliminated in the first round of voting with Buenos Aires then winning the hosting rights over Medellin. It became clear from comments and advice from friends that there was a reluctance within the IOC to award another event to Britain so soon after the London Games. A reminder of the emotions involved in the bidding business could be seen in the eyes of the young kids from Glasgow who, of course, thought that all their efforts, and their presence, would mean that Glasgow would win. Rosemary and I went down to their hotel later on in the evening and helped to put smiles back on young faces.

The competition for the 2020 host city election was an even more intense affair. The session in Buenos Aires in September would be the last one with Jacques Rogge as president of the IOC. He had enjoyed a distinguished term with a range of different but successful Games in Athens, Beijing, London, Salt Lake City, Turin, and Vancouver. Although perhaps lacking the vision of Samaranch, his predecessor, and nothing like as skilled a politician, he had been a hard-working and careful president. A president of the IOC is elected for an initial term of eight years and has an option of re-election for a further term of four years. If the president completes the full twelve years permitted and thus an election occurs only once in a generation of members, the choice of a successor leads to a full list of candidates.

Nominations had been received from Thomas Bach (Germany), Sergey Bubka (Ukraine), Richard Carrion (Puerto Rico), Ser Miang Ng (Singapore), Denis Oswald (Switzerland). and C. K. Wu (China). Their manifestos had been delivered to all the voting members, and discussions took place in many different corners of rooms, both discreetly and in full view. The IOC seemed to be insistent that a revised set of rules was required to police the election, and for the first time, candidates would make individual presentations to the membership. It had taken some time to ensure that the revised rules were sufficiently clear and fair for all the candidates. From a relaxed position as a mere observer, I had enjoyed making some contributions to deliver these rules.

In February 2013 in Lausanne, the candidates all addressed the IOC's extraordinary session, but it had been held in private and there was much ensuing media interest with a great deal of analysis and speculation about whether the presidential result at the subsequent Buenos Aires session in September would affect the city's outcome.

At the extraordinary session, the executive board also had to deal with the choice of candidate from the sports movement to take over the presidency of the World Anti-Doping Agency (WADA) under the constitutional rotation system between public authorities and sport. I had served on the WADA board and its executive since the inception of the agency in 1999 and made discreet inquiries among my WADA colleagues about my future role. Similar inquiries among my sports colleagues indicated that many people seemed to believe that I should put my name forward with a fair chance of being elected.

When the IOC sought requests for candidates, I was joined by Patrick Schamasch, the former IOC medical director, and at the very last minute by Edwin Moses, the former 400-m hurdles Olympic champion and president of the United States Anti-Doping Agency. We submitted our own brief manifestos, and having left the room during the agenda item, I was called back to be told that the decision was that I should be the sole nominee from the sports movement for election at the WADA board meeting during the world conference on doping in sport in Johannesburg in November.

Nerves became strained as the members gathered for their 125th IOC session in Buenos Aires. The host city election was to be the first item on the agenda on 7 September. The IOC would hold short polite meetings on 6 September with the senior members of the delegations from the three cities, and Jacques Rogge asked me if I would join him at these meetings and do 'the blah, blah blah bit'. All three cities were formally welcomed and wished 'Good luck'.

At around 10 p.m. that evening, I was asked if I could possibly meet Prime Minister Abe from Japan regarding a question he had about his presentation the following day. In the Tokyo room, he welcomed me warmly and asked, 'Do you think I should mention the Fukushima incident in my presentation tomorrow?' The Fukushima incident was the 2011 nuclear accident at the Fukushima Daiichi nuclear power plant in Ōkuma, Fukushima Prefecture, Japan. The event was caused by the 2011 Tōhoku earthquake and subsequent tsunami. It had been the most severe nuclear accident since the Chernobyl disaster of 1986.

My answer was short and clear. 'Yes, Prime Minister and my advice is that you should do so with full details of how the disaster is being handled, otherwise you might not win.' I was politely dismissed and found out the following day that Abe had thought my comment to be too harsh. Even so, his advisers had told him that I was right. On the following day, he dealt with Fukushima fully and clearly.

The presentations, live on world television, were impressive. Tokyo, its prime minister, and its athlete speakers were excellent. Madrid's presentation was led by Prince Felipe, an Olympian who had competed as part of the Spanish sailing team at the Barcelona Games in 1992. He had been a strong supporter throughout the whole bidding process and made a distinct impression, peering down on the members from his commanding 6-foot 5-inch height. For Istanbul, Prime Minister Erdoğan failed to capture the excitement that, for many months, had been generated by its bid committee.

With only three cities, the voting process was expected to be short. However, in the first round, Madrid and Istanbul both scored twenty-six votes. In the second round, Istanbul defeated Madrid with forty-nine votes to forty-five and proceeded to the final vote when Tokyo won with sixty votes to thirty-six.

The Tokyo win was greeted with great enthusiasm in Japan, and Prime Minister Abe was given much praise for his presentation, which dealt in detail with Fukushima. Support for Madrid seemed to have been affected by constant public commentaries on the weak Spanish economy, and Istanbul was certainly affected by the recent political problems and unfortunately timed doping cases, which I had spent some time dealing with. After consoling the defeated cities, I eventually appeared at the Tokyo party where I enjoyed a glass of wine with Abe. He was subsequently to invite me to a dinner in London during his visit to the UK, when we managed to discuss some happy memories.

The rest of the session agenda contained the standard reports from future organising cities and the very last report from London. Only Seb had travelled to Buenos Aires, and Princess Anne and I joined him at the speakers' table as he showed a splendid video and spoke with his normal style and grace. We were unlikely to get any questions, but there was fulsome praise from President Rogge and, to my great surprise, a long-standing ovation from the room.

The second happy presentation came from the sport of wrestling. Following the review of the London Games and comments from international federations, wrestling had been removed from the Olympic Programme, resulting in a serious review of its priorities. Applications to join the programme were also received from baseball/softball and squash. The three sports ran their own campaigns, and to the surprise of many, wrestling was able to procure the unusual joint support of both Presidents Putin and Obama. Wrestling is a popular sport in Russia and in the college sport system in the USA. Wrestling comfortably won the vote to be reinstated onto the programme.

The IOC presidential election was held at the end of the session. In the first round of voting, there was a tie in votes between Singaporean Ng Ser Miang and C. K. Wu (Wu Ching-kuo) of Chinese Taipei, with Ng Ser Miang winning the vote-off. In the second round, Thomas Bach achieved the required majority with forty-nine votes, well ahead of Richard Carrion on twenty-nine. Bach had run a very controlled and efficient campaign. With his consummate language skills and vast experience in his many appointments within the IOC, he was certainly the favourite going into Buenos Aires. The news broke soon after the end of the session that one of the first people to call and congratulate Bach was President Putin, a gesture which was not to be forgotten over the next few years.

The fourth world conference on doping in sport was held in Johannesburg in March 2013. It had a full agenda of reports from WADA committees and was to consider the ultimate approval of the next version of the world anti-doping code, which would come into effect on 1 January

2015. The consultation process had involved 525 pages of suggestions from stakeholders and had covered many issues. The revised code would increase sanctions to four years for serious offences, and the criterion for inclusion of a drug on the prohibited list was defined to be that it had the effect of enhancing performance. A new offence of 'prohibited association' would be introduced to indict the involvement of doctors, coaches and others in doping offences. The revised code was approved.

The meeting formally agreed my election as the new president of WADA from 1 January 2014, with Vice President Dr. Makhenkesi Stofile from South Africa. The conference had been a success with a remarkable degree of unity of opinion and had listened with interest to an address from Thomas Bach, the new president of the IOC. As I was about to leave for home, I went to see my predecessor, John Fahey, to thank him for all his efforts over the previous six years and to say goodbye. At the end of our short meeting, he said, 'By the way, I have renewed the Director General's contract.' This came as a surprise as I would have thought that as the new president and also the chair of the finance and administration, I might have been involved in that decision.

28

WADA:
Troubles Emerge

Thomas Bach had begun his IOC presidency with the clear signal that he wished to be involved at the centre of all Olympic deliberations and decisions. In early November 2013, he had arranged an Olympic movement coordination meeting with senior representatives of the key stakeholders to create an open and ongoing dialogue on topics of interest.

The agenda included the fights against doping, match-fixing and illegal betting, the sports calendar, autonomy, and good governance in the Olympic movement. The IOC executive board had already submitted its views on the world anti-doping code and insisted on its zero-tolerance policy. The meeting also asked me, as the new WADA president, to strengthen the role of WADA on research and as a service organisation. This request revealed the conflict felt by some between that role and the role of 'regulator'. There was also a call for closer cooperation between international federations (IFs) and national anti-doping organisations (NADOs) and between NADOs and national governments.

Bach travelled to the Johannesburg world conference on doping in sport and made a powerful speech in which he suggested that the IOC would like to change the emphasis from the 'fight against doping' to 'the protection of the clean athlete'. This change of emphasis proved attractive to the conference, and it was clear that the IOC would be more involved. The plea for more cooperation was also clearly understood as the anti-doping organisations in the world had been developing their services and efficiencies to avoid the duplication of efforts. The position of the IOC was to become clearer within a few weeks.

The IOC executive board held a retreat in Montreux over three days to consider in detail a proposal from the president to launch what was to be called Agenda 2020. This was to be a wide-ranging programme covering almost every aspect of the current IOC responsibilities and to provide a strategic framework for future actions. The proposals for discussion were organised around five clusters:

Nurturing the uniqueness of the Olympic Games
Athletes, at the heart of the Olympic movement
Olympism in action: Make Olympism alive 365 days a year
The IOC's role: unity in diversity
IOC structure and organisation

It was clear that our new president had given much thought to the broad reach of the detailed items for discussion. After the base proposals had been accepted by the IOC session, it was understood that, in practice, they would take several years to deliver. The proposals were wide-ranging and would involve many changes: the host city selection process for the Olympic Games, to the Sports Programme of the Games, Games management, a new online Olympic channel, a youth strategy, an education strategy, a review of the whole structure and membership of the IOC, and many other elements.

The initial proposals to protect clean athletes would be based on a zero-tolerance policy against doping, including the following:

1. Seamless cooperation with WADA, including reviewing code compliance incentives and sanctions.
2. Fostering more deterrence by ensuring more effective testing in quantity but also quality; more targeting, more outside competition; more intelligence, and sufficient investment in research.
3. Implementing more prevention by clarifying the roles and different responsibilities between different entities: WADA, IOC, NOCs, and NADOs.

In general terms, the points or principles would enhance much of the work that WADA was undertaking, but the emphasis on cooperation was noted. It was clear that I would be expected to give a WADA report to each executive board meeting.

Looking back over the previous thirteen years of involvement with the agency, I began to appreciate that although I had a 100 per cent attendance record at WADA meetings and had taken part in most of the debates, my principal role had been to look after its finances. As president, I would now have to develop a much wider understanding of all activities undertaken by WADA and with a new understanding that they were likely to increase in scale and number.

Despite a busy travel programme throughout 2013, I took myself to Montreal in late December and met the directors and staff in our headquarters. This was my first appearance in Montreal in the depths of a Canadian winter and to my surprise met a fellow guest who was the director of the Jamaican anti-doping agency. The temperature, much worsened by the wind chill, dropped to around -30 degrees Celsius. That was difficult for me but almost impossible for him, and I could only recognise him by peering inside a large bundle of mobile clothing to find the minimally exposed brown face of a man who was almost too cold to speak.

I spent most of the two-day visit with David Howman, WADA's director general, and tried to visit all the departments providing the different activities. Coming from a legal background and with a sporting involvement with the International Tennis Federation, David was a fully engaged and competent director general of the agency. He understood the many complexities it faced and was well known in the anti-doping community.

His management style was to accept responsibility for a large percentage of the issues that presented themselves, and frequently said, 'Just leave it to me'. In my view, he travelled incessantly, although I made allowances for his New Zealand nationality and his wish to make the occasional trip home. In fairness, he had never been much involved in financial issues and allowed me to argue the case for additional resources. Although my responsibilities had been finance and administration, in practice, David took responsibility for almost all administration and, in all honesty, was not a good delegator to his staff.

The administration of WADA was based around a series of standing committees, each with a director, covering athletes, finance and administration, health medical and research, science, legal, government relations, standards and harmonisation, communications, national anti-doping (NADO) and regional anti-doping (RADO) organisations, international federations, and regional offices. The regional office in Lausanne looked after our dealings with the international sports federations, which, as well as the IOC, were mostly based in the city.

I found that our staff were a committed and hard-working group who had gained much respect for their ability to handle the ever-greater pressures on their workload. However, I was aware of a feeling among our sporting stakeholders that their relationships with WADA could be closer. The efficient IFs had good anti-doping practices and experience from their own sports and were, in the main, supportive of WADA. There were others who seemed less committed to clean sport or had budget problems in allocating the necessary funds to maintain their own anti-doping departments. We also had to deal with a large number of 'recognised IFs' who did not benefit from the Olympic television money and for which anti-doping was a necessary but expensive challenge.

In an attempt to improve relationships, I wrote to all presidents of the Olympic international federations, offering to meet them personally and to discuss any specific issues they had. That seemed to go down well. As the new code would come into force on 1 January 2015, part of the discussions would be to confirm that WADA had distributed its model rules to all IFs and that we offered assistance to any IF in its adoption into its own rules.

We had already begun work on creating a sport-specific testing programme to introduce different tests for different sports, and even different events; the necessary consultation was being planned. In January 2014, I attended the biennial conference of the regional anti-doping organisations (RADOS), which was hosted in Kuwait, where all fifteen RADOS were in attendance, representing 123 different countries.

In addition to its list of responsibilities, WADA also held the obligation to present, on an annual basis, the list of prohibited substances involved in doping offences. This task involved wide consultation with the scientific, medical, and legal communities. The list had to be published in time to come into effect on 1 January each year, and great care was taken to ensure major changes would be understood before they come into force.

A further and associated responsibility was to accredit, and, frequently to re-accredit, the thirty-seven laboratories which had been granted approval, a duty inherited from the previous programme run by the IOC. To link many of its responsibilities together, WADA created, developed, and improved ADAMS (the Anti-Doping and Administration System), a computer-based system to be used by the signatories to the world anti-doping code.

I confess to ongoing difficulties caused by the financial implications of constant changes in the development of the system, not least when several anti-doping organisations had their own systems that were not completely compatible with ADAMS. The attempts to provide a possible interface to link the different systems only served to increase the challenges of how

WADA developed and delivered the system, not least to the athletes who used it for their 'whereabouts' responsibilities. Clearly, there was much work to do.

February 2014 took the Olympic world to Sochi for the Olympic Winter Games. Eighty-eight NOCs took 2,873 athletes to compete in ninety-eight events in seven sports. The main Olympic Park was built in Sochi, a resort beside the Black Sea, which, as a result of its sub-tropical climate, had, for a Winter Games, a somewhat unusual average temperature of 8.3 degrees in February. The Olympic Park housed the Olympic Village and six indoor venues plus the broadcast and media centres. The main stadium was to hold both opening and closing ceremonies, then be converted into a stadium for matches in the 2018 Football World Cup. The park was further converted to hold Russia's Formula 1 racetrack.

The mountain cluster for the snow-based sports was developed at Krasnaya Polyana, roughly one hour distant from Sochi, which contained the skiing and sliding venues. Team GB sent fifty-three athletes who produced outstanding results from a country with no home snow and little ice. Pride of place went to Lizzy Yarnold with her gold medal in the skeleton event, but success was also achieved in the curling rink with a silver medal for the men's team with David Murdoch as skip and a bronze for the women skipped by Eve Muirhead. The four-man bobsleigh team and Jenny Jones in the slopestyle event both won bronze medals. Team GB's great success justified the investment in winter sport that had been a long-held ambition.

After the Games, it became clear that the direct cost of the Games and all the necessary infrastructure had totalled an estimated $51 billion—an extraordinary amount. The original Sochi estimate had been $12 billion, which was 50 per cent higher than Vancouver in 2010. In fact, the much-discussed cost of $51 billion was three times greater than that of the 2012 London Summer Games.

Sochi's organising committee claimed that its operating budget was modest and had shown a profit. To be fair, the much greater part of the overall cost was a result of the domestic decision to invest in the development of Sochi as an attractive future destination, together with the stated plans to develop winter sport facilities to serve Russian athletes of the future. The new Olympic Park—plus the extension to the airport, a new motorway and railway line to the mountain venues, with a new town built to serve them at the bottom of the hills—clearly involved huge expenditure.

In retrospect, the IOC failed to explain that most of the costs were structural investment decisions taken by Russian politicians and not necessary for a Winter Olympic Games. The public impression that $51 billion had been spent on the Games was to become a real problem for the IOC as future host city candidate cities found themselves presented with understandable local opposition to such high numbers.

During the Games, joined by a party of the leading laboratory directors who had been invited to the Games, I visited the anti-doping laboratory built in Sochi, which was a satellite laboratory to the accredited laboratory in Moscow. The laboratory was in a newly constructed building in the Olympic Park and the Russian director, Grigory Rodchenkov, was pleased to show us around. I had previously met Rodchenkov at the new Moscow laboratory during the 2013 World Athletic Championships. Rodchenkov took great pride in showing his fellow scientists his new building in Sochi and displaying the range of brand-new equipment, which had been purchased and installed for the Games. His fellow laboratory directors were green with envy at the scale of the investment.

We had no idea that morning or at any time during the Sochi Games, that the laboratory would be central to one of the most sophisticated doping scandals of all time. At the next WADA executive committee meeting held in Montreal on 17 May 2014, the first occasion when I was chairman, the minutes revealed that in his report, our director general said that 'The Winter Olympic and Paralympic Games had been very successful events for WADA'.

He was referring to the success of the WADA independent observer teams at both Games and the outreach teams that deliver the WADA message to the athletes in the Olympic villages. They were systems that would help ensure that the anti-doping programmes in the future would be enhanced and would help protect clean athletes.

In addition to its normal workload, the WADA board and management had to deal with several additional responsibilities. One in particular arose from the approval at the Conference in Johannesburg of the new world anti-doping code, which was to come into force on 1 January 2015. The existence of the revised code and a specific date for its enforcement caused much discussion about how and when compliance with the new code should be dealt with. To determine the essential aspects of compliance in the initial steps, it was agreed that priority had to be given to monitor the compliance to the code of its signatories' rules so that the provisions of the revised code could come into effect on a worldwide basis.

The requirement to monitor the large number of signatories resulted in the creation of a compliance advisory group under the chairmanship of René Bouchard, a Canadian civil servant with knowledge of both WADA and the monitoring process. At that early stage of the debate, 'compliance' would be based on the acceptance of the rules under the code but did not deal with any possible effects of a non-compliance. The philosophical position would be to encourage compliance rather than punish non-compliance. This was a new position—one that would have repercussions in years to come.

WADA had also to deal with requests for advice on the increasing issues around investigations. We had been able to make use of a secondee from Interpol, Mathieu Holz, assisting WADA's chief investigator, Jack Robertson, a former drug enforcement official from the USA. The specific issues in investigations included how an anti-doping organisation (ADO) could store and use the intelligence it gathered, how this could be transferred across borders, and how relationships could be developed with law enforcement agencies. There had been requests from ADOs for WADA assistance in training, and we had gathered much experience in the field of data-protection from the new rules within the European Union.

On a much more positive note, the IOC had made an offer to provide $10 million of additional funding for anti-doping research, with the request that this amount be matched by the governments of the world, with decisions to be taken by governments by the end of March 2016. We explained the generous offer from the IOC and asked our member governments for assistance, and, over many months, managed to raise a further $6.45 million, so that a total of roughly $13 million would be available for enhanced research efforts.

The fund would be available in addition to the normal annual allocation to research made by WADA, which, regrettably, had come under pressure as demands on the level of WADA activities increased without the necessary parallel increases in contributions. Despite my Scot's reputation for care with money, I had not been overly successful in this area. My successor, Francesco Ricci Bitti, president of the International Tennis Federation, was to prove much better.

In August 2014, I received my first indication that there could be doping problems in Russia. I received an email from the Russian Ministry of Sport, saying that they wanted to meet because it had important information about 'incorrect interaction (abuse of authority) between the IAAF and ARAF (the Russian Athletic Federation)'. On 19 September, accompanied by Olivier Niggli, our COO and general counsel, I met with Russia's deputy minister of sport, Yuri Nagornykh, in Lausanne.

Nagornykh informed us that he had held meetings with Mr Valentin Balakhnichev, president of ARAF but also the treasurer of the IAAF, and wished to inform us of the information he had received. This information contained the following accusations:

> Since 2011, ARAF has been blackmailed by the IAAF.
>
> The system had been put in place at the IAAF level so that athletes with an abnormal blood passport profile would be allowed to continue to compete in exchange for cash payments made to the IAAF.
>
> These accusations concerned at least six athletes whose names were identified to us.
>
> The system was introduced and orchestrated by the son (Papa Massata Diack) of the IAAF President (Lamine Diack) and his lawyer (Habib Cissé).
>
> That the money was apparently paid by the athletes' agents to ARAF and then given to those involved within IAAF.

We were able to identify that for the six athletes named, no results management appeared to have been undertaken by the IAAF. The athletes' biological passport system had only been introduced in September 2012, and IAAF had refused to use ADAMS for the management of its profiles so that WADA was not able to monitor the passport profiles until later in 2013.

Responsibility appeared to rest exclusively with the IAAF. We wrote up the verbal evidence given to us and sent the signed statement to the chairman of the IAAF ethics commission. It seemed to us to be an attempt by the Russian authorities to protect Balakhnichev, but our only course of action was to refer the matter to the IAAF's ethics body, which we knew already had an ongoing investigation into the issue.

The IOC session in 2014 was held in December in Monaco, and the major item on the agenda was the consideration and approval of the twenty-four recommendations made under Agenda 2020, originated at the retreat in Montreux twelve months earlier.

As we arrived in Monaco, I was made aware of a television programme to be shown on 14 Friday by Das Erste, the flagship channel of the German television broadcaster, ARD, investigating major breaches of the WADA regulations in Russia.

With the assistance of one of the IOC's staff, who could speak German, I managed to watch the programme as it was live on air. The content was clear enough, but even more apparent and damaging was the many media comments the following morning. I called David Howman in Montreal and we identified that there was a serious issue to be faced. He suggested at once that we should announce a formal WADA investigation, and I asked him if we had received any similar reactions. He told me that we had received a letter from USADA (the US anti-doping agency) and 'a few phone calls'. I asked for more reaction when it arrived, but never heard from him again.

As I was involved in presenting one of the Agenda 2020 resolutions, I decided that I should think through our reactions for at least thirty-six hours. On Monday, I spoke again with David, and we agreed that we would have the proper legal authority to begin our own investigations on 1 January, when the new code came into force with the appropriate powers. I have subsequently been accused of delaying action to begin an investigation, mainly by Jack Robertson, but that accusation is completely without merit.

Within a few days, we had invited Dick Pound to chair an independent commission to investigate the Das Erste allegations. He was to be joined by Richard McLaren, a fellow Canadian lawyer, and Günter Younger from German law enforcement, both of whom were to become very involved in the process. The investigation started immediately at the beginning of January with the power granted to WADA in the new code. It could not have started earlier.

The Das Erste allegations were supported by evidence from a Russian doping officer, Vitaly Stepanov, and his wife and former athlete, Yuliya. It was the first time I had ever heard their names, but as the crisis developed, I took the time to ask Montreal exactly what contact we had had with them and when. An examination of our records indicated that there had been an initial contact with Vitaly in 2010, with intermittent contact in the ensuing years, but the advice given to him was that clear evidence was required before WADA could act. At the time, Vitaly only knew that— encouraged by her coach, Vladimir Mokhnev—his wife had been doping and he had not disclosed to her that he was speaking with WADA.

Under the rules in place at that time, WADA would have been obliged to pass the allegations to RUSADA, which would have been very unhelpful and even dangerous to Vitaly and his wife. His ability to deliver the required evidence was delayed until his wife was herself subject to a doping violation in her own country. Thereafter, Vitaly shared his actions with her, and together, they decided to collate their evidence, most of which was gathered by Yuliya in secret tape recordings. At the time, given the lack of investigative power from WADA, Jack Robertson, probably with the consent of David Howman, suggested to Vitaly that he take his story to Das Erste.

For understandable reasons, the Stepanovs had been able to arrange to leave Russia and were rightly hailed as brave and special people. They arrived in the United States, and I was happy to sign off on a financial loan package that helped them establish a base in their new country. Vitaly spoke to a WADA executive meeting by video link to protect his identity and location, and we were involved in supporting Yuliya's claim to be able to compete in athletics as she could no longer be affiliated with the Russian Athletic Federation.

As they became established in the United States and found employment, they repaid the loan from WADA to avoid any conflict of interest. Based on the Das Erste allegations and the evidence from the Stepanovs, the Pound commission was instructed to examine and report on possible breaches of WADA regulations in the sport of track and field athletics. The anti-doping world and sport in general faced a bombardment of new problems. WADA was firmly in the firing line, and I was stood front and centre as the volleys came in.

Dealing with the Das Erste allegations and creating the Pound independent commission were almost instant reactions. At the same time, and for the previous few years, we had been dealing with a more complex and far-reaching problem in Brazil. We were aware that the NADO in Brazil was less than effective and that this presented real problems in the build-up to the Rio de Janeiro Olympic Games in 2016.

We had a board member in WADA who had connections to the Brazilian NADO but seemed to be powerless to help. Brazil had also invited Luis Horta, an anti-doping expert from Portugal to join them in the NADO in Rio, and once again, we had hopes of the necessary improvement. The specific problem was that the Olympic Games risked major issues if a robust system of testing Brazilian athletes could not be put in place before the Games. A further complication was a series of issues with the laboratory in Rio, which would be required to be operating efficiently before the 2014 Football World Cup and the 2016 Olympic Games.

The laboratory had been suspended in 2012, and after improvements had been implemented, it was re-accredited in May 2015. The effect had been to force FIFA to send any samples for analysis, which were collected during the 2014 World Cup, to an accredited laboratory in Europe. While this arrangement was not ideal, FIFA could do this as there was always a definite period between matches in a world cup, which gave time for the anti-doping analysis to work properly. Such a system could not work during an Olympic Games because of the rapidity of the events.

We were told that a new building would be made available for the Rio laboratory, but this would involve major issues in the installation and preparation of the necessary technical equipment. Subsequently, the laboratory was to run into major problems, and its full accreditation was only finalised close to the opening of the Games.

In April 2015, I returned once again to the appointment of the independent commission to investigate the allegations against the Russian Anti-Doping agency. I was asked by senior figures in the IOC to try to refute comments coming from Russia that WADA was 'at war' with Russia. It seemed at the time to be a not unreasonable request as we were not 'at war' with Russia, and I chose to send a carefully worded email to Natalia Zhelanova, the assistant to Vitaly Mutko, the Russian sports minister. She served on one of the WADA standing committees and was our normal contact in the country.

The email dealt almost entirely with the creation of the independent commission and an assurance that this in no way represented a 'war'. I had met the Russian sports minister during the 2013 World Athletics Championships, when he explained that Russia had changed its anti-doping legislation and had been active in prosecuting athletes who had committed doping offences. I made mention of these facts in the email. The favour requested by the IOC seemed to have had the desired result as no further aggressive comments appeared. Reflection is, of course, a very exact science as those words were to prove.

In August 2015, a copy of my email was leaked to journalists in both Germany and the United Kingdom. The media comments were presented to suggest that I was 'soft' on Russia and that I did not want to disrupt the friendly relationship with the Russian sports minister. The comments were very damaging to my own reputation and to the strong position that WADA had taken. My explanation that I was dealing almost entirely with the work of the independent commission and that this had no further political implications was not regarded as a strong position to defend.

With mature reflection, I realised that, with the advantage of hindsight, I would have omitted some of the softer expressions I had included in the email. They were not happy times. The episode was to be quoted back to me for years to come. As the Russian doping crisis developed, Natalia Zhelanova disappeared from any formal position, her whereabouts not known to this day, but Minister Mutko became fully involved in attempts to deny Russian activities and was eventually promoted to be deputy prime minister, with a different portfolio of responsibilities.

Media interest always declines, and in calmer days, I began to think through how the leak of the email had happened. A close analysis of comments made, or significantly not made, in Russia made me question why anyone in Russia would have achieved any real benefit from putting this document in the public arena. Very few people in WADA had been aware of the email sent in April and this was confirmed by a search of our own email traffic around that time. I was left with the rather unhappy possibility that the leak had come from Montreal and not Moscow.

This was confirmed by the fact that the time on the email was the time in Glasgow when it was sent and not the time in Moscow (two hours later with the time difference) when it was received. The leaked email was one that had been forwarded but not a copy of the original email sent to Russia. I had a very clear idea who had done it but it was difficult to prove. The affair had cost me dearly and left my own reputation damaged. During those calmer moments, the only proper moral from the affair dawned on me that 'no good deed ever goes unpunished'.

In the middle of all the hysterics over Russia's doping scandal, the IAAF had elected Seb Coe as its new president to succeed the soon-to-be disgraced Lamine Diack. The campaign for the presidency—one of the most significant positions in sport—had been long and close with a narrow victory for Seb over Sergey Bubka from Ukraine, the former Olympic and world champion in pole vault. With their own impeccable athletics careers and records behind them, and with both candidates committed to the election, the two campaigns were extensive, resulting in a 115 to ninety-two win for Seb. However, his victory placed him in an unenviable position, where doping would confront him from day one.

This was to become apparent on the release of the independent commission report, which we organised in Geneva in reaction to European media interest and its consideration by the WADA board at its next meeting in Colorado Springs in November 2015.

The independent commission presented its report to a packed press conference in Geneva on 9 November. The report contained 323 pages and was a detailed presentation of its inquiries involving a complete range of interested parties from WADA itself to the Russian Sports Ministry. There was extensive reporting on all the organisations in Russia involved in drug testing and its management, including the Moscow laboratory and its director and staff.

The report corroborated the evidence made public in the Das Erste television programme and set out in detail the overall structure of anti-doping and its underlying intended strengths and weaknesses. The report was to serve as a volume of information from which improvements in the structure of anti-doping could be made.

Of prior importance was the list of specific recommendations covering the Moscow laboratory, RUSADA, ARAF, the Russian Federation, the IAAF, and WADA itself:

> For the Moscow laboratory, the director Dr Rodchenkov should be removed and that its accreditation should be revoked.
>
> For RUSADA, it should be declared non-compliant, to remain in effect until a comprehensive report into the failures identified by the Commission have been resolved.
>
> For ARAF, it should be declared non-compliant with the code and that it should undertake an internal investigation regarding its officials, coaches and athletes who were identified.
>
> For the Russian Federation, the Russian Ministry of Sport shall ensure that RUSADA and any eventual accredited laboratory should have adequate budgets to ensure an effective anti-doping programme. That all steps be taken to remove and prevent any actions by state agencies that may affect the independence of the anti-doping programme.
>
> For the IAAF, that it should introduce the position of a chief compliance officer and the position of an ombudsperson to whom other personnel can have access for advice and assistance.
>
> For WADA, that it shall take all the actions recommended in the Independent Commission Report. That Russian membership on the Foundation Board and all committees and working groups shall be excluded.

There were sixty-two recommendations in total, and they provided a framework for the organisations involved as they faced up to the detailed criticism. In practice, they provided what was to become a 'roadmap' for WADA as it faced the task of rebuilding the anti-doping structures in Russia. In retrospect, the comments on the need for WADA to have sufficient powers to compel its stakeholders to accept a much stronger compliance regime were prescient, as was the recommendation that WADA required much greater powers and abilities to conduct investigations. Both were to be implemented, but in the fullness of time.

The comments in the report that indicated government knowledge and potential interference in both RUSADA and the laboratory were given prominence in media reports and were to become a theme throughout the future years of recovery. Confirming the information already given to me and to Olivier Niggli by the deputy minister of sport from Russia in late 2014, the report also stated that the commission had found evidence of possible criminal conduct on the part of some officials, but as they had no powers to deal with these, it had referred them to Interpol, which then invited French law enforcement organisations to conduct a separate investigation. Ultimately, the investigations would, in September 2020, lead to the imprisonment of IAAF president Lamine Diack, his son, and several others on charges of corruption.

The November WADA board meeting was held in Colorado Springs and dealt with the initial and important recommendations from the independent commission. The meeting noted that the director of the Moscow laboratory had resigned, that the accreditation of the laboratory had been withdrawn, and that the IAAF had suspended the Russian Athletics Federation.

In the remarks on the commission report, some in the meeting wanted the commission to continue to work and deal with assumed irregularities across all Russian sport. This would have been difficult to deliver as the costs of the exercise and the need for detailed evidence would be issues. In an attempt to set in motion a procedure which might satisfy the requests, it was agreed that an appeal would be made to governments for finance to allow further investigations to be undertaken. The reluctance to institute such a comprehensive investigation instantly produced strong criticism from Travis Tygart of the United States Doping Agency, which was to become a feature of life in WADA for the foreseeable future.

There was one outstanding matter. A further television documentary and an article in the London Times had accused the IAAF of ignoring potential doping offences after the revelations which appeared from what was claimed to be an IAAF database, and which had brought many comments from both media and scientists. To help Seb Coe and to make use of the investigative skills of the independent commission, I had extended its terms of reference and its original mandate. After proper investigation, the Pound Commission reported that the blood profiles that had been the subject of the documentary were not a database as such and could not have been relied on for proof of anti-doping violations.

When added to the 2015 cycling independent reform commission report on doping issues in cycling and further accusations about the conduct of Alberto Salazar, one of the world's leading athletics coaches, the issue of doping in sport had generated a plethora of troubling headlines. I was concerned that this might continue for some time, and it did.

29

Russia:
The Ruin of Sport

The prediction that media headlines would continue after the publication of the Pound report was to prove to be depressingly accurate. The confirmation that the largest country in the world had been cheating in the sport of athletics became an irresistible subject for investigative journalists. Life settled into a programme of explaining facts and the reality of future actions.

There was also the need to raise substantial additional revenue to allow WADA to fund the inevitable new investigations which were likely to emerge from Russia. We knew the demands on us to expand the Pound report to cover all sports in Russia but to do so when we were trying to establish an improved anti-doping system in Russia to replace the suspended RUSADA.

It became clear that establishing an effective system from outside Russia without having responsible anti-doping experts on the ground in the country would prove to be completely ineffective. We had received the expressions of regret from Russian officials and their assurances of future cooperation, all delivered after the publication of the report. However, these did nothing to convince us that trust could be established without major change. Dick Pound had referred to the comments from Moscow as 'changing the deck chairs on the *Titanic*!'

To establish the necessary hands-on arrangements in Russia, we were able to agree contracts with Peter Nicholson from Australia and Leva Lukosiute-Stanikuniene, the director of the Lithuanian Anti-Doping Agency, to move to Moscow and to lead an independent new anti-doping agency. Sergey Khrychkov, from the Council of Europe was appointed to the board of the new agency, and UK Anti-Doping (UKAD) was contracted to produce a test-distribution plan and to ensure that efficient testing was carried out in Russia as part of an agreed 'road-map' to future compliance.

The developments all made sense but took time. A further ARD documentary in March 2016 contained more damaging allegations. It claimed that an individual from RUSADA gave advance warning to athletes of testing plans; that an individual connected with the Russian Athletics Federation (ARAF) was providing banned substances to athletes; and that a coach, sanctioned after the Pound report, was still operating as a coach in Russia. The documentary escalated the clamour for rapid action and made demands on the task force created by the IAAF to investigate the allegations in its own sport. The WADA athletes' commission declared its demand for further investigations into all sport in Russia, adding to the need to produce the necessary finance.

Although it did not compete with the Russian crisis, a further Eastern European substance appeared, with dramatic effect. The news broke that Maria Sharapova had tested positive at the Australian Open Tennis Championships for a drug called meldonium. The drug had been on the WADA monitoring list since 2015, but known before then, and had been put on the prohibited list from 1 January 2016. Sharapova claimed that she had not been informed by her team of advisers that the drug had been placed on the list, but the concentration in her sample indicated a clear breach of regulations. After much wrangling and an appeal to the Court of Arbitration for Sport, she was banned from tennis for fifteen months.

The drug was manufactured only by a Latvian Pharmaceutical Company called Grindeks and was not approved by any other regulator in Europe or by the United States. It was the practice of drug manufacturers to supply evidence of excretion of the drug but that had not been the case with meldonium. As a matter of urgency, WADA had initiated studies to determine how long the drug would stay in the body and be discovered by a test. As a result of these studies and in reaction to the large number of positive tests, it had been decided that any cases below a minimal concentration level (below 100 nanograms per millilitre of urine) following 1 January 2016 (when meldonium was put on the prohibited list), would be assumed to produce a finding of no fault or negligence, by the athlete. This was a pragmatic decision and the correct one, but the confusion led to yet more criticism.

It was hard to imagine that the Russian scandal could become worse, but it did—in early May in a United States TV programme and more revelations in *The New York Times* of claims by Grigory Rodchenkov of organised cheating affecting other sports in Russia, as well as at the Sochi Winter Games. These bombshell statements described a state-run cover-up of drug offences at Sochi, involving the replacement of tainted urine with clean samples collected months earlier involving at least fifteen Sochi medal winners.

Rodchenkov claimed that he had invented a special three-drug cocktail, given to Russian athletes, which was difficult to trace. Claims that there was involvement of the FSB, Russian security services, and the official sports ministry made the revelations even more serious than the ARD television allegations some eighteen months before. I heard of these reports while chairing a meeting of the WADA executive committee.

Somebody was making a long intervention on a research proposal, and I took the opportunity to check my mobile phone. This revealed *The New York Times* article in all its horrors, but it would at least allow me to claim that I knew nothing about them when questioned at the post-meeting press conference. WADA decided almost immediately to establish a second independent investigation and invited Richard McLaren, who had been a member of the Pound Commission, to undertake the tasks. His appointment was announced on 19 May.

The mandate of the McLaren Report (to be called the Independent Person (IP) report) was to establish the following:

1. There has been manipulation of the doping control process during the Sochi Games, including but not limited to, acts of tampering with the samples within the Sochi laboratory.
2. Identify the modus operandi and those involved in such manipulations.
3. Identify any athlete that might have benefited from those alleged manipulations to conceal positive doping tests.
4. Identify if this modus operandi was also happening within the Moscow laboratory outside the period of the Sochi Games.
5. Investigate Evidence or information held by Grigory Rodchenkov.

McLaren was given a target date for a first report of 15 July 2016, so that a factual basis could be provided upon which all interested parties might act prior to the Olympic Games in Rio. This McLaren Report was a contentious issue for the IOC, which asked me if it would be possible to delay the Report until after the Rio Games. That would have been a wrong decision and potentially even more damaging, although it was to become a very public justification for the IOC process on Russian participation in Rio.

As the public debate continued, WADA had to work through the retirement of David Howman, who wished to return to his native New Zealand after ten years as director general. We advertised the position widely and received a large number of applications, which were reduced to a final list of two external candidates and two internal. The small appointments committee enjoyed a long day of interviews in the Sofitel at London Airport, and unanimously recommended Olivier Niggli, the present chief operating officer and senior counsel to be the new director general. David left with our thanks and good wishes, and Niggli continued with the complex legal situation involving Russian cheating, which he had been leading for WADA for several months.

In the three months before the first report from McLaren was due, the media had a field day in speculating on what the report would say and on what sanctions could be imposed. All the old accusations of lack of decision by WADA re-emerged with personal attacks on me and Seb Coe of the IAAF. There were also statements of support for Russia and appeals that it should avoid any hard sanctions, many coming from people with clear conflicts of interest in the situation.

The McLaren Report was delivered to me and promptly published at a packed press conference in Toronto. The list of offences first contained in *The New York Times* in May was confirmed but in forensic detail, to the surprise and strong reactions from both sport and the media. As the report covered only a short period of time, it was clear that a fuller, more comprehensive report would follow. However, the shortened initial report had to be published because it contained vital information that was directly relevant to the full suspension of ARAF by the IAAF and would permit important decisions to be taken about Russia's future involvement in sport.

The McLaren Report dealt with the offences attributed to the Moscow laboratory, covering a period from 2011 to 2015. The laboratory became involved in the organisation of what the report, somewhat wryly, called 'the disappearing positive methodology'. It was a devious system whereby samples that indicated the possibility of a prohibited substance were either removed or destroyed with a result shown to WADA in its ADAMS system that the test had been negative.

The highly damaging and detailed information that the actions of the laboratory were controlled and implemented on orders from the ministry of sport was devastating. When potentially damaging results were uncovered in the laboratory, information was passed to the ministry, it would decide whether the sample would be destroyed or whether it would be simply allowed to continue its normal analysis. The effect of this was to ensure that no damaging evidence against Russian athletes could be found. There was also evidence that several questionable samples had been destroyed and some removed before a planned visit by WADA inspectors. The names of the minister for sport, his deputy, the FSB official, and all others responsible were made public.

The report also dealt with the detailed process established for Russian athletes prior to and during the Sochi Winter Games. Once again under ministry control, a system of collection of clean urine had been in place for many months so that during the period of the Games, it would be possible to swap any genuine urine sample with possible evidence of cheating by replacing this from the stored clean urine. The process was overseen by the FSB and allowed for the swapping procedure to take place at night when the WADA observer was not present in the laboratory nor were any other outside experts. The FSB had perfected a technique whereby the caps of the sample bottles could be removed and replaced without displaying any evidence to the naked eye.

Rodchenkov had been interviewed by McLaren, and part of his evidence indicated that he had developed a more effective system of administering a doping substance to an athlete than had been the practise in Russia prior to 2010. By that time, the quality of steroids and other performance-enhancing drugs that the coaches were providing to their athletes was becoming suspect. Rodchenkov developed his steroid cocktail in such a way that it could avoid detection. The cocktail consisted of three steroids that were dissolved in alcohol—Chivas whisky for the men and vermouth for the women. The cocktail was then swished in the mouth of the athlete so that it could be absorbed by the buccal membrane and was then spat out, with the effect lasting only three to five days. The successful use of this cocktail was confirmed by analysis of samples at the London Games.

The report provided details of analyses completed on samples that showed the presence of prohibited substances, all of which were entered into the ADAMS system as negative. To the increasing dismay of the readers and the audience, the report then indicated how the laboratory-controlled process had been effective and had application to the London 2012 Olympic games, the World University games in Kazan in 2013, and the Moscow IAAF world championships of 2013.

The organisation's control and length of the doping programme appeared to have been generated by the very poor performance of the Russian team in the 2010 Vancouver Olympic Winter Games. As Sochi was to be the host in 2014, a decision had been taken to ensure that the host country would win many medals. The effect of the programme developed by Grigory Rodchenkov and applied by the ministry of sport was to damage Olympic sport in 2012 and at least two other major events.

Reactions to the report were instant and widespread. The IOC reacted firmly by introducing sanctions on affected Russian officials, advising against future events in Russia, and instituting a disciplinary commission to report on the involvement of officials within the Russian sports ministry and other person persons mentioned in the McLaren report. Significantly, it became clear that the IOC were reluctant to accept a blanket ban on the Russian team but would consider passing decisions on eligibility to the respective international sports federations.

A reaction from Vitaly Mutko (the Russian sports minister) could only be interpreted as a form of last-minute appeal against sanctions. Mutko offered and requested cooperation to help Russia deal with their doping problems. WADA held a telephone meeting of its executive committee and asked it to consider a recommendation that as WADA had no powers to decide on eligibility for international competition, they should invite the IOC to consider declining entries to the Rio games from the Russian Olympic committee.

At no stage did WADA ever use the phrase 'blanket ban'. The Olympic charter used the word 'refuse' rather than the word 'decline', but the WADA proposal was to use the softer word. At that teleconference call, when all ten members were available, five from the sport movement and five from government, Francesco Ricci Bitti spoke briefly on the sensitivity of the situation. No other opinion was expressed from the sports movement. The government representatives were unanimous in their view that the WADA proposal with its particular wording should be submitted to the IOC, and this was done.

As the members of the IOC gathered for the session before the opening of the Rio games, it became clear that the IOC had decided to take a rather harder line. President Thomas Bach indicated that the IOC was not responsible for the timing of the McLaren report, nor were they responsible for the allegation that different information that was offered to WADA several years before was not followed up. Nor was the IOC responsible for the accreditation or supervision of anti-doping laboratories.

On the opening day of the session, there was a short IOC executive board meeting when the president informed us that a number of members wished to discuss the Russian situation. I did not fully appreciate how that discussion would be conducted. For the first ninety minutes of the session, and after an introduction from the chairman, many members made critical comments on the situation, at least three of which were personal attacks on me, and the atmosphere became strained and unpleasant.

I was aware that some of the IOC staff had been seen passing notes to different members; this was confirmed by my own WADA staff who were sitting at the back of the room. This had all the appearance of an organised and premeditated campaign. This was rather confirmed by an accidental meeting in the men's room at the coffee break when one of my staff watched a senior member of the IOC management embrace the then president of the Russian Olympic Committee, Alexander Zhukov, with the words, 'we did it, didn't we?'

I had been offered, by the chairman, the opportunity to respond to all of the comments and said clearly that I would do so but during my formal WADA report to the session, which was on the agenda for later that day. In the following coffee break, I took up two of the personal comments and both IOC members then apologised for what they had said. To add to my confusion, one of the apologies said, 'I was not talking about you; I was talking about Pound'. This rather stupid comment served only to confirm the attack on WADA.

During the lunch break, I confirmed views with Olivier and his staff, and we formulated the necessary response to the session, which I delivered, and which appeared to be accepted and certainly without question. During the following press conference and after many questions from the large media attendance, I refused to disagree publicly with many of the comments that had been made but stressed that the creation and delivery of his report had been completed within the time given to Richard McLaren and that its contents demanded a reaction. It had been a very unpleasant experience and left a nasty taste.

The IOC then passed all decisions on eligibility for the games to the IFs whose own decisions were then passed to a special IOC committee, consisting of Uğur Erdener, Juan Antonio Samaranch, and Claudia Bokel—all three members of the executive board. Claudia was the retiring chairman of the IOC athletes' commission, with strong views on clean sport. The small commission accepted all the IF decisions, probably by two votes to one. The public attacks on WADA and the following decisions on which athlete could compete caused almost universal media criticism of the IOC.

The result was that for Rosemary and me, the Rio games were a strange experience as some of my long-standing colleagues were unsure of their reaction to the stance I had taken. They may not have known that I took no part in the IOC executive teleconference meetings before the games as

Thomas declared me to be conflicted, and I was not allowed to contribute to the debates and chose not to make any public comment. The IOC chose to be vindictive and suffered the public consequences. It was not the best of moments for the IOC.

Team GB did much to make us both feel better by delivering the remarkable result of winning more medals than they had won in London four years earlier. The Rio games contained over 11,000 athletes from 207 NOCs, including for the first time Kosovo, South Sudan, and the Refugee Olympic Team, competing in twenty-eight sports, including for the first time for many years golf and rugby sevens. The team was 360 athletes strong and enjoyed the pre-Games training camp at Bello Horizonte, about a one-hour flight from Rio where the facilities of the Minas Tennis Club and all their assistance played a part in the outstanding success.

Regrettably, my other duties did not allow the normal efforts to watch every sport with a British competitor, but I still managed a few of the highlights. Swimming is the major sport in the early days of any Olympic games, and on this occasion, Team GB won five silver medals and a wonderful gold for Adam Peaty in the 100-m breaststroke. Rowing was held on a lake below the famous statue of Christ where another three gold medals and two silvers were won, one of them a remarkable fourth silver medal for Katherine Grainger.

Having been active for some years in favour of the return of golf since the games of 1904, I was interested to see the new course developed by the organisers with lots of help from the International Golf Federation and the PGA Tour in USA. Justin Rose had been an enthusiastic member of Team GB and a supporter of the return to the programme of his sport, despite the declared fears from some of his fellow golfers about the chances of a Zika virus. No mosquitos were found anywhere near Rio during the games. Justin's gold medal was richly deserved and the perfect conclusion for golf.

The second returning sport of rugby sevens saw good crowds at the stadium in Deodoro, and the British seven excelled themselves by reaching the final, to lose to the Fijians who won their first ever Olympic medal. The princess royal, a rugby enthusiast as patron of the Scottish Rugby Union, had selected this event as a potential medal presentation and made me laugh when she explained her concern that she would be unable to reach up to these huge men at the top level of a very high podium. The happy Fijians solved the problem by kneeling.

We were also lucky in our visits to gymnastics and delighted in the winning of two gold, one silver, and three bronze medals. The resurgence of British gymnastics was completed by the outstanding performances of Max Whitlock in the floor exercises and pommel horse events.

Andy Murray, and his brother Jamie, shared a room in the village, and Andy succeeded, eventually, in winning his second Olympic Gold medal in a long, hard fought final against Juan Martin del Potro of Argentina. Rosemary and I got to the tennis arena a bit late as I had been involved in a golf medal presentation, to find that no seats were available in the Olympic family area. A kind IOC assistant gave us two tickets down in the crowd of Argentinian supporters, and we were warmly welcomed but easily silenced by the raucous del Potro supporters. In front of us were another non-Argentinian couple who turned out to be Paul and Alison Deighton, relaxing in Rio after all the exertions of running London in 2012.

Rosemary had been an international hockey player, so a visit to hockey was a must. We went out to Deodoro to see the Team GB women in their quarter final, which they won. Sally Munday, the irrepressible secretary of GB Hockey, insisted we came back two nights later for the semi-final, which they also won. The final was firmly in the diary, and we helped to swell a British crowd, many from athletes in other sports, but were hugely outnumbered by the orange-clad thousands from Holland. It would be fair to say that Holland was favourite and looked like that for prolonged periods of the match, but GB's ability to defend, score on the few occasions it was able to, positioning, and capacity to outthink and outscore in the final, very nervous, shoot-out produced one of the most exciting and satisfying moments of the Games.

At the end of sixteen days of competition, medals for Team GB were also won in athletics, badminton, boxing, the canoe disciplines, diving, equestrian, judo, shooting, Taekwondo, trampolining, and triathlon, all adding up to the amazing total of twenty-seven gold, twenty-three silver, and seventeen bronze medals—second place in the unofficial medal table. Those marvellous days and the extraordinary haul of medals had taken a long time to mature but were unlikely ever to be surpassed.

The IOC coordination commission met with the Rio organising committee each morning, and Thomas Bach had invited his vice presidents to attend the meetings. This meant that, for me, every day started with a meeting of up to one and a half hours dealing with a range of issues that impacted on the delivery of good Games. For example, on the first morning of the Games, the first session of gymnastics finished before all the paying spectators had been able to enter the venue through the security system. This could be regarded as a teething problem but served notice of problems to come.

Much more serious was the situation in the village where the contractor appointed to clear all used toilet paper from the apartments was unable to fulfil his contract, leaving a potential hygiene problem, which was very worrying. While there was much sympathy for the organising committee, it became clear that there were underlying problems, including, long-term financial issues, which were to become serious just before the opening of the Paralympic Games.

On the morning after the closing ceremony, held in the huge Maracana Stadium, the IOC held the second part of its session, dealing with the election of the athletes to the IOC that had been held during the Games. The meeting also allowed the presentation of small gifts to those members leaving a range of positions, and I smiled politely on receiving my gift from Thomas Bach at the end of my seven years on the executive board. In his defence, it is fair to record that after the unhappy occasion at the start of the original session, it had taken him around thirty-six hours to make gentle approaches, which I interpreted as modest apologies for previous conduct.

The fallout from the IOC decisions on Russia in Rio began almost as soon as we got home. Many individuals were encouraged to contribute, and it appeared that none was reluctant to do so. The recurrent theme was the suggestion that WADA required to be reformed, and proposals came thick and fast. The IOC view, publicly supported by many of its senior members, was that a new form of 'integrity unit' might take over the anti-doping responsibility. The NADOs had their own view that there should be no control of doping matters by people with responsibility for promoting their own sports. In response to many comments, WADA arranged a 'Think Tank' meeting in Lausanne with wide representation to begin discussion of all the issues involved in 'The Way Forward'. WADA had also met with Richard McLaren and had discussed the timing and delivery of his full report.

That Russia would not sit back quietly and hope the problem would go away was confirmed in mid-September when a major leak was announced of the use of therapeutic use exemptions (TUEs) by athletes taking part in the Rio Games. TUEs are legitimate exemptions, which allow athletes to take substances for medical/health reasons.

The leak was organised by hackers from Russia called the Fancy Bears, who managed to get access to a data file prepared by WADA but used by the IOC medical experts in Rio, which contained the details of TUEs, not simply in Rio, but of all athletes ever allowed their use. The hackers chose to concentrate on medallists from the United States, followed by

Great Britain, creating the clear impression that the TUE system allowed many athletes to cheat, not just those from Russia. The reaction may have helped attitudes to calm down, and at an Olympic summit in October, there was general agreement on a need for a separation of powers between a regulatory body and a testing body. The position of WADA as the regulator was confirmed as was its need for increased powers, although the possibility of a new testing authority under the control of WADA raised several complicated questions.

Tensions were to continue when I was subject to another public attack at the annual meeting of all NOCs at ANOC (Association of National Olympic Committees) in Doha in November. Once again, the move was orchestrated by factions within the IOC. On this occasion, I actually sat in the body of the meeting, watching the attack being organised from the top table by a senior IOC official. Regrettably, WADA had delayed a decision to suspend the Doha laboratory, and the announcement was made just as I arrived in Doha, which did not help. I dealt with that attack immediately after the meeting in a private encounter with the president of ANOC, Sheikh Ahmad, who instantly backed off from what had been said. That was helpful but had not been delivered in public.

In addition, WADA had published its normal independent observer's report into the anti-doping processes in Rio, which were the responsibility of the IOC. There had been a number of weaknesses that had been difficult to overcome, but the WADA re-accreditation of the Rio laboratory only fifteen days before the Games led to positive comments as the laboratory had performed extremely well. All these issues added to never-ending opportunity for the media to present a situation of discord and turmoil. Thomas Bach and I were to resolve these issues, and many more, at a private meeting in Lausanne. This was a Thomas Bach 'four eyes meeting', at which I was able to express my own strong feelings about IOC complicity in the attacks on me. We agreed to move on and his press release after the meeting recorded:

> There was a very positive atmosphere in our meeting today, and I am very happy that any perceived misunderstandings could be clarified. We agreed to work closely together to strengthen the fight against doping under the leadership of WADA.

The Bach discussion had followed a meeting of the IOC executive board, when I was invited to appear and to contribute to a discussion on what my priorities might be for the next three years if my mandate as president of

WADA was to be renewed. Some of the members hinted that they would like to make conditions attached to such a renewal, but I explained that as I regarded myself as the 'independent' president of WADA, and that I would commit only to my best efforts to deliver an effective anti-doping system. This was accepted and the IOC wrote to WADA to confirm its support of my renewal.

The November meeting of the WADA executive board was hosted in my native city of Glasgow and, as you might expect, had a very heavy agenda. The meeting heard a report from Russia, presented by Vitaly Smirnov, its long-standing member of the IOC. He reported on the steps that had been taken in Russia since the Rio Games, which involved changes in domestic legislation and the creation of his own committee of investigation. The meeting then considered a whole range of suggestions and reports under the general heading of 'The Way Forward'. These were to include the outcomes of the WADA think tank on governance, which had been held in September; the proposals from the Olympic summit; reports from various government forums; the proposals made by the NADOs; and the opportunity for proposals to be made from members.

One of the suggestions was a wish from the IOC to reinstate the Osaka rule into the world anti-doping code dealing with eligibility for the Olympic Games. This would have been contentious, and we managed to defer this until after legal opinions were taken.

A detailed paper had been produced, which set out a roadmap and initial timelines for the way forward. This set out in detail the work streams that would be necessary under a list of headings:

1. Compliance. The chairman of the compliance review committee presented a detailed paper on potential improvements to the compliance regulations. At that time, they were based mainly on dealing with non-compliance with the code or international standards. The suggestion was that further requirements for compliance were necessary so that routine breaches of compliance with the Code were a first stage. This was to be followed by a second stage, in which significant components of the anti-doping programme were not aligned with the code. A third and more serious stage would cove deliberate attempts to circumvent the rules. This third case would require predictable and appropriate sanctions. If these improvements could be agreed, WADA would then have sufficient powers to implement a proper system of compliance. The meeting approved the paper and its proposals, the first step to a major improvement.

2. Investigations. It was reported that to enable WADA to develop its capabilities and professional intelligence gathering, that Gunter Younger, who had been a member of the Pound Commission had been hired and was forming a team around him to deal with these requirements. Further work would be required to give the investigations team complete independence within the WADA management framework.

3. Testing. It was also reported that a proposal from the IOC had been made to create a potential independent testing authority. WADA had agreed to investigate the possibility and had put together a steering committee which would report in due course.

4. Whistleblowing. The WADA legal department presented the first draft of a whistleblowing policy, which would be created in association with the investigations department. The draft document had been circulated for consultation to internationally recognised experts in the field of whistleblowing and data protection.

5. Governance. There had been much discussion of this at the Think Tank and at the executive committee and many members expressed their opinions. The result was to create a special group with wide representation to discuss all the issues, a decision which was to take a considerable time to reach agreed conclusions.

The combination of these proposed changes and the detailed compliance, investigations, and whistleblowing policies were seen as a significant WADA response to the criticism it had faced.

The meeting also formally nominated me as president for a further three years. Regrettably, Dr Stofile from South Africa had died, and the position of vice president had to be filled. The meeting was informed that governments had decided on one candidate, and Linda Hofstad Helleland, the Norwegian minister for sport, was elected. She was a controversial figure in the sports community in Norway, but she was a protégé of Thorhild Widvey, the current executive committee member from Norway, who was highly regarded.

My re-election was derided, yet again, by David Walsh in *The Sunday Times*. David had been a constant critic of the cheating in Russia, very supportive of the Russian whistle-blowers, and constantly critical of my own position, even though I had no knowledge of the WADA actions from 2010 to 2014. Each Sunday, I would look at the sports section of the paper and on good days would contact my brother, Allan, to say that this was a 'Walsh-free Sunday'. In fairness, both WADA and I had been supportive of the Stepanovs, who had provided vital information.

Becoming more than a little exasperated, I wrote to David, pointing out that in his last five articles, he had made five factual errors. I told him that we were really both strongly in favour of clean sport, and that I would be happy to meet him in London. He never replied, but the flow of criticism stopped.

30

Confusion Before Conclusion

The year 2017 started with reactions to the publication in December 2016 of the second and complete McLaren Report. The first report had been presented in July 2016 and had made the following key findings:

1. The Moscow Laboratory had operated, for the protection of doped Russian athletes within a State-dictated failsafe system, described in the report as the Disappearing Positive Methodology.
2. The Sochi Laboratory had operated a unique sample swapping methodology to enable doped Russian athletes to compete at the Games.
3. The Ministry of Sport had directed, controlled, and overseen the manipulation of athletes' analytical results or sample swapping, with the active participation and assistance of Russian state security organisations, the FSB, CSP and both Moscow and Sochi laboratories.

In the report, there was information and evidence about the involvement of at least 1,000 athletes across all sports and about the effects of cheating on the 2012 London Olympic Games and the Universiade and IAAF world championships in 2013. The report also included detailed evidence of individual cases and an evidence disclosure package, providing the possibility for cases to be prosecuted against a number of athletes. Details were provided of the hitherto unknown method of opening sample bottles and suggested that the methods used had operated in Russia from 2011 until 2015.

The report opened an almost never-ending list of potential anti-doping actions that were to dominate sport for the next three years. Clearly, the decision by WADA to begin a process to help establish an effective, independent anti-doping agency in Russia had been the correct course of action and even more badly needed than at first realised.

The IOC had reacted by creating two disciplinary commissions under the chairmanships of senior French judge Guy Canivet and Swiss IOC member Denis Oswald, respectively. They were asked to investigate the overall allegations of corruption and to deal with individual cases to be prosecuted by the IOC. McLaren had agreed to provide evidence to these two commissions where required.

WADA continued to develop its own roadmap towards renewed compliance of RUSADA, by using the presence of appointed international experts, resident in Moscow, and the services of UKAD to develop testing plans and their delivery. The impact and fallout from the problems in Russia were to dominate the work of WADA and influenced many of the steps already agreed to deliver 'The Way Forward'. The normal executive committee and board meetings in May 2017 set the template for all this work.

The major challenge to WADA was to develop an improved system of compliance, which had been agreed in principle at the previous meetings in November 2016. The compliance review committee (CRC) had a new chairman, British sports lawyer Jonathan Taylor, and he presented his paper setting out a proposed international standard for compliance, which would allow WADA to investigate situations of non-compliance and to take appropriate actions. The standard, for the first time, detailed a list of potential sanctions to apply to those organisations that became non-compliant.

To find out exactly the current situation on compliance, WADA distributed an audit questionnaire to 307 anti-doping organisations, all round the world, which had become signatories to the world anti-doping code. They had all been returned and provided the basis for the proposed new standard. WADA would create a compliance task force and monitor compliance of all signatories and report any breaches to the CRC.

Under existing conditions, every effort would be made to resolve any issues of non-compliance, but if this proved to be impossible, a system of graded and proportionate sanctions would be introduced. The CRC would recommend to the WADA executive committee that a signatory was non-compliant, and unless accepted by the signatory, WADA would then have to make that assertion to the Court for Arbitration in Sport, where the sanction would be decided. Articles 15 and 23 of the code would have to be amended to ensure acceptance of such a decision by all signatories.

The proposal to create a new international standard was agreed and the process then distributed to all interested parties in a consultation process.

The WADA meetings also considered reports, suggestions, and progress on the governance working group which indicated that the process would be long and complicated as there were many different views to be considered. The group had been unanimous in recognising the role of WADA as the world regulator, but more time was required to discuss the structures within WADA of the different board, executive committee, and standing committees and the positions of the officers and their election.

The laboratory accreditation group was certainly making progress in dealing with the thirty-four accredited laboratories in the world, not all of which were working at full capacity. There would be improvements in the financial stability required for accreditation and an emphasis on quality across all laboratories.

The working group on the creation of an international testing authority (ITA), suggested by the IOC, had made its recommendations of an organisation established under Swiss law, funded by the IOC and with a board of five people with two independent members, one of which would be chairman. It was noted that Valérie Fourneyron, the former French sports minister and former chair of the WADA health, medical and research committee had agreed to be chairman. The ITA would have to establish its own business model for its services to international federations. WADA would have a non-voting seat on the ITA board.

Former cross-country skier, Canadian Beckie Scott, the chair of the WADA athletes' committee, delivered her regular report, with agreement on the proposed new compliance standard but introduced the wish of the athletes' commission to prepare and present a charter of athletes' rights. The idea had been first raised and discussed at an athletes' meeting during the annual WADA symposium in March. This would require a wide consultation with athletes, and it was suggested that the IOC athletes' commission should be involved as the proposal appeared to be based on anti-doping issues but might develop a wider interest. The athletes' committee was also supportive of the new whistle-blower policy and the framework developed for the investigations department to ensure its independence.

The legal department reported on its investigations into the inclusion in the world anti-doping code of an article based on the previous Osaka rule, under which an athlete subject to a doping suspension would be ineligible for selection for an Olympic Games. WADA had consulted Jean-Paul Costa, an eminent French judge in the European Court of Human Rights, who had previously advised on the code. His view was that the case law from CAS on this subject confirmed the inclusion of the requested rule would create disproportionate sanctions and the suggestion should not be accepted.

The meetings also agreed that work should start on another new international standard, but on this occasion on the important subject of 'education'. There had also been information from the governments that the vice president, Linda Helleland, wished to establish a system of better coordinating the views of the governments at WADA meetings, which was to develop into the 'One Voice' project. This development, and almost all the other items for discussion, resulted from the damaging fallout from the Russian situation.

What was to be a normal item on all future agendas was a report on the current situation in Russia. Progress had been made in the reformation of RUSADA, but testing of athletes was complicated by a lack of capacity and service providers in Russia. With assistance from UKAD and the Finnish anti-doping agency, twenty new doping control officers were being trained. The current situation in Russia had been reported to the CRC, which had recommended that the new RUSADA should have an independent chair and vice-chair. Yelena Isinbayeva, a double Olympic champion pole vaulter, had been nominated as chair by the Russian Olympic Committee, but this had been strongly opposed by WADA as she could in no way be described as independent, and the position was withdrawn.

Conflict-of-interest policy for RUSADA was another challenge, and there was a clear need to access the athlete biological passport samples in the Moscow laboratory. This had been arranged. Having regard to all the circumstances, it was agreed that if Russia could satisfy the four conditions discussed, then RUSADA should be allowed to restart testing under the control of the international experts and UKAD. It was one small step forward. The agenda set out above was to remain in place for the next two years as everything that was said or done regarding the Russian sanction was a matter for media debate.

However, in the IOC world, there was a very public debate on the choice of Olympic host cities in July after Budapest had withdrawn its candidature for the 2024 Games. This was the third withdrawal after Hamburg and Rome had both decided not to proceed. The IOC was faced with a complex problem, but after the evaluation committee report, it decided to award both the 2024 and 2028 Games at the same session—to Paris for 2024 and Los Angeles for 2028.

Obviously, discrete negotiations had taken place, as Los Angeles seemed happy to accept the decision to delay until the end of the decade, a position 'sweetened' by a payment from the IOC of $160 million for youth sports development in the city. For once, anti-doping and Russia were never mentioned.

In August, WADA published the final version of the 'Road Map to Code Compliance', indicating the improvements that would be needed in Russia before its compliance could be renewed. Central to this document was an acceptance by Russia of the McLaren Report and this declaration of contrition was supported in principle by the IAAF, and by the International Paralympic Committee, which had both suspended the Russians. Regrettably, the document brought about an almost immediate statement from Russia that they would not publicly acknowledge the McLaren Report.

The situation became, if anything, even more confused when WADA decided that it would take no further action in an investigation into ninety-six individual athletes who were implicated in the Russian doping scandal. These cases were related to athletes already investigated and cleared by different international federations stretching back to before the previous Olympic Games in Rio. The available evidence was insufficient to support the assertion of an anti-doping rule violation against ninety-five of the athletes (only one case proceeded).

A group of NADOs had called for Russia to be banned from the Pyeongchang Winter Olympic Games in 2018, but the demand was less than helpful as we were working through an agreed roadmap with the Russian authorities, and of course, the suggestion went down badly with the IOC.

Cheating in the Olympic world raised its ugly head again when the authorities in Brazil announced that they had arrested Carlos Nuzman, president of the Brazilian Olympic Committee, and his general director, Leonardo Gryner, for alleged involvement in a vote-buying scandal during the successful Rio bid for the Games eight years earlier. The allegations involved Nuzman and Lamine Diack and a company established by Diack's son, Papa Massata Diack, funded by a Brazilian businessman, Arthur de Menezes Soares Filho (nicknamed 'King Arthur') to help solicit the votes of African IOC members; Frankie Fredericks, an athlete member from Namibia had been suspended in connection with the same issue. There was public protest from some members, and both Nuzman and the Brazilian Olympic Committee were suspended. The outcome of the investigations and subsequent trials is still not decided.

There was intense interest in the build-up to the Pyeongchang Games and in the ultimate IOC decision on the participation, if any, of the Russian

Olympic Committee and its athletes. WADA's investigation department was asked to vet all Russian athletes and support team members listed as potentially going to Pyeongchang. This work primarily relied on detailed analysis of the laboratory information management system (LIMS) from the Moscow laboratory covering a period from 2012 to 2015 that WADA had obtained from a whistle-blower. The database was very large and would take some time to analyse.

The next opportunity to consider progress in the rebuilding of RUSADA and its compliance came at the meetings in Seoul in November 2017. At the request of the new minister for sport in Russia, former Olympic fencer Pavel Kolobkov, I confirmed a requested invitation to him and to Alexander Zhukov, the president of the Russian Olympic Committee, to make presentations to both the executive committee and foundation board.

In their presentations, both Russian officials covered the improvements that had been made in RUSADA and the anti-doping structure in Russia, which had been aided by the international experts and assistance from UKAD. However, Zhukov stated clearly that it was impossible for Russia to accept the McLaren Report. The chair of the CRC then reported on the three conditions for reinstatement that were outstanding: the issue of access to closed cities; acceptance of the McLaren Report; and access to the data in the Moscow laboratory. As these conditions had yet to be satisfied, the meeting maintained the suspension of RUSADA, although it acknowledged that much work had been done to make it operationally effective.

On a positive note, the new international standard on compliance was approved, along with the necessary changes to the code. The renewal of the agreement with Montreal to retain the headquarters of WADA in the city was confirmed, although some slight concerns were raised by the IOC members because of the presence of so many international federations with offices in Lausanne. The decision provided a welcome degree of certainty as the costs and efforts of an international bidding process for a new home were avoided, to say nothing of the potential disturbance to the lives of around one hundred employees in Montreal, which had been a very cost-effective venue for the last ten years.

The challenges of the eligibility of Russian athletes for Pyeongchang became even more complicated when the Court of Arbitration for Sport upheld the appeals of twenty-eight Russian athletes from disciplinary procedures of the IOC arising from doping offences at Sochi. Another eleven cases lost their appeal as they were the cases with excess salt detected in their samples. The IOC was very irritated at the CAS decisions and considered a further appeal to the Swiss federal tribunal.

It emerged that during the establishment of the CAS arbitration panel, an appeal against an IOC-selected arbitrator had been upheld but that no such appeal was made by the IOC against the Russian appointed arbitrator. The decisions were very disappointing as they created some lack of acceptance and doubt about the strength of the evidence presented in the McLaren Report. For WADA, it was a real problem as these legal decisions reinforced the total refusal of Russia to accept the McLaren Report, an agreed condition of renewed compliance. Even more problems were brewing.

For the Pyeongchang Games, the IOC suspended the Russian Olympic Committee but allowed the participation of 'neutral' athletes from Russia under the acronym of OAR—Olympic athletes from Russia. WADA had provided the IOC with evidence on the doping involvement or history of around 100 separate Russian athletes and they were refused participation.

With no direct involvement in Pyeongchang, I could relax and enjoy some sport, watching ninety-two NOCs compete in 102 disciplines in seven sports. A very cold opening ceremony was enlivened by the United Team from both South and North Korea, which selected a 'unified' women's ice hockey team, who enjoyed themselves without any noticeable success.

Team GB was fifty-six athletes strong with one gold and four bronze medals won. The skeleton squad was outstanding with Lizzy Yarnold winning her second gold medal while Laura Deas and Dom Parsons won bronze, as did Izzy Atkin in women's slopestyle and Billy Morgan in big air. Eve Muirhead finished in fourth place in women's curling and Elise Christie had a series of heart-breaking losses in the short-track skating events. The results were excellent and showed much promise in the new snowboarding and freestyle events.

The IOC decided to lift the suspension of the Russian Olympic Committee just after the finish of the Sochi Games. I had suggested to the IOC in Sochi that a longer term of suspension offered an opportunity to press the Russian authorities to accept the conditions of the WADA roadmap, but clearly to no avail, and the almost daily saga of dealing with the standoff was to continue.

Each March, WADA held its annual symposium in the large auditorium of the SwissTech Convention Centre in Lausanne, which gave us the opportunity to present a form of a 'State of the Union' message to the large assembly of the anti-doping community. Our position on Russia was stated very clearly: WADA would require the satisfactory delivery of the two remaining conditions.

This symposium also heard from our vice president, Linda Helleland, who requested a special place on the agenda. She had not been active with WADA as an organisation since her election in November 2016 and seemed to find the problems of anti-doping too complex to meaningfully get involved. She seemed to regard her vice president position as a means of self- promotion. In Lausanne, she read a speech with strong criticism of the IOC and IFs over their handling of the Russian crisis. This was interpreted by some observers as her first public statement in a campaign to become the next president of WADA.

One of the delegates to the symposium was Yuri Ganus, the newly appointed director of RUSADA, who seemed to understand the requirement for the independence of RUSADA, a situation which would be difficult to deliver in Russia. He came from a legal background and was to prove to be an excellent administrator as he built the international connections that would help him and his organisation in their difficult operational tasks.

For the executive committee meeting in May 2018, the vice president had prepared and put on the agenda a request that WADA should instigate and fund yet another independent review of the anti-doping system in light of the Russian crisis. She reported that the paper had been discussed at length by the governments at their pre-meeting and stressed that the proposal required the agreement of the sports movement. It became clear that the details contained in her proposal had not been unanimously accepted by the governments, and a second short paper containing some amendments had been prepared with a request that it be circulated just before the meeting.

The issue of late papers being discussed had caused difficulties at a previous meeting in Paris, and there was a general view that the second additional paper should not be considered. After a full debate, it was clear that the sports movement did not believe that another independent review was necessary, and the matter was postponed for further consideration at the next executive committee meeting in September. The argument and the division within the WADA executive were becoming clear. Within a few days, Linda Helleland announced, via the BBC, her intention to stand for the presidency of WADA at the next world conference on doping in sport to be held, at the invitation of the young Polish sports minister, and former 400-m runner, Witold Banka, in Katowice in Poland.

Just before the executive committee meeting, I received two letters from Moscow. The first came from Pavel Kolobkov the Russian minister for sport, and listed the changes in anti-doping programmes in Russia, the creation of a new anti-doping laboratory, the restoration of the operations of RUSADA, and repeated confirmation that access to the samples in the Moscow Laboratory was in the hands of the investigative committee of the Russian Federation. A second letter from Kolobkov was also signed by the president of the Russian Olympic Committee, Alexander Zhukov, and the president of the Russian Paralympic Committee, Vladimir Lukin.

In the letter, they acknowledged the suspension of the Russian Olympic Committee and the findings of the IOC Schmidt Commission, which was the successor to the original Canivet Commission, charged with investigating the allegations of institutionalised cheating in Russia; the conclusion was very much in line with the results of the McLaren Report. The letter also commented on the McLaren Report and the manipulations and practises it contained, stating that they were carried out without their knowledge or authorisation. It also claimed that appropriate actions had been taken and would be taken against the individuals concerned. Both letters were acknowledged. The tone of the letters appeared to be rather more conciliatory than previous letters and both were sent to Jonathan Taylor, chairman of the compliance review committee (CRC) for his attention.

The increasing tensions caused by the Russian affair and the different opinions on how they should be faced, appeared again at the global athlete forum organised by the WADA athletes' committee in Calgary in June 2018. Initially, we received a number of complaints from athlete bodies that appeared not to have been invited, and steps were taken to explain and rectify any omissions.

To answer questions, Olivier Niggli and I were invited for a part of the first session only but were then requested to leave the meeting. Part of the agenda discussed the proposed athletes' charter and the consultation process that had employed the US company, Fair Sport, which had been established by an unknown group of US investors with the help of Johann Olav Koss of Norway, a former quadruple gold medallist speed skater and a good friend of the WADA vice president.

The results of the forum were decided by a small group of people in a very undemocratic fashion and the record of the discussions indicated a consistent theme of anti-Russian views. All these tensions were aggravating feelings of discord between the WADA athletes' committee and the IOC athletes' commission, four of whom were appointed to the WADA board as representatives of the sports movement, with one sitting on the executive committee.

The CRC, very ably led by Jonathan Taylor, an experienced London-based lawyer with much experience in anti-doping cases, decided, based on the discussion that had taken place during the May 2018 foundation board meeting, to consider whether any steps could be taken to find a solution to the apparent impasse with Russia on the final two conditions on the roadmap. Without a solution, WADA had no legal basis for potential sanctions that would deal with extended Russian exclusion. The CRC decided to try to break the impasse as the only way to deliver progress and to move matters forward in such a way that any Russian failure to deliver would be dealt with under the new standard for compliance.

The CRC met in Montreal and agreed unanimously to two revised conditions and wrote officially to Olivier Niggli, the director general in June. Based on that decision, I wrote formally to the Russian sports minister on 22 June, who took many weeks to respond, but slightly to my surprise, he accepted the offer on 13 September. The two revised conditions were as follows:

> 1. That the Russian authorities acknowledged the findings of the Schmidt Commission, including in particular the finding that 'a number of individuals within the Ministry of Sport and its subordinated entities' were involved in the manipulations of the anti-doping system in Russia.
> 2. That the second condition would be satisfied if the Russian authorities committed unconditionally to provide to WADA by a specific date the access to the data and samples sought by WADA in the Moscow Laboratory. This would provide an authentic copy of the analytical data stored on the hard drives of the laboratory instruments that generated the LIMS data and access to the samples stored at the laboratory for retesting purposes.

I was pleased that after literally years of effort, an agreement seemed possible to finalise the creation of an effective anti-doping system in Russia, rather than doing nothing and risking that the continued suspension of RUSADA could last indefinitely. This was always going to be a better option to deliver good anti-doping processes in Russia rather than do nothing and risk a return in Russia to the bad old days of institutional doping.

It was also pleasing that our highly regarded CRC had been unanimous in its recommendations, including Beckie Scott, the chair of our athletes' commission. Based on their suggestions I wrote to our executive commission, giving them all the information, which would be the basis for a decision at the next executive committee meeting in Mahe in the Seychelles in September. Following that, there had been no reaction at all from any member of the executive committee to the detailed proposals that would appear on the agenda.

As a volunteer in the administration of sport, I found the conduct of many in their reactions to Russian cheating had been pretty challenging, but part of the reaction became seriously unacceptable. The Dutch police, and Swiss and Canadian secret services, had been investigating the possibility of a hacking of WADA meetings held in Lausanne in September 2016, and in response to a request for cooperation, I found that one day I had five members of the UK National Crime Agency in our house at Bridge of Weir, west of Glasgow, to check on all my communications equipment—PC, laptop, iPad, and mobile phone—plus a two-hour interview.

I had never complained before about my involvement in sport, but that conviction was sorely tested when I was informed that one of the suspected hackers was the same GRU thug who had been identified as one of the two who was charged with the poisoning of the Skripals in Salisbury. Sometimes, volunteering leads to a step too far.

We had arranged to hold the normal September meetings of our executive in Mahe in response to an invitation from the vice president of the country and one of the members of our board, to meet at least close to the African continent. To our immense irritation, the BBC carried the agenda and supporting papers in a clearly organised leak, which forced us to release official copies and to respond to the immediate hysteria. The proposal on the agenda to consider the removal of the suspension of RUSADA under the two specific conditions encouraged much criticism; leaking continued right up to the date of the meeting. The CRC held its own separate conference call on 13 September when there appeared to be continued unanimity, but Beckie Scott then resigned her membership of the CRC the next day.

As you might imagine, the meeting was tense as feelings on both sides were running high. A proposal from the governments was made to postpone any decision until the next meeting, a not unusual tactic in the political world, but one which was not supported by the sports movement. The postponement proposal was narrowly defeated, and the meeting then had to consider and decide on the carefully worded recommendation from the CRC.

A firm date was added that Russian authorities would have to accept, which gave WADA access to the data by 31 December 2018, or they would again be declared non-compliant, but on this occasion under the rules of the new standard for compliance that gave WADA increased powers. A vote was taken, and the CRC recommendation was approved by nine votes to two, with one abstention. The opposing votes of Oceania and vice president Helleland were instructed to be disclosed.

The reactions to the decision, but as always in favour of a blanket ban, were instant and predictable. Some rather more balanced views recognised that progress had been made but with conditions that imposed real duties of delivery and that WADA had operated correctly in terms of both its powers and agreed processes. It was disappointing to read of David Howman's comment that we had put 'money over principle'. He should have known better. Our former investigator, Jack Robertson, joined the ranks of the complainers with a repetition of his claims of 'lack of action'. Robertson omitted to mention that he had been dismissed for leaking important papers to a friend a few years before (by David Howman at the time).

Led by Travis Tygart, CEO of USADA, and organised with the assistance of Fair Sport, a one-day conference on anti-doping was held in the White House in Washington. It attracted an audience of selected invited guest, mainly NADOs that were opposed to the Seychelles decision, and a number of sports ministers seemingly attracted by the venue.

Of course, WADA was not invited, and journalists were instructed to maintain the news under strict embargo until the last minute—so much for transparency from the White House. Linda Helleland attended, without informing me, but I had to make it clear to her that she attended as an individual and not as a representative from WADA. Helleland had announced her intention to stand as the next president of WADA and was in campaign mode as she knew by then that Witold Banka, the young Polish sports minister, would also be a candidate.

We then had to face a public accusation from Beckie Scott that she had been 'bullied' by disrespectful comments during the Seychelles meeting. I immediately responded to her by saying that I took her allegations very seriously and would be happy to discuss them with her at the next meeting planned for Baku in just a few weeks.

When I arrived in Baku and met with Scott as arranged, I found that she was accompanied by two members of the athletes' committee and a Benjamin Chew, a lawyer from Brown Rudnick LLP, a US-based legal firm, which acted for Fair Sport. The presence of a lawyer had not been announced and his name had been registered by the New Zealand representative, Clayton Cosgrove, as if he was part of the New Zealand delegation. It was only by pure luck that one of our staff identified the name given by New Zealand as being a US lawyer representing Beckie Scott. I did not regard it as a great example of fair play and ethical behaviour. She had been a long-serving member and chair of our athletes' committee; following her own experience in only winning Olympic bronze behind two Russian athletes, who were subsequently suspended for doping with the gold being reallocated to Scott, she was a strong supporter of clean sport. I was disappointed and surprised that she had chosen to escalate her complaint.

I had studied the minutes of the Seychelles meeting very carefully as I had been concerned that as chairman, I had allowed members to engage in bullying. I had chaired literally hundreds of committee or board meetings and had never believed that in any of them I had allowed bullying to take place. The minutes and the recording of the Seychelles meeting disclosed that contributions to the debate on the Russian matter had been firm but controlled and the process had been followed correctly. The agenda item that appeared to have caused the accusation was the report of the Athlete Committee by Beckie Scott.

The minutes recorded that she had expressed criticism of the IOC athletes' commission and had complained about the attitude of its members to the athlete forum, which had been organised in Calgary. Slovak skeet shooter Danka Barteková, a member of the IOC athletes' commission and the WADA board, had responded politely; the debate that followed involved opinions on the forum content and success with a view on the ongoing work required to deliver the requested athletes' charter.

In an immediate response to Scott's email and complaint, the matter had been referred to an organisation called Relais Expert-Conseil, a Montreal company specialising in 'psychological intervention in the workplace'. The company commented on the existing WADA policy to 'prevent harassment and promote a healthy work environment', which applied to the WADA staff. The consultant conducting the review had access to both the Seychelles minutes and recordings and concluded that 'there was no bullying or belittling at the meeting'.

Scott had continued to make public statements about her allegations in the media, and WADA had received a letter from Brown Rudnick LLP threatening legal action if a more formal independent inquiry was not established. Opinion had been taken from our Canadian lawyers who stated that, as the request had come from a US-based firm, that WADA should take advice in that country. This recommendation was considered and agreed during the board meeting in Baku.

To comply with that instruction, we appointed Covington, a well-known international firm of lawyers with a specific reputation for conducting the type of inquiry that Scott (and subsequently, Edwin Moses, the American double gold medal-winning 400-m runner and chair of our education committee) had demanded. We knew Covington only by virtue of some work it had done for us in the area of European data protection legislation. We had no prior connection with the New York firm, which were instructed to conduct the requested inquiry. Covington worked entirely independently of WADA management and interviewed thirty-two witnesses. This included twenty-nine of the forty people who had attended the Seychelles meeting and involved the audio recording of that meeting.

Regrettably, both Beckie Scott and Edwin Moses refused to be interviewed as their lawyers tried to insist that they be allowed to cross-examine witnesses and that the entire evidentiary record be made public. Those conditions were not acceptable as they set out a process which would have been a lawsuit and not an investigation. The Covington Report was submitted to WADA on 15 May 2019 and contained the central conclusion that, 'Ms Scott was not bullied or harassed at the 20th of September executive committee meeting'.

In considering the report, both I, as president, and Linda Helleland, as vice president, were regarded as conflicted and did not attend that part of the executive committee meeting. The same applied to the New Zealand member who had tried to include Beckie Scott's lawyer as part of the New Zealand delegation in Baku.

Edwin Moses claimed in an article in the *Sydney Morning Herald* on 18 October 2018 that he had been told to 'shut up' by the late Patrick Baumann at the May 2018 WADA board meeting. I had dealt personally with that claim in a discussion with Moses at the education conference in Beijing, with Catherine McLean (our communications director) as a witness. I reminded him that Baumann had asked at that meeting if the chairs of the athlete and education committees were allowed to speak, and that my ruling was that they attended meetings without a vote but were allowed to speak. He made no comment.

These developments turned out to be disruptive, and after examination, their claims turned out to be untrue. The whole process was disappointing for WADA management and staff and only served to accentuate the deliberate campaign of protest against WADA after its decision to reinstate RUSADA. The thought has always been at the back of my mind that those who claimed to defend their views on the delivery of clean sport, might just, on occasions, consider how much benefit could have been delivered to clean sport by the several million dollars of costs involved in these inquiries. In fact, the campaign was a deliberate attempt to orchestrate a destabilisation of the WADA organisation and its leadership.

In the Baku meetings in November, progress could be reported on the access to the Moscow laboratory, the major outstanding condition that remained to be satisfied in RUSADA compliance. There would also be a full audit of RUSADA, which was planned for December. This meeting also considered the further development of the athletes' charter and agreed rules for the election of the next president, who would come from the government side of WADA's stakeholders but including criteria to ensure the independence of the ultimately successful candidate.

The WADA appointed inspection team, led by Barcelona-based research scientist and experienced anti-doping expert, Dr Toni Pascual arrived in Moscow on 17 December but found that they were unable to collect the required data from the laboratory. The delay was stated as being because of the lack of certification of the team's equipment under Russian legislation. We made strong representations to the Russian authorities, who indicated on 24 December that a second visit would be accommodated, and this was strongly supported by Yuri Ganus, the director general of RUSADA.

A second WADA team arrived in Moscow on 9 January and successfully extracted all the necessary data and left Russia on 17 January. The inevitable storm of protest on 'missing' the agreed date of 31 December was dealt with by Jonathan Taylor and the CRC who explained that, under the international standard for compliance, it was always allowed that a stakeholder informed of a critical non-compliance would be allowed a short period in time to respond to that assertion of non-compliance, which had been made formally on 31 December. It was crucial that due process be followed so that any resulting ban would hold up in court.

Russia had provided access to the essential data by 17 January 2019. A telephone conference of the executive committee was arranged for 22 January 2019, and starting at 5 a.m., I chaired the meeting from the office of the general manager of Thunderbird Country Club in California. The recommendation from the CRC that no further sanction should be declared was accepted without dissent. Linda Helleland later announced that she was opposed.

The WADA team brought back 24 terabytes of data—an enormous amount of information—and began the long and complex process of verifying and authenticating the data it now held. The process of uploading the data took until early March when a comparison became available. The volume of data was equivalent to 400,000 hours of music or 5,200 DVDs. In April, we were able to announce that 2,200 samples had been removed from the Moscow laboratory to another accredited laboratory, an action that would assist the preparation of resulting cases to be prosecuted by international federations.

It was a pleasure to attend the annual WADA symposium in March and to make a speech setting out and justifying the decisions taken on RUSADA compliance and to offset, at least in part, the criticism we had suffered until the successful extraction of the Moscow data. I had made it absolutely clear that I would take no part in the process agreed among the governments over the selection of their candidate for the presidency of WADA but watched with great interest.

The *ad hoc* European committee for WADA, the CAHAMA (the *ad hoc* European committee for the World Anti-Doping Agency) selected former 400-m runner Witold Banka of Poland over Linda Helleland of Norway, the current vice president, and Flemish politician, Phillipe Muyters from Belgium. The voting was twenty-eight, sixteen, and five votes respectively. Banka's nomination was then approved by the European Council of Ministers despite interference by Helleland, who tried to get a second vote at that level. Marcus Diaz from the Dominican Republic was also a candidate and at a meeting of the governments in May—a decision had been taken that Mr Banka would be the sole nominee for election as the president of WADA from 1 January 2020. In that election, the votes had been ten for Banka to eight for Diaz.

By July, our intelligence and investigations department were able to predict that 300 athletes had been identified with the most suspicious samples from data retrieved from the Moscow laboratory. Evidentiary packages were being prepared for IFs, and up to 100 might be included in the first wave. Clearly, the decision to place all the emphasis on the data from the laboratory was correct and delivering the necessary evidence. Even David Walsh of *The Sunday Times* was complimentary.

However, the WADA investigative team had found evidence that the data may have been manipulated and began a process of providing information on its findings to the CRC the provisional views of which were presented to the executive committee at its meeting in Tokyo in September 2019. Additional information and analysis would be required, and great care taken to ensure that due process was undertaken. This information led the CRC to open a fast-track compliance procedure on 17 September 2019 and the Russian authorities were given the opportunity to provide responses to a list of detailed and technical questions.

After this process had been completed, the CRC reached the following conclusion in its long report:

When the evidence is viewed in its totality, the inescapable conclusion is that, while some deletions and alterations of the Moscow data took place as early as July 2016, multiple further deletions and alterations were made after the date of the Mahe meeting on September 20th, 2018. After that announcement but prior to making the Moscow data available to WADA, efforts were undertaken in the Moscow laboratory (particularly between 25th November 2018 and 16th January 2019) (1) to sanitise the Moscow data of key analytical data and remove the ability to recover crucial evidence; and (2) to plant fabricated evidence falsely incriminating Dr Grigory Rodchenkov and Dr Timofei Sobolevsky (Rodchenkov's assistant) in criminal conduct. The perpetrators then went to significant lengths to cover their tracks. As a result, this outrageous conduct would have gone undiscovered but for the detailed digital forensic analysis conducted by the WADA independent experts.

Based on its detailed twenty-six-page report, the CRC recommended to the executive committee on 22 November 2019 that a formal notice be issued to Russia, asserting its failure to comply with agreed conditions, aggravated by deliberate tampering with evidence and setting out consequences and reinstatement conditions. This would be dealt with by an extraordinary executive meeting, finally arranged for 9 December.

In the interim, the anti-doping world met in Katowice, Poland, for the fifth world conference on doping in sport. The meetings dealt with the approval of an amended and stronger world anti-doping code, a donation of a further $5 million from the IOC for storage of samples, and a further $5 million for research and investigations, to be matched by governments. They also reviewed progress on the governance reforms, the charter of athletes' rights; the new legislation going through the US Congress called the Rodchenkov Act; and the election of Witold Banka as the new WADA president and of Yang Yang, a distinguished Olympic gold medallist from China, as vice president.

I had not been involved in any of the governance debates as the topics frequently covered the role of the president and I wanted to avoid any accusations of conflict of interest. The problems with the athletes' charter proposals reflected a failure of coordination with the IOC athletes' commission, which had presented its own athletes' declaration of rights without any real mention of anti-doping—the subject that the WADA athletes' committee was supposed to deliver. This breach in communications and trust was unhelpful.

The Rodchenkov Act was designed to deal with doping conspiracies, and more specifically was giving the US extra-territorial jurisdiction over the entire world, allowing allow criminal prosecution in the US against anybody but the athlete in cases of doping anywhere in the world. The act granted territorial jurisdiction to US-based organisations, but after an amendment, it did not apply to any of the major sports in USA nor any of its college sport that probably accounts for 90 per cent of US athletes. The hypocrisy of that deliberate amendment was hard to accept and would become an issue for the future.

The extraordinary executive committee meeting was held in Lausanne on 9 December 2019, with arrangements made unnecessarily complicated by rail strikes and other disturbances in Paris, the original venue. The agenda was short and clear. Jonathan Taylor presented the long and detailed report from the CRC, which, yet again, after its distribution to the members of the executive committee, had been leaked to the media, forcing WADA to release a short press release.

The attacks on WADA had continued. Comments from members were strongly in favour of the recommendation and very complimentary about the work done by the WADA investigators. Linda Helleland spoke about the error in the Seychelles decision and her wish for a blanket ban, but that she would support the CRC recommendation. Beckie Scott, who had called in to the meeting, spoke on behalf of athletes, who, she suggested, had not been sufficiently considered.

In his responses, Jonathan Taylor dealt with both comments to justify the part of the recommendation that would allow 'clean athletes' to compete. This part of the decision had to be based on conduct from 2011 to 2015 (the original doping and cover up of doping) that may not affect current athletes. He stressed that athlete opinion had been considered. The meeting showed that all sportspeople and governments agreed unanimously with the recommendation, and some of us went off to yet another packed press conference.

The media knew the results of a successful assertion of non-compliance. It was recommended that Russia could not take part in Olympic Games and world championships for a period of four years. Russia could not have delegates appointed to the boards of code signatories or any world championships. Russia could not host or bid for events covered by the decision or to bid for the 2032 Olympic Games, nor could any Russian flag be flown. These sanctions would apply to officials of the Russian Olympic Committee and Russian Paralympic Committee. Some Russian athletes might be able to compete as neutral athletes under certain circumstances relating to knowledge from the data collected from the Moscow laboratory. Russia would pay a substantial fine.

After a very short opening and explanatory speech, which contained a few very pointed words, we only needed to summarise the above points at the press conference:

> This decision is designed to punish the guilty parties and sends the message that it will not be tolerated. It stands strong against those who cheated the system, while protecting those that did not. Russia was afforded every opportunity to get its house in order and re-join the global anti-doping community for the good of its athletes and of the integrity of sport, but it chose instead to continue its stance of deception and denial.

We had few questions and only the occasional request for personal interviews. The journey home allowed me the luxury of relaxation after a compelling and serious result. Five years of discord had placed strains on many different relationships, both within WADA, but more importantly among countries and sports organisations that had been impacted by Russian actions. Sometimes, it was quite hard to get critics to remember that it was not WADA that was doping athletes in Russia.

Investigations and subsequent proof that cheating had been endorsed and even organised at a high political level in Russia, presented acute problems to sport, which was not always too keen to accept and resolve them. The saga also presented the media with an almost unique platform for investigation and comment.

Having rationalised all that, I came to the personal conclusion that the attempt to resolve the impasse with Russia, and to make a clear condition on the need for access to the data was the correct decision. This presented the possibility of proper, legal processes to deal with those athletes who had cheated. I never thought that a complete, blanket ban in the hope that Russia would come crawling back full of contrition was a realistic option.

The following day, I happened to read an article in an informed sports website which contained the following tribute to my role in the saga:

> He leaves on a high note. Proceedings in Lausanne on Monday, under the full glare of the global media spotlight, on the whole displayed the World Ani-Doping Agency (WADA) at its best. Sir Craig Reedie, who steps down at the end of this month after six years in the presidential hot seat, can take much satisfaction from this final act of his tumultuous term. The mood of measured, competent determination was a far cry

from the chaos and animosity of the countdown to Rio. It may well be that the most significant attainment of the 78-year-old Scots stretch in sports impossible job will lie in the team of highly motivated specialists assembled under his stewardship. They are represented by the herculean labours of lieutenants such as Gunter Younger, the investigations expert, Jonathan Taylor the legal brains and Olivier Niggli, the low-profile director general who helped knit everything together. Knowing when and how to delegate is an important, usually underrated facet of leadership and one far too little practised in the paranoid ego heavy universe of international sport. While I personally think Sir Craig initially overestimated the extent to which other officials with influence in the politically sensitive world of elite performance would always act with the sense of honour that has been a hallmark of his own long career, once disillusioned he showed both the self-knowledge to recognise, he did not have all the answers and the humility and good sense to secure the services of top practitioners in the fields required. He has also drawn on deep reserves of tenacity, which he possesses in abundance, even if this is sometimes underappreciated owing to his unfailingly gentlemanly demeanour.

I thought, 'that will do nicely' and settled down to pack my bags for our annual air miles trip to our Californian golf club.

Epilogue

Throughout the pleasure in recalling through these pages over seventy-plus years in sport, it became clear that the communication and presentation of sport has been one of its most fundamental changes. As a very young school enthusiast, sport was communicated in newspapers, which I never read, or by radio, which I seldom listened to. If you were lucky enough to have access to a television set, or even own one, through no more than two channels, you might have seen—although it did not like it at the time—a distinctly grainy, black and white picture.

Then, in only a few years, the dramatic explosion in the awareness of sport was fuelled by the significant development of broadcasting in colour and by the huge increase in sports events that appeared because of the innovations of the jet engine and the communications satellite. Consequently, watching the best athletes in competition all around the world was transformative for both sport and its vast audience. We now live in an age of almost unlimited sports networks and via the digital delivery of myriad sports to whatever device you may have—some very large, some astonishingly small. It is no wonder that sport is a worldwide phenomenon of massive interest and great excitement.

Opportunities to play and use attractive facilities are part of modern life in organised societies. Like so many, my two grandsons play regular soccer in well-run community clubs in Kent. Even those less privileged, living in deprived parts of the world, seem to be able to find some open spaces where football, cricket, or other uncomplicated sports can be played. So, the world over, sport provides refuge, relaxation, and togetherness like no other aspect of life.

Yet with all the modern technology that makes sport available and the many new sports that continue to appear, we still celebrate the traditional and historic events that defy the passage of time. Each year, the grand slam tennis events, the major golf tournaments, and the national football and rugby cup finals and leagues provide an annual feast of excitement and involvement. In North America, the World Series and the Superbowl do the same, as do countless other national favourites around the world. International sport federations have developed their own regional, continental, and world championships and cups, which lead to ecstatic national celebrations for winning nations.

Sport has developed into a hugely lucrative commercial opportunity for both private and public investment and provides huge employment benefits on a worldwide basis, while governments—almost all of them—understand the benefits of sport's contribution to a healthy and happy society and to national pride and invest in it appropriately.

Regrettably, the seductive lure of success for countries, teams, and individuals has, over many years, encouraged a widespread culture of cheating through the abuse of performance-enhancing drugs and the increasing impact of corruption and match-fixing. The challenges have been recognised and there are, with varying degrees of success, efforts underway to counter the threats.

Throughout all this development and technological progress, the Olympic Games have provided an opportunity to celebrate a unique historical occasion, which brings the world together in the celebration of sport.

It is hard to believe that Baron Pierre de Coubertin and the small group of men who met in the Sorbonne in Paris in 1894 had the wisdom and belief to restore the Ancient Olympic Games in a modern format, and that we still enjoy them nearly 130 years later. Even more astutely, they chose to protect the independence of the modern Olympic Games by ensuring that entry to the events should be determined by each country's national Olympic committee, organisations recognised by the guardians of the Games and their ethics, the International Olympic Committee. This revolutionary decision has been of the greatest value to the Olympic movement and to world sport.

Despite wars and political protests, the Games have survived and grown to embrace 206 national Olympic committees in the greatest celebration of sport and our common humanity, in both summer and winter conditions. Cities and countries have benefitted in many different ways from the opportunity to organise the Games, and we have all enjoyed the thrill of witnessing the best of the world's young people taking part in their chosen sport. In an ever more complex world, the IOC, itself a venerable institution, has defended the spirit of sport and the Olympic values and by doing so has been able to fund the development of sport around the world.

For me, it has been the greatest personal reward to be part of the process of the development of sport over many years with significant interest in a certain sport, a particular country, and, laterally, in the IOC itself and international sport. Sport is special to almost all of us and understood and valued in many ways. Whether individual or collective, a personal challenge or an Olympic final, the joy of victory can be unbounded, while the disappointment of defeat builds character and makes us stronger.

Perhaps my appreciation for the power of sport is best illustrated by a story told to me by Seb Coe during our wonderful Olympic Games in London in 2012. Just to see how the transport services were working in practice, on occasions, Seb would travel from his central London hotel to the main venues by taking the Jubilee Line from Green Park underground station to the Olympic Park at Stratford.

One morning, he sat down beside a man in the rather bright purple uniform of a 'Games Maker', 2012's terrific volunteer army. Seb found out the man was a doctor and a volunteer at one of the competition venues. 'What persuaded you to volunteer?' said Seb. The doctor replied, 'I was on duty on 7th July 2005 during the terrorist attacks on London. So I volunteered, because now I have seen the worst of man and the best of man.'